COLLEGE OF MARIN LIBRARY
KENTFIELD, CALIFORNIA

WITHDRAWN

WITHDRAWN

WAR AND CONSCIENCE IN THE NUCLEAR AGE

Also by Sydney D. Bailey

Christian Perspectives on Nuclear Weapons
How Wars End (2 vols)
The Making of Resolution 242
The Procedure of the UN Security Council
Voting in the UN Security Council
The General Assembly of the United Nations
The Secretariat of the United Nations
A Short Political Guide to the United Nations
British Parliamentary Democracy
Ceylon
Parliamentary Government in Southern Asia
Naissance de Nouvelle Démocraties
Peaceful Settlements of International Disputes

War and Conscience in the Nuclear Age

Sydney D. Bailey

St. Martin's Press   New York

© Sydney D. Bailey 1987
All rights reserved. For information, write:
Scholarly & Reference Division,
St. Martin's Press, Inc., 175 Fifth Avenue, New York, NY 10010

First published in the United States of America in 1988

Printed in Great Britain

ISBN 0–312–01345–0

Library of Congress Cataloging-in-Publication Data

Bailey, Sydney Dawson,
War and conscience in the nuclear age/Sydney D. Bailey.
p.   cm.
Bibliography: p.
Includes index.
ISBN 0–312–01345–0 : $32.50
1. War—Moral and ethical aspects.   2. War—Religious aspects—
Christianity.   3. War (International law)   4. Just war doctrine.
I. Title.
U22.B25   1987
172′.42—dc 19

87–18755
CIP

For Brenda

Contents

Appendices and Tables

Abbreviations

ABM	Anti-Ballistic Missile
BW	Bacteriological (Biological) Weapon
CBW	Chemical and Bacteriological (Biological) Weapon
CD	Conference on Disarmament
CEP	Circular Error Probable
CS gas	Orthochlorobenzylidene malononitrile (chemical harassing agent)
CTB	Comprehensive Test Ban
CW	Chemical Weapon
EMP	Electro-Magnetic Pulse
ERW	Enhanced Radiation Weapon (neutron bomb)
FM27-10	US Department of the Army, Field Manual, *The Law of Land Warfare*, 1956
GA	UN General Assembly
GAOR	General Assembly Official Records
IAEA	International Atomic Energy Agency
ICBM	Inter-Continental Ballistic Missile
ICRC	International Committee of the Red Cross
ILC	International Law Commission
MAD	Mutual Assured Destruction
MIRV	Multiple Independently-targetable Re-entry Vehicle
MRV	Multiple Re-entry Vehicle
NPT	(nuclear) Non-Proliferation Treaty
PNE	Peaceful Nuclear Explosion
RV	Re-entry Vehicle
SALT	Strategic Arms Limitation Talks
SC	UN Security Council
SCOR	Security Council Official Records
SLBM	Submarine-Launched Ballistic Missile
UNESCO	United Nations Educational, Scientific and Cultural Organisation
UNRWA	United Nations Relief and Works Agency for Palestine Refugees in the Near East
WHO	World Health Organisation

Glossary of Military and Disarmament Terms

anti-ballistic missile (ABM)	missile designed to intercept and destroy an incoming warhead
atomic weapon	*see* nuclear weapon
ballistic missile	a missile which travels outside the earth's atmosphere, following an elliptical trajectory for much of its flight
battlefield weapon	weapon used in direct military combat on land
biological weapons (BW)	living organisms or infective material intended for use in warfare to cause disease or death in humans, animals, or plants
centrifugation	a method of enriching natural uranium
chemical weapons (CW)	chemical substances – whether gaseous, liquid, or solid – employed in combat because of their direct toxic effects on humans, animals, or plants
circular error probable (CEP)	the radius of a circle within which half the weapons are expected to fall, used to indicate accuracy
Conference on Disarmament (CD)	negotiating body, based in Geneva, which is composed of 40 states, including all the nuclear-weapon powers
conventional weapon	weapon other than chemical, biological, or nuclear
co-operative measures	measures taken by one side to enhance the other side's ability to verify
cruise missile	a guided missile which travels in the earth's atmosphere, similar to an unmanned aircraft

CTB — comprehensive (complete) ban on testing nuclear weapons in all environments

deterrence — the prevention of hostile military action by fear of counter-attack

enhanced radiation warhead (ERW) — a thermonuclear weapon so designed as to increase the initial radiation and reduce the other effects

enriched uranium — uranium which has been purified from 0.7% in natural form, perhaps to over 90%, almost certainly by gaseous diffusion or centrifugation

escalation — an increase in the intensity and scale of military action

fall-out — particles contaminated with radioactive material, descending to the earth's surface following a nuclear explosion

firestorm — the merging of many separate fires to form a large mass fire from which hot gases rise in a single column, leading to inrushing winds which prevent the fire from spreading but add fresh oxygen so that its intensity increases

first strike — a military operation carried out on the attacker's own premeditated initiative: often used more narrowly to refer to a pre-emptive operation aimed at knocking out within a very short period of time all or part of an enemy's nuclear strike capability

fission — process whereby the nucleus of a heavy atom splits into lighter nuclei with the release of substantial amounts of energy

flexible response — the ability to respond to provocation or aggression at an appropriate level, whether nuclear or conventional, first put forward as

	an alternative to massive retaliation in the early 1960s and officially adopted in 1967 as the basis of NATO's strategy
fusion	process whereby light atoms combine to form a heavy atom with the release of very substantial amounts of energy
gaseous diffusion	a method of enriching natural uranium
half life	the time required for radioactivity to decay to half of its original value
inter-continental ballistic missile (ICBM)	a ballistic missile consisting of booster, one or more re-entry vehicles, penetration aids, a post-boost vehicle in the case of a MIRVed missile, and warhead(s), with a range exceeding 3000 miles
kiloton (kt)	measure of the explosive yield of a nuclear weapon equivalent to 1000 tons of TNT
megaton (Mt)	measure of the explosive yield of a nuclear weapon equivalent to one million tons of TNT
multiple independently-targetable re-entry vehicle (MIRV)	carried on a single missile but with warheads capable of being directed against separate targets considerable distances apart
multiple re-entry vehicle (MRV)	re-entry vehicle of a ballistic missile, capable of being directed against a single cluster of targets
mutual assured destruction (MAD)	the situation in which both sides are capable of inflicting massive damage even after absorbing a first strike
mutual deterrence	situation in which both parties are deterred from launching an attack for fear of retaliation
national technical means	procedures and equipment for verifying compliance with an agreement

neutron bomb	*see* enhanced radiation warhead
nuclear weapon	a weapon in which energy is released by the fission or fusion of atomic nuclei
peaceful nuclear explosions (PNEs)	application of nuclear explosions for such peaceful purposes as digging canals, creating underground cavities, etc
Polaris	a submarine-launched intermediate-range ballistic missile of US manufacture, originally designed to carry three non-MIRVed warheads, first deployed in 1960; sometimes used loosely to describe the submarines on which the missiles are carried
pre-emptive strike	a military operation mounted in expectation of enemy attack and designed to minimise its effects
rapid re-load	the capability to fire a second missile within a short period of time
reactor	an apparatus designed to produce energy by the fission of atomic nuclei
re-entry vehicle (RV)	the part of a ballistic missile which carries the warhead into the earth's atmosphere at the end of its trajectory
reprocessing	the separation of plutonium from the spent fuel elements from a nuclear reactor
Strategic Arms Limitation Talks (SALT)	between the United States and the Soviet Union which began in 1969, seeking to limit the strategic nuclear forces
security assurance	declaration not to use nuclear weapons in defined circumstances
separation	the separation of plutonium from other substances of the spent fuel of a nuclear reactor
silo	underground missile shelter

somatic	related to the body
Standing Consultative Commission (SCC)	US–Soviet consultative body established in accordance with SALT
strategic weapons	weapons of last resort able to reach an enemy's homeland: customarily used to refer to ICBMs, SLBMs, and bomber aircraft of intercontinental range, sometimes also to ABMs designed to counter ICBMs or SLBMs
tactical	carried out in immediate support of military operation (NATO is tending to give up this term)
terminal guidance	guidance provided in the final, near-target phase of the flight of a missile
thermonuclear weapon	a weapon in which energy is released by the fusion of atomic nuclei
threshold test ban	agreement not to test underground nuclear weapons with a yield exceeding 150 kts, 1974
Tlatelolco, Treaty of	treaty designed to keep Latin America free of nuclear weapons, 1967
toxins	poisonous substances which are products of organisms but are inanimate and incapable of reproducing themselves
Trident C4	a submarine-launched intercontinental ballistic missile of US manufacture with up to 8 MIRVed warheads, first flight-tested in 1977; sometimes used loosely to describe the submarines on which the missiles are carried
Trident D5	improved version, longer range, more warheads
uranium enrichment	*see* enriched uranium
warhead	that part of a weapon which contains the high explosive, nuclear,

chemical, or biological material or device

yield — the energy released in an explosion, measured in tons of TNT, kilotons (kts), or megatons (Mts)

Acknowledgments

In writing this book, I have learned most on some crucial issues from those whose opinions differ from my own. I am grateful to friends in the British Council of Churches, the Council on Christian Approaches to Defence and Disarmament, the International Institute for Strategic Studies, and a panel of the American Society of International Law for forcing me to think about the Nürnberg principles and the potential contradiction between individual conscience and national consensus.

I have also appreciated the help of many colleagues in obtaining books, journals, and documents. I thank, in particular, Nicole Gallimore and John Montgomery in the library of the Royal Institute of International Affairs; Vivian Hewitt, formerly librarian at the Carnegie Endowment for International Peace; Diane Jumet in the office of the UN Secretary-General; Dominique Junod and Bruno Zimmerman, from the International Committee of the Red Cross; Jiri Toman, of the Henry Dunant Institute in Geneva; and Judith Baker and Diane Hendrik, in the Quaker UN Office in Geneva. I am grateful to the Catholic Central Library in London and the Catholic University of America Press for advice about English translations of Latin works, and the library at Friends House, London, and the Friends Historical Library, Swarthmore College, Pennsylvania, for help in tracking down records of what Quakers call the Holy Experiment.

Other friends (and, in two cases, complete strangers) suggested ideas to follow up, read and commented on the first draft of parts of the book, or helped in other ways. Some prefer that I not mention their names. To them, and to the following, I express warm thanks: Sir Hugh Beach, Geoffrey Best, Jack Boag, François Bugnion, Carl Builder, William Epstein, Jacques Freymond, Graham Gibbs, Guerman G. Gventsadse, the Rev. Richard Harries, the Rev. Anthony Harvey, Sir Arthur Hockaday, William Douglas Home, Michael Pakenham, Sir Michael Quinlan, Joseph Rotblat, Georg Schwarzenberger, Nicholas Sims, Duncan Wood, and the late Bishop B. C. Butler OSB.

The publications of the Stockholm International Peace Research Institute (SIPRI) have been invaluable.

S. D. B.
June 1986

Introduction

There are four kinds of contradiction in the principles and laws governing military activities. One, which has two aspects, is between promise and performance, between words and deeds. There is, in the first place, the contradiction between the obligation which states have assumed under international treaties not to resort to armed force, as against the way states actually behave. The UN Charter is a treaty to which most of the world's sovereign states have adhered and the obligations of which over-ride obligations under other international agreements (Art. 103 of the Charter). One of the obligations under the Charter is not to use force against the territorial integrity or political independence of any other state (Art. 2(4)). Those are fine words, to be sure, echoing the Kellogg-Briand renunciation of war as an instrument of national policy; but when we examine the deeds of states since 1945, we find that there have been many armed conflicts in disregard of UN Charter obligations. According to the Nürnberg Charter and a resolution of the UN General Assembly, to wage war in violation of an international treaty is a *crime against peace* (see Appendices 1(a) and 13).

A second aspect of the contradiction between theory and practice, between words and deeds, concerns the obligations assumed by states under international humanitarian law as against the way states actually behave when they engage in military operations. To take one example, it is abundantly clear from treaties in the Hague and Geneva streams of law, and in resolutions of the UN General Assembly, that it is prohibited to make direct attacks on civilians, prisoners of war (POWs), wounded and sick combatants, medical services, military chaplains, or other non-combatants. Those also are fine words, but it is apparent from the reports of the International Committee of the Red Cross, and what we know from the media in our own country, that military operations are often conducted in substantial disregard of the principle of non-combatant immunity. The British manual of military law states plainly that it is a generally recognised rule of international law 'that civilians must not be made the object of attack directed exclusively against them' (para. 13). Governments do not deny that international law prohibits direct attacks on non-combatants. Indeed, it is significant that when states violate this or other rules of international law, they do not deny that such acts are contrary to the

1

laws of war, but justify the violation on the ground that the enemy had committed a prior illegality, or even that the action was intended to put an end to the war quickly and thus to save lives.

International law is not simply what scholars write in books. Its sources include treaties, judicial decisions, and 'the general principles of law recognized by civilized nations', but also 'international custom, as evidence of a general practice accepted as law' (Art. 38 of the Statute of the International Court). Does that mean, then, that if enough states violate the principle of non-combatant immunity often enough, direct attacks on non-combatants would thereby become licit and be recognised as 'international custom … a general practice accepted as law'?

Surely not. Such attacks would violate other sources of international law, including treaties (the Hague and Geneva Conventions) and judicial decisions (the Nürnberg judgment), as well as a general principle of law recognised by civilised nations and to be found in most military manuals. Indeed, I know of no occasion in the past forty years when a government has claimed that direct attacks on non-combatants are or should be regarded as 'international custom' or 'a general practice accepted as law', though governments continue to make, or threaten to make, such attacks. A recent study prepared for the Rand Corporation, which is not usually squeamish on defence issues, concluded that the policy of mutual assured destruction depends on acts which would be unlawful under the international law of armed conflicts.[1] According to the Nürnberg Charter, to violate the laws or customs of war is a *war crime* (see Appendix 1(b)).

But there is another contradiction which is encountered when states or other entities engage in military operations and which is apparent in the main treaties governing the conduct of armed conflict – the Hague Conventions of 1899 and 1907 on the laws and customs of war on land, the four Geneva (Red Cross) Conventions of 1949, the Hague Convention of 1954 on the protection of cultural property, and the two Additional Protocols of 1977 to the Geneva Conventions, as well as in the Charter of the Nürnberg Tribunal. There is, on the one hand, the pressure of military exigency. The treaties do not use identical language for this pressure, but the meaning is the same – the necessities of war,[2] military necessity or necessities,[3] imperative or urgent or unavoidable or absolute military necessity or necessities,[4] the arbitrary judgment of military commanders.[5] Against these pressures must be set 'the usages established among civilized peoples, the laws of humanity, the dictates of the public conscience'.[6]

The conflict between the necessities of war and the laws of humanity was referred to in one of the earliest humanitarian instruments, the St Petersburg Declaration of 1868. The wording quoted at the end of the last paragraph is taken from the Martens Clause, which formed part of the Hague Convention of 1899 on the laws and customs of war on land, and has been repeatedly re-affirmed in subsequent treaties. The Hague Convention of 1899 was known to be incomplete when it was adopted, and it has in any event been overtaken by advances in military technology; but it was to apply until a more complete code of the laws of war could be issued. Parts of the laws of war have been developed and codified since 1899, but the task is by no means complete. There is, for example, no rule of international law dealing specifically with the use of nuclear weapons, though the UN General Assembly has issued a number of recommendations on the subject (see Appendix 4). Military commanders must often face acutely difficult decisions when seeking to give appropriate weight to military necessity, while at the same time avoiding actions which might cause unnecessary suffering or superfluous injury, as well as actions which might cause excessive harm to non-combatants as an indirect effect of a legitimate military attack.

In examining these contradictions, I have come to realise the close connection between the Just War doctrine as an ethical concept, as a norm of international law, and as the humanitarian basis of Red Cross and Red Crescent agencies (chapters 1–4). The International Committee of the Red Cross avoids using the expression *Just War*, as it is so frequently misused by those who want to justify their own side by resort to a slogan. The Just War concept has, nevertheless, a clear meaning in the Christian tradition, and I see no sufficient reason for seeking an alternative expression. Moreover, it should be stressed that the Just War doctrine is composed of restrictions and prohibitions rather than permissions.

I have sought to show in chapters 3 and 4 that there is no longer an adequate reason for separating the law of the Hague (conduct of military operations) from the law of Geneva (humanitarian protection of and aid to the victims of war). Whatever their original sources, the two streams of law have now merged.

I have made clear in chapter 5 that arms control and disarmament agreements necessarily include measures for effective international control. Three main kinds of verification are envisaged or used: on-site inspection, national technical means, and consultative procedures. It should be obvious from chapters 3 and 4 that human rights and humanitarian treaties also need proper supervision to ensure compliance, and also sanctions in the event of grave breaches. Most of the humanitarian norms for armed conflict are clear: what we still need are effective mechanisms of verification and implementation. This may eventually mean supplementing the International Court of Justice at the Hague, which deals with states and international organisations, with an international criminal court before which could be brought individuals accused of breaches of humanitarian law or other international crimes.

In chapter 5 I review some of the reasons for negotiating on the control and reduction of weapons, describe the negotiating machinery which now exists, review some of the difficulties of reaching agreement when there are major military asymmetries, and refer also to the role of unilateral initiatives and tacit understandings. I then turn to the conclusions of two UN studies on nuclear weapons, the materials and installations needed for nuclear explosions, the launching platforms and delivery vehicles, the financial costs of acquiring nuclear weapons and the dangers of proliferation, and I describe what it is believed would be the effects of using nuclear weapons and the durability of some radioactive substances released in nuclear explosions. I then examine the various processes which have been the subjects of international negotiation and agreement: research, testing, development, manufacture, stockpiling, transfer, and deployment of weapons, and their destruction or dismantling. While the central strategic balance has been remarkably stable, this has been due to separate national or alliance decisions and procedures rather than to substantial supervised disarmament. Reasonable security for the two alliances could be assured at balanced but much lower levels of weaponry. The results of negotiating over forty years are hopeful in the context of the difficulties to be overcome but miniscule in the context of the dangers that remain.

As the world moves hesitantly from arms control to minor or interim measures of reduction or restraint, and even more hesitantly along the tortuous path to substantial reductions, we have to ask whether there are any weapons or methods of war which violate ethical and legal norms so clearly that they should be unreservedly prohibited. And if, in spite of all efforts at peace-making and peace-keeping, wars still occur, are there any restraints which civilised nations should observe, unilaterally or on a reciprocal basis?

This book began life in 1967 as a one-page summary for a Quaker committee of those categories of persons entitled to protection and immunity from direct attack in armed conflict under the Hague and Geneva Conventions. It was then revised and expanded to nine pages for a conference in Oxford in 1968 of the Council on Christian Approaches to Defence and Disarmament (CCADD), and was further revised and expanded to nineteen pages for another CCADD conference in the Netherlands in 1969. It was later considered by a panel of the American Society for International Law. Some of this material then formed the basis for a book entitled *Prohibitions and Restraints in War* which was published in 1972 under the auspices of the Royal Institute of International Affairs. This has been out of print for about a decade.

In a review of that book published in *International Affairs*, Alastair Buchan expressed regret that I had not injected more of my own views into it.

> It would have been invaluable to have had, in addition to meticulous research and multiple quotations…, [Bailey's] own assessment of what that intractable body, the international community, great powers and small, stable and unstable societies, democracies and dictatorships, will or will not accept by way of codified restraints in war and conflict, what is enforceable and what is not. One can only hope that this is for a later volume.

The selection of material for any book necessarily represents a personal opinion; beyond that, I have in the main preferred to provide the basic material on which the reader can make up his or her own mind. Moreover, I doubt whether my personal views are very interesting or very important, and I know that they have often been immature and incoherent, even if held with passion and tenacity. I have exercised less restraint this time and expressed my own views on some issues, sometimes explicitly, as in chapter 6, but more often by implication. Some of the issues to which Alastair Buchan drew attention will remain intractable so long as governments put short-term advantage before long-term interest.

Those absolute pacifists who believe that war is in all circumstances immoral devote their main energies to its prevention and, when it occurs, to personal abstention, and have tended to regard the drawing up of humanitarian rules by which it should be conducted as a distraction from their main task or even as positively dangerous, because an effort of this kind might seem to imply that war can be made civilised. Most of those who hold that war may in certain circumstances be the lesser evil believe that it should not be conducted without limit or restraint. Increasingly during the past century, governments have issued declarations or negotiated agreements to prohibit unilateral resort to armed force or to ensure that, if armed conflict does occur, it is conducted with discrimination and proportion.

That is the third contradiction: between the belief that all-out war is too terrible to serve any rational or just purpose, and the belief that precisely because all-out war is so terrible, civilised human beings must seek to subject it to limitations. The dilemma is that the more war is subject to restraints, the more 'thinkable' it becomes. If war is more 'thinkable', is it therefore more likely? Or, on the contrary, should we make war as monstrous as human ingenuity can contrive in the hope that the 'unthinkability' of war would exercise a deterrent effect?

The fourth contradiction, or possible contradiction, is between loyalty to the state or community and obedience to conscience. For most of us, this dilemma has never arisen, though we may admire those elsewhere who have put conscience first – Claus von Stauffenberg, Dietrich Bonhoeffer, and the other anti-Hitler plotters in Nazi Germany; Chief Albert Luthuli and the campaigners against unjust laws in South Africa; Alexander Solzhenitsyn, Andrei Sakharov, and the other Soviet dissidents.

For almost all of us, there *could* conceivably come a point where we would refuse on grounds of conscience to undertake a particular task: a Catholic doctor might refuse to perform an abortion, a Quaker scientist might decline to do research on germ warfare, an ordinary citizen might in certain cases refuse jury service if capital punishment were re-introduced, and so on.

In a democratic society, conscientious abstention of this kind is respected as much as possible. During the second world war, the law in Britain provided that those who sincerely objected to serving in the armed forces on conscientious grounds should be exempt from military service. It is a privilege to live in such a country, and some conscientious objectors may have been troubled that their contemporaries in 1939–45 were fighting and dying for a way of life that included the right not to fight.

How does the citizen behave where the system does not allow for conscientious objection? In what circumstances should we put individual conscience above superior orders or the law itself? Is civil disobedience ever a responsible option? Or, to carry the train of thought a stage further, is it ever a duty to conspire against unjust or oppressive rulers? At what point would we face the choice between obeying God rather than men?

All I would insist on here is that for many people in the world, these questions are not simply theoretical, they are real, immediate, and existential.

In this book, I review four of the contradictions arising in armed conflict: between words and deeds when states decide to resort to armed force and in the actual conduct of military operations, between military necessity and the demands of humanity, between making war more horrible and therefore unthinkable or more humane in the hope that thinkable war enhances deterrence, and between loyalty to the national consensus and obedience to conscience.

The UN Charter affirms that 'We the peoples' are determined to 'save succeeding generations from the scourge of war...'. The obligations and activities reviewed in this book are no substitute for the primary goal of the United Nations, which often seems impossible but always is necessary.

1 The Just War in Christian Ethics

Let hope keep you joyful; in trouble stand firm ...
Call down blessings on your persecutors ...
Never pay back evil for evil ... . If possible, so far as it lies
with you, live at peace with all men.

Paul's letter to the Christians in Rome
(*New English Bible*)

THE EARLY CHURCH

The doctrine of the Just War had its origin in Christian ethics more
than 1000 years before Hugo Grotius began to clothe it in legal forms.

The first Christians did not perform military service, being more
concerned with their religious tasks than with the secular affairs of the
Roman Empire. The spirit of Christ was to transform the life of the
individual. The essential social groupings were the family and the
Church; within these, Christian principles were to have absolute
validity. All other elements of human existence, including the state,
belonged to 'the world'. The unbeliever was in bondage to 'the world',
and only Jesus Christ could free him. Christian hope was based on the
faith that individual men and women would be saved, but the
redemption of 'the world' would not become visible until the return of
Christ. This would inaugurate 'the next world', when God's perfect
rule over all creation would be established. The earthly life of
Christians was a period of preparation for full sainthood; their real
citizenship was in heaven.

During the period of waiting until the Second Coming of Christ,
believers were to be sober and industrious, content with their earthly
circumstances, in all things submissive – young to old, women to men,
servants to masters, and all to Caesar. Governmental authority,
although pagan, was accepted as a divine institution and was to be
obeyed so long as this did not conflict with Christian conscience.

Almost all Christian writers before the fourth century took it for
granted that service in the army was incompatible with Christian

principles. 'The Lord ... in disarming Peter, unbelted every soldier', wrote Tertullian (about 200 AD). If a soldier were converted to Christianity, he was expected to give up military service. '[Once] we have embraced the faith and have been baptized, we either must immediately leave military service (as many have done); or we must resort to all kinds of excuses in order to avoid any action which is ... forbidden' (Tertullian again). Several cases are recorded by both Christian and non-Christian writers of converted soldiers suffering martyrdom.[1]

The early Christians thus did not bear arms, but they did not usually condemn the use of arms by the unconverted if this were necessary for the purpose of maintaining an orderly fabric of society.

Critics of Christianity maintained that the Christian attitude was irresponsible. They argued, first, that Christians accepted the benefits of Imperial Rome but were unwilling to meet all the obligations of citizenship. How would the Emperor be defended, asked Celsus (about 180 AD), if everybody were to embrace such a utopian religion? When asked how Christians should act when others were fighting, Tertullian said that the life of the Christian was to be of the quality that made war unnecessary, and that he was to pray for those who served righteously as soldiers. Origen (3rd century) put it like this:

> We ... are much more helpful to the king than those who go into the field to fight ... . And none fight better for the king than we do. We do not indeed fight under him, although he require it; but we do` fight on his behalf ... by offering our prayers to God.

It was not surprising that the enemies of Christianity thought that this was to leave the dirty work to the unenlightened.

The other charge (and it was one that was to be made against Christian pacifists repeatedly, up to our own day) was that the practice of Christianity actually increased the number of wars. Sometimes the argument was that popular hatred of Christianity was itself a cause of war; in Saint Augustine's time, and particularly after the sack of Rome by Alaric in 410, it was said that the effect of Christian teaching was to weaken the will and capacity to resist aggression.

Arnobius (4th century) rebutted the first charge in these words:

> Actually, regarding the wars which you say were begun on account of hatred of our religion, it would not be difficult to prove that after Christ was on earth, not only did they not increase but in great

measure were reduced as a result of the repression of fierce
passions. ... We have learned from his teachings ... that it is better to
suffer wrong than be its cause.

The situation was to change radically during the fourth century. The
first Christians had assumed that the pagan world of Caesar was
wicked and doomed, that its redemption had to await the return of
Christ. But the Second Coming was delayed and then, to the
amazement of the Christians, the Emperor was converted. Not only
that, Constantine ascribed his victories in war to the fact that he had
adopted the Christian faith: assuredly those who believed in the God
of the Christians would prosper, claimed Constantine, and pagans
would suffer nothing but misfortune.

All this was to throw the Church into confusion. Some retreated into
monasticism. Some joined utopian sects which were regarded as
heretical, and in due course died or were coerced out of existence. The
majority took the view that this was a fulfilment of Biblical prophecy
and that they should seize the opportunity to extend the frontiers of
Christianity into the political realm, even if this meant some
modification in putting into practice the high ethical standards of the
Christian gospel. In 380 the Emperor Theodosius I declared that
Catholic Christianity was the state religion of the Roman Empire.
Non-Christians were but 'foolish madmen' and should be 'branded
with the ignominious name of heretics'. They would be punished with
'the chastisement of the divine condemnation' as well as with 'the
punishment which our authority ... shall decide to inflict'. Christians
were learning to live with the ambiguities of politics. The emblem of
the cross was inscribed on the shields of Roman soldiers, and early in
the fifth century non-Christians were excluded from serving in the
army.

SAINTS AMBROSE AND AUGUSTINE

The pioneer in asserting the claims of the Church in the post-Constant-
inian era was Saint Ambrose, bishop of Milan (339–97). 'For the first
time in history we find a representative of the Church entering the
secular arena. ... Never before had the claims of the Church been
asserted in so daring and uncompromising a manner.'[2] Ambrose had
been elected bishop of Milan by popular acclamation in 373, although
he was a layman and had not at the time been baptised. Indeed, his

promotion in the Church from baptism and confirmation, via deacon and presbyter, to bishop, took place within the space of a week.

Ambrose wrote of the blessings of peace, but accepts the necessity of going to war in a just cause and 'when driven to it by the wrongs received'. Restraint is to be shown during the conduct of war and after victory. '[Justice] must even be preserved in all dealings with enemies … . But a deeper vengeance is taken on fiercer foes, and on those that are false as well as those who have done greater wrong.' Ambrose lays great stress on justice, which accords with nature, and 'is binding, even in war'. Clergy are to take no part in fighting 'for we have our thoughts fixed more on the duty of the soul than on that of the body'. He assured the Emperor Gratian of his prayers for the victory of Roman arms, but ten years later he did not hesitate to write a stern letter rebuking the Emperor Theodosius for the massacre of 7000 inhabitants of Thessalonica in retaliation for a seditious outbreak which had led to the murder of a number of officers of the garrison. Theodosius was excommunicated by Ambrose until he had shown public penance.

Saint Augustine (354–430) further developed the ideas put forward by Ambrose, but he did not pretend to be a systematic thinker. He was essentially a polemicist, and his most important works were written to combat heretical and schismatic tendencies – Manicheans, Donatists, Pelagians. These splinter groups varied greatly, but the one thing they had in common was the notion that it is obligatory and possible to be faithful to the gospel in this life, a rejection of the dilution of Christian discipleship which seemed inseparable from wholehearted participation in the affairs of 'the world'. They saw themselves as a holy remnant, undefiled and unspotted by the relativisms and ambiguities of secular affairs. Augustine, by contrast, was an enthusiastic exponent of involvement and responsibility.

Augustine's ideas of the Just War were by no means original. In rejecting the pacifism of the early Church, he was only giving a Christian flavour to Greek philosophy and Roman practice. Time and again in his writings, he insists that if fighting were contrary to Christian teaching, Christ would have told those soldiers he encountered to lay down their arms.

Augustine starts from the premiss that order is a very great good, and is a prerequisite of justice. If order is threatened or disturbed, the Christian is not allowed to kill in a private capacity, but may do so at the command of the lawful authorities: 'I do not approve of killing [in self-defence] unless one happens to be a soldier or public functionary ... [acting] according to the commission lawfully given him, and in the manner becoming to his office.' Killing is also permitted at God's express command. He attaches great importance to the duty of obedience to the lawful authorities and considers that a soldier is 'innocent' even if he obeys an unrighteous command on the part of the ruler.

'Just wars [wrote Augustine] are usually defined as those which avenge injuries, when the nation or city against which warlike action is to be directed has neglected either to punish wrongs committed by its own citizens or to restore what has been unjustly taken by it.' It is the adversary's wickedness which makes a cause just: 'If the victory fall to the wicked (as sometimes it may) it is God's decree to humble the conquered, either reforming their sins, or punishing them.' God is at all times sovereign, 'ending [wars] sooner or later as He wills'.

Men ought to hate war and desire peace, but real peace will not be achieved in this world, 'because the mutability of human estate can never grant any realm an absolute security'. Real peace will be possible only in the heavenly city 'whose king is truth, whose law is love, whose measure is eternity'. Augustine wrote often that, though war is the contrary of peace, war's only purpose is to secure peace. Yet he is clearly uncomfortable with this paradox, and insists that 'it is a greater glory to destroy war with a word than men with a sword'.

The Christian is to wage war with moderation, to show mercy to prisoners and the defeated, 'especially where no disturbance of peace is to be feared'. If an earthly state observes Christian teachings, 'even war will not be waged without kindness'. Augustine makes an interesting distinction between the possession of weapons (deterrence) and their use (war-fighting). Christ had told Peter to take a sword, but rebuked him when he used it to cut off Malchus' ear. 'Doubtless it was mysterious that the Lord should require them to carry weapons, and forbid the use of them. But it was His part to give the suitable precepts, and it was their part to obey without reserve.'

Augustine was continually trying to rebut the charge that Christian doctrine is not adaptable to the customs of the secular realm, and it is here that his writings are least satisfactory. How is a state which claims to be based on Christian principles, he asks, to implement the precept to return evil with good, to turn the other cheek, to go the second mile? Augustine gives three answers. First, if the advice of Christ had been followed, the Roman state would have been founded, sanctified, strengthened, and enlarged very much more successfully than had been the case under non-Christian rulers. Let those who say that

Christian teaching is opposed to the welfare of the state consider how differently things would have turned out if only rulers and judges, parents and children, masters and slaves, tax-collectors and tax-payers, had followed Christian teaching: the critics would be forced to admit that nothing would provide more effectively for the safety of the realm than to observe Christian teaching. The Roman Empire had become rich and famous 'by natural virtues without true religion'; how much more might have been added if men had been Christian.

Secondly, the purpose of overcoming evil with good is to show how temporal things are to be despised for the sake of faith and justice. The intention must be to love both the victim and the aggressor, to bring the offender to repentance rather than to overcome him by force. But, adds Augustine without further explanation, 'we often have to act with a sort of kindly harshness, when we are trying to make unwilling souls yield, because we have to consider their welfare rather than their inclination'.

Thirdly, the precepts of Christ refer to the interior disposition of the heart rather than to the outward act.

SAINT THOMAS AQUINAS, VITORIA, CAJETAN, AND SUÁREZ

For many centuries, the Christian Church had almost nothing but the scattered writings of Ambrose and Augustine as a basis for the Just War doctrine. The decretals of Gratian of Bologna (twelfth century) provide the beginning of systematic thought about the Christian concept of the Just War, and between the thirteenth and sixteenth centuries the Just War doctrine was further elaborated and refined. Conditions were laid down about the requirements of the doctrine, both as regards the purposes for which a Just War could be fought, the procedure by which it should be initiated, and the manner in which it had to be conducted.

Saint Thomas Aquinas (1226–74), like Augustine, starts from the assumption that war is opposed to charity, and then asks 'whether it is *always* a sin to wage war' (my italics). With admirable lucidity, Thomas writes that war may be just (or justified) if three conditions are satisfied.[5]

(1) The authority of the sovereign by whose command the war is to be waged. It is not the business of a private individual to declare war, he wrote, because he can seek redress of his rights from a tribunal.

(2) A just cause is required, namely that those who are attacked should deserve it on account of some fault.

(3) It is necessary that the belligerents should have a rightful intention, so that they intend the advancement of good or the avoidance of evil.

The first explicit requirement in point of time to be added to the three conditions of Thomas Aquinas was that for a war to be just, the ruler ought to be so sure of the degree of his power that he is morally certain of victory. War brings so many evils in its train that it is wicked to cause or permit these evils, and then fail to secure the good ends for which the war is fought. The Spanish Jesuit Francisco Suárez (1548–1617) claimed that the requirement about certainty of victory had been first put forward by Thomas de Vio Cajetan, an Italian Dominican (1469–1534), but the passage in Cajetan to which Suárez refers deals with superstitious amulets. In any case, Suárez considered that Cajetan had been too rigorous in his demand for moral certainty. First, because from a human standpoint, such a degree of certainty is almost impossible of realisation. Secondly, because it may be in the interest of a state not to await such certitude, 'but rather to test its ability to conquer the enemy, even when that ability is somewhat doubtful'. Thirdly, because if complete certainty were required, 'a weaker sovereign could never declare war upon a stronger'. Suárez considered that a ruler should avoid an *offensive* war if there was not a 'probable expectation of victory, or one equally balanced as to the chances of victory or defeat'. A *defensive* war might be attempted without such certainty or balance of chances, because in that case 'it is a matter of necessity'.

Three further conditions of a Just War were made explicit by a succession of gifted Spanish neo-scholastics, especially Francisco de Vitoria (c. 1480–1546) and Suárez.

The first additional condition was that a serious effort must be made to resolve the matter at issue by peaceful means before resorting to force. Vitoria keeps coming back to the need for caution and prudence. 'Not every kind and degree of wrong can suffice for commencing a war.' Before embarking on war, the ruler must make 'an exceedingly careful examination' and must listen to the opinions of those who are opposed to going to war. 'For it is the extreme of savagery to seek for and rejoice in grounds for killing and destroying men whom God has created and for whom Christ died. But only under compulsion and reluctantly should [the ruler] come to the necessity of war.' Vitoria insists that those whose conscience is against the justice of a war may not serve in it '*whether they be right or wrong*' (my italics).

It might be thought that Vitoria was only emphasising the requirements of Thomas Aquinas that a just cause and rightful intention are necessary. Suárez, however, carries the idea of proportionality a stage further. War, he wrote, brings so many misfortunes in its train and is so often carried on in an evil fashion that it requires many justifying circumstances to make it righteous. The only just and sufficient cause is 'a grave injustice which cannot be avenged or repaired in any other way'. Before a ruler goes to war, he must call to the attention of the opposing state the existence of a just cause, and must seek suitable reparation. If the other state agrees to make reparation, the ruler 'is bound to accept it, and desist from war, for if he does not do so, the war will be unjust'.

In the light of these requirements, Vitoria and Suárez both raise the question whether a war can be just on both sides. Both answer that, apart from ignorance, this is impossible.

The final conditions relate to the actual conduct of war and comprise two distinct principles: proportion and discrimination. These were implied but not spelled out in the writings of Augustine and Thomas Aquinas. Suárez put it like this: 'The method of its conduct must be proper, and due proportion must be observed at its beginning, during its prosecution and after victory.' When Vitoria and Suárez held that the conduct of war should be 'proper', they mainly had in mind the immunity of the innocent from direct attack, but all writers of the period follow Thomas Aquinas in distinguishing between two effects of an act, one of which is intended, while the other is beside the intention – the law of double effect. 'Now moral acts [wrote Thomas] take their species according to what is intended and not according to what is beside the intention, since this is accidental.'[4]

All Christian theologians agreed that it was unlawful to slay the innocent directly and intentionally. Vitoria defined the innocent as including women, children, 'harmless agricultural folk', 'the rest of the peaceable civilian population', 'foreigners or guests who are sojourning among the enemy', clerics and members of religious orders. Suárez points out that the immunity of religious persons and priests is by canon law; he substitutes 'ambassadors' for 'foreigners or guests' (by the law of nations rather than natural law); and he adds among those who should be immune 'all unable to bear arms ... [and] those who are able to bear arms, if it is evident that ... they have not shared in the crime nor in the unjust war'.

The law of double effect was put to some odd purposes in the Middle Ages as, indeed, it is in our own day. Domingo de Soto (1495–1560) followed Aquinas in holding that there were two consequences of self-defence, 'the preservation of one's own life and the destruction of another's, of which the former was intended, the latter was accidental'. But the more usual application nowadays has been to say that the killing of enemy soldiers is intended, while the accidental killing of civilians in the course of military operations is unintended.

The real problem, then as now, was whether it was lawful to engage in a military operation in which the death of innocent people could be expected, even though it was not intended. The modern version of this question is whether those who hold the Christian version of the Just War doctrine may, in order to maintain nuclear deterrence, threaten to attack military targets in the knowledge that if deterrence fails and strategic nuclear weapons are used, civilians will be injured or killed as a collateral effect. Paul Ramsey has answered the question in this way: 'Certainly there can be justified destruction of an entire city that is an indirect consequence of the destruction of a military installation. The destruction of a city may be a collateral effect, an accompanying, unavoidable result of bombing military targets.'[5]

Vitoria and Suárez both accept that innocent people may be slain as an indirect effect or collateral circumstance. Vitoria considered that it was permissible to kill innocent people in the course of storming a fortress or city, but this conclusion evidently troubled him, for he added:

> Great attention, however, must be paid to the point already taken, namely, the obligation to see that greater evils do not arise out of war than the war would avert. For if little effect upon the ultimate issue of the war is to be expected from the storming of a fortress or fortified town wherein are many innocent folk, it would not be right, for the purpose of assailing a few guilty, to slay the many innocent ... . In sum, it is never right to slay the guiltless, even as an indirect and unintended result, except when there is no other means of carrying on the operations of a just war ... .[6]

Vitoria goes on to consider whether it is lawful to kill the innocent from whom some danger is apprehended in the future; 'for example, the children of Saracens are guiltless, but there is good reason to fear that when they grow up they will fight against Christians'. He writes that although such killing 'may possibly be defended', it is in no wise right. It is 'intolerable that any one should be killed for a future fault'. Similarly it is not lawful to kill innocent hostages.

Suárez held that the intentional slaying of the innocent is always illicit. 'No one may be deprived of his life save by reason of his own guilt.' All kinds of harm may be inflicted on an enemy 'provided that these ... do not involve an intrinsic injury to innocent persons, which would be in itself an evil'. The death of innocent people is acceptable only if it is 'not sought for its own sake, but is an incidental consequence'.

A few Catholic writers in the United States have questioned whether the principle of non-combatant immunity is now an essential part of the Just War doctrine. William O'Brien, for example, argues that the principle that non-combatants are immune from direct intentional attack is not derived from some first principle of natural law, but arose out of the practice of individuals and states in the late medieval and early Renaissance period. The principle was possible, he writes, because of the material facts of war at the time the principle was being made explicit. It was a restraint hallowed by custom rather than as 'the result of deductive moral reasoning'.[7] Strict adherence to it today would mean, in O'Brien's view, abandoning both the concept of nuclear deterrence and the possibility of fighting a nuclear war against a nuclear enemy. O'Brien, and also Richard Shelly Hartigan, would hold that the principle of non-combatant immunity must today be subordinate to the over-riding obligation to deter or defeat an aggressor.

O'Brien and Hartigan are a minority, nevertheless, and the weight of opinion is that non-combatant immunity is an integral part of the Just War doctrine. The principle was reaffirmed by the Second Vatican Council in the following terms: 'Any act of war aimed indiscriminately at the destruction of entire cities or extensive areas along with their population is a crime against God and man himself. It merits unequivocal and unhesitating condemnation.'[8]

The principle of discrimination has in practice meant regarding combatants as guilty and non-combatants as innocent. In insurgency and counter-insurgency warfare, the traditional distinction between soldier and civilian is blurred, and the principle of discrimination is more difficult to apply. Moreover, the invention of weapons of mass destruction introduces a further difficulty, since it is difficult to use these weapons in such a way that only military targets are harmed.

The Just War doctrine at the time of the Reformation may be said to have required seven conditions to be satisfied for a war to be justified:

jus ad bellum (justice in going to war)

(1) War can be decided upon only by the legitimate authorities.

(2) War may be resorted to only after a specific fault and if the purpose is to make reparation for injury or to restore what has been wrongfully seized.

(3) The intention must be the advancement of good or the avoidance of evil.

(4) In a war other than one strictly in self-defence, there must be a reasonable prospect of victory.

(5) Every effort must be made to resolve differences by peaceful means before resorting to the use of force.

jus in bello (justice in conducting military operations)

(6) The innocent shall be immune from direct attack.

(7) The amount of force used shall not be disproportionate.

It is interesting that the United Nations, without explicit reference to the Just War tradition, has adopted very similar principles for its own peace-keeping operations.[9]

LUTHER AND CALVIN

The Christian version of the Just War doctrine entered the Protestant tradition at the time of the Reformation. Luther, like Augustine, was a polemicist and dealt with the problem haphazardly in books, tracts, and sermons, written between 1523 and 1530, with such vivid titles as *Whether soldiers, too, can be saved.* Calvin, in this respect more like Thomas Aquinas, was a systematic thinker and dealt succinctly with the question in a couple of pages of his *Institutes of the Christian Religion* (1536).

Luther with great force, and Calvin with more restraint, start from the assumption that governmental authority is divinely instituted and must be obeyed. The citizen is not bound to obey the ruler if the ruler is in the wrong; but if there arise cases of doubt, and if citizens 'cannot with all diligence find out, they may obey him [the ruler] without peril to their souls'. War should be fought 'at the emperor's command, under his banner, and in his name. Then everyone can be sure in his conscience that he is obeying the ordinance of God.' The magistrate (ruler), wrote Calvin, 'does nothing by himself, but carries out the very judgments of God ... ; all things are done on the authority of God who commands it'.

Both Calvin and Luther seem to regard as illicit what is nowadays sometimes called the Just Revolution. Calvin writes that rulers are 'the guardians and defenders of the laws' and should overthrow all who seek to undermine the authority of the laws: the only justification for rebellion is that the ruler is tyrannical. Luther opposed rebellion conducted in the name of Christianity: 'war and uprisings against our superiors [or 'overlords', as he writes elsewhere] cannot be right'.

Following the Catholic tradition, Luther and Calvin insist that rulers may resort to war only 'to execute ... public vengeance [as Calvin puts it] ... , to restrain the seditious stirrings of restless men, to help those forcibly oppressed, to punish evil deeds ... , to defend by war the dominions entrusted to their safe-keeping'. Recourse to arms should arise from 'concern for the people alone'. When men allege that war is a great plague, wrote Luther, they should consider how great is the plague that war prevents. It is 'a small misfortune that prevents a great misfortune'.

Luther expressly makes the point emphasised by the neo-scholastics on the need to be sure of victory.

> If we are not going to make an adequate, honest resistance that will have some reserve power, it would be far better not to begin a war, but to yield lands and people ... without useless bloodshed, rather than have him [the Turk] win anyhow in an easy battle and with shameful bloodshed ... .

Luther and Calvin both insist on the need to seek a peaceful resolution of disputes before resorting to arms. Calvin warns the ruler not to seek occasion to take to arms lightly 'unless they are driven to it by extreme necessity'. Surely, he writes, 'everything else ought to be tried before recourse is had to arms'.

As to the actual conduct of military operations, Calvin and Luther give different advice. Calvin warns rulers against 'undue cruelty' and 'giving vent to their passions'. 'Rather, if they have to punish, let them not be carried away with headlong anger, or be seized with hatred, or burn with implacable severity. Let them also ... have pity on the common nature in the one whose special fault they are punishing.' But he also warns against imprudent leniency and quotes a Latin tag to the effect that it is indeed bad to live under a prince with whom nothing is permitted, but much worse under one by whom everything is allowed.

Luther, in more bloodthirsty vein, writes that it is 'both Christian and an act of love to kill the enemy without hesitation, to plunder and burn and injure him by every method of warfare until he is conquered'. Almost as an afterthought, he adds 'except that one must beware of sin, and not violate wives and virgins'.

Both the Reformers accept the need for Christians to bear arms, and Luther urges Christians to offer their services as hangmen, constables, judges, lords, or princes. The profession of the soldier is 'right and godly', and children are especially urged not to 'despise, reject, or do away with soldiers...and those whose business is war'. Every occupation 'has its own honour before God'.

Calvin prefaces his discussion of the problem of war by admitting that it is 'a seemingly hard and difficult question' since the law of God forbids all Christians to kill. Luther asks why Christ and the apostles did not bear the sword, and answers briskly, 'You tell me, why did Christ not take a wife or become a cobbler or a tailor'.

If an office or vocation were to be regarded as disreputable on the ground that Christ did not pursue it himself, what would become of all the offices and vocations other than ministry, the one occupation he did follow? Christ pursued his own office and vocation, but he did not thereby reject any other.

Although Christ did not bear or prescribe the sword, 'it is sufficient that he did not forbid or abolish it but actually confirmed it'.

WILLIAM PENN'S 'HOLY EXPERIMENT'

Through all the centuries, there was always a minority of Christians which believed that the Church made a disastrous compromise at the time of Constantine, and that it can recover its original vitality only by unequivocal loyalty to the total demands of the teachings of Jesus, whatever the consequences. But the mainstream of Christian thinking has held that fourth-century Christians were right, that there can be no going back to the 'innocence' of the early Church.

What the man or woman in the street wants to know, however, is not whether pacifism is an authentic position for a Christian, but whether it works. Some pacifists would claim no more than that pacifism is right for them, a vocation: probably the majority of pacifists see pacifism as a practicable policy, and indeed the early Quakers tried to build a state on pacifist principles in Pennsylvania – what William Penn and his fellow-Quakers called 'The Holy Experiment'.

Penn wished to return to the 'purity' of the early Church, but not by withdrawing from politics. 'True godliness', he once wrote, 'don't turn men out of the world, but enables them to live better in it, and excites their endeavours to mend it.' His policy received its first major test in

1689 – a request that Pennsylvania should make preparations for defence. The initial reaction of the Quaker members of the Council was to belittle the gravity of the threat. Said John Simcock, 'I see no danger but from the bears and wolves'. When the issue could no longer be evaded, the Quakers decided to state their personal attitudes as a matter of conscience and to abstain from voting, but Simcock made it clear that they did not want to tie the hands of others; 'they may do every one what they please'.

In 1693, when the English Crown had resumed control over Pennsylvania, there came another request for funds, but Governor Benjamin Fletcher agreed that those who had scruples about supporting war could give money which might be used for other purposes and 'not be dipt in blood'. The Assembly refused to vote funds until other matters had been attended to, but in the end a money bill was approved.

Meanwhile, Penn in London promised that he would transmit to the Council and the Assembly of the colony all messages from the English Crown, and he said that he had no doubt that the colony would supply such men or money as the Crown considered necessary for the safety of America.

Requests for money or men continued to trouble the Pennsylvania Quakers. In 1695 the General Assembly in the colony said they would vote funds only if a new constitution were adopted, whereupon Governor Fletcher dissolved the two Houses. In 1696 £300 was voted in the expectation that it would be used to buy food and clothes for distressed Indians. The following year Pennsylvania was asked to supply 80 men or £2000 for defence, but a joint committee of the two houses replied by drawing attention to the fact that they had contributed £300 the previous year.

In 1709, the issue arose once again, and the Quakers held an informal meeting to decide their attitude: ' ... notwithstanding [that] their profession and principles would not by any means allow them to bear arms; yet it was their duty to support the Govmt of their Sovereign the Queen ... and therefore that they might and ought to present the Queen with a proper sum of money.' £500 was appropriated, which led to a sharp response from Governor Charles Gookin: 'Words alone, I assure you, Gent., are not much valued by the ministry at Home, and £500 from Pennsylvania will add ... but little weight.' The Quakers might have scruples about war, he said, but that should not prevent them from being generous in their gifts to the Queen. No conscience could be pleaded to prevent the grant of a sum 'in some measure worthy of Her Royal acceptance'.

What is an *ad hoc* decision the first time it is taken easily becomes a precedent. When money was requested for military purposes, the first reaction of Friends in Pennsylvania was to deny that the situation was dangerous. When this argument had exhausted its utility, Friends claimed that the measures contemplated were provocative. If a request for funds were persisted in, they said that their grievances should be considered first, or that it was inconvenient for the Assembly to meet, or simply that they could not afford the money. When prevarication would no longer suffice, funds were usually voted, at first on the understanding that they would not be used for military purposes, but after 1709 simply as a present for Queen Anne or King George.

The attitude of Friends to military service is illustrated by a phrase which occurs several times in the laws of Pennsylvania: 'the people called Quakers who, though they do not, as the world is now circumstanced, condemn the use of arms in others, yet are principled against it themselves.'

I do not want to belittle the Quakers of Pennsylvania or the principles they tried to put into effect, but to show how difficult it is to convert a personal vocation into a public policy. Penn's Holy Experiment is remembered for its pioneering achievements in such matters as religious toleration, respect for the rights of the Indians, and a humane penal system. But Pennsylvania could not be isolated from the external situation. The colony posed no threat to others, but the Quakers of that day learned, as each generation has learned since, that their task is not to create a peaceable kingdom as a sanctuary into which to escape from the wars and rumours of wars which threaten the rest of mankind. The clear implication of Penn's essay *Towards the Present and Future Peace of Europe* (1693) is that pacifism is not enough. Men and women must also build the institutions of peace.

WAR IN THE TWENTIETH CENTURY

The vocation and witness of Christian pacifists has perhaps become more relevant as war has become more terrible. At the first Assembly of the World Council of Churches in 1948, three positions held by Christians were outlined: that there is a duty to maintain the rule of law, by force if necessary; that 'modern warfare, with its mass destruction, can never be an act of justice' (a form of nuclear pacifism); that some Christians refuse all military service as 'an absolute witness against war and for peace' (total pacifism). The Assembly admitted its 'deep sense of perplexity in the face of these conflicting opinions' and by implication accepted that any of the three is legitimate for Christians.

The Second Vatican Council of the Roman Catholic Church, in addition to stating and elaborating the Just War position, praised those who renounce the use of violence provided that this can be done without injury to the rights and duties of others or of the community itself. The Council thought it right that the law should make humane provisions for the case of those who for reasons of conscience refuse to bear arms, provided that they accept some other form of service to the human community.

It is evident that the Churches are as perplexed as others in the nuclear age. It is not easy to use modern strategic weapons without violating the principles of discrimination and proportion. A nuclear weapon causes harm by heat, blast, and initial radiation in a rough circle around the point of explosion. A 500 kiloton bomb over the Ministry of Defence in London, for example, would cause extensive third-degree burns to exposed people in Leytonstone 4.9 miles away and would damage most houses in Edgware 6.8 miles away. The early residual radiation released in the first 24 hours would be blown down-wind, possibly for several hundred miles: with a typical north-west wind, radioactive contamination from a 500 kiloton bomb over central London could well reach France and Belgium within a day. The remaining delayed radiation and fall-out would be sucked into the upper atmosphere and fall to the ground indiscriminately world-wide. In addition, the partial destruction of ozone in the stratosphere would lead to enhanced ultra-violet radiation which would penetrate towards the surface of the earth, supplementing the radiation released by the explosion. Radiation is known to induce cancer, to harm foetuses in the womb, and to damage reproductive organs, thus leading to genetic defects in future generations.

Two other effects of a nuclear explosion may be mentioned: the generation of an electro-magnetic pulse which damages radio, telephone, and electrical circuits: the electro-magnetic pulse from a nuclear explosion at an altitude of 300 miles above Frankfurt would destroy unprotected integrated circuits in the whole of Europe. Secondly, the rise of minute particles into the atmosphere as a result of a substantial nuclear exchange might well, on plausible assumptions, cause a drop in the mean continental temperature in the northern temperate zone by as much as 25° centigrade, leading to what has been called a 'nuclear winter'.

It hardly needs saying that nuclear weapons pose an especially acute problem for those who take the Just War tradition seriously. The V-1 and V-2 bombs of the second world war had explosive yields of less than one ton. The nuclear bombs used against Hiroshima and Nagasaki in 1945 had yields of 12,500 and 22,000 tons respectively. War-heads now exist more than one thousand times as powerful as the nuclear bombs used against Japan. The United States tested a weapon with a yield of 15 megatons (15 million tons) at Bikini Atoll in 1954, and the Soviet Union tested a 58 megaton weapon (58 million tons) in 1961.

For many centuries states have practised deterrence, the notion that if you want peace, you should prepare for war. A military capacity is no longer enough, however: it has to be accompanied by a credible declaratory policy that succeeds in convincing an adversary that it would be foolish to assume that the threat is idle. This leads to the paradox for nuclear-weapon states that peace is preserved by the knowledge that the failure of deterrence could lead to escalating violence culminating in mutual annihilation.

Western nuclear-weapon states insist that elaborate precautions have been taken to prevent unauthorised or accidental use, and that uncontrolled escalation is not inevitable; but this is a plausible hope, not a certainty. Moreover, one is entitled to ask if the threatened acts will accord with Just War criteria for military operations. Western spokesmen do not now threaten to attack civilians 'as such' if deterrence should fail, but they have been careful never to say that indirect harm to non-combatants would meet the proportionality test of the Just War doctrine. For understandable reasons, British governments have not revealed much about targeting plans.

There was always a gap between what the Just War theorists said and what the men of action did. There are some who now claim that Just War principles have lost their relevance, that it is absurd in the modern world to apply principles first enunciated in totally different circumstances sixteen hundred years ago. And it is easy to deride the Just War position, to maintain that in an era of long-range missiles with nuclear war-heads, it makes no sense to talk of confining attacks to enemy combatants and military targets or to insist that military operations shall never be excessive. But the fact is that the non-pacifist Christian has only two options: to argue that there need be no moral restraints on the right to go to war or on the conduct of military operations so long as the cause is just or, following the Just War tradition, to accept limitations and prohibitions on war-making. In theory at any rate, a version of the Just War doctrine is today, explicitly or implicitly, the ethical position of almost all non-pacifist Christians.

But practice does not always coincide with theory, especially in time of war, and during the second world war there were only a few Christians in Britain and the United States who took completely seriously the requirements of the Just War: notably, Bishop George Bell of Chichester in Britain[10] and Father John Ford SJ, of Weston College in the United States.[11] After the war, the Just War tradition became better known among English-speaking Protestants, initially as a result of a pioneering study by a US Methodist scholar.[12]

I have reviewed elsewhere the responses of Christian Churches to the nuclear predicament.[13] I was myself a member of a Church of England working party which, using Just War criteria, recommended that Britain should withdraw in stages from all direct association with nuclear weapons,[14] although this recommendation was rejected by the General Synod (1983). The Roman Catholic Church has issued a series of documents in different forms on the ethics of deploying or using nuclear weapons, including Pope John the twenty-third's letter *Pacem in terris* (1963), the document of the Second Vatican Council entitled 'Pastoral Constitution on the Church in the Modern World' (*Gaudium et Spes*, 1965), Pope John Paul II's message to the United Nations (1982), and the pastoral letter of the US bishops 'The Challenge of Peace: God's promise and our response' (1983).[15] From these sources, one may summarise the view of the Catholic mainstream, and of many Protestants as well, as follows:

1. *Legitimacy of war to defend justice.* 'The fact of aggression, oppression and injustice in our world ... serves to legitimate the resort to weapons and armed force in defence of justice.' (US bishops' letter, para. 78).
2. *Rejection of nuclear war.* 'We see with increasing clarity the political folly of a system which threatens mutual suicide, the psychological damage this does to ordinary people, especially the young, the economic distortion of priorities ... . But it is much less clear how we translate a No to nuclear war into the personal and public choices which can move us in a new direction ... ' (US bishops' letter, para. 133).
3. *Modern war anachronistic.* In the atomic age, the idea that war is any more a suitable way of righting wrong is contrary to reason (*Pacem in terris*). 'All these considerations compel us to undertake an

evaluation of war with an entirely new attitude ... . It is our clear duty, then, to strain every muscle as we work for a time when all war can be completely outlawed by international consent.' (*Gaudium et Spes*, arts 80, 82). 'To evaluate war with a new attitude, we must go far beyond an examination of weapons systems or military strategies.' (US bishops' letter, para. 67).

4. *Deterrence.* Many people regard the accumulation of arms for the purpose of deterrence as 'the most effective way by which peace of a sort between nations can be maintained at the present time. Whatever be the case with this method of deterrence, men should be convinced that the arms race in which so many countries are engaged is not the best way to preserve a steady peace ... . Rather than being eliminated thereby, the causes of war threaten to grow gradually stronger.' (*Gaudium et Spes*, art. 81). Nevertheless, deterrence based on balance can be judged morally acceptable, not as an end in itself but as a stage on the way to progressive disarmament. At the same time, we should not be satisfied that this is the way to preserve peace, as it is always susceptible to the real danger of explosion. (Pope John Paul II to the United Nations). 'There are moral limits to deterrence policy as well as to policy regarding use ... . Nuclear deterrence should be used as a step on the way to progressive disarmament.' (US bishops' letter, paras 178, 188.3).

5. *Difficulty of keeping war limited.* 'We express repeatedly in this letter our extreme scepticism about the prospects for controlling a nuclear exchange, however limited the first use might be. Precisely because of this scepticism, we judge resort to nuclear weapons to counter a conventional attack to be morally unjustifiable ... . Even the "indirect effects" of initiating nuclear war are sufficient to make it an unjustifiable moral risk in any form ... . There must be no misunderstanding of our profound scepticism about the moral acceptability of any use of nuclear weapons ... . As a people, we must refuse to legitimate the idea of nuclear war.' (US bishops' letter, paras 131, 153, 193, 194).

6. *Conduct of military operations.* 'A justifiable use of force must be both discriminatory and proportionate ... . To wage truly "total war" is by definition to take huge numbers of innocent lives. Just response to aggression must be discriminate; it must be directed against unjust aggressors, not against innocent people caught up in a war not of their making ... . It is not morally acceptable to intend to kill the innocent as part of a strategy of deterring nuclear war ... . No Christian can rightfully carry out orders or policies deliberately aimed at killing

non-combatants. Under no circumstances may nuclear weapons or other instruments of mass slaughter be used for purposes of destroying population centres or other predominantly civilian targets.' (US bishops' letter, paras 104, 144, 147–8, 178). Any act of war indiscriminately directed to the destruction of whole cities or vast areas with their inhabitants is a crime against God and man, which merits firm and unequivocal condemnation. (*Gaudium et Spes*, art. 80).

7. *Conscience and the secular authorities.* 'Since the right to command is required by the moral order and has its source in God, it follows that, if civil authorities legislate for or allow anything that is contrary to that order and therefore contrary to the will of God, neither the laws made nor the authorizations granted can be binding on the consciences of the citizens, since *God has more right to be obeyed than men.*' (*Pacem in terris*). Actions which deliberately conflict with the all-embracing principles of universal natural law, as well as orders commanding such actions, are criminal. 'The courage of those who openly and fearlessly resist men who issue such commands merits supreme commendation.' (*Gaudium et Spes*, art. 79).

8. *Conscientious objection to war.* 'We cannot fail to praise those who renounce the use of violence in the vindication of their rights ... provided that this can be done without injury to the rights and duties of others or of the community itself .... Moreover, it seems right that laws make humane provisions for the case of those who for reasons of conscience refuse to bear arms, provided however, that they accept some other form of service to the human community.' (*Gaudium et Spes*, arts 78–9).

9. *Urgent need for disarmament.* 'The production and the possession of armaments are a consequence of an ethical crisis that is disrupting society in all its political, social and economic dimensions .... True disarmament, that which will actually guarantee peace among peoples, will come about only with the resolution of this ethical crisis .... It is important and right that every serious proposal that would contribute to real disarmament and would create a better climate be given the prudent and objective consideration it deserves. Even small steps can have value that would go beyond their material or technical aspects .... Indulgence in rhetoric, in inflamed and impassioned vocabulary, in veiled threat and scare tactics can only exacerbate a problem that needs sober and diligent examination .... I re-affirm my confidence in the power of true negotiations to arrive at just and equitable solutions. Such negotiations demand patience and

diligence and must notably lead to a reduction of armaments that is balanced, simultaneous, and internationally controlled.' (Pope John Paul II to the United Nations). 'Justice, then, right reason and humanity urgently demand that the arms race should cease; that the stockpiles which exist in various countries should be reduced equally and simultaneously by the parties concerned; that nuclear weapons should be banned; and that a general agreement should eventually be reached about progressive disarmament and an effective method of control.' (*Pacem in terris*).

10. *The role of the United Nations*. 'It is Our earnest wish that the United Nations Organization ... may become ever more equal to the magnitude and nobility of its tasks, and that the day may come when every human being will find therein an effective safeguard for the rights which derive directly from his dignity as a person, and which are therefore universal, inviolable and inalienable rights.' (*Pacem in terris*).

PROBLEMS OF THE JUST WAR

The seven principles of the Just War doctrine are easy to understand but difficult to satisfy in practice. There is no space to examine all of the difficulties in depth, but I briefly review five of them.

(1) proportionality

The concept of proportionality sometimes leads to confusion as it is used in three quite different senses. There is, in the first place, proportionality in reprisal action: the principle that when military reprisals are undertaken in response to an illegality by the other side, one of the requirements is that the scale of reprisal should not exceed the scale of the violation. This means that a future act should not exceed the scale of a past act: the decision which a military commander has to take may be difficult, but he at least has a standard against which his response is to be measured.

Secondly, there is proportionality in war-fighting (*jus in bello*). The principle here is that no act of war should be undertaken if the harm to be expected would be excessive in relation to the military advantage anticipated. This is inevitably a subjective test, because unlike events have to be compared – for example, an attack which in the ordinary way would be excessive might be explained and justified as a means of ending a war quickly and thus saving lives, as in the US atomic attacks on Japan in 1945. The British Council of Churches, in a report published in 1946, commented that this argument 'undoubtedly has weight' but that it is one of peculiar danger 'since it can be used to justify any kind of barbarity.'[16] Proportionality in war-fighting requires difficult decisions by military commanders, though the notion of minimum force is understood in some armies.

The problem of proportion in this second sense is that to assess proportionality requires a cool Cartesian calculation in time of crisis and danger. This can be illustrated by an extract from George Orwell's diary. Following his experiences in the Spanish Civil War, Orwell had fancied himself as a strategic thinker, and in his diary during the second world war, he was constantly weighing up military options. In March 1941, Orwell thought that the choices for Britain were between holding on to Libya at whatever cost and sending a major force to Greece. It would be appalling to lose Libya, he thought, and there were few purely military advantages from sending a force to Greece; but to help Greece would demonstrate that Britain would come to the aid of a European country struggling to maintain its independence. 'Everyone who thinks about the matter is torn both ways.' After weighing up the pros and cons, Orwell's conclusion was as follows: 'I am in favour of putting all our eggs in one basket and risking a big defeat, because I don't think any defeat or victory in the narrow military sense matters so much as demonstrating that we are on the side of the weak against the strong.'[17] British troops had, in fact, landed in Greece nine days before Orwell wrote.

The concept of proportionality in the third sense is in decisions whether to go to war or not (*jus ad bellum*). This use of proportionality was well expressed in the Pastoral Letter of the US Roman Catholic bishops: 'proportionality means that the damage to be inflicted and the costs to be incurred by war must be proportionate to the good expected by taking up arms' (para. 99). This involves a comparison between two complex sets of hypothetical events in the future, events which are quite different in kind. On one side of the equation (to oversimplify greatly) might be an estimated financial burden of £10 billion plus 100,000 combatant casualties and 100,000 civilian casualties: on the other side of the equation might be the expectation of saving a nation with 10 million inhabitants from an alien, totalitarian invader; and in practice, of course, the calculation would be vastly more complicated as there would be many additional costs and possibly a few additional benefits on both sides of the equation. And there is always the possibility of going to war and thus incurring the costs, and then failing to secure the main benefit.

Decision-makers who rely on consequentialist ethics often have to make cost-benefit analyses of this kind, though usually on a lesser scale; and not to act is also a decision, with possibly momentous consequences. But to compare the effects of unlike acts, such as surrender to oppressive government and resort to nuclear war, is to ask a lot of mere mortals.

(2) double effect

Thomas Aquinas distinguished between different effects of an act, one or more effects being intended by the doer and one or more effects being 'beside the intention, ... accidental'. This is a concept with which we are all familiar, as when a medical procedure has side effects which may be foreseen by the practitioner but which may be undesirable: for example, an aspirin tablet to cure a headache which irritates a sensitive stomach lining or an injection before a tooth is extracted which causes momentary pain. Military operations often have double or multiple effects – for example, a legitimate air attack on an ammunition dump which causes indirect harm to a nearby maternity hospital.

A special moral difficulty arises, nevertheless, when the harm is not only indirect but is also inevitable and foreseen. All of the delayed radiation from a nuclear explosion is inevitable and foreseen, and some of it will almost certainly cause bodily harm to innocent persons now living and genetic harm to future generations. In one sense, the harm is an accidental side-effect which, while foreseen, may not be wished for or intended by the person authorising or undertaking the nuclear attack; but it might also be argued that an effect which is certain and foreseeable cannot easily be thought of as 'beside the intention ... accidental'.

This is a difficult issue for those who believe that it is possible to use nuclear weapons in accordance with Just War principles. The usual solution is to say that indirect effects are permissible so long as the unintended harm is proportionate in the second sense indicated above (proportionality in *jus in bello*).

(3) intention, threat, and bluff

It is necessary to distinguish carefully between intention, threat, and bluff. An intention is a decision, whether announced or not, to perform an act in the future: I will wash the dishes tonight. A threat is a declaration that an unpleasant act will be performed in defined circumstances: I will stop your pocket money if I find you ill-treating an animal. A bluff is a declaration of intent in the hope of affecting the behaviour of another person but without the firm intention of performing the unpleasant act if the threat is disregarded, as when Solomon said 'divide the living child in two'.

Does deterrence depend on intention, or threat, or bluff, or simply on uncertainty as to whether the deterrer will or will not, in defined circumstances, perform an act of which he is capable? While there may possibly be an element of bluff in the declared intention to use nuclear weapons in certain circumstances, I think we may safely eliminate it as a major component of deterrence. Bluff does not usually work the second time.

Uncertainty is a more important element in deterrence: when two sides have the capability of destroying each other, and when both have told the other that an unprovoked attack will lead to immediate nuclear retaliation, both may be uncertain whether the other will match deeds to words, and this may play a part in deterring them from acting in such a way as to invite a nuclear response.

From an ethical point of view, however, I think we should regard deterrence as depending on the threat to use nuclear weapons in certain eventualities, backed by the resolute intention of using them if the threat fails to deter: in other words, a conditional intention.

The question then has to be asked whether it is moral to threaten or have the conditional intention of performing an act which would be immoral if performed. Assume for the sake of argument that torture would be wrong in all circumstances. Would it be a moral act to have the conditional intention of using torture in a just cause: that is to say, declaring the intention of resorting to torture in certain eventualities, not as a bluff but with the firm intention of doing so if the threat fails to bring about the desired result? This is a difficult issue on which thoughtful and humane people disagree, but my own view is that if an act would be wrong, a conditional intention to perform the act would also be wrong. When republican prisoners in Northern Ireland went on hunger strike, Father Herbert McCabe maintained that because it is wrong to intend directly to take one's own life, it must be wrong to threaten to do so, 'for the threat is nothing but the announcement that under certain conditions [a man] will do this thing that is wrong.'[18]

How, then, should a person who accepts Just War principles view the conditional intention to use strategic nuclear weapons which is implicit in NATO's deterrence policy?

The most straightforward position is taken by those who believe that any act of war conditionally intended must be consistent with the Just War principles of discrimination and proportion. These people I refer to below as Just War deterrers. The difficulty for them is to conceive of a use of nuclear weapons which would fully meet *jus in bello* criteria and yet would impress an enemy as being militarily significant.

There are several alternative positions. Some consider that, while all acts of war actually committed should accord with *jus in bello* principles, a threat to use strategic nuclear weapons need not do so as it will never be necessary to perform the act. They hold, as do many Just War deterrers, that what deters is the *possibility* of nuclear retaliation, not the *certainty*. One difficulty for them is to convince a potential enemy that the threat is not bluff. If they do not succeed and the threat fails to deter (which they believe will never happen), they have not escaped the moral predicament, simply postponed it to a later stage.

Others take the view that it is often necessary to choose the greater good or lesser evil, that the prevention of war in the nuclear age must take precedence over other moral considerations, even if this results in the paradox of threatening to do something which would be immoral if it had to be done; that while we must do all we can to respect discrimination and proportion if deterrence fails, we sometimes have to be prepared to violate one or both of these principles if this is necessary to prevent a greater evil. The holders of this position believe that, in a tragic and imperfect world, it may sometimes be necessary to choose the lesser evil or greater good, even if this means performing an act which on the face of things would be immoral. Although some distinguished philosophers have sought to justify such a line of reasoning, I find it difficult to square it with the demands of Christian ethics.

Others would accept the last position but would carry it a stage further and maintain that if nuclear deterrence is inconsistent with *jus in bello* principles, so much the worse for *jus in bello*, that we have inherited these principles from an age that did not know and could not have foreseen total war or absolute weapons. These would be willing to abandon one or both of the traditional *jus in bello* criteria if that should be necessary to prevent submission to an unjust aggressor.

My own view, for what it is worth, is that no position is wholly free from difficulty but that the non-pacifist Christian is on firmest moral ground if the threats implicit in nuclear deterrence are confined to acts which would be moral if committed; and, according to the Just War tradition, this means that the threatened acts should conform to the *jus in bello* principles of discrimination and proportion.

(4) deterrence, war-fighting, and war-winning

A military strategist who takes the Just War tradition seriously would base deterrence on the conditional intention of performing acts which would accord with the *jus in bello* principles of proportion and discrimination. To threaten or conditionally intend to perform acts which would violate the deterrer's own conscience is not credible and will hardly deter. If the simple fact of possessing weapons is to have a deterrent effect, there must also be a credible doctrine about use. When defence experts put forward scenarios for fighting a war, it is often difficult for the ordinary lay person to know whether this is merely a bit of declaratory deterrence or whether the military capability is not maintained for deterrence at all but for war-fighting and war-winning; and the difficulty is compounded if the military capability is nuclear. Has nuclear war become thinkable?

The truth probably is that the deterrer can never get the balance right, that rational and restrained discussion of war-fighting may enhance deterrence but that loose and excessive talk about war-fighting, and particularly cheap talk about prevailing in nuclear war, may disturb domestic or allied opinion and seem grossly provocative to the other side.

(5) just on both sides?

The Just War concept is criticised by some as providing inadequate guidance in the contemporary world. On the other hand, it may be held that the Just War doctrine (as G. K. Chesterton wrote of the Christian ideal in general) has not been tried and found wanting, it has been found difficult and left untried. It would be contrary to reason to believe that a war can be just on both sides, so that every war is necessarily unjust for one side if not for both. Why is it, then, that Christians can be found on both sides of so many past wars, proclaiming the justice of their own cause and regarding those on the other side as misguided and wicked?

Vitoria and Suárez were surely right in holding that a war cannot be just on both sides. My own view is that the failure of Christian leaders in all ages to make it plain when their own side fails to meet the demands of the Just War represents a major ethical scandal. Would that the Churches had been as outspoken and clear in this regard as they have been in upholding their understanding of Christian standards in sexual matters.

2 The Just War in International Law

> All things are uncertain the moment men depart from law.... War ought not to be undertaken except for the enforcement of rights; when once undertaken, it should be carried on only within the bounds of law and good faith.... In order that wars may be justified, they must be carried on with not less scrupulousness than judicial processes are wont to be.
>
> Hugo Grotius

HUGO GROTIUS: THE FATHER OF INTERNATIONAL LAW

It is hardly possible to exaggerate the contribution which Hugo Grotius made to the foundation of international law as a subject in its own right, worthy of academic study, distinct from moral theology, and with immediate practical applications in the relations among rulers. Grotius was a great innovator, not because he disregarded the work of his predecessors and contemporaries, but because he brought their disparate work into coherent relationship. He was a man of extraordinary scholarship, and in his work on the law of war and peace – *De jure belli ac pacis* (1625)[1] – he cites or quotes from the works of Greek, Roman, and Jewish classical writers: Homer, Euripides, Herodotus, Thucydides, Xenophon, Plato, Aristotle, Demosthenes, Cicero, Virgil, Horace, Livy, Ovid, Seneca, both Plinys, Josephus, Plutarch, and Tacitus. He quotes from fifty-two of the Bible's seventy-five books, as well as from the Apocrypha. He was fully acquainted with the writings of the early fathers of the Church: Justin Martyr, Tertullian, Origen, Lactantius, and Saints Ambrose, Jerome, Chrysostom, and Augustine. He was also steeped in the writings of the schoolmen and quotes Thomas Aquinas, Cajetan, Domingo de Soto, and Luis Molina; and he mentions in particular that among the theological works he had studied were those of Vitoria (p. 22). He refers more than once to the writings of his Spanish Catholic contemporary Suárez, and he tells us that he had obtained the works of Ayala and Gentili. He was a Protestant, belonging to a moderate

Calvinist group, but it is noteworthy that he does not quote from the
writings of Calvin or Luther. He warns his readers against the dangers
of receiving with approval everything written by famous authors; often
they are simply under the influence of their feelings. But 'when the
schoolmen agree on a point of morals, it rarely happens that they are
wrong' (pp. 28, 100).

Grotius wrote in a way that both shocked and fascinated the
traditionalists, for he was a man of independent judgement. He did not
look for authority in a church or creed or political ideology, but in the
conscience of the individual. *De jure belli ac pacis* was first published in
Paris in 1625. It was on the Roman Catholic Index from 1626 until
1896, but within a century of its first publication, Dutch, French,
German, and English translations had appeared. The Latin text, with
an abridged English translation by William Whewell, was published by
the Cambridge University Press in 1853.

The reason why Grotius wrote this remarkable book was, as he
correctly expressed it, that before his time 'no one has treated [the
mutual relations among rulers of states] in a comprehensive and
systematic manner'. He considered that these relations were governed
by two distinct systems of law, which 'writers everywhere confuse'.
First, there is the law of nature, natural law, which is based on right
reason; secondly, there is the law of nations, which is derived from the
law of nature. This law of nations has received its obligatory force from
'the will of all nations, or of many nations'. Grotius considered that
what he wrote 'would have a degree of validity even if we should
concede ... that there is no God, or that the affairs of men are of no
concern to Him' (pp. 9, 13, 24, 26, 44).

Grotius also recognises a third system of law, municipal law (pp.
24, 44, 192, 234, 385, 707–9, 713, 788–9), but he sometimes
confuses the reader by referring in addition to a fourth system, what he
calls the rules of love or the law of the gospel (pp. 63–81, 94, 182,
234–7, 759).

In his early years Grotius had been concerned with a case before the
Prize Court involving the Dutch East India Company, some of whose
members were Mennonites. The Mennonites were then, and are
today, pacifists, rejecting all use of armed force. From his contact with
these worthy people, Grotius realised that any serious study of the law
of war written by a Christian must come to grips with the question
of whether it is possible to wage war without violating Christian
principles. The practice of the majority of Christians might have
provided him with a sufficient answer, for Christians seemed to have

no greater scruples about going to war, or about the methods of waging it, than pagans or adherents of other faiths. Indeed, this was something which greatly shocked Grotius.

> Throughout the Christian world I observed a lack of restraint in relation to war .... I observed that men rush to arms for slight causes, or no cause at all, and that when once arms have been taken up there is no longer any respect for law ... ; it is as if, in accordance with a general decree, frenzy had openly been let loose for the committing of all crimes. (p. 20)

When good men are confronted with such ruthlessness, he writes, they are likely to go to the other extreme and forbid all use of force. He feared that his fellow countryman, Erasmus, had yielded to this temptation. Grotius was too wise to think that the truth lay at the mid point between extreme opinions.

> The very effort of pressing too hard in the opposite direction ... does harm, because in such arguments the detection of what is extreme is easy, and results in weakening the influence of other statements which are well within the bounds of truth. For both extremes therefore a remedy must be found, that men may not believe that nothing is allowable, or that everything is. (p. 20)

In order to consider the question of the use of force as a matter of Christian ethics, Grotius goes back to the time of Jesus and the experience of the early Church. When soldiers came to John the Baptist, 'he did not bid them withdraw from military service, as he must have done if such was the will of God'. If it had been the purpose of Jesus absolutely to do away with capital punishment and war, 'he would have expressed his purpose with words as plain and explicit as possible'. The reason Jesus rebuked Peter for using a sword against Malchus at the time of his arrest was that 'he [Peter] was taking up arms against those who were coming as representatives of the public authority' (pp. 65, 71, 95) – a more plausible explanation than Augustine's!

Grotius insisted that, for the Christian, a greater degree of moral perfection is required than is enjoined by the law of nature alone. The law of the gospel makes it impermissible for the Christian to use force in personal self-defence, 'for Christ bids us submit to a blow rather than do harm to an aggressor'. No true Christian should, of his own accord, enter upon a public office which may require him to have to decide upon the shedding of blood, for Christian goodness is manifested by seizing every opportunity to show mercy (pp. 27, 86–7, 178, 486).

Grotius does not deny that the early Church was pacifist. 'The early Christians, fresh from the teachings of the Apostles..., both understood the Christian rules of conduct better, and lived up to them more fully, than did men of later times.' Little by little, he writes, the interpretation of the law of the gospel was adjusted to the customs of age, and by the time of Constantine, there is no lack of writers who hold the opinion that Christians may lawfully resort to war. Many bishops were very alert guardians of discipline, but 'we do not read that there was a single one who ... sought to deter either Constantine from inflicting the death penalty and engaging in war, or Christians from military service' (pp. 84, 86, 153, 182). (What Grotius wrote may be technically correct, but there were Christians who were faithful to the pacifism of the early Church at the time of Constantine.)

But it was not the intention of Grotius to furnish a system of ethics; he was asking what can be learned from the law of nature and the law of nations about the relations between states and rulers. Grotius takes it for granted that the intentional killing of an innocent person is forbidden; 'it is necessary that he who is killed shall himself have done wrong'. Grotius then asks if there are any exceptions to the general prohibition of taking human life, if it is 'ever lawful' or 'ever permissible' to wage war. Grotius answers his own question by saying that it is permissible to use force 'as a just penalty or in case we are able in no other way to protect our life or property'. Such force may be used only in such a way that it 'does not violate the rights of others'. Not all wars, he writes cautiously, are at variance with the law of nature, 'and this may also be said to be true of the law of nations' (pp. 33, 51–90, 723).

Like the schoolmen, Grotius assumed that a war of self-defence is justified, that a state may respond with force if attacked. 'The right of self-defence ... has its origin ... in the fact that nature commits to each his own protection' (p. 172).

Three other causes are given which may make a war just. First, 'for the enforcement of rights' (p. 18). Secondly, to seek reparation for injury (pp. 170–1, 186). Thirdly, to punish the wrong-doer (pp. 171, 489, 502, 504). Yet not every wicked act should necessarily be punished; 'many reasons ... admonish us to forego punishments'. There may be occasions when 'to refrain from the exercise of one's right is not merely praiseworthy but even obligatory, by reason of the love which we owe even to men who are our enemies'. Love for our neighbour often prevents us from pressing our right to the utmost limit. The obligation to forgive rests upon us with special weight 'when either we too are conscious ... ourselves of some sin, or when the sin committed against us is the result of some human and pardonable weakness, or when it is sufficiently clear that he who has wronged us is repentant'. All these reasons for leniency have their origin in 'the love which we owe to our enemies'. In any case, there should always be a prudent calculation of likely consequences. If a particular course of action is likely to have both good and bad consequences, 'it is to be chosen only if the good has somewhat more of good than the evil has of evil' (pp. 568–70, 572, 601) – which is to ask a lot of mere mortals! Moreover, Grotius adds two further warnings. First, there may exist a just cause for going to war, but the war may be unjust because of the wrong intention of the one who engages in hostilities (p. 556). Secondly, a war may be undertaken for a just cause, but may become unjust because it gives rise to unjust acts (pp. 718–9).

Grotius follows the majority of medieval theologians by holding that morally a war cannot be just on both sides, except where ignorance is present, but he distinguishes between ethical justice and legal justice. Many things are done 'without right and yet without guilt' (pp. 565–6).

A war is not just unless it has been sanctioned by the lawful authorities, and it is also 'necessary ... that it should be publicly declared' and proclaimed by one of the parties to the other. The reason why public declarations are required is to avoid resort to force to settle private quarrels. The twin requirements of the sanction of the lawful authorities and public declarations of war must both be satisfied; 'one without the other does not suffice' (pp. 91, 633, 639).

A prudent ruler will not go to war without a reasonable expectation of victory. Even if the cause is right, it is of the highest importance that the necessary resources should be available. Even if one has made a commitment to an ally one is not 'bound to render aid if there is no hope of a successful issue'. War ought not to be undertaken 'save when the hope of gain [is] greater than the fear of loss' (pp. 575–6, 581–2).

Military alliances are permissible, but not of an unconditional character. Aid should not be rendered 'for any sort of war without distinction of cause', and it is not permissible to entice or force anyone to anything which it may not be permissible for him to do. A war formally declared against a ruler is declared at the same time against 'all his subjects', and 'all who will join him as allies' (pp. 585, 622, 638).

Grotius is reluctant to concede that there can be a just revolution comparable to a just war, except where judicial procedures are not available. It is

> much more consistent with moral standards, and more conducive to the peace of individuals, that a matter be judicially investigated by one who has no personal interest in it, than that individuals, too often having only their own interests in view, should seek by their own hands to obtain that which they consider right .... (p. 91)

It is not permissible 'for either private or official persons to wage war against those under whose authority they are', although if the lawful authorities issue an order which is contrary to the law of nature or the commandments of God, it should not be carried out. It is not even permissible for a private citizen to put down by force or kill a usurper of sovereign power, except where the usurper has seized power by means of an unlawful war and contrary to the law of nations, and 'no promise has been given to him, but possession is maintained by force alone'. It is a weighty question how to choose between independence and peace, between life and liberty, but private individuals ought not to take it upon themselves to decide such questions, since it involves the interest of the whole people. Even when the right of sovereignty is in dispute, the private citizen should 'accept the fact of possession'. Grotius points out that although the administration of the Roman Empire was often in the hands of extremely bad men, and there was no lack of pretenders who sought to rescue the state, the early Christians 'never associated themselves with [these] attempts'. Those who from a lawful cause have come into personal or political slavery 'ought to be satisfied with their state' (pp. 92, 138, 144, 159–63, 551, 573, 781).

A ruler desirous of winning friends should strive for a reputation for having undertaken war 'not rashly nor unjustly', and of having waged it in 'a manner above reproach'. A nation is not foolish which does not press its own advantage to the point of disregarding the law common to all nations, for no state is so powerful that it may not some time need the help of others. The state which transgresses the laws of nature and of nations cuts away the bulwarks which safeguard its own future peace (pp. 16, 20).

Grotius devotes a great deal of attention to the immunity of the innocent, and his list of those he regards as innocent is a long one. It includes children, women (unless they have committed a crime which ought to be punished), old men, all those whose manner of life is opposed to war such as those performing religious duties and 'those who direct their energies to literary pursuits', farmers, merchants, artisans and other workmen, prisoners of war, and neutrals. Military commanders are to forbid plundering and 'the violent sack of cities and other similar actions' which cannot take place without harming many innocent people (pp. 173, 734–40, 756, 783, 790).

Grotius accepts the law of double effect as it had been formulated by Thomas Aquinas: 'many things follow indirectly, and beyond the purpose of the doer'. Thus it is permissible to bombard a ship full of pirates or a house full of brigands, even if innocent women and children are thereby endangered. At the same time, we must take care regarding what happens beyond our purpose, 'unless the good which our action has in view is much greater than the evil which is feared, or, unless the good and the evil balance'. In all cases of doubt, we should favour that course which has regard for the interest of another rather than our own (pp. 600–1).

Among the methods of war which Grotius considers to be expressly forbidden are the use of poison, the use of falsehood or deception, except perhaps to save the life of an innocent person, deliberate terrorism, and attacks on 'things of artistic value [and] things which have been devoted to sacred uses', including 'structures erected in honour of the dead'. Also forbidden is the harming or killing of hostages. A hostage is permitted to try to escape, unless he has given a pledge not to do so in order that he might have more liberty; but prisoners captured in a just war should not try to escape. Rape is contrary to the law 'not of all nations, but of the better ones'. Among Christians, rape should be subject to punishment, even in time of war (pp. 539, 617, 619, 651–3, 657, 740–1, 743, 751, 753, 768, 828–9).

It is not permissible to injure or kill to prevent a future offence, unless the danger to life or property is 'immediate and imminent in point of time'. It is quite untenable to take up arms against a power which, if it becomes too great in the future, may be a source of danger. Those who justify 'anticipatory slaying' are greatly deceived, and deceive others; while it is permissible to kill him who is making ready to kill, the man is more worthy of praise who prefers to be killed rather than to kill. The idea that the possibility of being attacked confers the right to attack (a pre-emptive strike) is 'abhorrent to every principle of equity'. Fear of an uncertainty cannot confer the right to resort to force. For protection from uncertain dangers, we must rely on 'Divine Providence and on a wariness free from reproach, not on force'. As for vengeance 'not as a retaliation for the past, but as a preventive for the future', Christ wishes us to forego this. 'Nature does not sanction retaliation except against those who have done wrong' (pp. 175–6, 184–5, 481, 504, 741).

In a just war, he who takes booty from the enemy becomes its owner 'witout limit or restriction'; but in an unjust war, things taken must be restored. Individual soldiers who capture anything acquire it for themselves 'when they are not in formation or engaged in executing an order'. But Grotius again insists that 'the rules of love are broader than the rules of law'. Humanity requires that those who do not share in the guilt of a particular war should be left with their possessions 'particularly if it is quite clear that they will not recover from their own state what they have lost' (pp. 664, 673, 683, 759, 778).

Those rulers who decide to stay out of a war have an obligation to be impartial and, in particular, to avoid increasing the power of him who supports a wicked cause. There are advantages in having one's neutral status recognised by treaty (pp. 786–7).

A truce does not end a state of war; it is 'an agreement by which warlike acts are for a time abstained from ... , a period of rest in war, not a peace'. During a truce, all acts of war are unlawful. If one party violates a truce, the other party is 'free to take up arms even without declaring war' (pp. 832, 834–6, 838).

Peace is to be highly valued, 'especially by Christians'. Throughout the whole period of war, the soul can be kept serene and trusting in God only if it is always looking forward to peace (p. 861).

Although, according to the law of nations, prisoners of war become slaves, both Christians 'among themselves' and Moslems 'among themselves' have agreed that prisoners shall not become slaves but shall be exchanged or freed when an appropriate ransom has been paid or some other agreement has been reached. Innocent prisoners are not to be killed or punished with undue severity, nor are tasks to be imposed upon them which are excessively severe (pp. 690, 696, 763–4, 769).

Those who go to war without a just cause deserve punishment, but they shall not be executed unless they have committed a crime which a just judge would hold punishable by death. Collective punishments are forbidden. 'It is not sufficient that by a sort of fiction the enemy ... be conceived as forming a single body.' On the other hand, responsibility for a wicked act does not rest solely on him who ordered it; responsibility is shared with those who granted it the necessary consent, or who helped it, or who furnished asylum, or who actually shared in committing the crime, or who gave advice or praise or approval, or who did not forbid it, or who failed to help the injured, or who did not dissuade when they ought to have done so, or who concealed facts which they ought to have made known – 'all these may be punished, if there is in them evil intent sufficient to deserve punishment'. Like Augustine and Thomas Aquinas, Grotius attaches importance to the intention behind an act, as well as to its intrinsic nature and likely consequences (pp. 522–3, 556, 600, 740–1).

In all these matters, Grotius insists on the supreme authority of the individual conscience. If an act is objectively just but the person who commits it considers it to be unjust, 'the act is vicious'. If those who are ordered to go to war consider that the cause is unjust, 'they should altogether refrain' (pp. 138, 558, 587, 622).

Indeed, Grotius is constantly advising moderation and magnanimity. It is better to acquit a guilty person than condemn one who is innocent. War is such a serious matter that the ruler should not be content with 'merely acceptable' causes, but only 'causes that are perfectly evident'. War is so horrible that 'only the utmost necessity, or true affection', can render it honourable. It is better to neglect care of our own lives in order to safeguard the life of another. Moderation is often an act of prudence. Even those who deserve punishment should be treated 'with goodness, with moderation, with highmindedness'. A conquered enemy should be shown clemency. When crimes have been committed which deserve death, 'it will be the part of mercy to give up something of one's full right because of the [large] number of those involved'. We should consider not only 'what the laws of men permit' but also 'what is right from the point of view of religion and morals'. Those displays of strength which are of no use for obtaining a right or putting an end to war 'are incompatible both with the duty of a Christian and with humanity itself'. Moderation 'gives the appearance of great assurance of victory' (pp. 559, 566–7, 586, 731, 733, 742–4, 755, 773, 776).

Grotius was writing a treatise on the law of war and peace, and much that he has to say about the law of peace lies outside the scope of the present work. Suffice it to note that Grotius considers how war may be avoided by creating the appropriate institutions for the peaceful settlement of disputes. Three ways of avoiding war are reviewed: a conference (that is to say, direct negotiations), arbitration, or decision by lot. 'Where judicial settlement fails, war begins' (pp. 171, 560–3, 823–4).

The whole structure of international law depends upon agreements being honoured, which is 'a rule of the law of nature'. 'Faith must be kept even with the faithless.' Whatever may be the terms on which peace is made, they ought to be preserved absolutely. If differences arise regarding the interpretation of an agreement, we should not depart from the natural meaning of the words, except to avoid an absurdity (pp. 14, 799, 855, 862).

Much could be written by way of comment on this fascinating treatise, but I will confine myself to two remarks. First, Grotius does not fail to remind his readers of the perfectionism of 'Sermon on the Mount' Christianity. For thirteen centuries, this emphasis has been confined to a few utopian sects, while the Christian mainstream had been more concerned with accommodating the law of the gospel to the requirements of the secular world. Yet here was Grotius, a Christian and a humanist, a man of the world, a professional bureaucrat, formulating a theory of international law, and yet constantly reiterating the need to love the enemy, to give him the benefit of the doubt, to be killed rather than to kill.

Secondly, the work of Grotius has well stood the test of time. Three and a half centuries later, the main thrust of his book is commonplace among international lawyers. There are, of course, aspects where the work of Grotius has been elaborated or refined or overtaken by events. Perhaps he should have taken a stronger line against looting. Perhaps he should have paid more attention to the protection due to prisoners of war and to the problem of reprisals. In an age which emphasises 'the inadmissibility of the acquisition of territory by war', as Security Council resolution 242 puts it, perhaps Grotius gives too much weight to the fact of possession. His discussion of what is now called 'the just revolution' is perhaps too much influenced by his passion for order and certainty. But criticism of particular defects does not detract from the seminal value of the work as a whole.

TOTAL WAR AND ABSOLUTE WEAPONS

It is impossible, within the scope of this book, to survey even in the most sketchy form the way others have built on the foundations laid by Hugo Grotius. His main contribution was to secularise what, until his day, had been considered to be a matter of moral theology or Christian ethics, but a matter in which practice had increasingly disregarded doctrine. In any event, there are two respects in which developments have made it increasingly difficult to apply one of the main principles which Grotius had taken over unaltered from Christian teaching: the idea that 'the innocent' should be immune from direct attack, 'the innocent' comprising all those taking no direct part in the actual conduct of hostilities.

The first development was that of total war, the idea that entire populations should be mobilised in the war effort, the transformation of war from a contest between full-time fighters into a struggle of peoples. War-time armies in the so-called developed countries are formed by conscripting all those who are physically fit and not engaged in activities essential to the war effort. In this century, conscription has been applied to women as well as to men. The productive capacity of the community is geared to winning the war, or at least avoiding defeat. Government-controlled propaganda is directed towards the unity of the national effort and towards undermining the will of the enemy. Party politics, normally regarded as essential to the democratic system, are put into cold storage for the duration of the war, so that the energies of the nation may be fully concentrated on military victory. If national territory is occupied by the enemy, underground resistance movements operate under cover of normality. Brave men and women infiltrate into enemy society to disrupt essential activities or to stiffen the will of the underground movement. So-called fifth columns prepare the way for a take-over of further territory.

In situations of this kind, what happens to the traditional distinction between civilian and combatant, innocent and guilty? It is only too easy to assume that the adversary is not the enemy's armed forces, but his whole society. And if his whole society is the adversary, it is argued, his whole society becomes a legitimate target for attack. If this results in injury to those who are unquestionably 'innocent', such as young babies, this is justified by recourse to the principle of double effect: the harm done to 'the innocent' was not intended, even though it was expected and indeed inevitable.

During the past generation, what had become increasingly acceptable in international armed conflicts has become commonplace in internal wars, in wars of national liberation, in insurgency and counter-insurgency. Thus we have the phenomenon of the man or woman, even the child, who is a peasant by day and a guerrilla fighter by night.

Accompanying this trend towards total war has been the invention of absolute weapons, by which I mean weapons which by their nature (range and power) cannot be used in a just and rational way and yet are made and deployed in order to deter others from using them. Even before the discovery of nuclear explosives and long-range missiles, the ability to attack enemy cities had made modern war different in kind,

and not simply in degree, from the traditional war between professional armies about which Augustine, Thomas Aquinas, and Grotius,
had written. 'The most radical and significant change of all in modern
warfare', wrote Father John Ford in 1944, 'is ... the enormously
increased power of the armed forces to reach behind the lines and
attack civilians indiscriminately.'[2] It is not denied that both sides
during the second world war resorted to terror-bombing against
civilians. Frits Kalshoven has made it plain that both Britain and
Germany made plans to bomb cities, but that the operational
decisions to begin were almost fortuitous. On 10 May 1940, German
aircraft dropped bombs on the town of Freiburg in the Black Forest
in the belief that they were somewhere near Dijon in France, more
than 100 miles to the south-west. On 14 May, the Germans bombed
Rotterdam, and the following day, the British war cabinet authorised
attacks on oil and railway targets in the Ruhr. On 24 August,
German aircraft dropped bombs on London, but against orders and
in the belief that they were somewhere else, and the next day British
aircraft bombed Berlin. This led in turn to German attacks on the
docks of East London on 5–7 September, announced in Germany as
reprisals for British attacks against German civilians. Kalshoven
concludes that 'certain characteristics' of British bombing were
'incompatible with the law as it stood', and that German attacks on
London were '*prima facie* unlawful according to the law of air
warfare in force at the time' and that he can find no justification for
this as a reprisal.[3]

When the decision had to be made about the first use of nuclear
weapons, the advice offered to President Truman by a group of
thoughtful and humane men, which included Henry Stimson and
George Marshall, was to use the first nuclear weapon as soon as
possible against a previously undamaged Japanese city containing a
military installation surrounded by houses and without explicit prior
warning (advice of the Interim Committee of the US War Department after its meetings on 31 May and 1 June 1945).

Deterrence depends on making a conditional threat, but to make a
threat does not necessarily mean that one will carry it out. If one is
told that nuclear deterrence does not include any conditional
'intention' along the lines suggested above, that states only pretend
to prepare nuclear retaliation, that the threat is only a matter of
declarations and semantics and will never be implemented, the
private citizen can only reply that he knows nothing of such a
well-intentioned subterfuge. The fact is that the credibility of

deterrence depends on convincing the other side that one has a firm resolve not to shrink from taking the action which one has declared one would take in defined circumstances.

It is the realisation of these facts which has given rise to a sort of nuclear pacifism. Those who take this view do not renounce all use of force; what they reject is the use of nuclear arms, with the risk of escalation up to weapons so powerful and so indiscriminate that it is difficult to conceive of their being used justly. Pacifism, whether a selective pacifism limited to particular weapons or particular methods of waging war, or the full-blooded and complete rejection of all use of force whatever the consequences for oneself or others, provides a way of escape from one set of dilemmas, only to face the pacifist with another set of dilemmas. Perhaps the most poignant fact with which the pacifist must come to terms is not that he or she may suffer as a consequence of the rejection of force, but that many of the victims will be totally innocent. But this is part of the human condition and is as true for the non-pacifist as it is for the pacifist.

ATTEMPTS TO OUTLAW WAR

It will seem to many a utopian dream to try to get rid of war simply by fiat, without first building the institutions of peace and eliminating the instruments of war. The League of Nations Covenant and the UN Charter recognise the interconnection between the three processes. Members of the League agreed 'to respect and preserve as against external aggression the territorial integrity and existing political independence of all Members' (Art. 10). States agreed not to resort to war without first trying to settle their disputes peacefully. War, or the threat of war, was not declared to be illegal but 'a matter of concern to the whole League' (Art. II(1)). Any resort to war in disregard of the Covenant was to be deemed 'an act of war against all other Members of the League' (Art. 16(1)).

The UN Charter seeks to distinguish between the legal and illegal use of force. It contains a commitment that 'Members shall refrain in their international relations from the threat or use of force against the territorial integrity or political independence of any State, or in any other manner inconsistent with the Purposes of the United Nations' (Art. 2(4)). Members agree to settle their disputes by peaceful means (Arts 2(3) and 33(1)), and Chapter VII of the Charter provides for machinery, which has largely remained a dead letter, for dealing with

threats to or breaches of the peace or acts of aggression. The last article
of Chapter VII declares that the right of individual or collective
self-defence remains unimpaired. Both the League and the UN pay
their respects to disarmament – in the case of the League to 'the
reduction of national armaments' (Art. 8(1)) and in the case of the UN
to 'a system for the regulation of armaments' (Art. 26) and 'possible
disarmament' (Art. 47(1)).

The most ambitious, if least realistic, attempt to outlaw war was the
Pact of Paris of 27 August 1928 (often known as the Kellogg Pact or
the Briand–Kellogg Pact). This committed the parties to a total
renunciation of war as an instrument of national policy. Its significance
was not that it would or could or did prevent resort to war; it was that the
initiative for it had come from the United States, which had decided to
stay out of the League of Nations.

On 24 October 1970 (United Nations Day), the UN General
Assembly adopted resolution 2625, to which was annexed a
Declaration and a set of principles of international law regarding
friendly relations and co-operation among states. Seven principles from
the Charter were chosen for progressive development and codification,
namely:

(a) that states shall refrain in their international relations from the
threat or use of force against the territorial integrity or political
independence of any state, or in any other manner inconsistent with the
purposes of the United Nations;

(b) that states shall settle their international disputes by peaceful
means in such a manner that international peace and security and justice
are not endangered;

(c) the duty not to intervene in matters within the domestic
jurisdiction of any state;

(d) the duty of states to co-operate with one another;

(e) the principle of equal rights and self-determination of peoples;

(f) the principle of sovereign equality of states;

(g) the principle that states shall fulfil their obligations in good faith.
That part of the Declaration regarding the renunciation of force is given
in full in Appendix 8.

INDIVIDUAL RESPONSIBILITY UNDER INTERNATIONAL LAW

If the international community is to prohibit all war, or aggressive war,
or war in defiance of obligations arising from treaties and other sources

of international law, or crimes against the peace, or methods of waging war which do not conform to the usages established among civilised peoples or are contrary to the laws of humanity or violate the dictates of the public conscience, then more is needed than simple promises by governments that neither they nor their citizens will use force for illegal purposes or in an illegal way. In the conditions of the second half of the twentieth century, to resort to war against another state except in self-defence or under the enforcement provisions of the UN Charter is a crime, in both the moral and legal senses of the word. Crimes within national societies are deterred by three kinds of force: the force of personal conscience, the force of public opinion, and the force of the police. In order that the community should accept the rule of law, those who are responsible for maintaining law are themselves subject to law; 'no man [wrote A. V. Dicey] is above the law, but ... every man, whatever be his rank or condition, is subject to the ordinary law of the realm and amenable to the jurisdiction of the ordinary tribunals'.

Comparable institutions are slowly being created for the international community, but it is increasingly accepted that international law is not confined to the relations among states, that an individual who commits an act which is a crime under international law is responsible therefor and consequently liable to punishment. Almost the first act of the UN General Assembly was to ask in resolution 3 that Members should arrest war criminals who had committed atrocities and 'cause them to be sent back to the countries in which their abominable deeds were done, in order that they may be judged and punished according to the laws of those countries'. At the suggestion of Secretary-General Trygve Lie, the General Assembly in resolution 95 affirmed 'the principles of international law' recognised by the Nürnberg Charter and the judgment of the Tribunal. The International Law Commission (ILC), which had been set up by the General Assembly to promote the progressive development and codification of international law, was asked to formulate the principles of international law recognised in the Charter of the Nürnberg Tribunal and to prepare a draft code of offences against the peace and security of mankind.

It hardly needs stressing that the Nürnberg Tribunal was established by the victors to try the vanquished. If Allied nationals committed crimes under international law during the second world war, they were not brought to trial before any international tribunal. It is notable, moreover, that the accused at Nürnberg were not charged with aerial bombardment of cities or torpedoing civilian ships, possibly because this would have exposed the prosecutors to the *tu quoque* argument. The Nürnberg Tribunal itself considered that its Charter was 'not an arbitrary exercise of power on the part of the victorious nations but ... the expression of international law existing at the time of its creation; and to that extent is itself a contribution to international law'. Nevertheless, a number of jurists considered that the Nürnberg procedure was partially defective. It is no doubt for this reason that the General Assembly was careful not to endorse the entire Nürnberg procedure, but only to affirm those 'principles of international law' which are to be found in the Charter and the judgment of the Tribunal.

In accordance with the directive of the General Assembly, the ILC formulated seven principles, as indicated in italic type below. Extracts from ILC's comments follow in indented paragraphs.[4]

Principle 1

Any person who commits an act which constitutes a crime under international law is responsible therefor and liable to punishment.

The Tribunal declared that international law imposes duties and liabilities on individuals as well as on states. 'Crimes against international law are committed by men, not by abstract entities.' 'The authors of these acts cannot shelter themselves behind their official position in order to be freed from punishment ....'

> [The first] principle is based on the first paragraph of article 6 of the Charter of the Nürnberg Tribunal which established the competence of the Tribunal to try and punish persons who, acting in the interests of the European Axis countries, whether as individuals or as members of organizations, committed any of the crimes defined in ... article 6. The text of the Charter declared punishable only persons 'acting in the interests of the European Axis countries' but, as a matter of course, Principle I is now formulated in general terms.
>
> The general rule underlying Principle I is that international law may impose duties on individuals directly without any interposition of internal law.

Principle II

The fact that internal law does not impose a penalty for an act which constitutes a crime under international law does not relieve the person who committed the act from responsibility under international law.

Once it is admitted that individuals are responsible for crimes under international law, it is obvious that they are not relieved from their international responsibility by the fact that their acts are not held to be crimes under the law of any particular country: ' ... the very essence of the [Nürnberg] Charter is that individuals have international duties which transcend the national obligations of obedience imposed by the individual State.'

This principle is a corollary to Principle I ...

The Charter of the Nürnberg Tribunal referred, in express terms, to this relation between international and national responsibility only with respect to crimes against humanity. Sub-paragraph (c) of article 6 of the Charter defined as crimes against humanity certain acts 'whether or not [committed] in violation of the domestic law of the country where perpetrated'. The [International Law] Commission has formulated Principle II in general terms.

The principle that a person who has committed an international crime is responsible therefor and liable to punishment under international law, independently of the provisions of internal law, implies what is commonly called the 'supremacy' of international law over national law. The Tribunal considered that international law can bind individuals even if national law does not direct them to observe the rules of international law ... .

Principle III

The fact that a person who committed an act which constitutes a crime under international law acted as Head of State or responsible Government official does not relieve him from responsibility under international law.

This principle is based on article 7 of the Charter of the Nürnberg Tribunal. According to the Charter and the judgment, the fact that an individual acted as Head of State or responsible government official did not relieve him from international responsibility. 'The principle of international law which, under certain circumstances, protects the representatives of a State', said the Tribunal, 'cannot be applied to acts which are condemned as criminal by international law ... .'

The last phrase of article 7 of the Charter, 'or mitigating punishment', has not been retained in the formulation of Principle III. The [International Law] Commission considers that the question of mitigating punishment is a matter for the competent Court to decide.

Principle IV

The fact that a person acted pursuant to order of his Government or of a superior does not relieve him from responsibility under international law, provided a moral choice was in fact possible to him.

This text is based on the principle contained in article 8 of the Charter of the Nürnberg Tribunal as interpreted in the judgment. The idea expressed in Principle IV is that superior orders are not a defence provided a moral choice was possible to the accused. In conformity with this conception, the Tribunal rejected the argument of the defence that there could not be any responsibility since most of the defendants acted under the orders of Hitler. The Tribunal declared: 'The provisions of this article [article 8] are in conformity with the law of all nations. That a soldier was ordered to kill or torture in violation of the international law of war has never been recognized as a defence to such acts of brutality, though, as the Charter here provides, the order may be urged in mitigation of the punishment. The true test, which is found in varying degrees in the criminal law of most nations, is not the existence of the order, but whether moral choice was in fact possible.'

The last phrase of article 8 of the Charter 'but may be considered in mitigation of punishment, if the Tribunal determines that justice so requires', has not been retained for the reason stated under Principle III ... .

Principle V

Any person charged with a crime under international law has the right to a fair trial on the facts and law.

The principle that a defendant charged with a crime under international law must have the right to a fair trial was expressly recognized and carefully developed by the Charter of the Nürnberg Tribunal. The Charter contained a chapter entitled: 'Fair Trial for Defendants', which for the purpose of ensuring such fair trial provided the following procedure:

'(a) The indictment shall include full particulars specifying in detail the charges against the defendants. A copy of the indictment and of all the documents lodged with the indictment, translated into a language which he understands, shall be furnished to the defendant at a reasonable time before the trial.

'(b) During any preliminary examination or trial of a defendant he shall have the right to give any explanation relevant to the charges made against him.

'(c) A preliminary examination of a defendant and his trial shall be conducted in, or translated into, a language which the defendant understands.

'(d) A defendant shall have the right to conduct his own defence before the Tribunal or to have the assistance of counsel.

'(e) A defendant shall have the right through himself or through his counsel to present evidence at the trial in support of his defence, and to cross-examine any witness called by the prosecution.'

The right to a fair trial was also referred to in the judgment itself. The Tribunal said in this respect: 'With regard to the constitution of the Court all that the defendants are entitled to ask is to receive a fair trial on the facts and law.'

Principle VI

The crimes hereinafter set out are punishable as crimes under international law:

The Tribunal was careful not to equate all internationally illegal acts or violations of international law as crimes: '... a criminal act is certainly an illegal act, but not every illegal act is criminal.' Nevertheless, the Tribunal held that acts prohibited by a treaty can be crimes even if they are not expressly designated as such in the treaty.

(a) *Crimes against peace*:
  (i) *Planning, preparation, initiation or waging of a war of aggression or a war in violation of international treaties, agreements or assurances*;
  (ii) *Participation in a common plan or conspiracy for the accomplishment of any of the acts mentioned under (i)*.

The wording of Principle VI(a) is essentially the same as that of Article 6(a) of the Nürnberg Charter: '... resort to a war of aggression is not merely illegal, but it is criminal'. 'To initiate a war of aggression ... is not only an international crime; it is the supreme international crime ... .' A war of aggression, declared the Tribunal, was already a crime in 1939. The Tribunal concluded that at least some administrative activities of high officials in territories occupied by aggressive war are tantamount to waging aggressive war.

Both categories of crimes [in Principle VI(a)] are characterized by the fact that they are connected with 'war of aggression or war in violation of international treaties, agreements or assurances'.

The Tribunal made a general statement to the effect that its Charter was 'the expression of international law existing at the time of its creation'. It, in particular, refuted the argument of the defence that aggressive war was not an international crime. For this refutation the Tribunal relied primarily on the General Treaty for the Renunciation of War of 27 August 1928 (Kellogg–Briand Pact) which in 1939 was in force between sixty-three States. 'The nations who signed the Pact or adhered to it unconditionally', said the Tribunal, 'condemned recourse to war for the future as an instrument of policy, and expressly renounced it. After the signing of the Pact, any nation resorting to war as an instrument of national policy breaks the Pact. In the opinion of the Tribunal, the solemn renunciation of war as an instrument of national policy necessarily involves the proposition that such a war is illegal in international law; and that those who planned and waged such a war, with its inevitable and terrible consequences, are committing a crime in so doing. War for the solution of international controversies under- taken as an instrument of national policy certainly includes a war of aggression, and such a war is therefore outlawed by the Pact.' ...

The Charter of the Nürnberg Tribunal did not contain any definition of 'war of aggression', nor was there any such definition in the judgment of the Tribunal. It was by reviewing the historical events before and during the war that it found that certain of the defendants planned and waged aggressive wars against twelve nations and were therefore guilty of a series of crimes. ...

The term 'assurances' is understood by the [International Law] Commission as including any pledge or guarantee of peace given by a State, even unilaterally.

The terms 'planning' and 'preparation' of a war of aggression were considered by the Tribunal as comprising all the stages in the bringing about of a war of aggression from the planning to the actual initiation of the war. In view of that, the Tribunal did not make any clear distinction between planning and preparation ... .

The meaning of the expression 'waging of a war of aggression' was discussed in the [International Law] Commission during the consideration of the definition of 'crimes against peace'. Some members of the Commission feared that everyone in uniform who fought in a war of aggression might be charged with the 'waging' of such a war. The Commission understands the expression to refer only to high-ranking military personnel and high State officials, and believes that this was also the view of the Tribunal.

A legal notion of the Charter to which the defence objected was the one concerning 'conspiracy'. The Tribunal recognized that 'conspiracy is not defined in the Charter'. However, it stated the meaning of the term, though only in a restricted way. 'But in the opinion of the Tribunal', it was said in the judgment, 'the conspiracy must be clearly outlined in its criminal purpose. It must not be too far removed from the time of decision and of action ... .'

(b) *War crimes*:
Violations of the laws or customs of war which include, but are not limited to, murder, ill-treatment or deportation to slave labour or for any other purpose of civilian population of or in occupied territory, murder or ill-treatment of prisoners of war, or persons on the seas, killing of hostages, plunder of public or private property, wanton destruction of cities, towns, or villages, or devastation not justified by military necessity.
(The ILC noted that Article 34 of the Fourth Geneva Convention on the protection of civilians prohibits the taking of hostages.)

The above is essentially Article 6(b) of the Nürnberg Charter. The Tribunal considered that the Charter gave expression to already existing international law. 'The law of war [the Tribunal declared] is to be found not only in treaties, but in customs and practices of States which gradually obtained universal recognition, and from the general principles of justice applied by jurists and practised by military courts. This law is not static, but by continual adaptation follows the needs of a changing world. Indeed, in many cases treaties do no more than express and define for more accurate reference the principles of law already existing.' By 1939, the rules laid down in the Hague Convention of 1907 'were recognised by all civilised nations, and were regarded as being declaratory of the laws and customs of war ... '. Violations of the provisions of the Hague and Geneva Conventions 'constituted crimes for which the guilty individuals were punishable'.

In a memorandum prepared by the UN Secretary-General in 1949, it was noted that the laws and customs of war are applicable even in an aggressive and therefore illegal war. The principle that violations of the laws and customs of war are international crimes, wrote the Secretary-General, 'has far-reaching implications.'

> The Tribunal emphasized that before the last war the crimes defined by article 6(b) of its Charter were ... covered by specific provisions of the Regulations annexed to The Hague Convention of 1907 respecting the Laws and Customs of War on Land and of the Geneva Convention of 1929 on the Treatment of Prisoners of War. After enumerating the said provisions, the Tribunal stated: 'That violation of these provisions constituted crimes for which the guilty individuals were punishable is too well settled to admit of argument.'

(c) *Crimes against humanity*:
Murder, extermination, enslavement, deportation and other inhuman acts done against any civilian population, or persecutions on political, racial or religious grounds, when such acts are done or such persecutions are carried on in execution of or in connexion with any crime against peace or any war crime.

In dealing with crimes against humanity, the Tribunal sought a compromise between two ideas. 'One is the principle of traditional international law that the treatment of nationals is a matter of domestic jurisdiction. The competing idea is the view that inhumane treatment of human beings is a wrong even if it is tolerated, encouraged or even practised by their own State, and that this wrong ought to be penalized on the international level ... .'

The Tribunal itself was careful to distinguish between acts committed before 1939, and acts committed during the war. To constitute crimes against humanity, the acts relied on before the outbreak of war must have been in execution of, or in connexion with, any crime within the jurisdiction of the Tribunal. The Tribunal therefore cannot make a general declaration that the acts before 1939 were crimes against humanity within the meaning of the Charter. In other words, the Tribunal found that crimes against humanity are accessory to crimes against peace and war crimes. Nevertheless, when the International Law Commission came to draft Principle 6(c), it decided to omit the words 'before or during the war', which were included in the Nürnberg Charter, and emphasised that 'crimes

against humanity ... may take place also before a war in connexion
with crimes against peace'.

The wording of the Nürnberg Charter makes it clear that crimes
against humanity can be committed both against the perpetrator's own
compatriots and against populations of other nationalities. The
Tribunal found that a person otherwise guilty of a crime against
humanity cannot effectively plead that his act was legal under domestic
law.

Article 6(c) of the Charter of the Nürnberg Tribunal distinguished
two categories of punishable acts, to wit: first, murder, extermination, enslavement, deportation and other inhuman acts committed
against any civilian population, before or during the war, and
second, persecution on political, racial or religious grounds. Acts
within these categories, according to the Charter, constituted
international crimes only when committed 'in execution of or in
connexion with any crimes within the jurisdiction of the Tribunal'.
The crimes referred to as falling within the jurisdiction of the
Tribunal were crimes against peace and war crimes.

Though it found that 'political opponents were murdered in
Germany before the war, and that many of them were kept in
concentration camps in circumstances of great horror and cruelty',
that 'the policy of persecution, repression and murder of
civilians ... was most ruthlessly carried out', and that 'the persecution of Jews during the same period is established beyond all doubt',
the Tribunal considered that it had not been satisfactorily proved
that before the outbreak of war these acts had been committed in
execution of, or in connexion with, any crime within the jurisdiction
of the Tribunal. For this reason the Tribunal declared itself unable
to 'make a general declaration that the acts before 1939 were crimes
against humanity within the meaning of the Charter'.

The Tribunal did not, however, thereby exclude the possibility
that crimes against humanity might be committed also before a
war. ...

In accordance with article 6(c) of the Charter, the above
formulation characterizes as crimes against humanity murder,
extermination, enslavement, etc., committed against 'any' civilian
population. This means that these acts may be crimes against
humanity even if they are committed by the perpetrator against his
own population.

Principle VII

Complicity in the commission of a crime against peace, a war crime, or a crime against humanity as set forth in Principle VI is a crime under international law.

The wording of Principle VII is a paraphrase of the last paragraph of Article 6 of the Nürnberg Charter. The Tribunal did not impose a collective responsibility on the members of any organisation, based solely on the fact of membership. To hold a member responsible for the criminal activities of his organisation, the Tribunal required some conduct on the part of the member which established his complicity in the activity.

> The only provision in the Charter of the Nürnberg Tribunal regarding responsibility for complicity was that of the last paragraph of article 6 which reads as follows: 'Leaders, organizers, instigators and accomplices participating in the formulation or execution of a common plan or conspiracy to commit any of the foregoing crimes are responsible for all acts performed by any persons in execution of such a plan.'
>
> The Tribunal, commenting on this provision ... said that, in its opinion, the provision did not 'add a new and separate crime to those already listed'. In the view of the Tribunal, the provision was designed to 'establish the responsibility of persons participating in a common plan' to prepare, initiate and wage aggressive war. Interpreted literally, this statement would seem to imply that the complicity rule did not apply to crimes perpetrated by individual action.
>
> On the other hand, the Tribunal convicted several of the defendants of war crimes and crimes against humanity because they gave orders resulting in atrocious and criminal acts which they did not commit themselves. In practice, therefore, the Tribunal seems to have applied general principles of criminal law regarding complicity. This view is corroborated by expressions used by the Tribunal in assessing the guilt of particular defendants.

These, then, were the seven Nürnberg Principles as formulated by the ILC and presented to the General Assembly in 1950. It might have been possible for the Assembly to have re-affirmed these Principles when they were first formulated; but if the matter were raised in the atmosphere prevailing in the General Assembly of the 1980s, there would undoubtedly be great pressure to extend the sixth Principle to cover inhumane acts resulting from the more virulent forms of racism. That, in itself, might be unobjectionable, but it would change the character of the Nürnberg Principles, which were intended to deal with war crimes and related offences, and not simply with grave violations of human rights.

The ILC had been invited in 1947 to undertake two other tasks: to prepare a draft code of offences against the peace and security of mankind (resolution 177); and to study the desirability and possibility of establishing an international judicial organ for the trial of persons charged with genocide or other crimes over which jurisdiction would be conferred by international conventions (resolution 260B).

During its regular session in 1950–1, the General Assembly took four decisions which bear on the subject matter of this book. First, it invited governments to submit written observations on the ILC's formulation of the Nürnberg Principles (resolution 488). Secondly, it deferred consideration of that part of the ILC report relating to a draft code of offences against the peace and security of mankind and requested the Commission, in its further work on the draft code, to take account of the observations made in the Assembly as well as any written observations by governments (resolution 488). Thirdly, it established a committee of seventeen states to prepare one or more preliminary draft conventions and proposals relating to the establishment and statute of an international criminal court (resolution 489). Finally (although first in point of time), it remitted to the ILC a Soviet proposal on the need to define aggression (resolution 378B).

From this point onwards, the four subjects were so inextricably intertwined that it was difficult to make progress on one aspect until progress was also possible on the other three. The General Assembly had, in effect, deferred consideration of the Nürnberg Principles until a definition of aggression had been agreed. As for a possible code of offences against the peace and security of mankind, the ILC prepared a draft for consideration by the General Assembly in 1951. The rather dismal story of the General Assembly's treatment of this item thereafter is as follows:

1951	item postponed
1952, 1953	item not on the agenda
1954	ILC submits revised draft but item postponed until aggression defined (resolution 897)
1955, 1956	no action
1957	written comments on ILC draft invited (resolution 1186)

1958–73	no action
1974	aggression defined, but no action on draft code of offences
1975, 1976	no action
1977	item postponed (resolution 32/441)
1978	written comments again invited (resolution 33/97)
1979	no action
1980	written comments again invited (resolution 35/49)
1981–5	written comments again invited; ILC asked to continue the work (resolutions 36/106, 37/132, 39/80, 40/69)

The United Kingdom has usually abstained from voting on these decisions.

There is now general agreement in the ILC that the code of offences should cover the most serious international crimes, whether such crimes are politically motivated or not. The Commission intends to consider first the criminal responsibility of individuals, and then, at a later stage, whether states or groups of states can be made legally responsible for the criminal acts listed in the code. The Commission will make a provisional list of the acts constituting serious breaches of international law and the international instruments in which these acts are regarded as international crimes. There are at present differences of view regarding a suitable judicial organ and a scale of penalties.

The item on an international criminal court also languished in the UN system for a good many years. The Committee appointed by the General Assembly to deal with the matter in 1950 itself established a subcommittee, which prepared a number of drafts for consideration by the full Committee; several governments submitted written comments on these drafts. All this material was submitted to the General Assembly in 1952. A wide divergence of view was expressed, and a new Committee was appointed to review the documentation and, in particular, to explore the implications and consequences of establishing an international criminal court (resolution 687). The Assembly, in other words, was asking to be told what would be the consequences of implementing the decision which it had taken in principle two years previously.

The new Committee duly prepared a fresh report. In 1953 the Assembly postponed a decision of substance, and in 1954 it postponed consideration of the report pending progress on related issues (resolution 898). The matter was deferred in 1956, and again in 1957 (resolution 1187).

The question of international criminal jurisdiction was raised in 1965 by Poland in connexion with the punishment of war criminals. The occasion which sparked off this event (or non-event, as it turned out) was the fear in Eastern Europe that the Federal Republic of Germany was on the point of enacting a law which would have provided that no further prosecutions for war crimes could begin after 1965. The law which was finally enacted in West Germany extended from 8 May 1965 to 31 December 1969 the period during which prosecutions could take place of previously undetected offences of the most serious kind, and in 1969 the deadline was further extended.

When Poland first raised the matter in 1965, these West German actions lay in the future. The Polish proposal was dealt with in the normal fashion. Studies were undertaken by the UN Secretary-General, and there were debates and decisions in the Commission on Human Rights, the Economic and Social Council, and the General Assembly. The Polish initiative had three results.

First, the General Assembly began the drafting of a document on the arrest and punishment of war criminals and persons who had committed crimes against humanity. This led in 1973 to the adoption of a declaration on international co-operation in the detection, arrest, extradition, and punishment of persons guilty of war crimes and crimes against humanity. According to Article 7 of the Declaration, states shall not grant asylum to any person where there are serious reasons for considering that he has committed a crime against peace,' a war crime, or a crime against humanity (resolution 3074).

Secondly, a Convention was prepared on the Non-Applicability of Statutory Limitations to War Crimes and Crimes against Humanity, and this Convention came into force on 11 November 1970 (resolution 2391). The original intention was to prepare a convention with the single object of ensuring that no statutory limitation should apply to war crimes, with the hope that this would act as a deterrent to the recurrence of the atrocities committed during the second world war. As the work of drafting proceeded, however, the definition of 'crimes against humanity' was extended to apply not only to those mentioned in the Nürnberg Charter, and to genocide as defined in the Genocide Convention of 1948, but also to inhuman acts resulting from the policy of apartheid. A British attempt to amend the definition to read 'war crimes of a grave nature and crimes against humanity as defined in international law' was heavily defeated, and the Convention was approved by 58 votes in favour, 7 against (including the UK), with 61 states abstaining or absent.

Thirdly, a proposal was initiated by Saudi Arabia whereby persons accused of war crimes or crimes against humanity should be tried by a tribunal consisting of judges from states not parties to the conflict, and that the right of asylum should be denied to a person found guilty of such crimes. The General Assembly decided that the proposal should be taken up 'at such time as it [the Assembly] resumes consideration of the question ... or at such other times as it deems appropriate' (resolution 2392).

The fourth item of the 1950 quartet was the Soviet proposal regarding the definition of aggression, and this eventually made progress. The issue had been first raised in 1950, soon after the North Korean attack on South Korea, and it was alleged that the Soviet move was diversionary in character. The matter lay dormant for a decade but was revived in 1967, at a time when the war in Viet Nam was escalating. There are, of course, intrinsic difficulties over defining aggression, direct and indirect, in such a way as not to lay up trouble for the future; but in 1974, the General Assembly was able to adopt a declaration to the effect that aggression is the use of armed force by a state against the sovereignty, territorial integrity, or political independence of another state, and that the first use of armed force constitutes *prima facie* evidence of an act of aggression. Among acts of aggression, whether or not there has been a declaration of war, are blockade, allowing territory to be used by others for perpetrating aggression, and the despatch of irregular forces or mercenaries. Aggression constitutes 'a crime against international peace', and it is not lawful to acquire territory or special advantage from committing aggression (resolution 3314, see Appendix 13).

Whatever may be the final fate of the 1974 definition of aggression, the seven Nürnberg Principles, a possible code of offences against the peace and security of mankind, and the question of international criminal jurisdiction, the question of penal sanctions against individuals who commit crimes against international law remains before the international community. The UN Secretary-General has stressed that breaches of the laws and customs of war involve the personal responsibility of those committing them; he has suggested that those who violate humanitarian instruments should be liable to penal sanctions after a fair trial 'on the national level'; and he has expressed the view that future humanitarian instruments will be more effective if they expressly provide for penal sanctions against violators.[5]

3 Human Rights in Armed Conflict

> Everyone has the right to life ...
> Universal Declaration of Human Rights, 1948

At its very first session, the UN International Law Commission rejected a proposal that it should attempt to codify the laws of war. The majority of the members of the Commission considered that as war had been outlawed, the regulation of its conduct had ceased to be relevant.

> The majority of the Commission declared itself opposed to the study of the problem at the present stage [1949]. It was considered that if the Commission, at the very beginning of its work, were to undertake this study, public opinion might interpret its action as showing lack of confidence in the efficiency of the means at the disposal of the United Nations for maintaining peace.[1]

The UN, after all, was created to keep the peace, and its Members have agreed to refrain from the threat or use of force in their international relations (Art. 2(4) of the Charter). But this does not mean that armed conflict has ceased. In the first place, the UN Charter does not impair the right of self-defence 'until the Security Council has taken measures necessary to maintain international peace and security' (Art. 51). Secondly, the UN is itself permitted to use armed force (Art. 42). Thirdly, armed conflict can occur between factions within a state, or between the authorities of a state and dissident groups; such conflict will not necessarily be contrary to any provision of the UN Charter. Finally, it hardly needs to be noted that states have resorted to the use of armed force against the territorial integrity or political independence of other states in disregard of their Charter obligations. There have been over 150 armed conflicts since 1945, and a new one breaks out roughly every three months.

TEHERAN CONFERENCE ON HUMAN RIGHTS AND UN GENERAL ASSEMBLY, 1968

Since 1968 attempts have been made to reinforce the work of national and international humanitarian agencies by resort to the human rights machinery of the UN. The first substantial discussion of the role of the UN regarding human rights in armed conflict took place in 1968 at the International Conference on Human Rights, one of the chief events of Human Rights Year. A resolution on the subject was proposed by India and co-sponsored by Czechoslovakia, Jamaica, Uganda, and Egypt. The resolution had a long preamble which, besides referring to various international legal instruments, noted that racist or colonial régimes 'frequently resort to executions and inhuman treatment', and considered that persons who struggle against such régimes 'should be protected against inhuman or brutal treatment and ... if detained should be treated as prisoners of war or political prisoners under international law'. The substance of the resolution called on states to accede to the relevant instruments; invited the General Assembly to initiate a study of existing agreements and the need for new ones; and asked the Secretary-General, after consultation with the International Committee of the Red Cross (ICRC), to urge governments to respect existing rules of international law.

The British representative at the conference expressed 'serious doubts' about the reference to colonial or racist régimes. He thought it was a mistake to make a direct link between 'freedom fighters' and prisoners of war, in the strict sense in which the ICRC had understood the latter expression. He asked for a separate vote on this part of the proposal, but it was approved by 68 votes to none, with 15 abstentions (mainly Western countries). The British representative then voted in favour of the resolution as a whole, which was adopted by 67 votes in favour and no negative votes. Switzerland abstained on the ground that the ICRC, the guardian of the Red Cross Conventions, had not been consulted; South Viet Nam also abstained.

The substance of the Teheran resolution was raised during the General Assembly later in 1968 in the form of a draft resolution sponsored by sixteen states. One paragraph of the proposal, which would have affirmed that the general principles of the law of war apply to nuclear and similar weapons, was deleted at the request of the Soviet Union. The amended proposal was then approved by the Assembly on 19 December 1968 (resolution 2444). The operative part of the resolution affirmed a resolution of the International Red Cross Conference to the effect that:

1.   The right of the parties to a conflict to adopt means of injuring the enemy is not unlimited (this is the essence of Article 12 of the

Brussels Declaration of 1874 and Article 22 of the regulations annexed to the Hague Conventions of 1899 and 1907 on the laws and customs of war on land).
2. It is prohibited to launch attacks against the civilian populations as such.
3. Distinction must be made at all times between persons taking part in the hostilities and members of the civilian population to the effect that the latter be spared as much as possible.

The Secretary-General was asked to do three things:

1. Study steps which could be taken to secure the better application of humanitarian conventions and rules in all armed conflicts;
2. Study the need for additional humanitarian conventions or other legal instruments;
3. 'Take all other necessary steps to give effect to ... the present resolution and to report to the General Assembly ... '

States which had not already done so were called upon to become parties to the Hague Conventions of 1899 and 1907, the Geneva Protocol of 1925, and the four Geneva Conventions of 1949.

The Secretary-General was a little slow off the mark in following up the 1968 decision of the General Assembly, but on 19 May 1969 he communicated the provisions of the resolution to member states, specialised agencies, UN bodies, and a number of non-governmental organisations. Twenty-one of the 126 member states had replied to his letter by the time his report went to press on 20 November 1969, some merely endorsing the Assembly's resolution or giving factual information about the conventions to which they were parties, others going into detail about additional steps which might be taken in the future. Many of the replies reflected the preoccupations of the government concerned: Britain sent the text of its draft convention to ban biological weapons (UN doc. A/7720, pp. 86–90); Mexico commended the treaty on the denuclearisation of Latin America (p. 80); the United States complained that North Viet Nam had been disregarding the Geneva POW Convention (pp. 90–3); Finland proposed that a study be undertaken of neutrality and the status of neutral nations (p. 76); UNESCO suggested that a study be made of the factors which contribute to the inadequacy of existing rules of international law, an appraisal of major innovative legal ideas regarding better application of existing rules, and a study of the range of conditioning processes necessary to ensure human rights in armed conflicts (p. 95). The World Health Organisation, the UN Children's Fund, and the UN High Commissioner for Refugees also sent letters. The ICRC sent a letter and communicated the text of six resolutions adopted at the 21st International Red Cross Conference (pp. 101–6).

UN REPORT AND DECISIONS, 1969

The decision of the General Assembly in 1968 had included three requests to the UN Secretary-General, who at the time was U Thant. The work was in fact done in the Human Rights Division of the UN Secretariat, and it is convenient to refer to the 1969 report, and those issued subsequently, by the short-hand expression 'UN report(s)' or 'Secretariat report(s)'.

The first UN report on human rights in armed conflict did not pretend to be more than preliminary and dealt with only a limited number of questions.[2] The UN Secretariat commented that constructive suggestions for remedial action had been relatively few, and that what was required was 'a relatively long-term United Nations endeavour' (para. 13).

The first chapter of the report makes the interesting point that the second world war 'gave conclusive proof of the close relationship which exists between outrageous behaviour of a Government towards its own citizens and aggression against other nations' (para. 16). The Secretariat then provided a historical survey of international humanitarian instruments, starting with the Geneva Convention of 1864 (sick and wounded in time of war) and going up to the nuclear non-proliferation treaty of 1968 (paras 36–69). The next chapter compared the four Geneva Conventions of 1949 and UN instruments in the field of human rights (paras 70–108). Chapter IV was concerned with the substance of the task entrusted to the UN Secretary-General (paras 109–227). The whole problem of humanitarian protection had become very difficult to handle because recent developments had threatened to blur traditional distinctions. The distinction between combatants and civilians was threatened by advances in military technology, and the distinction between international and internal wars had been becoming less clear (para. 131).

An issue of special concern to the United Nations was whether the UN as an entity should formally accept the obligations of the Geneva Conventions in its peace-keeping operations. In 1963, following the fighting in Katanga, the Council of Delegates of the ICRC had passed a resolution recommending (a) that the UN should be invited to adopt a solemn declaration accepting that the Geneva Conventions apply equally to UN Emergency Forces as they apply to the forces of parties to the Conventions; (b) that the governments of countries providing contingents to the UN should, as a matter of prime importance, give their contingents 'adequate instructions on the Geneva Conventions as well as orders to comply with them'; and (c) that the authorities responsible for UN contingents should agree to take all necessary measures to 'prevent and repress' any infringements of the Conventions. This matter was raised again in 1969 in the letter of the ICRC to the UN Secretary-General, in which it proposed that the UN should itself formally undertake to apply the Geneva Conventions and other humanitarian rules in operations in which UN forces are engaged. 'Such a gesture would have value as an example' (para. 114 and p. 102).

In issuing regulations for UN forces in the Middle East, the Congo (Zaire), and Cyprus, the Secretary-General had stipulated that such forces should observe 'the principles and spirit of the general international conventions applicable to the conduct of military personnel'. At the same time, he had insisted that training and discipline of troops in UN operations had rested with each national contingent, and that progress would come from a wider acceptance of humanitarian conventions by contributing states rather than by having the UN undertake 'obligations whose discharge would involve the exercise of an authority it had not been granted' (pp. 101–6 and para. 9). It is a pity that none of the UN Secretaries-General has found it possible to evolve a formula which would go at least part of the way to meeting the long-held views of the ICRC in this respect.

The 1969 report contained a number of proposals of 'areas where it would appear that useful studies might be undertaken', including the clarification or strengthening of existing instruments; the preparation of new instruments for the better protection of civilians, prisoners, and combatants; the problem of internal armed conflicts; the use of napalm and other weapons said to cause unnecessary suffering; and relief activities (paras 109–227). These matters were all to be discussed in greater detail in the UN report in 1970.

The 1969 report did not become available until the first week of December, by which time the General Assembly had almost completed its session. The report was considered rather hurriedly at three meetings of a committee of the Assembly. There was general appreciation for the preliminary report and a wish that the study should be continued. Pakistan and Tanzania proposed that in any future work 'special attention' should be given to the protection of those engaged in 'conflicts which arise from the struggle of peoples under colonial and foreign rule for liberation and self-determination' (which I will hereafter refer to by the short-hand expression 'wars of national liberation'). This amendment was approved by 48 votes (Afro-Asian and Communist countries) to 17 (West plus Japan), with 28 abstentions. The draft resolution was approved in plenary meeting on 16 December 1969 by 91 votes to none (resolution 2597). The UK was among 23 abstainers, who were presumably opponents of the Pakistani-Tanzanian amendment. The resolution asked the Secretary-General to continue the study, to consult and co-operate with the ICRC, and to present a further report in 1970.

UN REPORT AND DECISIONS, 1970

The second UN report was in many ways a model of how the UN Secretariat should conduct studies and, on the basis of those studies, put forward proposals for action or further research. Some of the proposals went beyond what governments were then willing to accept, but this should not in itself be a reason for the Secretariat to refrain from reviewing various courses of action and inaction.

It may be useful to start with one matter which was dealt with in a preliminary way in 1969 and more conclusively in 1970. While it is true that the UN and regional instruments on human rights on the one hand and the four Geneva Conventions of 1949 on the other hand complement each other, the protection afforded by the two sets of instruments is not identical. Common Article 3 of the Geneva Conventions of 1949 sets out minimum standards to be applied in conflicts not of an international character (what I will in future refer to as internal wars). These standards go further in some respects than the UN Covenant on Civil and Political Rights in that they provide for judicial guarantees which may not be suspended in periods of armed conflict and expressly prohibit the taking of hostages. The UN Covenant, on the other hand, goes further than common Article 3 in that it would apply at all times, in all places, and to all individuals without distinction as to nationality or status. The Covenant also expressly prohibits retroactive penal legislation.

The 1969 report had stressed that a common feature of the four Geneva Conventions and UN human rights instruments is that they 'appear to belong to the category of treaties setting forth "absolute obligations"'. In other words, the obligations are unconditional and do not depend on reciprocity (A/7720, para. 82). The UN Secretariat concluded that the four Geneva Conventions should, as far as possible, remain untouched. Nevertheless, they showed 'certain imperfections, inadequacies and gaps', and it was suggested that the UN should institutionalise procedures for acting 'specially in fields in which the International Committee [of the Red Cross] cannot operate' (UN doc. A/8052, paras 14–17).

The UN Secretariat reviewed what could be done to ensure better humanitarian protection for protected persons. Civilians are especially exposed if they find themselves close to the battle zone, which may itself be constantly fluctuating. The Secretary-General had tentatively suggested in 1969, as had Austria, that sanctuaries or zones of refuge should be established for those civilians not taking part in hostilities (A/7720, paras 145–52 and p. 73), and this idea was elaborated in more detail in the 1970 report (A/8052, paras 45–87). The proposals for verification of civilian sanctuaries were to some extent adapted from the arrangements in the Hague Convention of 1954 for the Protection of Cultural Property. The Secretariat suggested that such civilian sanctuaries should be registered with an international authority and be subject to 'an effective system of control and verification'. They should bear 'special markings and insignia, clearly visible and recognizable'. Free access should be granted to official inspectors at all times, and the inspectors would be empowered to order an investigation of any suspected violation. The inspectors should be permitted to fix a time-limit for rectification which, if not complied with, could lead to the lifting of the protection and immunity. Shelter should be given in such sanctuaries to 'civilians taking no part in hostilities and in no way contributing to the war effort'. The zones would be 'completely disarmed and demilitarized' and should contain no large industrial or administrative establishments, no important communications or transport facilities, and no installations which might be put to military use. They should be demarcated in such a way that belligerents would secure no military advantage from their existence. Sanctuaries should be immune from attack, possibly even in internal wars. The Secretary-General suggested that the matter should be given 'a comprehensive analysis and study in depth ... by a group or committee of qualified experts' with a view to the preparation of a Protocol to the Geneva Conventions of 1949 or a separate international instrument (paras 45–87).[3]

The other main proposal for the better protection of civilians would have involved the setting out of a code of standard minimum rules, complementary to the obligations which states had already assumed (paras 34–44). Such a code would need to define those entitled to protection as civilians, but such definition should be irrespective of nationality and should expressly apply to refugees and stateless persons. The main intention would have been to prohibit attacks directed against civilians as such, indiscriminate terrorising or destruction, and the use of civilians as an object of reprisal. There would need to be arrangements to prevent abuse, such as using civilians as a shield for military attacks or permanently placing armed forces or military installations in cities or areas with large civilian populations.

In 1969 the Secretary-General had mentioned the problem of 'terror bombing' and suggested a study of 'the effects of this kind of military operation within their legal context … and the question of defining limits' (A/7720, para. 143). In the suggested minimum code for the protection of civilians put forward a year later, the Secretariat proposed 'the specific prohibition of the use of "saturation" bombing as a means of intimidating, demoralizing and terrorizing civilians by inflicting indiscriminate destruction upon densely populated areas'. In addition, the report reiterated that belligerents have an obligation to take precautions to ensure that the objective to be attacked is not the civilian population. The purpose would be to reduce to a minimum or avoid entirely harming civilian populations in the vicinity of a military objective (A/8052, para. 42).

As for the humanitarian protection of prisoners of war, the Secretariat considered the Third Geneva Convention of 1949 to be 'generally … sound', but it was pointed out that the question whether a person qualifies for the protection of the Convention is unilaterally decided upon by the capturing power, and that there might be advantages in allowing an international agency 'to advise and give guidance' on the eligibility of persons for POW status. Other suggestions were that prisoners should not be interrogated until they had received medical attention; that all brutal methods of interrogation, including the giving of drugs, alcohol, or similar agents, and deprivation of food and rest, should be prohibited; and that the power to impose the death sentence on prisoners 'should be exercised with the greatest moderation and if possible prohibited altogether'. It was suggested that, even in guerrilla fighting, persons should not be sentenced to death merely for acts, such as killing their enemy in open fight, which may reasonably be expected of combatants and which are committed in accordance with the laws and customs of war. In the case of internal conflicts, the Secretariat favoured the gradual elimination of capital punishment inflicted on combatants solely on the ground of having espoused the cause of either party to the conflict (paras 104–7, 111(c), 114–21, 182, 184, 190, 191).

The humanitarian protection of combatants raises many difficult questions. Some of these arise from the near impossibility of distinguishing between a 'ruse of war', which is permitted under the Hague Regulations (Art. 24) and to 'kill or wound treacherously', which are among the acts 'especially prohibited' (Art. 23(b)). The Secretariat considered that a more precise rule was needed on this. It was also necessary to clarify the prohibition of 'the improper wearing of military insignia and uniform', as well as the prohibition of declaring that 'no quarter' will be given (paras 101–3, 108–9). The Secretariat considered that the Hague Regulations should be updated and adapted to modern conditions, either by their revision as a whole, by the preparation of 'an additional Protocol to the Geneva Convention [sic], or an independent international instrument'. The elaboration or amendment should define and if possible extend the definition of protected combatants; define what is inadmissible as 'treacherous' conduct; elaborate the existing prohibition of killing or wounding the disabled enemy; define how a combatant can clearly make known his intention to surrender; and replace the rule forbidding the declaration that 'no quarter' will be given by the positive obligation to proclaim 'that the disabled enemy will be protected under the laws and customs of war'. The Secretariat admitted the 'practical difficulties and complexity of the task' and emphasised the need for international procedures to verify the implementation of existing and any new provisions (paras 111–13).

Both civilians and combatants would benefit from the prohibition of weapons or methods of war which cause unnecessary suffering, which are 'especially prohibited' under the Hague Regulations (Art. 23(e)). The Secretariat noted in 1969 that this problem must be dealt with in large measure by means of arms control and disarmament, but it was pointed out that incendiary weapons such as napalm cause needless suffering unless their use is accompanied by 'special precautions', and it was tentatively suggested that 'the legality or otherwise of the use of

napalm' called for special study (A/7720, paras 183–201). This
proposal was repeated in 1970, the Secretariat then favouring the idea
of a study of 'the precise effects of the use of napalm on human beings
and the living environment ... with a view to curtailing or abolishing
such uses of the weapons in question as might be established as
inhumane' (A/8052, paras 122–6, 152).

Perhaps the most difficult group of questions concerned internal
wars, guerrilla fighting, and the use of armed force by groups engaged
in national liberation struggles. The Secretariat had emphasised in the
1969 report that while the distinction between international and
internal conflicts may be of great importance from the point of view of
international law, this may not be the case when it comes to the
securing of humanitarian standards. It was also pointed out that the
'traditional distinction between international war formally
declared ... and purely internal conflicts [had become] less clear'. A
matter for further study should concern the elaboration of a new
international instrument providing protection for civilians in those
internal armed conflicts 'of international concern' (A/7720, paras
104, 131, 168–77). The UN Secretariat elaborated this proposal in
some detail in 1970, dealing in the main with the need to clarify and
strengthen common Article 3 of the Geneva Conventions. On one
point, there seemed to be substantial agreement among the experts
who had been consulted. While foreign military intervention can have
the effect of transforming an internal conflict into an international
one, it is often difficult to assess whether intervention is in fact taking
place, especially if it is covert or in the guise of 'volunteers' or
mercenaries. Another difficulty of definition arises because common
Article 3 comes into effect only in the case of 'armed' conflict, and
some experts wanted to see the application of Article 3 in certain
situations of conflict where there has been no actual recourse to
weapons. One possibility would have been to widen the expression
'armed conflict' so as to cover the operations of 'any movement
which ... aims at overthrowing the Government by the use of arms
[or] changing the form or structure of the State by modifying the
Constitution or basic laws of the State or part thereof'. The Secretariat
commented that some experts would regard all 'struggles for
self-determination, and liberation from colonial and foreign rule ... as
international' (paras 130–47).

One difficulty about giving protection to persons actively engaged in
internal hostilities, indeed in all armed conflicts, is that the wider the
definition of those claiming the benefits of combatant status, the wider

the definition of those who may legitimately be attacked. The Secretariat examined the expression used in common Article 3, 'persons taking no active part in the hostilities', and asked whether any persons, in addition to those named in Article 3 for illustrative purposes, should be regarded as 'not actively participating in the hostilities'. It was proposed that the protection of Article 3 should apply to all those whose conduct and activities have no relation to the conduct of hostilities, those whose assistance or participation was given under duress, and those who 'merely express opinions criticizing the Government or favouring the objectives of the uprising'. It was also suggested that Article 3 should be extended so as to afford protection to medical and relief personnel; to allow the free passage of food, clothing, and medical supplies; and to allow detainees to send and receive family messages and to receive relief (A/7720, paras 148–56).

The Secretariat's first report (paras 202–27) considered the general problem of securing effective implementation of agreed norms, and this problem was considered in greater detail in the 1970 report (A/8052, paras 157–62, 185–6, 238–58). Reference has already been made to the proposal that an international agency might in some circumstances advise whether persons claiming POW status do in fact qualify for the protection given by the Third Geneva Convention. The Secretariat noted that determining whether a given situation comes within the purview of common Article 3, that is to say, is an internal conflict, is 'complex and delicate'. Among the suggestions for dealing with this was that advice on this point should be available from 'some international body ... offering full guarantees of competence, independence and impartiality' (paras 116, 157–62, 191(e)).

Guerrilla warfare may be an element of an international conflict, as was the case of the underground and partisan movements in the second world war, or it may be resorted to in civil and other internal wars. The Secretariat suggested in the first report that an expert study should be made to advise whether new rules were needed to confer the status of 'protected' combatants upon guerrilla fighters not eligible for protection under the Geneva Conventions; but it was pointed out that the possibility of doing this depends to a large extent on whether the guerrillas themselves apply humanitarian norms (A/7720, paras 158–67). In the second report, the Secretariat suggested that if guerrilla groups do not have adequate facilities for holding prisoners, they might hand them over to an allied or neutral state. Guerrillas should afford full respect and freedom of action to medical and relief personnel (A/8052, paras 166–7, 181). The Secretariat commented that 'the international provisions in force concerning the definition of protected combatants contain discrepancies, are not always precise enough and may lend themselves to difficulties of interpretation'. The Secretariat reiterated the proposal for a study in order to 'ascertain and clarify' the meaning of existing texts, to bring them into better harmony with each other, and to broaden their scope so as to cover certain categories of combatants not protected. In addition, the Secretariat put forward for study some tentative suggestions for broadening the definition or interpretation of privileged combatants in international conflicts (paras 89–98, 174–80, 183, 189, 191(b), (e), and (f)).

Among other suggestions for further consideration was that Article 23 of the Hague Regulations, which lists acts which are especially forbidden, should be construed or amended so as to prohibit 'the killing or harming of all persons who participate actively in international conflicts, at the time of surrender or capture' (paras 107, 111, 168–73, 191(a)).

An important section of the 1969 report had dealt with the role of protecting powers. The UN Secretariat had suggested that there was a pressing need for measures to improve and strengthen the system of international supervision and assistance to parties to armed conflicts in their observance of humanitarian norms. Among the proposals of the Secretariat in 1969 were the following: (a) widening the effective choice of methods of supervision and assistance available to the parties; (b) establishment of a new organ or organisation for supervision and assistance; (c) extension of the role of protecting powers to additional humanitarian functions; (d) recourse to international organisations as substitute for protecting powers; (e) creation of official panels of states willing to act as protecting powers. In addition, the General Assembly or the ICRC might, by resolution, emphasise the fact that protecting powers, in addition to safeguarding the interests of the parties, are agents of the international community (A/7720, paras 202–24). In the second report, the Secretariat suggested that these questions should receive further study, and it was emphasised that this section of the report was necessarily of a tentative character, merely outlining alternative possibilities, with emphasis on co-operation with the governments concerned. Any new organ or agency should help in applying not only the existing rules of the Geneva Conventions but also the norms set by UN instruments on human rights. It might also undertake tasks arising from new international instruments, such as advising on those eligible for POW status and whether an internal conflict exists, as well as administering and verifying civilian sanctuaries. The ICRC would not necessarily be able to assume additional functions beyond its present humanitarian responsibilities. The role of protecting power embraces diplomatic and political functions, and the ICRC might find the role of conciliator or mediator more congenial than acting as representative of one of the belligerents or of the international community. Perhaps the UN, it was suggested, constituted 'the most authentic and comprehensive expression of the international community'. If a UN organ or agency were created, it would need to have a degree of autonomy so that it could act independently and impartially. The executive head should be guided by a committee of highly qualified personalities of international renown and unquestioned integrity (paras 186, 191(d), 240–7).

The final substantive question dealt with concerned medical and relief assistance. The UN Secretariat had suggested in 1969 that guidelines should be formulated aimed at improving the efficiency, strengthening the co-ordination, and expanding the scope of relief activities in situations of armed conflict. If a UN body were created as an organ of protection as suggested above, either the UN organ, or a non-UN humanitarian organisation, might act as co-ordinator between various relief agencies. This would, of course, require careful handling so as to avoid overlapping with the ICRC (A/7720, paras 153–5, 225–7). In the second report, the UN Secretariat suggested that the UN might 'in appropriate cases' co-ordinate and execute relief activities. This might necessitate the creation of an autonomous organisation, guided by 'a committee of highly qualified personalities of international renown and unquestioned integrity ... who would adequately represent the major legal and social systems of the world' (A/8052, paras 42(j), 44, 247–8).

A programme as ambitious as that outlined by the Secretary-General in his two reports would have needed:

1.   Wide dissemination and publicity for existing humanitarian instruments, especially to military personnel (paras 251–6);
2.   More effective implementation of existing instruments, including improved means of reporting and verification (paras 238–50);
3.   A review of existing reservations to humanitarian conventions to see whether any of these reservations can now be withdrawn (para. 257);

4. Expert studies on several important matters, such as civilian sanctuaries, the effects of using incendiary weapons on human beings and the living environment, the effects of terror bombing and the possibility of defining limits, the humanitarian protection of civilians in internal armed conflicts, the humanitarian protection of guerrilla fighters, and an extended use of protecting powers (paras 83–7, 126, 186);
5. The preparation of amendments or protocols to existing instruments, or of entirely new instruments (paras 18, 163–5, 192–3).

The UN debate on the 1970 report was complicated by repeated attempts on the part of some representatives to discuss particular armed conflicts, especially those in South East Asia and the Middle East, and also, though to a lesser extent, the question of guerrilla fighters in Southern Africa. In the end, however, on 9 December 1970, the Assembly was able to approve five separate resolutions.

The first dealt with the protection of journalists engaged on dangerous missions in areas of armed conflict: it was adopted by 85 votes to none, with 32 abstentions (mainly Communist or Afro-Asian states) (resolution 2673). This issue had arisen because of the disappearance of seventeen foreign journalists in Cambodia (Kampuchea) earlier in 1970. The resolution recalled those provisions of the Geneva Conventions of 1949 affording 'certain types of protection... to journalists' and requested the Commission on Human Rights, at its next session and 'as a matter of priority', to consider the possibility of preparing a draft international agreement to be adopted 'as soon as possible', to ensure the protection of journalists engaged on dangerous missions. The abstaining states made it clear that they did not object to the principle of devising better measures to protect journalists, but they questioned whether this matter needed such high priority, and they wished to ensure that only *bona fide* journalists would be protected and not persons engaging in political or military activities under cover of the journalistic profession.

The second resolution had been introduced by the Sudan and co-sponsored by Ceylon, India, and the Soviet Union. It condemned countries which engage in aggressive wars and disregard the principles of the Geneva Conventions of 1949 and the Geneva Protocol of 1925 on chemical and biological weapons; affirmed that 'participants in resistance movements and freedom-fighters in Southern Africa and territories under colonial and alien domination and foreign occupation' should, if arrested, be treated as POWs; and recognised the need to develop additional international instruments providing for the protection of 'civilian populations and freedom-fighters' (resolution 2674). The resolution was adopted by 76 votes (mainly Afro-Asian and Communist states) to 1 (Portugal).

The third resolution had originally been submitted by Norway, and was adopted by 109 votes to none. It affirmed eight basic principles for the protection of civilian populations in armed conflicts, 'without prejudice to their future elaboration within the framework of progressive development of the international law of armed conflict' (resolution 2675: for text, see Appendix 9).

The fourth resolution, sponsored by the United States and 11 others, was adopted by 67 votes to 30. It called on all parties to an armed conflict to comply with the Geneva Convention relating to POWs; endorsed the continuing efforts of the ICRC to secure the effective application of the Convention; requested the Secretary-General 'to exert all efforts to obtain humane treatment for prisoners of war'; and urged compliance with particular provisions of the Convention regarding the repatriation of sick and wounded prisoners, and humane treatment of prisoners not repatriated (resolution 2676).

The fifth resolution, which was introduced by Britain and co-sponsored by 12 other states, called upon all parties to any armed conflict to observe the rules laid down in the Hague Conventions of 1899 and 1907, the Geneva Protocol of 1925, the Geneva Conventions of 1949, 'and other humanitarian rules applicable in armed conflicts'; urged states which had not already done so to adhere to 'those Conventions'; expressed the hope that the expert conference to be convened in 1971 by the ICRC would 'consider further what development is required in existing humanitarian laws applicable to armed conflicts', and requested the Secretary-General to report on the results of the ICRC expert conference 'and on any other relevant developments' (resolution 2677).

UN REPORTS AND DECISIONS, 1971-7

The third UN report was issued just before the UN General Assembly convened in 1971. The UN effort to make progress on human rights in armed conflict was beginning to run out of independent steam, and the most useful contribution seemed to be to support and reinforce the work of the ICRC in devising new international instruments to supplement the four Geneva Conventions. Indeed, one of the 1971 reports of the UN Secretariat was in the main a summary of a conference of government experts convened by the ICRC to consider the reaffirmation and development of international humanitarian law applicable in armed conflicts. The ICRC experts had considered the protection of civilians (UN doc. A/8370, paras 30–92) and combatants (paras 93–7), the protection of the sick and wounded (paras 138–9), prohibition and limitation of means of warfare (paras 98–108), guerrilla warfare (paras 131–3), national liberation struggles (paras 134–7), internal wars (paras 109–30), and respect for humanitarian conventions and rules (paras 141–58). A second report of the Secretariat was concerned exclusively with the protection of journalists engaged in dangerous missions in areas of armed conflict, supplemented by a report of a working group of the UN Human Rights Commission on the same subject.

On the basis of these reports, the General Assembly adopted three resolutions on 20 December 1971. The first, sponsored by Sweden and 11 other states, called again for respect for the humanitarian rules applicable in armed conflicts, re-affirmed the right of fighters in national liberation wars to be treated as POWs, invited the ICRC to continue work on the two draft Protocols to the Geneva Conventions, and asked the Secretary-General to prepare a report on napalm and other incendiary weapons (resolution 2852). The second resolution, initiated by Britain and co-sponsored by Japan and New Zealand, was in part repetitive, and in part procedural. There was, however, a sting in the fourth operative paragraph, which called on states 'as a matter of priority' to review any reservations they had made to existing international instruments. Most of these reservations had been made by Communist states, and they tried, but without success, to have the paragraph deleted (resolution 2853). The third resolution, spearheaded by France and co-sponsored by 8 others, repeated the invitation to the UN Commission on Human Rights to draft a convention on the protection of journalists engaged in dangerous missions (resolution 2854).

The main report of the Secretariat in 1972 summarised the most recent work of the ICRC on the reaffirmation and development of international humanitarian law. There were also UN reports in 1972 and subsequently on the protection of journalists, and this matter was in the end dealt with in 1977 in Additional Protocol I to the Geneva Conventions (Art. 79 and Annex II).

The Secretariat also issued in 1972 a first-class report on incendiary weapons. These weapons cause most distress when used in developing countries, where medical resources are modest, so that casualties have little chance of receiving effective aid and where widespread malnutrition, chronic anaemias and other deficiencies increase the susceptibility to exposure (UN doc. A/8803, paras 104(a), 119, 130, 182). Napalm appears to cause an exceptionally high proportion of deaths, so that it is 'one of the most lethal weapons in existence today': incendiary weapons against Japan during the second world war were between five and twelve times as destructive as high-explosives (paras 104(b), 114, 155). Recovery from burn injuries is slow and patients are in great pain (para. 104(c)). Incendiary weapons 'characterize the savage and cruel consequences of total war' (para. 185).

On 29 November 1972, the General Assembly welcomed the report on incendiary weapons and deplored the use of napalm and other incendiary weapons in all armed conflicts (resolution 2932; see also resolutions 3076, 3255, 3464, 31/64, and 32/152). On 18 December, the Assembly adopted a new resolution calling on states to observe the rules of international humanitarian law, supporting the work of the ICRC, and asking the UN Secretary-General 'to prepare as soon as possible, a survey of existing rules of international law concerning the prohibition or restriction of use of specific weapons' (resolution 3032). Britain abstained in both votes.

The Secretariat reported again in 1973 on ICRC activities as well as on the recommendations of a number of non-governmental organisations, including a memorandum on incendiary weapons which I had prepared for the UN and which was submitted through the Friends World Committee for Consultation. The full text of the memorandum is in Appendix 12: the summary prepared by the UN Secretariat reads as follows.[4]

> The writer of this memorandum feels that direct and premeditated attacks against non-combatants are contrary to international law no matter what weapons are used in such attacks. He suggests that this general rule should be reaffirmed in an instrument concerning attacks carried out by means of incendiary weapons and containing, *inter alia*, international implementation provisions which would reaffirm the Nürnberg principles on criminal responsibility and provide an international complaints procedure.

I also suggested the drafting of a standard wording on incendiary weapons for inclusion in manuals of military law.

The General Assembly had perhaps hoped that the survey of international law which it had requested in 1972 would be a brief and succinct document. In the event, the survey comprised some 300 pages of text. It was, nevertheless, a useful compilation for legal experts.

The authors stressed that the impulse to humanise armed conflict 'responds to certain fundamental principles long recognized by international law and frequently reaffirmed', so that their 'universal validity' seems 'beyond any reasonable doubt in contemporary international law' (A/9215, vol. I, p. 13). At the same time, modern weapons are cruel and tend to obliterate the distinction between combatants and civilians (p. 14). The authors reviewed the rules governing military operations, stressing that the choice of means and methods of combat is not unlimited (p. 17), and that it is prohibited to make direct attacks on non-combatants (pp. 18, 94–111, 209), to cause unnecessary suffering or superfluous injury (pp. 17, 204–8), or to resort to treachery (pp. 19, 209–10). The authors reviewed in detail international law governing

    nuclear weapons (pp. 41–67, 147–65)
    poisons (pp. 29, 115–9)
    chemical and bacteriological (biological) weapons (pp. 29–39, 120–133)
    incendiary weapons (pp. 40, 138–46)
    land mines and booby traps (pp. 186–8)
    delayed action weapons (pp. 191–2)
    fragmentation bombs (p. 186)
    projectiles of various kinds (pp. 39, 134–8)
    balloons (pp. 68–9)
    missiles (pp. 69–79, 188–91)
    naval weapons (pp. 80–93, 193–201)
    bombardment from air, land, or sea (pp. 165–85)
    weather modification (pp. 201–3)
    the establishment of demilitarised areas (pp. 112–4)

The compilation also contained a number of national and international judicical decisions, selected resolutions of the UN General Assembly, and the text of relevant articles of the ICRC's draft Additional Protocols to the Geneva Conventions.

The General Assembly approved two resolutions on 12 December 1973, the first repeating support for ICRC efforts, urging national liberation movements to participate in the conference to consider the draft Additional Protocols to the Geneva Conventions, and calling again for compliance with international humanitarian rules (resolution 3102). The second resolution proclaimed the legitimacy of national liberation struggles and asked that captured combatants in such struggles should be accorded POW status (resolution 3103). Britain voted in favour of the first resolution, against the second.

During the next four years, 1974–7, the UN Secretariat reported on the sessions of the diplomatic conference on humanitarian law and in 1977 provided the texts of the resolutions and final act of the conference and of the two Additional Protocols (see below, Chapter 4). Each year during this period, the General Assembly adopted supportive resolutions, in 1974 approving as well a declaration on the protection of women and children in emergency and armed conflict (resolution 3318, see Appendix 14), in 1974 and 1975 welcoming the ICRC decision to convoke conferences on indiscriminate or excessively injurious weapons (resolutions 3319 and 3500), in 1976 urging all participants in the diplomatic conference 'to do their utmost to reach agreement' (resolution 31/19), and in 1977 welcoming the successful conclusion of the diplomatic conference and noting the recommendation that a special conference be called on prohibiting or restricting indiscriminate or excessively injurious weapons (resolution 32/44; see also resolutions 31/64 and 32/152).

The efforts of the United Nations spread over the decade '1968–77 undoubtedly had a beneficial effect in facilitating and reinforcing the work of the ICRC in supplementing the Geneva Conventions by the two Additional Protocols – although relations between the UN and ICRC Secretariats were often strained. In addition, the UN produced a technical report which formed a basis for the Convention and Protocols on indiscriminate and excessively injurious weapons, drafted provisions to cover journalists on dangerous missions, and approved two sets of principles, one for the protection of civilians in armed conflicts (1970) and one on the protection of women and children (1974) (Appendices 9 and 14).

Yet there is a paradox about all this work, a contradiction between words and deeds, between what states say and what states do. Some UN Members spoke and voted in favour of resolutions urging states to accede to named humanitarian instruments, and yet failed to take their own advice. To be specific, 26 of the states which in 1973 voted in favour of resolution 3103 calling on states to acknowledge and comply with the Geneva Protocol of 1925, had not themselves acceded to the Protocol ten years later. And, as I will demonstrate in Chapter 4, some states which have formally accepted the obligations of humanitarian instruments have in practice failed to carry out their obligations under them.

HUMAN RIGHTS IN TERRITORIES OCCUPIED BY ISRAEL

While these discussions were taking place, the world had not been free of armed conflict. There had been major wars in Viet Nam and Kampuchea, between Federal Nigeria and Biafra, between India and Pakistan leading to the establishment of Bangladesh, between two Arab states and Israel, and some twenty-five lesser wars. There had been decisive military intervention in Czechoslovakia, Uganda, Cyprus, Western Sahara, East Timor, and Afghanistan; liberation movements had gained control in Angola and Mozambique; and there had been a rising tide of violence in South Africa and Namibia, as well as military incursions from South Africa into neighbouring states. Tension in the Gulf had been growing, with several armed clashes between Iraq and Iran, and civil war had broken out in Lebanon. There had been major military coups in Chile and Ethiopia, armed conflict in the Horn of Africa, and political violence in many other parts of the Third World. There had been hijackings and kidnappings. UN peace-keeping forces had been functioning in Cyprus, Sinai, and on the Golan Heights, and UN observers had been deployed in Kashmir and the Middle East.

In some of these cases, the UN has exercised humanitarian responsibilities; in some there has been UN conciliation, mediation, or good offices; in many cases, UN organs had engaged in debate and passed resolutions. But it was unprecedented for UN organs to decide to investigate directly the application of humanitarian principles during armed conflict or in occupied territory after the cessation of hostilities, as happened after the 1967 war in the Middle East. Initially there were two different UN bodies of inquiry, which on the face of things was an unnecessary duplication of effort. One body, which was established by the General Assembly in 1968 and has been reappointed every year since then, is the Special Committee to investigate Israeli practices affecting the human rights of the population of the occupied territories (hereafter referred to as the Special Committee). The other body was set up by the Human Rights Commission in 1969 and was known as the Special Working Group of Experts established under resolution 6(XXV) (hereafter referred to as the Working Group).

It would be tedious to recount in detail the work of these two bodies, but some information is necessary about the circumstances in which they were set up. On 14 June 1967, immediately after the Six Day War, the UN Security Council recommended to the governments concerned 'the scrupulous respect of the humanitarian principles' contained in the Geneva Conventions of 1949 (resolution 237). On 4 July 1967 the General Assembly welcomed this resolution 'with great satisfaction' (resolution 2252).

On 27 September 1968 the question of territory occupied by Israel was debated in the Security Council at the request of Pakistan and Senegal, and the Council asked the Secretary-General to send a special representative 'to the Arab territories under military occupation by Israel', and asked the government of Israel to receive him and 'to cooperate with him and to facilitate his work' (resolution 259). On 14 October the Secretary-General reported that Israel was not prepared to co-operate with the proposed mission unless its mandate were to include the treatment of both Arabs *and Jews* in *all* the states which had taken part in the June war. U Thant therefore reported that he was unable to give effect to the Security Council's decision.

In spite of this rebuff, the General Assembly decided on 19 December 1968 to establish the Special Committee already referred to, the membership to be determined by the President of the General Assembly. The government of Israel was asked to receive the Committee, co-operate with it and facilitate its work, and the Committee was asked to report 'as soon as possible and whenever the need arises thereafter' (resolution 2443).

Before the Special Committee could be appointed, the President of the 1968 session of the General Assembly, Emilio Arenales of Guatemala, died following an operation for a brain tumour, and the question arose as to how the committee should be appointed. The government of Israel has alleged (and there is no reason to doubt the truth of this) that before his death, Arenales had

approached a large number of Member States ... but, at the time of his death, had not been successful ... on account of the refusal of a great many Member States to accept such an invitation .... In the communication addressed to ... Israel ... on 6 March 1969, the late President of the General Assembly himself expressed his view that the establishment at that juncture of the special committee would add 'further causes of friction to the already tense situation in the Middle East'.[5]

The situation facing the UN upon the death of Arenales was not covered by the General Assembly's Rules of Procedure, nor were there any exact precedents. U Thant, acting under the article of the Charter which designates him as 'chief administrative officer of the Organization', felt that he had no alternative but to consult the 126 Members in writing, with the following result: 25 states did not reply and 4 'abstained'; 3 favoured convening a special session of the Assembly to decide on another method for constituting the Special Committee; 13 favoured postponing the matter until the next session of the Assembly due to convene four months later; 64 favoured designating one of the Vice-Presidents to make the appointment; 12, 'in line with the spirit ... of the rules of procedure', wanted to invite the government of Guatemala to designate the chairman of its delegation for the next session and ask him to make the appointment; and 5 were willing to accept either of the last two *ad hoc* procedures.

The Secretary-General noted that 'more than an absolute majority' (64 out of 126) preferred a procedure which was 'consonant with the spirit' of the Charter and rules of procedure: the designation of one of the Vice-Presidents to undertake the appointment. Accordingly, a meeting of all the Vice-Presidents of the previous General Assembly session (the Vice-Presidents are states, not individuals) was held on 23 June 1969, and they decided to entrust the appointment of the Special Committee to Dr Luis Alvarado of Peru. On 12 September 1969, four days before the 1969 session of the Assembly was due to convene, it was announced that Ceylon (Sri Lanka), Somalia, and Yugoslavia had agreed to serve. By this time, the Security Council had again called on Israel to observe the Geneva Conventions and international law governing military occupation (resolution 271).

Israel strongly objected to the procedure adopted to deal with the unprecedented procedural situation, as well as to the composition of the Committee:

In view of the one-sided character of the resolution [of the General Assembly] ... all uncommitted States that were approached refused to serve on the Committee. The only countries willing to become members of the Committee were Somalia, Yugoslavia and Ceylon. None of the three countries have diplomatic relations with

Israel. ... Somalia even denies Israel's right to independence and sovereignty.[6]

Meanwhile, the problem of the occupied territories had been raised in the UN Commission on Human Rights, which on 4 March 1969 had set up the Working Group mentioned earlier, asking it to investigate allegations that Israel had violated the Fourth Geneva Convention on the protection of civilians. The Working Group had six members appointed as individuals, the identical membership of an *ad hoc* Group which had previously reported on conditions in Southern Africa. Before the Working Group could report to its parent body, however, another General Assembly session had been held, at which it was revealed that the Assembly's Special Committee had been unable to do more than elect a chairman. A resolution in stronger terms than the previous year was adopted by the Assembly on 11 December 1969, which recorded 'grave concern' at reports of violations of human rights in territories occupied by Israel; condemned practices such as collective punishments, destruction of homes, and deportations; called upon Israel 'to desist forthwith from its reported repressive practices'; and asked the Special Committee to 'take cognizance' of the Assembly's new resolution on the matter (resolution 2546).

At this stage, then, there existed two UN bodies to investigate the application of humanitarian principles in territories occupied by Israel: not surprisingly, both bodies received full co-operation from Arab governments and the Arab League. Both bodies consulted representatives of the ICRC and visited refugee camps in Syria and Jordan, and both also asked the UN agency for Arab refugees (UNRWA) to provide information. The Commissioner-General of UNRWA expressed his understanding and sympathy with the needs and purposes of the Working Group, but he doubted whether its requests fell 'within the terms of the [Agency's] mandate, or are consistent with the activities as conducted at present at UNRWA'. The Special Committee expressed dismay at this apparent lack of co-operation and suggested that UNRWA should be authorised to 'make ... information available, without condition, to investigating bodies'.

The failure of UNRWA to disclose information regarding conditions prevailing in the occupied territories ... might appear to be a dereliction of a humanitarian duty. If, however, the policies of UNRWA preclude the organization from furnishing any evidence ... , the Special Committee must either accept the situation ... or seek some change of policy.[7]

Neither investigating body was able to visit territory occupied by Israel, which informed the Working Group that there was no basis for co-operation. Israel took the same view of the Special Committee: 'The history of this matter has from the beginning been tainted with political bias and procedural irregularity': Israel therefore refused to co-operate.[8]

Besides hearing witnesses, the two bodies examined documentation including, in the case of the Working Group, specific Egyptian complaints of violations of the Geneva Conventions. The Working Group stated that it was 'not in a position to verify juridically the allegations which were received' and that the evidence presented to it was 'one-sided', because of Israel's refusal to recognise or co-operate with it. Nevertheless, the Working Group felt able to evaluate the evidence proferred. The Special Committee also felt that, despite the absence of co-operation on the part of Israel, it had created 'a basis upon which a responsible opinion can be given'.

The Working Group issued its report in stages in January and February 1970. It was of the opinion that the Fourth Geneva Convention of 1949 was being violated by Israel; that persons were being detained without trial; that houses and villages had been destroyed after the cease-fire; and that people had been expelled or transferred from their homes. It recommended that the Fourth Geneva Convention be fully implemented; that allegations of torture, looting, and pillage should be investigated by the Israeli authorities and those found responsible suitably punished; that deported or transferred persons should be allowed to return home under UN supervision; that detainees should be brought to trial at an early date; that confiscated property taken in a manner inconsistent with the Geneva Convention should be restored to its owners; and that the Israeli authorities should refrain from demolishing houses for reasons not provided for in the Convention, and should provide compensation in all cases of houses demolished in violation of the Convention.[9]

The Special Committee had sought to define the human rights which the Security Council had described as 'essential and inalienable' on 4 June 1967 (resolution 237).[10] The Committee concluded that these rights are those affirmed in the Universal Declaration of Human Rights and those deriving from the express provisions of the 1949 Geneva Conventions. The Committee's general verdict was that the situation of the refugees in the occupied territories was 'grim'. The Special Committee believed that Israel 'hoped to enervate the [Arab] community by depriving it of intelligent and active leadership' by means of deportations and expulsions, thereby reducing it 'to a state of passive subservience'. There was 'considerable evidence' of infringements of the right of persons living in the occupied areas to remain there and of the right of those who fled to return to their homes. Israel had been pursuing a policy of 'collective and area punishments ... imposed indiscriminately'. While not contesting the right of the occupying power under the Fourth Geneva Convention to restrict the freedom of those who pose a threat to security, the Committee considered that this power was 'being abused' in that it was exercised too freely. Individuals were being held in detention 'for indefinite, prolonged periods' and administrative detainees and ordinary prisoners were treated alike. The Committee heard several allegations of destruction of houses and buildings ('in many instances ... unwarranted') and of confiscation and expropriation of property. Although such destruction is prohibited by the Fourth Geneva Convention 'except where such destruction is rendered absolutely necessary by military operations' (Art. 53), Israel had 'unscrupulous recourse' to military necessity in carrying out 'this wanton destruction'. Evidence had also been presented of 'widespread looting'. The Special Committee concluded that Israel had been violating human rights in the occupied territories: 'the fundamental violation ... lies in the very fact of occupation'. The weight of international public opinion should be brought to bear to persuade the Israeli government to desist from violations. It recommended that there should be 'a further and more thorough study of ... the entire question of the protection of human rights in occupied territories', and asked that 'sufficient professional and other staff' should be assigned to the Special Committee should it be necessary to visit the Middle East again.

On 13 November 1970 a brief statement was circulated by the government of Israel commenting on the Committee's report. Israel reiterated her objection to the procedure followed in setting up the Committee, which had resulted in its serving as 'a tool of Arab propaganda'. The Committee had 'proceeded to organize a spectacle of hearing "evidence" from ... pre-selected, coached and rehearsed witnesses'. In the case of one witness, Israel provided detailed information to refute the Committee's allegation. This witness, a resident of Gaza, had alleged that he had been given an anaesthetic and castrated by an Israel doctor (A/8089, para. 104). Israel contended that the witness had undergone two operations performed by Arab surgeons for the removal of his testicles before the June war. Israel maintained that it possessed a copy of a report by Professor Muhamad Safawat, dated 28 July 1966, stating that the hope of the witness for a transplant operation was illusory (A/8164).

But to demonstrate that one charge was false was not to undermine the main tenor of the Special Committee's report. Indeed, Israel's brusque reply to a report of some 130 pages showed how contemptuously Israel viewed the activities of the Special Committee.

The two UN reports were submitted to the parent bodies in 1970. The Human Rights Commission approved its Working Group's report on 23 March. Israel was condemned for refusing to apply the Fourth Geneva Convention, and called on to take measures to rectify the situation. The Working Group was asked to 'continue to investigate and report', and Israel was called on to receive the Working Group and co-operate with it.

It was, perhaps, a strange decision to continue the mandate of the Working Group when the General Assembly's Special Committee had been entrusted with an almost identical task. In the event, the Working Group did not issue a further substantive report, and the debates in the Human Rights Commission thereafter were based on the reports of the Special Committee.

At the request of Iraq, the report of the Special Committee was placed on the agenda of the General Assembly. When the report was being considered, a representative of the Palestinian Arabs was permitted to address the Assembly's committee 'without such authorization implying any recognition of the Delegation ... '.[11] A resolution sponsored by 8 Afro-Asian states was approved in plenary on 15 December by 52 votes to 20 (resolution 2727). By the resolution, the Assembly asked the Special Committee to continue its work 'pending the early termination of Israeli occupation of Arab territories', to consult the ICRC, and to report 'as soon as possible and whenever the need arises'. Israel was again asked to receive and co-operate with the Committee, and it was decided to resume consideration of the matter in 1971.

As noted earlier, the Special Committee has been re-appointed at each annual session of the General Assembly, and the subsequent reports to the next session take a standard form. Each report begins with an explanation of its mandate;[12] an explanation of how the Special Committee's work has been organised; the oral evidence and written information received, as well as information derived from printed sources; a comparison of the evidence and information with the obligations under the Hague Convention of 1954 on the protection of cultural property and the Fourth Geneva Convention of 1949 on the protection of civilians, with particular reference to the behaviour of agents of the occupying power, the Convention's prohibition of collective penalties and reprisals, rights of protected persons, transfers of population, destruction of property, treatment of prisoners, and sanctions under the Convention for grave breaches (Arts 29, 33, 47, 49, 53, 64, 76, 146–7); the Special Committee's conclusions; together with a number of factual annexes. From time to time, special issues have been dealt with. The reports in 1976 and 1977, for example, included technical reports on the destruction of Quneitra (A/31/218, paras 316–20 and Annex III, A/32/84, paras 242–4 and Annex II). The 1984 report included the full text of an Israeli report on the activities of anti-Arab vigilantes on the West Bank (the Karp report, A/39/591, paras 149–54 and pp. 107–23). The reports from 1979 to 1984 included sections on judicial remedies (A/34/631, paras 323–63; A/35/425, paras 260–88; A/36/579, paras 49–50; A/37/485, paras 216–43; A/38/409, paras 313–50; A/39/591, paras 308–24).

The conclusions in 1985 were essentially the same as in previous years. Israel was continuing to treat the occupied territories as part of the state of Israel by establishing settlements, expropriating property, encouraging a Palestinian exodus, and by denying Palestinians the right to return. There had been a steady decline in respect for human rights, so that the cycle of violence was bound to continue and the situation would remain explosive (A/40/702, paras 321, 326).

The General Assembly has adopted 63 resolutions on human rights in territories occupied by Israel since the June war in 1967. Britain has sometimes voted in favour of these resolutions and has sometimes abstained, but has never voted against.

The predicament for those states which believe that Israel has repeatedly failed to respect certain humanitarian norms in the occupied territories is to discover a means of inducing Israel to amend its policies, rather than to give emotional satisfaction to the critics. To drop the matter would seem to the Palestinians a great betrayal, yet to condemn Israel every year in increasingly forceful language does not have the effect of improving the lot of the people under occupation. Most Israelis have ceased to listen to raucous critics, especially those from countries with dismal records on human rights. Until the modern age, states which were able to occupy territory were entitled to substitute their own authority for that of the defeated enemy. The doctrine now is that to wage war contrary to the UN Charter confers no rights and that, in particular, it is inadmissible to acquire territory by war. The UN Security Council has called on Israel to withdraw from territories occupied in 1967, but has also affirmed the right of all states in the Middle East to live in peace within secure and recognised boundaries.[13] So long as Israel continues to occupy territory beyond the 1949–67 armistice lines and fails to apply all the requirements of the Fourth Geneva Convention in the territories which it occupies, it is likely to remain a pariah in the UN system, a status not substantially mitigated by offers to negotiate with its Arab neighbours without preconditions.

4 International Humanitarian Law

> The [Hague] Conference is unanimous in thinking that it is extremely desirable that the usages of war should be defined and regulated. In this spirit it has adopted a great number of provisions which have for their object the determination of the rights and of the duties of belligerents and of populations, and for their end the reduction and softening of the evils of war, so far as military necessities permit. It has not always been possible to come to an agreement that henceforth all these stipulations should apply to all practical cases. On the other hand, it could not possibly be the intention of the Conference that unforeseen cases should, in the absence of written stipulations, be left to the arbitrary decision of those who commanded the army. In awaiting the time when a complete code of the laws of war may be elaborated and proclaimed, the Conference considers it opportune to state that in cases not provided for in the Articles of this date, populations and belligerents remain under the safeguards and government of the principles of international law, resulting from the customs established between civilized nations, the laws of humanity, and the demands of public conscience ... —Statement submitted by Fedor Fedorovich Martens, the Russian legal expert, to the Hague Conference on 20 June 1899 which, with stylistic amendments, was incorporated in the preamble to the Hague Conventions of 1899 and 1907 on the laws and customs of war on land, the last sentence of which was also incorporated in the four Geneva Conventions of 1949, the two Geneva Protocols of 1977, and the Convention on indiscriminate or excessively injurious weapons of 1981.

International humanitarian law applicable in armed conflict has been codified in two parallel streams known, somewhat confusingly, as the law of Geneva and the law of the Hague. The law of Geneva was designed to ensure respect, protection, and humane treatment of those who are taking no direct part in the fighting (wounded, sick, or shipwrecked combatants, medical services, military chaplains, prisoners of war, and civilians) while the law of the Hague laid down the rights and duties of belligerents, including prohibitions and restrictions governing the conduct of military operations. Part of the confusion to which I refer arises from the fact that the law of the Hague includes instruments identified with other cities (the St Petersburg Declaration of 1868, the Geneva Protocol of 1925 on chemical and bacteriological (biological) weapons (CBW), and the 1981 Geneva Convention and Protocols on indiscriminate or excessively cruel weapons).

It is implicit in the Martens declaration, used as the epigraph to this chapter, that belligerents are bound by the principles of the laws and customs of war whether or not they have expressly accepted the instruments of the Hague or Geneva streams of law. The British government regards the Hague law as part of customary international law and therefore binding on states: as for the Geneva law, the official British view is that, while this reflects generally-accepted principles, its detailed provisions are binding only on parties to the Conventions and Protocols.

THE LAW OF GENEVA

The codification of the law of Geneva began over a century ago. The Geneva Conventions have been as follows:

1864   For the amelioration of the condition of the wounded in armies in the field

1906   For the amelioration of the condition of the wounded and sick in armies in the field

1929   1. For the relief of the wounded and sick in armies in the field

2. Treatment of prisoners of war

1949   1. Amelioration of the condition of the wounded and sick in armed forces in the field

2. Amelioration of the condition of wounded, sick, and shipwrecked members of the armed forces at sea

3. Treatment of prisoners of war

4. Protection of civilian persons in time of war (This was the first Red Cross Convention expressly to protect civilians. It applies in the main to persons who, in case of armed conflict

or occupation, find themselves in the hands of a foreign belligerent power or under foreign occupation (Art. 4) but in some respects also to 'the whole of the population of the countries in conflict' (Art. 13).

1977   1. Additional Protocol I to the Geneva Conventions, dealing with international armed conflicts.

2. Additional Protocol II relating to internal wars. Part of the purpose of the Protocols was to codify more extended protection for civilians (Additional Protocol I, Arts 48–79, Additional Protocol II, Arts 13–18).

There were in 1986 163 parties to the Geneva Conventions, the last state to become a party being Saint Christopher and Nevis. On 28 May 1986, Benin became the 59th party to Protocol I and the 52nd party to Protocol II; some states ratified or acceded with reservations and/or declarations.

The idea that POWs should receive humane treatment is, of course, much older than the Conventions which seek to give effect to the idea. Dr Samuel Johnson, writing in 1759 in a pamphlet on French POWs in British hands towards the end of the Seven Years' War, held that the only argument against treating French POWs humanely, was that 'while we are relieving Frenchmen, there remain many Englishmen unrelieved; that while we lavish pity on our enemies, we forget the misery of our friends.' But, wrote Johnson, 'the relief of enemies has a tendency to unite mankind in fraternal affection; to soften the acrimony of adverse nations, and dispose them to peace and amity ... '.[1]

The Geneva Conventions of 1949 now in force were prepared at a diplomatic conference convened by Switzerland. The First Convention replaced the Geneva Conventions of 1864, 1906, and 1929 on sick and wounded combatants. The Second Convention replaced the Tenth Hague Convention of 1907 for the adaptation of the principles of the Geneva Convention of 1906 to maritime warfare. The Third Convention of 1949 replaced the Geneva POW Convention of 1929 and is complementary to the relevant provisions of Hague Conventions II of 1899 and IV of 1907 on the laws and customs of war on land. The Fourth Convention broke new ground in that it was the first expressly to protect civilians who, in case of armed conflict or occupation, find themselves in the hands of a state of which they are not nationals (Art. 4). Like the Third Convention, the Fourth supplements the relevant provisions of the Hague Conventions of 1899 and 1907.

There are certain provisions common to all four Geneva Conventions. The parties undertake 'to respect and to ensure respect for' the Conventions 'in all circumstances' (Art. 1). The Conventions apply to 'all cases of declared war or of any other armed conflict ... ' even if the state of war is not recognised by one of the parties, and also to cases of 'partial or total occupation' (Art. 2). Certain minimum provisions apply in the case of armed conflict not of an international character (Art. 3). There are common provisions about the inalienability of the rights of protected persons (non-renunciation of rights), the role and activities of the International Committee of the Red Cross, the duties of protecting powers or their substitutes, conciliation procedures in the event of conflicting interpretations, the repression of abuses and infractions, and the fact that the obligations of the Conventions continue in operation until POWs and civilian internees are repatriated or military operations have ceased (I, 5–7, 9, 11, 49–52; II, 6–7, 9, 11, 50–3; III, 5–7, 9, 11, 129–31; IV, 6–8, 10, 12, 146–9).[2] The final provisions define the procedures for signature, ratification, and entry into force and for subsequent accessions (I, 55–64; II, 54–63; III, 133–43; IV, 150–9). Denunciation takes effect one year after notification, except when the party is involved in an armed conflict, in which case denunciation shall not take effect until peace has been concluded and all protected persons have been repatriated. In any case, denunciation in no way impairs the obligations which the parties are bound to fulfil 'by virtue of the principles of the law of nations, as they result from the usages established among civilized peoples, from the laws of humanity and the dictates of the public conscience' (the Martens Clause) (I, 63; II, 62; III, 142; IV, 158). The parties agreed to disseminate the text of the Conventions and to include the study of them in their programmes of instruction, so that their principles might become known (I, 47; II, 48; III, 127; IV, 144).

The Conventions are based on the principle that persons who are placed *hors de combat* and those who are taking no active part in hostilities shall have their lives spared and shall in all circumstances be treated humanely. The taking of hostages, executions without regular judgment, torture, cruel or degrading treatment, and reprisals against persons protected by the Conventions, are prohibited (I, 3, 46; II, 3, 47; III, 3, 13; IV, 3, 32–4).

Wounded and sick, both military and civilian, shall be respected, as shall all medical personnel, hospitals sheltering wounded and sick, vehicles transporting them, and medical equipment allotted to them.

The emblem of the Red Cross or the Red Crescent is the sign of this protection, and it shall be used for no other purpose. Military chaplains must also be protected. Medical personnel and chaplains are, for their part, bound to refrain from committing acts harmful to the enemy (I, 12, 15, 19–21, 24–7, 32–6, 38–44; II, 12, 18, 22–4, 36–9, 41–5; IV, 16–22).

Military personnel and auxiliaries who are captured or who surrender must have their lives spared. They must at all times be treated humanely and in particular must receive the necessary food, clothing, and medical care. They shall be permitted to correspond with their families. The capturing authority will communicate the names of POWs to the Central Tracing Agency of the ICRC, which will be allowed to visit prisoners and arrange for them to receive relief. If penal proceedings are undertaken against a POW, the protecting power must be notified. Representatives of the protecting power are authorised to follow the judicial proceedings and to provide the POW with an advocate or counsel. In the event of the death penalty being pronounced, the sentence shall not be carried out until at least six months after the protecting power has been notified of the sentence. In the absence of a protecting power, the ICRC may be asked to assume the tasks normally entrusted to the protecting power (III, 4, 13–20, 70, 72, 78, 101, 104–5, 107, 123, 126).

Civilian wounded and sick, as well as civilian hospitals and their personnel, shall be the object of particular respect and may be placed under the protection of the Red Cross or Red Crescent. Civilians in occupied territory must, so far as circumstances permit, be enabled to live in a normal manner. Deportations, pillage, and indiscriminate destruction of property in occupied territory are prohibited. Civilians may be interned only for imperative reasons of security, and conditions shall be of no less a standard than those in POW camps (IV, 16–22, 33, 41–3, 49, 53).

The two Additional Protocols to the Geneva Conventions represented the consummation of a major effort by the ICRC, which began soon after the adoption of the Conventions in 1949, and which culminated in four sessions of a diplomatic conference convened by Switzerland in 1974–7. The final session was attended by 110 states and three national liberation movements (Palestine Liberation Organisation, Panafricanist Congress, South West Africa People's Organisation). Additional Protocol I, concerning international armed conflicts, applies in situations described in the Geneva Conventions, but there is an extension to cover as well 'armed conflicts in which peoples are fighting against colonial domination and alien occupation and against racist régimes ... ' (Art. 1). The authority representing a people engaged in such armed conflict may undertake to apply the Geneva Conventions and Additional Protocol I by means of a unilateral declaration (Art. 96). Moreover, while the Hague and Geneva Conventions granted combatant status to irregular fighters who use a fixed distinctive sign or emblem recognisable at a distance and who carry their arms openly, Additional Protocol I requires only that irregular fighters distinguish themselves from civilians while engaged in an attack or a military operation preparatory to an attack, and that arms shall be carried openly during a military engagement or during such time as they are visible to the other side prior to an attack (Art. 44). These provisions are interesting for two reasons: first, they go much further than previous instruments in legitimising national liberation struggles, in particular, by making Additional Protocol I applicable by reference to the purpose of armed conflict rather than its objective character; and, secondly, national liberation struggles are regarded as international rather than internal armed conflicts. Additional Protocol I breaks new ground, moreover, in denying combatant status to mercenaries (Art. 47).

Additional Protocol I reaffirms the prohibition in the Hague Regulations on using arms or methods of fighting which cause superfluous injury or unnecessary suffering (Art. 35), prohibits methods of warfare likely to cause 'widespread, long-term and severe damage' to the natural environment (Art. 55), and clarifies arrangements for the protection and humane treatment due to wounded, sick, and shipwrecked combatants, including new procedures for identifying and giving immunity to medical aircraft and vehicles, and better provisions for providing information about combatants missing or killed in action (Arts 8–34 and resolutions 17, 18, and 19 of the diplomatic conference, 7 June 1977).

Additional Protocol I forbids resort to perfidy (Art. 37), abuse of the red cross or similar emblems (Art. 38), declaration that no quarter will be given (Art. 40), or attack on a person parachuting from an aircraft (Art. 42). Combatants who are *hors de combat* shall receive protection (Art. 45), but spies and mercenaries are not entitled to claim POW status (Arts 46–7).

Britain, France, and the United States made clear their view that Additional Protocol I does not regulate or prohibit the use of nuclear weapons, and this view was not openly and formally challenged. A resolution was passed at the conference calling for action to prohibit weapons with indiscriminate or excessively injurious effects (resolution 22, 9 June 1977), and this led shortly afterwards to a Convention banning or restricting the use of incendiary weapons, mines, booby traps, and weapons releasing fragments which cannot be detected by X-rays.

There are detailed provisions in Additional Protocol I for the protection of civilians against the effects of hostilities, including the prohibition of indiscriminate attacks, area bombing, and attacks designed to spread terror (Arts 48, 51–2), attacks on cultural objects and places of worship (Art. 53 and resolution 20, 7 June 1977), the destruction of crops, food, and other objects indispensable to survival (Art. 54), and attacks against installations containing dangerous forces (Art. 56). Military commanders are to do everything feasible to prevent direct or indirect harm to civilians and are not to cause incidental harm to civilians which would be excessive in relation to the concrete and direct military advantage anticipated (Arts 57–8). Provision is made for the immunity of non-defended localities and demilitarised zones (Arts 59–60), civil defence personnel (Arts 61–7), relief organisations (Arts 68–71), refugees and stateless persons (Art. 73), and journalists (Art. 79 and Annex II). Women and children are to have special respect (Arts 76–8), and there is an article setting out minimum humanitarian standards, including the prohibition of torture, hostage-taking, and collective punishments (Art. 75). The ICRC and other humanitarian organisations are to be granted the necessary facilities to carry out their activities (Art. 81). Personnel entitled to immunity and protection are to carry identity cards (Annex 1).

Provision is made for the appointment of protecting powers or substitutes (Art. 5), and there are the usual provisions for disseminating the Geneva Conventions and the Protocol (Arts 6, 83, and resolution 21, 7 June 1977), and for bringing the Protocol into effect (Arts 92–5). Procedures for dealing with breaches are more stringent than in the Geneva Conventions (Arts 85–91).

Additional Protocol II deals with internal wars or, to be more precise, 'non-international armed conflicts'. The original draft had been quite detailed, but it was not much to the liking of many Third World countries, which feared that the restrictions in the draft on methods of combat and the rules on the protection of civilians would limit the means which governments could use to repress internal conflict. At the final session of the diplomatic conference, Pakistan (with encouragement from Iraq, Canada, and the United States) introduced a simplified draft, about half the length of the text previously under consideration, and this (with minor amendments) was approved by consensus.

Additional Protocol II recalls international instruments relating to human rights and is said to develop and supplement common Article 3 of the Geneva Conventions regarding armed conflict not of an international character. The Protocol applies to conflicts in the territory of a party 'between its armed forces and dissident armed forces or other organized armed groups' which control territory and so are able to carry out 'sustained and concerted military operations', but not covering 'situations of internal disturbances and tensions, such as riots, isolated and sporadic acts of violence ... '. Additional Protocol II does not detract from state sovereignty or the responsibility of a government to use legitimate means to maintain or re-establish law and order, or to defend national unity and territorial integrity (preamble and Arts 1 and 3). There is a general article setting out minimum standards of humane treatment similar to the corresponding article in Additional Protocol I, but also expressly prohibiting slavery, rape, and acts of terrorism (Art. 4). As in Additional Protocol I, it is prohibited to declare that no quarter will be given (Art. 4). Children are to receive 'the care and aid they require' (Art. 4). Persons whose liberty has been restricted are to be treated humanely (Art. 5), and there shall be no sentences or penalties 'except ... by a court offering the essential guarantees of independence and impartiality'. The death penalty is not to be pronounced on pregnant women, mothers of young children, or persons under 18 (Art. 6). The draft contained a provision to the effect that in sentencing those who had taken part in hostilities, account should be taken of the fact that the accused had respected Additional Protocol II, but this was deleted, as was the prohibition of reprisals, and articles which would have prohibited methods or means of combat causing superfluous injury or unnecessary suffering or severe damage to the natural environment. Additional Protocol II is to be applied without discrimination ('without any adverse distinctions', Art. 2).

Wounded, sick and shipwrecked persons are to be respected and protected 'whether or not they have taken part in armed conflict' (Arts 7–8), and medical and religious personnel are to be respected and protected and 'granted all available help' (Arts 9–11).

There are provisions to ensure that civilians are protected against the dangers arising from military operations. Civilians are not to be the object of attack, and there shall be no violence designed to spread terror

(Art. 13). Additional Protocol II prohibits attacks on cultural objects and places of worship (Art. 16) or on installations containing dangerous forces (Art. 15), and destruction of crops, foodstuffs and other objects indispensable to the survival of civilians (inserted by a vigorous initiative of the Holy See) (Art. 14). There shall be no forced removal of civilians 'unless the security of the civilians involved or imperative military reasons so demand' (Art. 17). A draft article requiring that those planning attacks should distinguish between civilians and combatants was deleted.

Additional Protocol II concludes with the usual provisions for entry into force (Arts 20–3) and for disseminating the Protocol as widely as possible (Art. 19).

One difficulty of securing full implementation of the law of Geneva is that the law of the Hague has not kept pace with military technology. Indeed, the ICRC has come to the conclusion that a clear distinction between the law of Geneva and the law of the Hague can no longer be maintained. The UN General Assembly has, by implication, taken the same view, in regarding 'Respect for Human Rights in Armed Conflicts' as a single subject and in calling in one paragraph for states to become parties to the Hague Conventions of 1899 and 1907 and the Geneva CBW Protocol of 1925 (which belong to the law of the Hague) and to the Geneva Conventions of 1949. The humanitarian effort now must encompass both fields of law.

An ICRC summary of the fundamental rules of international humanitarian law applicable in armed conflict is given in Appendix 15(a).

THE LAW OF THE HAGUE

The law of the Hague comprises the St Petersburg Declaration of 1868, the Hague Conventions of 1899 and 1907 on the laws and customs of war on land, the Geneva Protocol of 1925 prohibiting the use in war of chemical and bacteriological (biological) weapons (CBW), the Hague Convention of 1954 on the protection of cultural property, and the Geneva Convention and Protocols of 1981 banning or restricting the use of weapons which are indiscriminate or cause excessive injury. The St Petersburg Declaration of 1868, the Geneva Protocol of 1925, and the 1981 Convention on indiscriminate or cruel weapons are also measures of arms control, but it is convenient to deal with them below.

Hague Convention II with respect to the laws and customs of war on land, with the annexed Regulations, was signed at the Hague on 29 July 1899. It was replaced, as between the contracting parties, by Convention IV, signed at the Hague on 18 October 1907. The 1899 Convention 'remains in force as between the Powers which signed it, and which do not also ratify' the 1907 Convention (Art. 4).[3] Britain ratified the 1899 Convention in 1900, and the 1907 Convention in 1909.

The Regulations annexed to the Conventions defined those who qualify for belligerent status (Arts 1–3) and also contain specific rules for POWs (Arts 4–20). The obligations of belligerents with regard to the sick and wounded are to be governed by the Geneva Convention of 1864 (Art. 21).

The Regulations especially forbid the use of poison or poisonous weapons; the killing or wounding of 'an enemy who, having laid down his arms, or having no longer means of defence, has surrendered'; the declaration that no quarter will be given; the improper use of a flag of truce, the national flag, the military insignia and uniform of the enemy, or the Red Cross emblem; the destruction or seizure of enemy property 'unless ... imperatively demanded by the necessities of war'; and the killing or wounding 'treacherously' of individuals belonging to the hostile nation or army – although 'ruses of war' and the employment of 'measures necessary for obtaining information about the enemy and the country' are permitted (Arts 23–4).

It is prohibited to attack or bombard undefended towns, villages, dwellings, or buildings. The Officer commanding an attacking force must do all in his power to warn the authorities before beginning a bombardment, 'except in cases of assault'. The pillage of a town or place is prohibited, even when taken by assault. In the event of siege or bombardment, 'all necessary steps must be taken to spare, as far as possible', buildings dedicated to religion, art, science, or charitable purposes, historic monuments, hospitals, and places where the sick and wounded are being collected, 'provided they are not being used at the time for military purposes' (Arts 25–8).

A section dealing with 'military authority over the territory of the hostile state' contains provisions for protecting the inhabitants of occupied territories. The occupying power must 'take all the measures in his power to restore and ensure, as far as possible, public order and safety, while respecting, unless absolutely prevented, the laws in force in the country' (Art. 43). Respect must be paid to family honour and rights, the lives of persons, and private property (which must not be confiscated), as well as religious convictions and practice (Art. 46). No 'general penalty' shall be inflicted upon the population on account of 'the acts of individuals for which they can not be regarded as jointly and severally responsible' (Art. 50). The provisions in the 1899 Convention on the internment of belligerents and the care of wounded in neutral countries (Arts 57–60) were transferred in 1907 to Convention V respecting the rights and duties of neutral powers and persons in case of war on land.

More than fifty states have ratified or acceded to or consider themselves bound by one or both of the Hague Conventions. But what is perhaps of greater importance is the judgment of the Nürnberg Tribunal, to the effect that by 1939 the rules of land warfare laid down in the 1907 Convention had been recognised by all civilised nations and were regarded as being declaratory of the laws and customs of war: this conclusion is repeated in the Foreword to the US manual of military law.[4] The International Military Tribunal for the Far East declared in its judgment that the 1907 Convention was good evidence of the customary law of nations.

We now move on half a century to the Convention for the protection of cultural property in the event of armed conflict signed at the Hague on 14 May 1954.[5] This elaborates some of the provisions of Article 27 of the Hague Convention of 1907 on the laws and customs of war on land; it was prepared at an inter-governmental conference convened by UNESCO.

As in the case of the Hague Conventions of 1899 and 1907 and the Geneva Conventions of 1949, it applies in the event of international armed conflicts (Art. 18), but it follows the Geneva Conventions in providing also for the application of certain minimum provisions in non-international armed conflicts (Art. 19). The parties undertake to refrain from using cultural property for purposes which are likely to expose it to destruction or damage, and to refrain from hostile acts against such property. They further undertake to prevent theft, pillage, or misappropriation of cultural property, and acts of vandalism. They agree not to requisition 'movable cultural property', and there is an unconditional ban on 'any act directed by way of reprisals against cultural property' (Art. 4).

The Convention grants special protection to 'a limited number of refuges [zones of sanctuary] intended to shelter movable cultural property [and] immovable cultural property of very great import-ance'. These refuges must be situated at 'an adequate distance' from any large industrial centre or important military objectives, and they are not to be used for military purposes (Art. 8).

The Convention, the annexed Regulations, and a Protocol create machinery for implementation, and provide for the function of protecting powers, for conciliation, and for the assistance of UNESCO. In 1985 there were 72 parties to the 1954 Hague Convention (including the Holy See) and 59 parties to the Protocol concerned with the safeguarding and return of cultural property which has been improperly exported during enemy occupation.

There was opened for signature in 1981 a Convention and Protocols prohibiting or restricting the use against civilians in international wars of certain weapons which have indiscriminate effects or which cause excessive injury, including mines, booby traps, and incendiary weapons, and all uses against both combatants and civilians of weapons which release fragments which cannot be detected by X-rays. An attempt was made to prohibit small-calibre weapons on the ground that these, like dum-dum bullets, cause excessive injury, but this was unsuccessful. There were 26 parties to the Convention and Protocols in 1986. It may be noted that the British Manual of Military Law states that fire weapons shall be directed solely against 'inanimate military targets' and that it is illegal to use them 'solely against combatant personnel'.[6]

The Hague law is based on principles which after eighty years still remain valid.
(1) The parties stated, in the preamble to the Hague Conventions of 1899 and 1907, their wish to preserve peace and prevent armed conflicts. But when, to use the wording of the Conventions, 'events' bring about an 'appeal to arms', the parties still desire to serve the interests of humanity and the needs of civilisation. The parties therefore considered it important to revise the general laws and customs of war, either by defining them more precisely or by confining them within 'such limits as would mitigate their severity as far as possible'. The Conventions were designed 'to diminish the evils of war, as far as military requirements permit ... '.

The preamble then recorded the failure of the parties to find agreement covering all the circumstances which might arise in practice; and yet they did not intend that, when unforeseen cases occur, the absence of a written agreement should mean that 'the arbitrary judgment of military commanders' should be decisive. The preamble sets out the so-called Martens declaration, named after the Russian jurist, Fedor Fedorovich Martens, which forms the epigraph to this chapter. In other words, the code contained in the Regulations was recognised to be incomplete: it was to be supplemented by principles applied in the interests of humanity and civilisation, even when these are not expressed in treaty form.

(2) The second basic principle of the Hague Conventions is to be found in Article 22 of the annexed Regulations: 'The right of belligerents to adopt means of injuring the enemy is not unlimited.' This principle had been affirmed in Article 12 of the Brussels Declaration of 1874. (Britain signed the Brussels Declaration but it did not receive enough ratifications to enter into force.)

This general rule that belligerents may not adopt unlimited means of injuring an enemy may be made concrete in three ways: limitations for the benefit of persons, target limitations, and limitations on weapons and their use.

(a) The limitations for the benefit of persons proceed from the basic principle of the Just War doctrine, namely, that combatants are the main force of resistance and a legitimate target of military operations, and that non-combatants shall neither participate in nor be subject to hostilities. Rousseau expressed the principle as follows:

> The object of war being the destruction of the enemy State, a commander has a perfect right to kill its defenders so long as their arms are in their hands: but once they have laid them down and have submitted, they cease to be enemies ... and revert to the condition of men, pure and simple, over whose lives no one can any longer exercise a rightful claim.[7]

If combatants who surrender are to be immune from attack, how much more those who never took up arms. The ICRC, after mature consideration, has concluded that if the principle of the protection of the civilian population is to be maintained, it should apply even to civilians engaged in 'non-peaceful' activities, such as scientists and workers in industries closely connected with the war effort. The ICRC admits that this would open the way to abuses, but holds that 'these are minor drawbacks compared with the danger of excluding the above categories from the civilian population'.[8] Additional Protocol I to the Geneva Conventions defines a civilian as any person who is not a member of organised armed forces, militias, volunteer corps, and resistance movements, and those who do not spontaneously take up arms to resist an invading force (Art. 50).

If civilians are not to be exposed to attack, belligerents should take every precaution to reduce to a minimum the damage inflicted on non-combatants during attacks against military objectives, and should not commit acts of destruction in such a way as to cause indirect harm to the civilian population disproportionate to the importance of the military objective under attack. For the attacking side, this requires careful choice and identification of military objectives, precision in attack, abstention from area bombing unless the area is exclusively military, abstention from attacking civil defence organisations, and (as required by Article 26 of the Hague Regulations and Article 57.2(c) of Additional Protocol I of 1977) the giving of warning in specified cases. For the side being attacked, it requires the evacuation of civilians from the vicinity of military objectives; civilians staying in or near military objectives or threatened areas do so at their own risk.

The prohibition of direct attacks on civilians presupposes that a distinction can be made between combatants and civilians. The fact is that the immunity of civilians is still one of the pillars of international law. Although there have been many examples of blatant disregard of the rule, no government has claimed that to do so is lawful. To the extent that violations have been defended, the argument has been that it was a reprisal for an unlawful act of an enemy or an exceptional measure dictated by over-riding considerations, such as the saving of human lives by putting an end to the war quickly.

The distinction between combatants and civilians cannot easily be maintained in an era of total war and absolute weapons. War is no longer the concern of professional fighters only: whole societies are mobilised to support the war effort. And modern weapons have some effects which are both indiscriminate and excessive in relation to any concrete and direct military advantage. The St Petersburg Declaration of 1868 solemnly affirmed that 'the progress of civilization ought to have the effect of alleviating as much as possible the calamities of war'. Unfortunately the progress of civilisation has not had that beneficial effect: it has, on the contrary, provided human beings with more effective instruments of slaughter – submarines, aircraft, long-range missiles, nuclear explosives, nerve gases, and the like. Mankind is no more secure than it was when the Hague Conventions were concluded eighty years ago: what has changed is that the price of failure has increased.

(b) Target limitations constitute a corollary of the group of limitations referred to above. The accepted rule is that attacks may be directed only against military objectives, that is to say, those of which the total or partial destruction would confer a distinct military advantage. The rule is stated in the 1907 Hague Regulations in the following terms: 'The attack or bombardment, *by whatever means*, of towns, villages, dwellings, or buildings which are undefended is prohibited' (Art. 25).[9] Additional Protocol I to the Geneva Conventions prohibits all indiscriminate attacks, area bombing, attacks designed to spread terror, attacks on cultural objects and places of worship, the destruction of crops, food, and other objects indispensable to the survival of civilians, and attacks against the natural environment or installations containing dangerous forces. Military commanders are to do everything feasible to prevent direct or indirect harm to civilians and are not to cause incidental harm to civilians which would be excessive in relation to the concrete and direct military advantage anticipated (Arts 51–8).

The present state of humanitarian law clearly has paradoxical results. The crew of a bombing plane may direct their weapons against a military target in a built-up area and, as an indirect consequence, may kill or injure tens or hundreds of thousands of 'innocent' civilians. If the plane is later hit by anti-aircraft fire, the crew may eject or bail out, and then claim the full protection of the Hague and Geneva Conventions from those who may have survived their attack.

On the initiative of Norway, the General Assembly on 9 December 1970 approved resolution 2675 containing eight 'basic principles for the protection of civilian populations in armed conflicts'. The text of the substantive part of the resolution is given in Appendix 9.

(c) As for limitations on weapons and their use, the basic principle of the Hague Law is that it is forbidden to use weapons which cause superfluous injury (1899 Convention), unnecessary suffering (1907 Convention), or which are excessively injurious (1981 Geneva Convention). This concept was derived from Article 13 of the Brussels Declaration of 1874. The aim when this text was adopted was not primarily to spare civilians, but to avoid causing suffering to combatants in excess of what is essential to place an adversary *hors de combat*. This is a very subjective test. What may seem 'necessary' to the attacker may seem quite 'unnecessary' to those attacked. Some of the most effective weapons are also the most cruel.

(3) Another principle, implicit in the Hague Regulations but explicitly affirmed in the Geneva Conventions and Protocols, and also explicit in the Nürnberg principles, is that international law imposes direct and personal obligations on individuals. A person who

violates international humanitarian law is responsible therefor and liable to punishment, and it is no defence to enter a plea of superior orders.

RETRIBUTION AND REPRISALS IN ARMED CONFLICT

Reprisals in time of peace are coercive measures for resolving conflict without resort to armed force; reprisals in time of armed conflict, usually known as belligerent reprisals, are acts of retaliation to compel an enemy to comply with the laws and customs of war. It is reprisals in this latter sense with which I am concerned here.

Military retribution is an act of counter-attack, punishment, or revenge. Any particular act of retribution may be open to question on prudential or humanitarian grounds, but so long as it conforms to the laws and customs applicable in armed conflicts, it is not illegal. Belligerent reprisals, by contrast, are acts which in ordinary circumstances would be regarded as violations of international law. The only justification for resorting to such unlawful acts arises from the prior commission of an illegal act by the enemy. The matter is put very clearly in the US military manual, *The Law of Land Warfare*: 'Reprisals are acts of retaliation in the form of conduct which would otherwise be unlawful, resorted to by one belligerent against enemy personnel or property for acts of warfare committed by the other belligerent in violation of the law of war, for the purpose of enforcing future compliance with the recognized rules of civilized warfare.'[10] A reprisal in time of war, then, has three tenses: a *past* act of warfare in violation of the law of war, a *present* act of retaliation in a form which would otherwise be illegal, in order to enforce *future* compliance with the recognised rules of war. The rationale behind reprisals has been that a belligerent should not be put at a disadvantage because the enemy breaks the rules.

Certain acts of belligerent reprisal are expressly prohibited. The Geneva Conventions of 1949 forbid reprisals against protected persons, namely, wounded, sick, and shipwrecked members of the armed forces, prisoners of war, and civilian persons in occupied territory or enemy nationals on the territory of a belligerent state (I, 46; II, 47; III, 13; IV, 33). The Hague Convention of 1954 on the protection of cultural property contains an absolute ban on reprisals (Art. 4). Resolution 2675 adopted by the UN General Assembly in 1970 affirmed that 'civilian populations or individual members thereof, should not be the object of reprisals' (see Appendix 9, para. 7). Additional Protocol I to the Geneva Conventions prohibits reprisals against wounded, sick, and shipwrecked combatants, civilians, objects indispensable to the survival of the civilian population, works and installations containing dangerous forces, cultural objects, places of worship, and the natural environment (Arts 20, 51(6), 52(1), 53(c), 54(4), 55(2), 56(4)). A Protocol to the 1981 Convention on indiscriminate or excessively injurious weapons prohibits the use of mines, booby traps, delayed action or remote control weapons against civilians 'by way of reprisals' (Protocol II, Art. 3(2)). It is probably now the case that the only legitimate reprisal in armed conflict is to use illegal weapons or methods of fighting against combatants or military objectives.

In a study on human rights in armed conflict in 1969, the UN Secretary-General drew attention to the risk that under the stress of armed conflict, the notion of reciprocity may lead to reprisals 'which may be themselves contrary to internationally proclaimed objectives of the humane treatment of civilians, prisoners and combatants, and the application of which should be forbidden or, to say the least, strictly circumscribed'. The international community should direct its efforts towards the development of 'internationally agreed standards'. In a report a year later, he suggested a total prohibition 'in all circumstances' of the use of the civilian population as an object of reprisal.[11] The declaration on some principles of international law, adopted by the UN General Assembly without dissent on 24 October 1970 as resolution 2625, reaffirmed the principle in the UN Charter that states should refrain in their international relations from the threat or use of force against the territorial integrity or political independence of any state, or in any other manner inconsistent with the purposes of the United Nations (Art. 2(4)), and added that 'States have a duty to refrain from acts of reprisal involving the use of force' (see Appendix 8). The United Kingdom accepted this unqualified wording on the understanding that the term 'force' denotes physical or armed force, and would thus accord with Britain's consistent interpretation of the term 'force' as used in the UN Charter.[12] The Security Council, in its resolution 188 of 9 April 1964, condemned reprisals as 'incompatible with the purposes and principles of the United Nations'.

It is not difficult to see how the admissibility of the notion of reprisals in peace or in war opens the way to abuse, and it can be plausibly maintained that it is now up to the UN Security Council rather than the victim to determine when an illegality has occurred and what form any reprisal should take. That certainly seems to have been the view of UN Secretary-General Dag Hammarskjold when he was trying to reinforce the cease-fire commitments in the Middle East in 1956.[13] Such a view is strengthened by the Security Council's repeated condemnation of particular acts of reprisal.

The ICRC has held that the only position it can adopt is to call for a complete prohibition of belligerent reprisals, with procedures for investigating alleged violations. But realising that an immediate prohibition of reprisals is not possible, the ICRC has drawn attention to 'limits ... formulated in the texts of qualified writers or in the publications of specialized institutions'.[14]

(a) Reprisals cannot be exercised unless the party alleging violation has offered the possibility of an enquiry and impartial observation of the facts;

(b) The scale of reprisals must not be out of proportion to that of the violation they aim at stopping;

(c) Reprisals must be carried out, so far as possible, only in the same field as that of the violation;

(d) They should in any case not be contrary to the laws of humanity.

Those writers who have given most attention to belligerent reprisals in practice as well as in theory are most sceptical of the utility of the concept. E. S. Colbert raised the question whether the doctrine of reprisals 'makes a contribution to the maintenance of law and order sufficiently great to outweigh its potentialities for abuse'. Frits Kalshoven considers that 'the balance of merits and demerits of belligerent reprisals has now become so entirely negative as no longer to allow of their being regarded as even moderately effective sanctions of the laws of war ... '. They are 'a complete anachronism' and 'a total prohibition ... is the only tenable proposition.'[15] Indeed, the man or woman in the street, unschooled in the niceties of international law, may well agree with Professor Telford Taylor that 'resort to crime in order to reform the criminal is an unappetizing method'.[16]

ATTEMPTS TO BAN THE USE OF CHEMICAL AND BACTERIOLOGICAL (BIOLOGICAL) WEAPONS (CBW)

I am concerned in this chapter with attempts to limit or prohibit the *use* of weapons: efforts to control research, development, testing, manufacture, stockpiling, deployment, and transfer of weapons are reviewed in chapter 5.

Chemical weapons are usually defined as those chemical agents employed for their toxic effects on humans, animals, or plants. This definition is intended to exclude incendiary and smoke weapons, which exert their primary effects through physical force, fire, deprivation of air, or reduced visibility, and which are better classified with high explosives. Chemical weapons include incapacitating agents (tear and harassing gases), defoliants, and herbicides. Some gases, such as CS, are used in aerosol form, and since 2 February 1970 British official spokesmen have sometimes referred to them as 'smokes'. One is reminded of the opening sentence of the standard British lecture on air raid precautions during the second world war. 'Gases are of three kinds: solids, liquids, and vapours.'

What most people call 'germ warfare' was referred to in the Geneva Protocol of 1925 as 'bacteriological methods of warfare'. There are, however, living organisms, in addition to bacteria, which can be used as weapons. To avoid misunderstanding, it is now customary to use the term 'bacteriological (biological) weapons'. A complication sometimes arises when the term 'biological agent' is used, since it might reasonably be held that human beings are biological agents.

The attempt to prohibit the use of chemical and germ weapons in war by means of specific legal instruments began over a century ago with the St Petersburg Declaration of 1868. Before the middle of the nineteenth century the law of war was entirely customary, and it is still often necessary to distinguish between legal obligations of a contractual nature which derive from international treaties, and obligations which are part of customary international law. One difficulty in the field of chemical and biological weapons is that some of the basic texts are ambiguous or inconsistent on this point.

Looking back more than a century, the St Petersburg Declaration seems to have been more important for the general principles it enunciated than for its specific provision – the prohibition of 'any projectile of a weight below 400 grammes [about 14 ounces], which is either explosive or charged with fulminating [flashing] or inflammable substances'.

The Declaration's preamble states the need for civilised nations to agree on technical limits 'at which the necessities of war ought to yield to the requirements of humanity'. There follow five principles, of which the first reads somewhat quaintly in the age of nerve gases and thermonuclear missiles: 'Considering that the progress of civilization should have the effect of alleviating as much as possible the calamities of war.' The second principle, by implication, affirmed the immunity of civilians from direct attack: 'the only legitimate object which States should endeavour to accomplish during war is to weaken the military forces of the enemy'. The remaining three principles were concerned with the protection of wounded combatants:

> Considering … that for this purpose [weakening the enemy's military forces] it is sufficient to disable the greatest possible number of men;
> That this object would be exceeded by the employment of arms which uselessly aggravate the suffering of disabled men, or render their death inevitable;
> That the employment of such arms would, therefore, be contrary to the laws of humanity.

It should be noted that the Declaration banned only projectiles *less* than the specified weight, on the ground that small projectiles would cause unnecessary suffering. Larger shells were permitted, because it was considered that the amount of suffering they caused was not disproportionate to the military advantages of employing them.

The next document bearing on CBW is the Brussels Declaration of 27 August 1874. This Declaration included the important statement which was later to become the second basic principle of the Hague Conventions: 'The laws of war do not recognize in belligerents an unlimited power in the adoption of means of injuring an enemy' (Art. 12). The Brussels Declaration also stated as 'especially forbidden' the use of 'poison or poisoned weapons' (Art. 13(a)).

The Regulations annexed to Hague Convention (II) of 1899 repeated the 1874 ban on unlimited warfare: 'The right of belligerents to adopt means of injuring the enemy is not unlimited' (Art. 22). The use of 'poison or poisoned arms' was again declared to be 'especially prohibited', as was the use of 'arms, projectiles, or material of a nature to cause superfluous injury' (Art. 23(a) and (e)). There was also concluded at the 1899 Hague Conference a separate declaration banning, on a reciprocal basis, the use of 'projectiles *the sole object of which* is the diffusion of asphyxiating or deleterious gases' (my italics). Britain ratified the 1899 Declaration on poisonous gases in 1907.

Hague Convention IV of 18 October 1907 was a slightly improved version of Convention II of 1899 on the laws and customs of war. The 1907 Convention reaffirmed that belligerents do not have the right to adopt unlimited means of injuring the enemy (Art. 22), and it was again declared to be 'especially forbidden' to employ poison or poisonous weapons, or to use arms, projectiles, or material calculated to cause unnecessary suffering (Art. 23(a) and (e)).

In spite of these rules, 6000 tons of lachrymators and 7000 tons of respiratory irritants were used during the first world war. In reaction against this, the post-war treaties attempted to carry the prohibition of poisonous or germ weapons a stage further, the wording used being significant in two respects. First, the weapons prohibited were defined as 'asphyxiating, poisonous or other [in French, *similaires*] gases and all analogous liquids, materials or devices [*procédés*]'. This was the wording destined to be used in the Geneva CBW Protocol of 1925. Secondly, the peace treaties asserted without qualification that the use of the specified weapons was already prohibited: 'The use of ... *being prohibited*, their manufacture and importation are strictly forbidden ... ' (my italics).

The same wording, 'asphyxiating, poisonous or other gases and all analogous liquids, materials or devices', was used in the Washington Naval Treaty of 1922, which was, however, never ratified by France and consequently did not enter into effect. The treaty declared that the use in war of the specified substances had been 'justly condemned by the general opinion of the civilized worlds'; it asserted that a prohibition of the use in war of these substances had been 'declared in treaties to which a majority of the civilized powers are parties'; in order that the prohibition should be 'universally accepted as a part of international law, binding alike on the conscience and practice of nations', the parties assented to the prohibition and agreed to be bound by it 'as between themselves'; and the parties invited 'all other civilized nations to adhere thereto'.

The 1922 wording was followed in all important respects in the Geneva CBW Protocol of 17 June 1925, but the parties agreed also 'to extend this prohibition [of the use of the specified chemical agents in war] to the use of bacteriological methods of warfare'. The 1922 reference to treaties 'to which a majority of the civilized powers are parties' was retained, except that 'civilized' was dropped. Moreover, instead of simply inviting others states to adhere, the 1925 Protocol commits the parties to exerting every effort to induce other states to accede. It should be noted *en passant* that the 1925 Protocol was a by-product of a convention on the supervision of the international trade in arms, ammunition, and implements of war, which never came into force.

Nobody would now claim that the Geneva Protocol was well drafted, either in English or French. It is by no means clear which paragraphs of the section relating to chemical weapons are declaratory of customary international law, and which are solely of a contractual nature. The fact that the chemical part is simply extended to bacteriological warfare would be easier to interpret if the chemical part were itself unambiguous. There is a great deal in the Protocol for lawyers to argue about, but the lay person will not go far wrong by regarding the Protocol as a no-first-use treaty, confined to the use of the specified agents in war. The Protocol does not prohibit research, manufacture, stockpiling, transfer, training, or – in practice – reprisals, and it does not ban the use of the specified substances in non-war situations. Needless to say, non-parties to the Protocol, and parties released from their obligations under it because of a breach by an adversary, remain bound by the customary law applicable in armed conflicts.

Britain ratified the Geneva Protocol in 1930. A good many states, including Britain, ratified with a reservation of reciprocity, which in Britain's case reads as follows:

> The said Protocol is only binding on His Britannic Majesty as regards those Powers and States which have both signed and ratified the Protocol, or have finally acceded thereto; The said Protocol shall cease to be binding on His Britannic Majesty towards any Power at enmity with him whose armed forces, or the armed forces of whose allies, fail to respect the prohibitions laid down in the said Protocol.

No state has ratified or acceded with a reservation limiting the types of chemical weapons to which the Protocol applies.

Before ratifying the Geneva Protocol, any government must ask itself precisely what substances are to be prohibited in war. The British government's conclusion on this matter was made clear in Parliament on 18 February 1930: 'Smoke screens are not considered as poisonous and do not, therefore, come within the terms of the Geneva Gas Protocol. Tear gases and shells producing poisonous fumes are, however, prohibited under the Protocol.'

A draft disarmament treaty being considered in 1930 contained an undertaking, subject to reciprocity, to abstain from the use in war of 'asphyxiating, poisonous or *similar* [other] gases, and of all analogous liquids, *substances or processes* [materials or devices]'.[17] On 18 November 1930 Britain submitted to the Preparatory Commission for the Disarmament Conference a memorandum to the effect that, basing itself on the English text of the draft treaty, the British government took the view that the prohibition of the use of gases in war included lachrymatory gases. The British memorandum, and a French note reaching a similar conclusion, were discussed in Geneva on 2 December 1930, and there was virtual unanimity in support of the view that the prohibition contained in the Geneva Protocol and the draft treaty applied to the use in war of tear gases; only the United States, not then a party to the 1925 Protocol, expressed reservations.

It so happened that a parliamentary question on the definition of poisonous elements under the Geneva Protocol was due to be answered in the House of Commons a fortnight after the Geneva debate. As background for answering the question, E. H. Carr, then in the Foreign Office, wrote a minute on the complication arising from the fact that 'the Americans ... do not regard the prohibition as extending to tear gas, *which apparently is harmless to health*' (my italics). Among those initialling the minute without dissent were Sir Robert Vansittart and Hugh Dalton.[18] In his reply to the question on 17 December, Arthur Henderson simply said that the exact substances which are prohibited are not defined, either in the Protocol or elsewhere.

The significance of the Carr minute did not become fully apparent until much later – indeed, not until 1970, when the British government interpreted the prohibition contained in the Geneva Protocol as not being applicable to CS gas. The tear gas available in 1930 was CN; Corson and Stoughton had synthesised CS in 1928, but it was not developed for use until the 1950s. It seems clear from Carr's minute that it was known to the British government in 1930 (the year Britain ratified the Geneva Protocol) that there existed tear gases not harmful to human health.

Be that as it may, the 1930 view that the prohibition of gases in war included tear gases continued to be the British position, and when Britain put forward a draft disarmanent treaty in March 1933, it was provided that the prohibition of the use of chemical weapons in war should apply to the use of 'toxic, asphyxiating, lachrymatory, irritant or vesicant [blistering] substances', that parties to the treaty would inform the proposed disarmament commission of 'lachrymatory substances intended ... for police operations', and that smoke or fog used for screening purposes was not included in the prohibition of chemical weapons 'provided that such smoke or fog is not liable to produce harmful effects under normal conditions of use'. On 8 June

1933 the Disarmament Conference decided to accept the British draft as a basis for future work, but as Hitler strengthened his grip in Germany, the inter-war disarmament effort lapsed into futility.

Interest in CBW revived in 1952, when the Communist states alleged that the United States had used germ weapons in Korea. A Soviet proposal in the UN Security Council to appeal to states to ratify or accede to the Geneva Protocol was not adopted (1 vote in favour, 10 abstentions), and a US proposal to refer the matter to the UN Disarmament Commission was withdrawn. The Soviet Union then vetoed two proposals, one of which would have asked the ICRC to investigate the charges, and the other would have condemned the fabrication and dissemination of false charges.[19]

During the 1960s, Britain favoured the separation of biological from chemical weapons, on the ground that the former had virtually never been used in war and a total ban could be imposed immediately. Britain therefore put forward a draft convention designed to prohibit not only the use of biological weapons in war, but also research directed towards production of biological weapons, manufacture, acquisition, and possession, and to eliminate stocks. Britain also made a diplomatic effort to persuade states to ratify or accede to the Geneva CBW Protocol. In 1966, there had been 48 parties, and this increased to 90 in 1971 and 105 in 1985.

In 1969, following the publication of a UN expert report on chemical weapons, UN Secretary-General Thant appealed to states to make a clear affirmation that the prohibition in the Geneva Protocol 'applies to the use in war of all chemical, bacteriological and biological agents (including tear gas and other harassing agents), which now exist or which may be developed in the future'. It was noticeable that the response by Britain's minister for disarmament to this appeal was cautious. British reservations increased as the weeks went by, particularly when British troops had to use CS in Northern Ireland, the first instance of the use of tear gas for riot control within the United Kingdom.

Uncertainty about the British position continued for some months, but on 2 February 1970, when replying to a seemingly innocuous parliamentary question about disarmament, the Foreign Secretary said that he would like to explain the government's view regarding the use of tear gases in war. He quoted the conclusion of the second Labour government in 1930 that smoke screens did not come within the Geneva Protocol: 'modern technology has developed CS smoke which, unlike the tear gases available in 1930, is considered to be not significantly harmful to man in other than wholly exceptional circumstances'. He then expressed the government's view that CS 'and other such gases' should be regarded as outside the prohibition of use in war contained in the Geneva Protocol. The next day the Prime Minister added that CS 'has been newly discovered or invented – whatever is the right phrase – since 1930'. While it is true that CS was not 'available' in 1930, it was known to the British government at that time that gases with the characteristics of CS existed.

Until government files are open to public inspection, we cannot be sure why the British government reached this decision. Many ordinary citizens no doubt took the view that it would be absurd not to use in war a chemical substance which British troops were using for riot control in the United Kingdom in time of peace.

Opposition to the decision announced in 1970 was based on three main considerations. First, there is an important distinction between use in peace and use in war. Tear gas is used in peace under strict controls and to avoid using more lethal weapons: the purpose is to reduce injuries and save lives. In war, tear gas may be used in conjunction with other weapons to increase the lethal effectiveness of the latter. Whatever may have been the original intention of the US authorities, it is beyond doubt that tear gases were used in South East Asia to enhance the effectiveness of conventional anti-personnel weapons. But the grave danger, as was shown in the first world war, is the risk of escalation from chemicals which merely irritate to those that cause serious injury, and then perhaps to those that kill (for example, nerve gases).

The second objection was to the method used to reinterpret an international treaty. Britain had taken the view when ratifying the Geneva Protocol in 1930 that the Protocol banned the use of tear gases in war, and had played a leading part in trying to persuade other countries to take the same view. A unilateral reinterpretation of an international treaty undermines the effort to build world order. The offence was compounded in this case because it followed so closely on U Thant's appeal and the vote of a substantial majority in the UN General Assembly urging states to respect the traditional view of the obligations contained in the Geneva Protocol.

The third objection followed naturally from the second. Britain had been establishing a reputation as a country genuinely committed to making progress in arms control and disarmament. Britain had proposed separating biological from chemical weapons, and dealing with the former by means of an immediate and total ban, but there were critics who said that the ulterior motive for this ploy was to make it easier for the United States to continue using harassing gases and anti-plant chemicals in Vietnam. The effect of the British proposal to separate biological from chemical weapons, said the critics, would not be to strengthen the Geneva Protocol, but to weaken it. If, as was alleged, Britiain's stance was having the effect of weakening the Geneva Protocol as it applied to chemical weapons, how could British delegates in international bodies convince the critics of Britain's good faith in giving priority to a treaty on biological weapons?

The British government can at any time return to the traditional interpretation of the Geneva Protocol. If doubts should exist regarding the precise scope of the Protocol, an authoritative opinion could be secured from the International Court of Justice.

Shortly before the British announcement about the scope of the Geneva Protocol, the Nixon Administration had been conducting a reivew of policy on CBW, and on 25 November 1969, the President announced that he was asking the Senate to advise and consent to US ratification of the Geneva Protocol of 1925. The United States took the view that the Protocol restricted but did not prohibit the use in war of riot-control agents and chemical herbicides.

In addition, Nixon announced that the United States was taking two unilateral steps regarding CBW.

(1) The United States would not be the first to use incapacitating or lethal chemical weapons.
(2) The United States renounced entirely the use of all biological weapons, would destroy stocks of such weapons, and would discontinue research on biological warfare except for research on 'defensive measures such as immunization and safety measures'.

Nixon also stated his support for the British draft convention on biological weapons, but would 'seek ... to clarify specific provisions of the draft to assure that necessary safeguards are included'. On 14 February 1970 it was announced that the US ban on biological weapons would also apply to biological toxins, which are chemicals even though 'the technology of their production resembles that of biological agents'. Toxins are not capable of reproduction.

This was an interesting example of how a unilateral act may stimulate and reinforce the negotiating process, for it soon led to the conclusion of a new Convention prohibiting the development, production, or acquisition of bacteriological (biological) and toxin weapons and for the destruction of stocks. Alleged breaches are to be dealt with by the UN Security Council. Nothing in the Convention is to lessen the prohibition of use contained in the Geneva Protocol. There were 100 parties to the BW Convention in 1986. I refer later in this chapter to Iraq's use of chemical weapons against Iran.

ATTEMPTS TO BAN THE USE OF NUCLEAR WEAPONS

Nuclear weapons were used twice in 1945, but those were relatively small atomic bombs. Some of the nuclear-weapon states now possess weapons more than one thousand times as powerful as those dropped on Japan and a million times as powerful as the conventional bombs of the second world war. The paradox of nuclear deterrence is that weapons are deployed in order to prevent others from using them, and each technological development by one side is matched almost at once by a similar development on the other side.

Proposals to ban the use of nuclear weapons naturally appeal to persons of humane sentiments or, if a ban could be universal and effective, to those who understand that any use of nuclear weapons against another nuclear-weapon state might quickly lead to mutual annihilation. NATO strategy is to deploy nuclear weapons in order to deter an attack by the Warsaw Pact's massive conventional forces. For this reason among others, the West resists all proposals for an unconditional ban on using nuclear weapons on the ground that a threat to use nuclear weapons, first if necessary, is needed in order to deter aggression with conventional arms. To the neutral and non-aligned countries, and to many pacifists and nuclear-pacifists, the stance of NATO is morally indefensible. If nuclear weapons were ever used, the harm could not be confined to the country attacked, for much of the delayed radiation and other effects would cause somatic or genetic injury to people far away from the area of conflict. Indeed, it might be thought by the non-expert that nuclear weapons were encompassed by the Geneva Protocol's ban on using liquids, materials, and devices analogous to chemical weapons, but this has never been seriously advanced.

In the early days of the UN, the problem of nuclear weapons revolved mainly around the radical US plan for placing nuclear operations under international ownership and control, and the Soviet slogan about banning the bomb, which was widely regarded at the time as a propaganda ploy. Serious debate and negotiation about disarmament date from 1954, when the Soviet Union agreed to take as a basis

2222222222

for discussion a comprehensive Anglo-French plan for verified disarmament by stages.

In 1961, as a result of an initiative by Ethopia, it was decided to separate the question of the use of nuclear weapons from other disarmament matters, and the UN Secretary-General was asked to consult governments with a view to convening a conference for signing a convention banning the use of such weapons.

Britain and the United States opposed this decision on the ground that deterrence depends on a determination to respond to aggression at whatever level is necessary, and that there should be no abrogation of the right of self-defence. The Western view was that paper promises not to use weapons which you possess and are training your armed forces to use are no substitute for concrete measures of arms control or disarmament. It was clear that Western governments wished to leave open the possibility of using nuclear weapons in response to a conventional attack.

The Soviet government has always adopted a simple view of this problem in its public pronouncements: that a convention to prohibit the use of nuclear weapons would be an important step on the road to their complete abolition.

The UN item regarding non-use of nuclear weapons has been continued at each annual session of the General Assembly, with Communist and Third World support and NATO opposition. The UN General Assembly has repeatedly condemned any use of nuclear weapons as contrary to the spirit and aims of the United Nations and to the rules of international law, and as a crime against humanity and civilisation (see Appendix 4). The British manual of military law states that there is no rule of international law dealing specifically with the use of nuclear weapons, so that use involves the application of the recognised principles of international law. The US manual states more categorically that the use of explosive atomic weapons 'cannot as such be regarded as violative of international law in the absence of any customary rule of international law or international convention restricting their employment.'[20]

The Treaty of Tlatelolco prohibits the use of nuclear weapons in Latin America, and a similar agreement has been drafted for the South Pacific area. The only other restrictions on use are in separate unilateral declarations by the first five nuclear-weapon states in 1978, undertaking not to use these weapons against non-nuclear-weapon states. In Britain's case, the assurance was not to use nuclear weapons against states which are parties to the Treaty on the non-proliferation of nuclear weapons or similar internationally binding commitments, except in the case of an attack on the United Kingdom, its dependencies, its armed forces, or its allies.

OPTIMISTS AND PESSIMISTS

Slaughter and devastation on the scale now feasible is beyond the human imagination. For the private citizen with humanitarian impulses and an optimistic outlook, the division of humanitarian law into the Hague and Geneva streams had a certain logic. For the pacifist minority, and for those like the ICRC who reject 'the very idea of war', as one ICRC document puts it, the obvious task has been to strengthen the law of Geneva, which is concerned with the protection of those not taking a direct part in hostilities, and at the same time to do what is possible in an imperfect world towards the abolition of war itself. Andrew Carnegie was so sure that war could be abolished in a foreseeable future that when he set aside $10 million to promote world peace, he was careful to instruct the trustees in his own distinctive spelling about what should be done with the money when that goal had been achieved.

> When civilized nations enter into such treaties as named, and war is discarded as disgraceful to civilized men, as personal war (duelling) and man selling and buying (slavery) hav been discarded within the wide boundaries of our English-speaking race, the Trustees will pleas then consider what is the next most degrading remaining evil or evils whose banishment – or what new elevating element or elements if introduced or fosterd, or both combined – would most advance the progress, elevation and happiness of man, and so on from century to century, without end, my Trustees of each age shall determin how they can best aid man in his upward march to higher and higher stages of development unceasingly, for now we know that man was created, not with an instinct for his own degradation, but imbued with the desire and the power for improvement to which, perchance, there may be no limit short of perfection even here in this life upon erth.

For those who may be less sanguine about achieving perfection at an early date, it has not been enough simply to develop and strengthen the law of Geneva for protecting non-combatants; there has been the further task of strengthening the law of the Hague, which seeks to make war less brutal. It is true that some unbending pacifists assert that it is vain to imagine that war can be made more humane when it is of its nature opposed to humane sentiments. But the mainstream of humanitarian opinion considers this view to be mistaken. The unlawfulness or immorality of the resort to force does not negate the legitimacy of the law of armed conflict, which seeks to lessen the consequences of the inability of the international community to prevent the use of military force. Jean Pictet, a veteran of the Red Cross movement, points out that no one questions the need for an efficient health organisation or a reliable fire brigade, 'but it is not for any love of disease or fire'. It is a basic assumption of all humanitarian efforts that evils which cannot be immediately suppressed should, if possible, be attenuated. The ICRC considers that all Red Cross work 'is a protest against violence'. Endeavours to abolish war and to protect its victims 'complete one another and must be conducted on a parallel'.[21]

IRREGULAR FIGHTERS AND INTERNAL WARS

It is necessary to start this section with some definitions. The Hague Regulations are declared to apply 'not only to armies, but also to militia and volunteer corps fulfilling [certain] conditions' (Art. 1). The first three Geneva Conventions of 1949 apply to 'members of the armed forces of a Party to the conflict as well as members of militias or volunteer corps forming part of such armed forces'. In addition, the first three Geneva Conventions cover 'members of other militias or other volunteer corps, including those of organized resistance movements…' (I, 13; II, 13; III, 4). Additional Protocol I regards conflicts against colonial domination, alien occupation, or racist régimes as international wars and grants combatant status to fighters who carry their arms openly during each military engagement or during such times as they are visible to an adversary while engaged in a military deployment prior to the launching of an attack (Arts 1(4), 44(3)). The UN General Assembly has, in a number of resolutions, called for the application of the Geneva Conventions to 'freedom fighters', 'participants in resistance movements and freedom fighters', and 'people captured during their struggle for freedom'. As noted in chapter 3, I will use the portmanteau words *irregulars* or *irregular fighters* for such clandestine underground fighters, partisans, guerrillas, or resistance groups, and the term *wars of national liberation* for armed conflicts against colonial domination, alien occupation, or racist régimes. The Geneva Conventions of 1949 and Additional Protocol II refer to 'armed conflicts not of an international character'. I often use a shorter expression, such as *internal armed conflicts* or *internal wars*.

It should be emphasised that there is no necessary connection between irregular fighters and internal wars. Irregulars have in the past taken part in inter-state conflicts of the classical kind. Some internal wars have been conducted solely by regular forces. But if one reviews the 150 or so armed conflicts since the second world war, one finds that a large number of them have been internal, and that irregulars have often taken part on one or both sides. Moreover, the frontier between internal and international wars is not always clear. Many legal experts would regard the intervention of foreign personnel as transforming an internal conflict into an international one, but there are ways of providing disguised aid by means of 'volunteers' and mercenaries – though mercenaries are denied combatant status under Additional Protocol I (Art. 47). The fact is that states are nearly always reluctant to admit that armed conflict is taking place within their borders and consequently that common Article 3 or Additional Protocol II come into force.

Both the Hague Regulations and the Geneva Conventions list four conditions which must be fulfilled by irregular fighters if they are to qualify for the protection afforded by the Conventions. These conditions were first formulated in the Brussels Declaration of 1874 (Art. 9). The purpose was to make a clear distinction between combatants and non-combatants, so that hostile action would be directed against combatants only, and secondarily to avoid a situation in which marauders or bandits, on capture, might claim POW status. The four conditions common to the Hague Regulations and the Geneva Conventions are:

(1) Irregulars must be 'commanded by a person responsible for his subordinates'.
(2) They must have 'a fixed distinctive sign [or emblem] recognizable at a distance'.
(3) They must carry their arms 'openly'.
(4) They must conduct their operations 'in accordance with the laws and customs of war'.

In addition, the Geneva Conventions apply to 'organised resistance movements'.

Additional Protocol I introduces a new element into the law of armed conflict by extending common Article 2 of the Geneva Conventions ('all cases of declared war or of any other armed conflict which may arise between two or more of the High Contracting Parties') to cover wars of national liberation. National liberation movements may undertake to apply the Geneva Conventions and Additional Protocol I by unilateral declaration (Art. 96(3)).

Another effect of the Additional Protocol I is to modify the second and third conditions common to the Hague and Geneva Conventions. It is now accepted that the nature of hostilities may make it impossible for an irregular fighter to distinguish himself with a sign or emblem recognisable at a distance and to carry his arms openly at all times. Nevertheless, he retains combatant status so long as he carried his arms openly during a military deployment before the launching of an attack and during each military engagement.

The requirements in the Hague and Geneva Conventions that irregular fighters shall conduct their operations in accordance with the laws and customs of war seem to me to raise very difficult questions. Regular armed forces, operating in accordance with printed manuals of military law, have been known to disregard 'the laws and customs of war'; irregular fighters, with no such manuals, and in some cases with minimal education and training, are likely to have no more than a rudimentary idea of 'the laws and customs of war'. Moreover, their opponents may be flouting these laws and customs.

On the other hand, it would be an entirely retrograde step to introduce the idea that 'the laws and customs of war' are losing or have lost their validity. These laws and customs, which are for the protection of combatants as well as non-combatants, should be made more precise and strengthened, not dispensed with.

It can hardly be disputed that in insurgency and counter-insurgency warfare, civilians may be more severely affected than in most forms of war. The purpose of the irregular fighter is often to demonstrate that the public authorities are incapable of governing. This can be accomplished by fostering discontent, but also by resorting to acts of terrorism such as the assassination of the élite on the other side. The fact that this may be done in a righteous cause, as in a struggle for equal rights and self-determination of peoples, does not alter the fact that deliberately to kill an innocent person is murder.

Additional Protocol I contains fundamental guarantees for humane treatment which are to be applied without discrimination and which prohibit 'at any time and in any place whatsoever' acts or threats of violence to persons and outrages upon personal dignity, including corporal punishment, torture, mutilation, murder, hostage-taking, and collective punishments (Art. 75(2)). Common Article 3 of the Geneva Conventions relating to internal wars also prohibit violence to life and person, in particular murder of all kinds, mutilation, cruel treatment, and torture; outrages upon personal dignity, in particular humiliating and degrading treatment; the taking of hostages; and the passing of sentences and the carrying out of executions without previous judgment pronounced by a regularly constituted court, affording all the judicial guarantees which are recognised as indispensable by civilised peoples. These 'minimum' requirements are supplemented in Additional Protocol II by a ban on acts or threats of violence against persons and outrages upon personal dignity, acts of terrorism, hostage-taking, slavery, collective punishments, and pillage (Art. 4(2)).

THE INTERNATIONAL RED CROSS

The International Red Cross movement consists of three elements. There is, first of all, the International Committee of the Red Cross (ICRC), initially known as the International Committee for aid to wounded soldiers, founded by five Swiss citizens in 1863 following the publication of Henry Dunant's *A Memory of Solferino*.

Secondly, there are the 139 national Red Cross or Red Crescent Societies, the most recent society to be recognised being that of the United Arab Emirates (27 August 1986). In order to be recognised, a national society must meet certain conditions. It must be constituted on the territory of a party to the first Geneva Convention of 1949, be the only such society, operate throughout the entire country and its dependencies, and be officially recognised by its own government. Membership must be open to all without discrimination, it must respect fundamental Red Cross principles, must adhere to the statutes of the International Red Cross, and must use the title and emblem of the Red Cross or the Red Crescent.

There is a society in Israel which uses as an emblem the Red Shield of David but in accordance with the last requirement mentioned above, this society has not been officially recognised by the Red Cross movement.[22]

The first conference of national Red Cross societies took place in

1867, and the societies formed the League of Red Cross and Red Crescent Societies in 1919, the third element of the Red Cross movement.

The three elements of the International Red Cross meet together, normally every four years, as the International Conference of the Red Cross. Sometimes people speak loosely of the International Red Cross when in fact they mean the International *Committee* of the Red Cross.

Article 4 of the Statute of the ICRC, as amended in 1973, defines the role of the ICRC as follows:

(1) The special role of the ICRC shall be:

(a) to maintain the Fundamental Principles of the Red Cross as proclaimed by the XXth International Conference of the Red Cross;

(b) to recognize any newly established or reconstituted National Red Cross Society which fulfils the conditions for recognition in force, and to notify other National Societies of such recognition;

(c) to undertake the tasks incumbent on it under the Geneva Conventions, to work for the faithful application of these Conventions and to take cognizance of any complaints regarding alleged breaches of the humanitarian Conventions;

(d) to take action in its capacity as a neutral institution, especially in case of war, civil war, or internal strife; to endeavour to ensure at all times that the military and civilian victims of such conflicts and of their direct results receive protection and assistance, and to serve in humanitarian matters, as an intermediary between the parties;

(e) to ensure the operation of the Central Information Agencies provided for in the Geneva Conventions;

(f) to contribute, in view of such conflicts, to the preparation and development of medical personnel and medical equipment, in co-operation with other Red Cross organizations, the medical services of the armed forces and other competent authorities;

(g) to work for the continual improvement of humanitarian international law and for the better understanding and dissemination of the Geneva Conventions and to prepare for their possible extension;

(h) to accept the mandates entrusted to it by the International Conferences of the Red Cross.

(2) The ICRC may also take any humanitarian initiative which comes within its roles as a specifically neutral and independent institution and consider any questions requiring examination by such an institution.

The ICRC is a self-perpetuating body in that membership is only by co-optation and is limited to Swiss citizens.

The Red Cross movement was initially concerned with the care of sick and wounded combatants on the field of battle. It later extended its concern to prisoners of war, and in 1949 there was adopted for the first time a Convention designed to ensure humane treatment of civilians in occupied territories. The two Additional Protocols of 1977 provide for further measures of protection in both inter-state and internal wars. In accordance with the last sentence of Article 4 of the statute of the ICRC, and often in the absence of formal agreement, the ICRC makes its services available for a wide range of humanitarian activities – protection and assistance to victims of inter-state or internal armed conflict or other disasters.

The ICRC has to act with great discretion in situations of political delicacy. During the conflict between Federal Nigeria and Biafra, for example, the ICRC was engaged in what was then its largest humanitarian effort since the second world war – and also 'the most thankless'. After the Nigerian air force had shot down a Swedish aircraft operating under ICRC responsibility, the ICRC's activity was almost completely paralysed. Fourteen ICRC delegates or pilots were killed on duty during this conflict.

In 1962, the Soviet Union suggested that the ICRC should check on the withdrawal of Soviet missiles from Cuba. The ICRC was willing to place inspectors at the disposal of the United Nations under certain conditions and if the parties agreed, but UN Secretary-General Thant was told that, while Cuba had no objection to ICRC inspection of Soviet ships at sea, 'Cuba was opposed to Red Cross inspection in Cuban ports'. The crisis was finally resolved some weeks later without a role for the ICRC.[23] The Soviet Union has vetoed two proposals in the UN Security Council which would have requested the ICRC to undertake tasks: the first in connection with allegations of the use of bacterial weapons in Korea (1952) and the second in connection with the shooting down of a US aircraft (1960).[24]

The primary task of the ICRC, as is made explicit in Article 4(c), (d), and (f) of its Statute, is in providing medical personnel and equipment in 'war, civil war or internal strife', and in working for the faithful application of the principle in the Geneva Conventions that those not taking part in the fighting are entitled to immunity from direct attack and must receive humanitarian treatment. The Fourth Geneva Convention provides for the establishment of 'hospital and safety zones' and 'neutralized zones' for both civilians and wounded or sick combatants (IV, 14–5), and Additional Protocol I provides for 'non-defended localities' and 'demilitarized zones' (Arts 59–60).

Sanctuaries of this kind were created by the ICRC, either alone or in co-operation with others, in Jerusalem in 1948,[25] in Dhaka in 1971,[26] and in Phnom Penh in 1975, and such zones were in process of being established in the Falkland Isles (Malvinas) and Argentina in 1982 when the cease-fire came into force.

All the elements in the Geneva stream of law contain national and international procedures for dealing with grave breaches. The ICRC's relief and related activities are given reasonable publicity but, when the ICRC undertakes more delicate tasks (such as visiting political prisoners), the general rule is that it seeks no publicity and reports only to the government concerned. The ICRC publicises the difficulties it encounters or its findings only if (a) the breaches of international humanitarian law are major and repeated, (b) its delegates have witnessed the violations with their own eyes or the breaches have been established by reliable and verifiable sources, (c) confidential representations to the governments concerned have not succeeded, and (d) such action would be in the interest of the victims.[27]

Alleged violations of the Geneva Conventions have been brought before the UN Security Council in connexion with the Bangladesh war (1971–2), the Middle East (1967 and since), and Iraq–Iran (1983 and since). The Security Council either appeals to the parties to respect the Geneva Conventions or, if the breach is reliably established, condemns the guilty party.[28]

The ICRC acts on its own initiative in reminding states of their humanitarian responsibilities in particular cases, whether these responsibilities derive from specific instruments or (in the words of the Martens Clause) 'result from the usages established among civilized peoples, from the laws of humanity, and the dictates of the public conscience'.

When visiting political detainees, ICRC delegates insist on being given a list of detainees before the visit or being granted facilities to compile it during the visit, on seeing all political detainees, on being enabled to talk with them freely and in private, and in repeating the visit as needed. If necessary and possible, delegates organise the transmission of family messages and assistance to detainees and their families. In the five-year period covered by the ICRC's annual reports for 1979–83, delegates visited POWs, captured civilians, and political detainees in no fewer than 45 states or territories, as shown in Table 1.

A glance at the ICRC histories by Pierre Boissier and André Dunand, the four official volumes on the astonishing work of the ICRC during the second world war, and the forty annual reports since

1945, makes clear that the ICRC undertakes an impressive array of routine tasks patiently and anonymously. Other non-governmental agencies complain that the ICRC is sometimes inclined to be standoffish and too self-assured, but this stance is no doubt inevitable. It would perhaps help if women played a larger role, but the ICRC conforms to the general style of public life in Switzerland.

As there have been some 150 conflicts since 1945 in which armed force has been used, it is impossible within the compass of this book to describe the ICRC's role in every case, but I review below four cases of exceptional ICRC responsibility: Korea (1950–3), the Cuban missile crisis (1962), the third Middle East war (1967), and Iraq–Iran (since 1980). Focusing on these four unusual cases can easily give a misleading impression. From the point of view of this book, however, it is necessary to review a number of those exceptional cases where the performance of states did not match promise, or where military necessity overcame the claims of humanity.

Korea   In Korea, the Unified Command tried to respect the provisions of the Geneva Conventions, except those relating to repatriation of POWs. By August 1951, after just over a year of fighting, the Unified Command had notified the ICRC of the names of 163,539 prisoners which it held. During the same period, North Korea had supplied the names of only 110 prisoners – though it became clear later that year that more than 11,000 POWs were held by the Communist side, and more than 11,000 were in fact released after the armistice in 1953. The ICRC was consistently denied access to POW camps in the North, and its activities in the South were sometimes interfered with. The ICRC delegate was distressed at the brutal treatment of civilian prisoners in the South, and on more than one occasion protested to the South Korean authorities. The ICRC also protested to the Unified Command that the use of collective punishments in POW camps was contrary to the Geneva POW Convention (Art. 87).

During the armistice negotiations at Panmunjom, North Korea and China suggested 'the formation of joint teams of the International Committee of the Red Cross' and the Red Cross of North Korea and China to assist in supervising POW exchanges after the armistice. The ICRC said the proposal was 'entirely untenable' as it would violate the neutrality of the ICRC, and it issued a statement making clear its independence of governments and other official bodies. The UN Command thought this episode had been an attempt to identify the

TABLE 1 *POWs, captured civilians, and political detainees visited by the ICRC, 1979–83*

Detaining state	1979	1980	1981	1982	1983
Afghanistan					
Angola		•		•	
Argentina		•			
Bolivia	•	•	•	•	•
Burundi		•	•		
Cape Verde Islands			•	•	
Chad	•	•			•
Chile	•	•	•		•
Colombia		•	•		•
Democratic Yemen	•		•		
El Salvador		•		•	
Ethiopia		•			•
Grenada			•		•
Haiti	•		•		•
Indonesia (including East Timor in 1982)		•	•	•	•
Iran		•	•	•	•
Iraq		•	•		•
Israel and the Occupied Territories			•		•
Jordan		•		•	•
Lebanon					•
Lesotho				•	•

Malaysia
Mauritania
Namibia
Nicaragua
Paraguay
Peru
Philippines
Poland
Rwanda
Somalia
South Africa (including the Homelands)
Southern Rhodesia (Zimbabwe)
Spain
Suriname
Switzerland (Soviet prisoners captured in Afghanistan)
Syria
Tanzania
Thailand
Uganda
United Kingdom (Northern Ireland in 1981 and 1983, Falklands/Malvinas in 1982)
Uruguay
Yemen Arab Republic
Zaire
Zambia

ICRC as an agency of the Unified Command. When allegations about bacterial warfare were made by North Korea and China, Dean Acheson suggested that these should be investigated by the ICRC: the ICRC, in an unusual move (which it perhaps later regretted), said that it would 'set up a Commission which will be under its direction', with 'every guarantee of moral and scientific independence ... by experts who have highest qualification', on the understanding that the two sides would co-operate. This was acceptable to the United States but not to the Communists, so the idea was dropped.[29]

Cuban missile crisis   The Cuban missile crisis of 1962 confronted the ICRC with acutely difficult decisions. The UN Security Council debated the matter at four meetings on 23–25 October, but thereafter the matter was dealt with by UN Secretary-General Thant, initially in correspondence with the three heads of government. At 4 am on the night of 30/31 October, the ICRC received a request from Thant to provide 30 inspectors to monitor the removal of Soviet missiles from Cuba. The idea of ICRC inspection had been raised by the Soviet Union the previous day, subject to the agreement of Cuba.[30]

This was an unprecedented request to the ICRC, outside the scope of its normal humanitarian duties, but the ICRC took the line that in a situation of exceptional gravity, it should do what it could to meet the request, though subject to certain conditions:

(1) All three parties explicitly, and the main maritime powers implicitly, should agree to the operation;
(2) The inspectors would be selected by the ICRC and placed at the disposal of the United Nations and subject to UN authority and control, but would at the same time have a large measure of authority;
(3) The emblem of the Red Cross would not be used;
(4) In no circumstances would there be resort to force;
(5) The operation would be consistent with Red Cross principles and the provisions of international law;
(6) The task could be carried out in a real and effective manner.

The ICRC understood from the United Nations that 'Cuba would give its agreement'.

Meanwhile, Thant had been to Havana for discussions with Prime Minister Castro and his colleagues. Castro's line was that ICRC inspection of Soviet vessels at sea was not the concern of Cuba, but there could be no ICRC inspection on Cuban territory. Thant was also informed that dismantling of Soviet missiles would be completed within two or three days. Three weeks later the ICRC was told that its help was no longer necessary.

Middle East   An exception to the general ICRC rule of no publicity was the publication in 1970 of a report on ICRC activities in the Middle East for the period June 1967 to June 1970. According to a UN Committee, part of this report had been leaked, so the ICRC decided to minimise the damage by publishing the full text.[31]

The ICRC found that, following the June War, problems relating to the treatment of the wounded and prisoners of war were settled 'relatively quickly'. Matters were different in the case of the application of the Fourth Convention concerned with civilians in occupied territories. The ICRC informed Israel in July 1967 that 'in its opinion the Fourth Convention was applicable'. Israel replied a year later that it wished 'to leave the question ... open for the moment'. To this day the government of Israel continues to hold this position, though many Israeli specialists in international law consider that it is legally incorrect, especially in regard to Sinai (while it was under Israeli occupation) and the Golan Heights.[32] Though Israel does not regard the Fourth Convention as applicable, it has claimed to be acting in accordance with its main humanitarian principles. The refusal of the Israeli government to apply the Fourth Convention has hindered the ICRC in seeking to prevent such prohibited activities as the destruction of houses and the deportation of protected persons.

The Fourth Convention prohibits destruction of property 'except where such destruction is rendered *absolutely necessary by military operations*' (Art. 53, my italics). It also prohibits the punishment of any protected person except for an offence which he or she has *personally* committed (Art. 33, my italics): in other words, indiscriminate or collective punishments are banned. The ICRC found that destruction of property was in fact carried out by Israel. When the ICRC delegate made representations to the Israeli Ministry of Defence about this, he was told 'that it was not for the ICRC to intervene in a question that affected directly the security of the State'. The ICRC took the view that, while deploring all terrorist attacks against civilians, such attacks were in themselves no justification for resorting to reprisals or any other form of collective penalties.

None of the parties to the Geneva Conventions directly involved in the Middle East conflict had availed themselves of the possibility of requesting a state or a neutral organisation to assume the functions of protecting power. Indeed, when the ICRC communicated with the states concerned with regard to the application of the Geneva Conventions, only the government of Jordan replied and then simply to say that 'it did not accept the ICRC's viewpoint'.

ICRC delegates were usually given freedom of movement to visit prisoners of war. All applications for information with regard to missing prisoners rapidly received official answers from the Israeli military authorities, and requests and suggestions were met in most cases by positive responses. The ICRC was able to arrange for the repatriation of all seriously wounded casualties before the end of 1967. After delay in some cases, 5,638 Arab POWs and 19 Israeli POWs were exchanged. Detainees and internees were visited, but ICRC delegates encountered difficulties in 1969 and 1970 in visiting Israeli prisoners held in Egypt; in 1970 the same problem was encountered in Syria.

There were greater difficulties over the repatriation of civilians, but 'some twenty-thousand persons were enabled to return to their homes on one side or other of the cease-fire lines'. Some 3,700 family reunions were permitted on compassionate grounds.

The ICRC had evidence of deportations from the Golan Heights, the West Bank of the Jordan, and the Gaza Strip. The Israeli authorities stated that in the case of the Golan Heights there had been no deportations, only 'voluntary departures'. As for the West Bank, those deported were Jordanian citizens engaged in activities detrimental to the interests of the state: deportation, in Israel's view, was more humane than internment. There had been transfers of population within the Occupied Territories, and in most cases the persons transferred had accepted compensation.

The ICRC took the view that 'at least by analogy' the provisions of the Fourth Convention should apply to Jewish communities in Arab countries. The ICRC delegate was able to visit Jews 'assigned to residence in camps' in Libya, and was in 'more or less constant touch' with three communities of Jews of Syrian nationality. The Egyptian government, on the other hand, would not permit ICRC delegates to visit interned Jews.

As the ICRC has not published comparable reports of other situations during and following armed conflict, it is impossible to judge whether its experience in the Middle East in 1967–70 was in any way typical. No country complied fully with the obligations it had assumed, yet no country was totally impervious to the appeals of the ICRC.

Iraq–Iran The war between Iraq and Iran raised many difficult and delicate problems regarding humanitarian norms. There were allegations by both sides about direct attacks on civilians and about inhumane treatment of POWs, and Iran alleged that Iraq had used chemical weapons, in violation of the Geneva CBW Protocol. United Nations experts carried out a number of investigations of alleged attacks on civilians. Although not all the charges could be verified, it was clear to the UN experts that both countries had made attacks which had caused damage to civilian targets. The allegation that Iraq had used chemical weapons was confirmed by UN experts in 1984 and again in 1986.

The ICRC does not normally publicize the difficulties it encounters or its findings on particular issues, but in exceptional circumstances the ICRC believes that its duty to the victims leaves it no alternative but to seek publicity. In May 1983, the ICRC issued a public appeal about grave and repeated breaches of international humanitarian law by both sides in the Iraq–Iran war (summary executions of captured soldiers, abandoning of the wounded on the field of battle, indiscriminate bombing of towns and villages) and the obstacles it had encountered in exercising its mandate under the Geneva Conventions. In February 1984, the ICRC issued a second memorandum making similar points. Also in 1984, the ICRC issued a report on the use on the battlefield of substances prohibited by international law and incompatible with humanitarian principles, and later issued a press release calling on both belligerents to cease bombing raids on civilian zones, even if in the form of reprisal or counter-reprisal. Finally, the President of the ICRC made a formal public statement about official allegations in Iran that the ICRC had been spying for Iraq, and he also reported that Iran had first obstructed and then suspended ICRC activities. This followed an incident in a POW camp in Gorgan in Iran, which caused Iraq to request a UN inquiry. Another group of experts was appointed by UN Secretary-General Pérez de Cuéllar. After a full investigation, the UN experts concluded that both Iraq and Iran had failed to uphold the standards and policies which they professed.

It is easy for the cynic to dismiss the Geneva Conventions as mere paper promises, but there can be no doubt that they influence the way governments behave at a time when national security is at stake.

The ICRC has no power other than the power of reason and humanity. It can appeal to a government's sense of compassion, but conscience is a very personal attribute. All governments have an interest in respect for law and would like if possible to implement their legal obligations, if for no better reason than the hope that they can rely on other governments to do likewise.

There are well-known defects in the present system of humanitarian law applicable in armed conflict. There is, unfortunately, widespread ignorance of its basic principles. There are some gaps in the law itself. What law there is could be more rigorously applied, and there could be more effective action in the case of grave breaches.

5 Disarmament

To disarm is an irregular verb with no first person singular and only a future tense.   Edouard Herriot

Arms control is a process or action, following a negotiated agreement or undertaken and declared unilaterally, to prohibit or limit the testing, manufacture, stockpiling, transfer, or deployment of specified weapons, or not to use them at all, or to use them only in reprisal.

Disarmament is a process or action, following a negotiated agreement or undertaken and declared unilaterally, whereby weapons already in existence are dismantled or destroyed or the materials diverted to peaceful uses.

The phrase 'general and complete disarmament' is popular with some committed disarmers but it is in one respect ambiguous. 'General' means either applying to all states or covering all weapons: 'complete' is not ambiguous and means total.

Governments, when they are serious about it and not just indulging in cosmetics and propaganda, pursue arms control and disarmament because they believe that this is one way of increasing national and international peace and security. Public opinion is often sceptical or indifferent: the subject is highly technical, a great deal of time is spent in producing a coherent national policy out of disparate and competing interests, negotiations with allies and adversaries seem endless, and the achievements often meagre; and in periods of acute international tension, it may seem more urgent to come to grips with the political difficulties of which arms are only a symptom.

There are, however, other considerations. Arms are sometimes an intrinsic source of tension – witness the Cuban missile crisis and the difficulties over the neutron bomb and intermediate-range missiles. Arms races are always expensive and usually destabilising. Moreover, the very process of negotiating about arms control and disarmament provides a means of communication between potential adversaries about those policies and actions which give rise to anxiety and often to over-reaction. The exchange of information during negotiations helps the parties to adjust those defence postures which the other side finds provocative, and to do so without impairing the security of one's own side.

135

The vast subject of arms control and disarmament becomes more complex every year, and many governments now have special sections or departments which specialise in the subject, whereas only thirty years ago, most officials privately regarded the matter with scorn, whatever they may have had to say in public. And it still remains true that, in many parts of the world, there are military people and civilians who think of disarmament as a plot to weaken their own side while the potential enemy improves his position.

In this chapter I want to illustrate the problem of prohibitions and restraints in war by considering the efforts which have been made to control the means of military combat. It can be argued that if one despairs of abolishing war in any conceivable future, then it is more important to ease particular crises or to seek agreement on general principles of restraint rather than to attempt to control weapons. Indeed, it has been said that very few of the prohibitions and permissions of the traditional code regarding the just use of force are susceptible of being embodied in treaties or agreements.[1] And it is true that even a total ban on a weapon, covering every phase from research and development to deployment and actual use in war, cannot alter the fact that once a weapon has been invented, it cannot be dis-invented. How to make it has become part of our permanent stock of knowledge.

At the same time, some weapons arouse especial revulsion in the public mind. On the other hand, chemical and nuclear weapons have been used in war. Moreover, it is difficult to use some modern weapons in accordance with the twin principles of discrimination and proportion, so that there are particular reasons of ethics and law for regarding their control as a matter of great urgency.

As a broad generalisation, one may say that weapons are neutral: moral and political issues arise only when someone intends, threatens, or decides to use them. At the same time nuclear, biological, and chemical weapons may be of such magnitude that one can understand why the possibility of their use should give rise to feelings of revulsion, and why it seems reasonable to make efforts to prohibit or limit their production, deployment, and use.

While the manufacture of chemical and biological weapons is within the capacity of many countries, that of nuclear weapons is, at the time of writing, an overt monopoly of five countries: the United States, the Soviet Union, the United Kingdom, France, and China. India had exploded a peaceful nuclear device, but any device that explodes may be directed to a target and used for military purposes. It is believed that Israel has the means of assembling nuclear weapons quite quickly, and possibly also South Africa. Pakistan, Argentina, and Brazil have been developing facilities for making material which could be used for weapons purposes. None of these six states is a party to the nuclear Non-Proliferation Treaty (NPT), and one or two of the parties to the NPT have hinted that they might abandon their non-nuclear status if external circumstances should warrant such a decision. It is not implausible to speculate that, if present trends continue, there are likely to be ten or a dozen nuclear-weapon states by the end of the century, most of the new nuclear powers being in unstable parts of the world.

Two substances have been used to cause a nuclear explosion: uranium-235 and plutonium-239. Uranium-235 exists naturally, but it has to be enriched from less than one per cent to something like 90% or more for use in a weapon. All the enrichment processes, such as gaseous diffusion and centrifugation, are expensive.

Plutonium-239 is made by irradiating uranium-238 in a nuclear reactor and then separating the plutonium from the spent fuel. A separation facility is also complicated and expensive.

Natural uranium is found in the United States, Canada, Australia, South Africa and Namibia, and in about ten other countries in commercial quantities, and presumably in the Communist world as well.

The launching platform for a nuclear weapon may be a fixed silo or mobile vehicle on land, an aircraft, a submarine, or a surface ship. Submarine-launched missiles are the least vulnerable to attack, whereas fixed land-based missiles may be no use unless they are used first, before they are attacked.

Ballistic missiles are rapid rockets in which the final stage travels to the target along a predetermined trajectory. Cruise missiles are like relatively slow pilotless aircraft which are guided to the target by an on-board computer.

The energy from a nuclear explosion is measured in kilotons or megatons (kts or Mts, a thousand or a million metric tons of conventional TNT). The bombs of the second world war, including the German V-1 and V-2 weapons, had yields of less than one ton. The nuclear bombs used against Hiroshima and Nagasaki had yields of 12.5 and 22 kts respectively. Polaris missiles, sixteen of which are deployed on one or more British submarines, were made in the United States but carry up to three British-made war-heads of about 200 kts each: the Trident D5 missile will also be made in the United States and will carry between eight and fourteen independently-targetable British-made war-heads of about 100 kts each.

The accuracy of a weapon is defined as Circular Error Probable (CEP), being the radius of a circle within which half the war-heads are expected to fall. If a weapon has a CEP of 200 metres, half the war-heads are expected to fall within 200 metres of the target and half outside a circle with that radius. The Polaris missile has a CEP of about 800 metres, the Trident D5 missile about 450 metres, and the Tomahawk cruise missile perhaps as little as 20 metres.

If a country wishes to manufacture nuclear weapons, it needs to make or obtain either highly enriched uranium or plutonium extracted from the spent fuel of a nuclear reactor; the ability to construct a device which will explode by fission or fusion; and the ability to construct a delivery vehicle for conveying the war-head to the target. Most of the basic information for these processes is now available in the open literature, but it is a flight of fantasy to imagine that a usable nuclear weapon can be constructed in a garage or cow-shed.

Making nuclear weapons is not cheap. A UN expert committee estimated in 1967 that a small nuclear capability would cost in the region of $560 million a year: that would correspond to about $3.4 billion at 1986 prices. Once a country has achieved nuclear status, however, the annual maintenance cost is not impossibly high. Britain's strategic nuclear forces represent 2 or 3 per cent of the defence budget, though the percentage is likely to double as the Trident programme proceeds.

If a nuclear weapon explodes above ground, about 50 per cent of the yield is in the form of blast and shock, 35 per cent in heat and light, 15 per cent in radiation. In the enhanced radiation war-head (the neutron bomb), the amount of yield in prompt radiation is increased from 5 to about 30 per cent, so that the weapon can be used against personnel in tanks, while causing less collateral damage to buildings.

Nuclear weapons cause harm by blast, heat, and prompt radiation in a rough circle around the explosion, harm by early residual radiation in an elliptical-shaped area down-wind from the explosion, and harm from delayed residual radiation and fall-out which is distributed indiscriminately world-wide. Residual radiation causes cancerous tumors, harm to foetuses in the womb, and damage to reproductive organs leading to physical and/or mental genetic defects in future generations. It is difficult to quantify the genetic harm as it depends on future mating decisions, but a UN committee of experts estimated in 1980 that atmospheric testing of nuclear weapons had then caused 'a global dispersion of radioactive debris from about 145 Mt of fission yield', leading to 'about 150,000 premature deaths world-wide', mainly in the Northern Hemisphere.[2] This would suggest one premature death from somatic or genetic causes for every kiloton of yield into the atmosphere, but I should stress that this is a layman's deduction on plausible assumptions, not a scientific estimate. A high-altitude explosion causes harm to integrated circuits over a wide area by electro-magnetic pulse (EMP), and it is likely that an extensive use of nuclear arms would have serious climatic effects (the so-called nuclear winter).

Radioactive substances produced by a nuclear explosion decay naturally, but at differing rates. The process of decay is measured by 'half life', the period of time for the radioactivity to have decayed to half of its original value. The half life of some substances produced by nuclear explosions are as follows:

iodine-131	8 days
strontium-90	28 years
carbon-14	5,730 years
plutonium-239	24,100 years

It is clear that nuclear weapons are uniquely destructive, and that some effects are uniquely indiscriminate. It is probably the case that nuclear weapons are unprecedented in that it is impossible to use them without harming innocent people from early residual radiation down-wind from the explosion and from delayed radiation and fall-out world-wide.

An expert UN committee, which included Lord Zuckerman, pointed out in 1967 that nuclear weapons have transformed the conduct of war. Air warfare has made it possible to destroy cities without first defeating the defending armies. Large megaton nuclear weapons have a greater destructive power than all of the conventional explosive that has ever been used in warfare since the invention of gunpowder, and the two superpowers in 1967 possessed more than enough destructive power to eliminate all mankind. The distinction sometimes made between tactical and strategic nuclear war would in practice be likely to be meaningless. Moreover, the disastrous effects of all out nuclear war could not be confined to the powers engaged in that war. Once the nuclear arms race begins, 'no size of programme ever satisfies'. Having acquired an unsophisticated nuclear-weapons system, a country is driven inexorably to produce more sophisticated and less vulnerable means of delivery. Spiralling arms races, concluded the experts, have no end and lead to phases of 'major insecurity'. The goal should be the total elimination of stocks and a ban on use. 'The ultimate question for the world to decide ... is what short-term interests it is prepared to sacrifice, in exchange for an assurance of survival and security'.[3]

A further UN expert study in 1980 confirmed the main conclusions of their predecessors. Nuclear arsenals were the equivalent of more than three tons for every human being. New weapons were emerging, not because of military needs, 'but because technology by its own impetus often takes the lead over policy, creating weapons for which needs have to be invented ... '. The more numerous the weapons, the more complex the systems, the more sophisticated the doctrines, 'the more likely it may be that the weapons may be used by mistake ... '. The experts questioned whether doctrines of deterrence would prove to be reliable instruments of control in a crisis.[4]

NEGOTIATING MACHINERY

A considerable number of diplomatic organs are concerned with arms control and disarmament. Some are forums for debate and make recommendations by voting: others are negotiating bodies which, except occasionally for minor procedural questions, proceed on the basis of unanimity.

The founders of the United Nations seem to have envisaged disarmament as coming within the purview of the Security Council. In order to establish peace with the least diversion of human and economic resources to armaments, the Security Council was to formulate plans 'for the regulation of armaments and possible disarmament' (Arts 26 and 47). It was intended that the Council should be assisted by the Military Staff Committee, composed of the Council's five permanent members, but though the Military Staff Committee meets once a fortnight, it has not reported any substantive work since 1948.

In the early days, atomic energy and conventional armaments were dealt with by two separate UN bodies, but these were dissolved in 1952, when the General Assembly created a Disarmament Commission (a committee of the whole) to deal with both conventional and nuclear arms. Disarmament is now debated every year in the First Committee of the UN General Assembly, which adopts between 60 and 70 resolutions, and in occasional session of the Disarmament Commission. There have been two special sessions of the General

Assembly devoted exclusively to disarmament (1978 and 1982), and there was established in 1972 a committee on the possible holding of a world disarmament conference. The Security Council still remains seized of items concerned with the regulation and reduction of armaments and the international control of atomic energy.

The main negotiating body is now the Conference on Disarmament, with 40 members, which meets in Geneva and reports to the General Assembly. There is also a UN committee on the Indian Ocean as a zone of peace, and several bodies have conducted or are conducting studies or research on such matters as the economic and social consequences of the arms race, the relationship between disarmament and development, zones free of nuclear weapons, reduction of military budgets, procedures for investigating alleged uses of chemical or biological weapons, military research and development, and the strengthening of international security. Outside the UN framework are bilateral negotiations on nuclear weapons between the United States and the Soviet Union (Geneva), negotiations on conventional force reductions in Europe between countries from NATO and the Warsaw Pact (Vienna), and disarmament and confidence-building in Europe as part of the Helsinki process (Stockholm).

THE ISSUES

Various processes are, in theory, susceptible to control:
(1) research, testing, and development of war-heads and the means of delivery;
(2) manufacture and stockpiling of weapons;
(3) transfer of weapons by gift or sale;
(4) operational deployment in particular regions or environments;
(5) use of weapons.
I have dealt in chapter 4 with efforts to limit or ban the use of chemical, bacteriological (biological), and nuclear weapons.

The usual means of controlling weapons is by negotiation leading to a treaty or other international agreement, but states may also act unilaterally, as did President Nixon over biological weapons, either to stimulate or reinforce the negotiating process or, more rarely, for Kantian moral reasons regardless of the response of others. Many states impose unilateral restrictions on their own policy regarding the sale or transfer of arms to non-allies.

One of the difficulties encountered in negotiation arises from the fact that nations of similar size may, for reasons of geography and history, deploy different kinds of military force. An island like Sri Lanka is likely to have a navy, while a land-locked country like Zimbabwe will give priority to land and air forces. Even when countries have defence forces of similar character and scale, there will be many asymmetries to take into account. Are military formations of identical size? A West German armoured division has twice as many men and tanks as its British equivalent. A US airborne division has more than twice as many men as the Soviet equivalent. And how is it possible to establish equivalences between different weapons and military capabilities? How many high-yield but relatively inaccurate nuclear bombs dropped by gravity from aircraft are equal to how many lower-yield but relatively accurate nuclear ballistic missiles launched from fixed silos or submarines? How compare a missile with one warhead, a missile with several warheads which can be directed only at a single target, and a missile with several warheads which can be directed independently at different targets? How is it possible to take account of less tangible factors like secrecy, discipline, reliability of equipment, and speed of maintenance?

THE RESULTS

If the negotiations on disarmament over the past three decades are assessed in the light of the difficulties to be overcome, the results may seem reasonably satisfactory: but if they are viewed in the context of the magnitude of the dangers from uncontrolled arms races, then the results are meagre in the extreme. In the first year of peace after the second world war, there was one country with nuclear weapons; the stockpile was almost certainly less than a dozen bombs; and the yield of the nuclear weapons then existing was measured in kilotons. Today there are five overt nuclear-weapon states, and probably two or three others with the capability to assemble nuclear explosive devices quickly; nuclear war-heads deployed or stockpiled are believed to exceed 50,000 in number; and about 1,500 of these war-heads are in the megaton range.

Because nuclear weapons cannot easily be used with discrimination and proportion, because war between nuclear-weapon states might escalate quickly from limited to massive use, and because the consequences of all-out nuclear war would be catastrophic beyond human imagining, it is natural that major attention should have been directed to bringing the competition in nuclear weaponry under control. This is perfectly understandable and necessary, but it leads to a situation in which more than 150 states which do not possess nuclear weapons, or do not provide a base for the nuclear weapons of allies, are provided with an alibi for doing nothing about regional arms races on the ground that priority should be given to the nuclear threat. The truth is that most states in the world *could* contribute to the disarmament process if they were so minded. Any ambassador worth his salt can think of a score of disarmament measures for others to carry out. As I wrote in a poem for the *Economist* thirty years ago

The rumours were spreading, the news was alarming,
While diplomats placidly talked of disarming,
Though everyone knew that concealed in their pockets
Were recent refinements in hydrogen rockets.
With candour commendable each one protested
At nuclear weapons that *others* had tested.[5]

Let us now turn to the five groups of processes listed under 'The Issues' (page 141).

(1) Research, testing, and development

It would be virtually impossible to verify a ban on *research* and *development*, even with the most intrusive kinds of on-site inspection, because research into defences against weapons clearly has to be permissible. It is, however, possible to prohibit or limit the *testing* of some weapons.

One special feature of nuclear weapons is that simply to test them above ground or in the oceans releases radiation which harms some people now living and causes genetic damage to generations yet unborn. A total prohibition on all testing of nuclear weapons, if it could be generally accepted and effectively enforced, would prove a formidable barrier to an increase in the number of states possessing their own nuclear weapons (horizontal proliferation) and would also prevent the further sophistication of nuclear weapons by countries already possessing them (vertical proliferation).

The Antarctic Treaty of 1959 (see Table 2*, no. 1) prohibits the testing of 'any type of weapons' as well as 'Any nuclear explosions'. The Treaty of Tlatelolco (no. 4) commits the parties to refraining from the testing of nuclear weapons and from encouraging or authorising such testing, directly or indirectly, in Latin America. The partial test ban treaty of 1963, to which the Soviet Union, the United Kingdom,

TABLE 2* *Arms control and disarmament agreements*[6]

		No. of parties (signatories only in nos 12, 14, and 17) in 1985
1	Antarctic Treaty, 1959	32
2	Partial test ban treaty, prohibiting nuclear tests in the atmosphere, outer space, and under water, 1963	110
3	Outer space treaty, 1967	83
4	Treaty of Tlatelolco and Additional Protocols, prohibiting nuclear weapons in Latin America, 1967	31
5	Nuclear Non-Proliferation Treaty, 1968	127
6	Treaty prohibiting the emplacement of weapons on the sea-bed and ocean floor, 1971	73
7	Convention prohibiting bacteriological (biological) weapons and toxins, 1972	99
8	Interim Agreement, Protocol, and agreed interpretations on the limitation of strategic offensive arms (SALT I), 1972	2
9	Anti-Ballistic Missiles Treaty, 1972	2
10	Establishment of Standing Consultative Commission, 1972	2
11	Protocol to the ABM Treaty, 1974	2
12	Threshold treaty and Protocol on underground nuclear tests, 1974	2
13	Declaration of Ayachuco, 1974	9
14	Treaty and Protocol on peaceful nuclear explosions, 1976	2
15	Convention prohibiting environmental modification for military purposes, 1977	45
16	Guidelines for nuclear transfers (the London Club), 1977	15
17	Treaty, Protocol, agreed statements, common understandings, and agreed memorandum and statements on the limitation of strategic offensive arms (SALT II), 1979	2
18	Agreement on the moon and other celestial bodies, 1979	5

*Figures in brackets in the text refer to numbered items in this table.

and the United States are parties (no. 2), prohibits tests of nuclear weapons 'in the atmosphere; beyond its limits, including outer space; or under water, including territorial waters or high seas; or in any other environment if such explosion causes radioactive debris to be present outside the territorial limits' of the state carrying out such tests. The 1974 threshold test ban treaty (no. 12) extended the partial ban to 'any underground nuclear weapon test having a yield exceeding 150 kilotons' (more than ten times the size of the Hiroshima bomb). The Soviet Union and the United States are the only signatories to the threshold test ban: it has not yet been ratified by the United States, but neither party has indicated an intention not to ratify. Britain has undertaken to observe the provisions of the ban, despite the fact that the United States has not ratified and that the ban is not yet legally in force. In any case, the United Kingdom uses US underground facilities for its tests, so that Britain is in effect limited to underground tests of nuclear weapons below 150 kts. A 1976 treaty between the two super-powers (no. 14), not yet ratified by the United States so not legally in force, established agreed arrangements for carrying out peaceful nuclear explosions, and the nuclear non-proliferation treaty (NPT) (no. 5) provided for international co-operation for ensuring that 'potential benefits from any peaceful applications of nuclear explosions will be made available to non-nuclear-weapon States ... on a non-discriminatory basis'. The 1972 convention on biological (bacteriological) and toxin weapons (no. 7) includes a ban on developing the specified agents.

(2) Manufacture and stockpiling

The attempt to stop the horizontal proliferation of nuclear weapons began with an Irish proposal in 1958 and culminated in the Non-Proliferation Treaty of 1968 (NPT) (no. 5). This was accompanied by a resolution of the Security Council on security assurances and three virtually identical statements made in the Council by the British, Soviet, and US representatives. The International Atomic Energy Agency (IAEA) established the safeguards procedures required under the NPT in 1971. Neither China nor France has ratified the NPT, but France has declared that it will in practice respect the treaty provisions.

The NPT contains three sets of obligations. The nuclear-weapon states undertake not to transfer nuclear weapons to any recipient whatsoever, or to assist or encourage non-nuclear-weapon states to manufacture, acquire, or control such weapons. The non-nuclear-weapon states undertake not to manufacture or acquire nuclear weapons, and to accept the safeguards system of the IAEA. All parties agree to co-operate in the development of the peaceful uses of nuclear energy, including nuclear explosions for peaceful purposes, and to negotiate further measures of nuclear disarmament.

It has sometimes been said that the NPT is 'discriminatory' in that it seeks to freeze permanently a situation in which five states possess nuclear weapons, while all other parties have to accept the status of not having such weapons and of being subject to IAEA controls. There is no denying the force of this, but it must at the same time be said that non-nuclear-weapon states derive advantages from the treaty; if that were not so, more than 120 of them would not have ratified it.

The Treaty of Tlatelolco (no. 4) is intended to prohibit the manufacture, production, storage, or any form of possession or control of nuclear weapons. The 1972 Convention on biological and toxin weapons (no. 7) includes a ban on production and stockpiling, but there is at present no ban on manufacturing or stockpiling chemical weapons.

(3) Transfer of weapons

As noted above, the NPT (no. 5) prohibits the transfer of nuclear weapons 'directly or indirectly', and this is buttressed by an agreement among the main nuclear suppliers in the so-called London Club (no. 16), who have agreed on 'fundamental principles for safeguards and export controls' for nuclear transfers to non-nuclear-weapon states including 'common criteria for technology transfers'. The Treaty of Tlatelolco (no. 4) prohibits the acquisition or receipt of nuclear weapons in Latin America. The convention on biological weapons and toxins (no. 7) prohibits the transfer of these weapons 'directly or indirectly', but there is at present no ban on transferring chemical weapons to others.

There have been a number of initiatives to limit or at least publicise the transfer of conventional weapons, but these have invariably run into opposition from recipients. Nine Latin American states agreed in 1974 (no. 13) 'to create conditions which will make possible the effective limitation of armaments and an end to their acquisition for offensive purposes ... '.

(4) Deployment

(a) environments
The outer space treaty of 1967, the agreement on the moon and other celestial bodies of 1979, and the treaty on the sea-bed and ocean floor of 1971 (nos 3, 18, and 6 respectively) prohibit placing nuclear weapons or other weapons of mass destruction 'in orbit around the earth', or on or in orbit around the moon and other celestial bodies, or 'on the seabed and ocean floor and in the subsoil thereof'.

(b) regions
The Antarctic Treaty of 1959 (no. 1) prohibits 'any measures of a military nature, such as the establishment of military bases and fortifications, the carrying out of military maneuvres' as well as the disposal of radioactive waste in Antarctica. The Treaty of Tlatelolco in 1967 (no. 4) is intended to prohibit the installation or deployment of nuclear weapons in Latin America. Two protocols call on nuclear-weapon states and on external states with territories in the zone to respect or apply the denuclearisation provisions. A zone free of nuclear and biological weapons is being created for the South Pacific, and the UN General Assembly has called for Africa and other regions to be free of nuclear weapons.

(c) numbers
SALT I between the two super-powers had two elements: an interim agreement limiting strategic offensive arms and a treaty limiting anti-ballistic missile systems (ABMs), supplemented by a protocol (nos 8, 9, and 11). The interim agreement established numerical limits for fixed land-based missiles and for submarines and submarine-launched missiles, but placed no limits on other missiles. Modernisation and replacement of missiles was permitted within specified limits. The ABM Treaty limited the parties to two ABM deployment areas each, subsequently reduced to one area each by the ABM Protocol.

SALT II (no. 17), which was intended to replace SALT I, comprised a treaty, protocol, agreed statements and common understandings, and an agreed memorandum and accompanying statements giving information on the numbers of strategic offensive arms held by the two super-powers in June 1979.[7]

Equal over-all numerical ceilings, and a number of sub-ceilings, were placed on specified strategic weapons. Both sides were required to dismantle some nuclear delivery vehicles, and there was a ban on constructing new ICBMs and restrictions on modernisation. A number of unusual or exotic nuclear weapons were not to be developed, tested, or deployed. Limits were agreed on flight-testing and on rapid re-load systems, and each side agreed to notify the other of certain test launches. Finally, the two powers agreed a number of principles and guidelines for future negotiations. SALT II was never ratified by the United States, but both sides undertook in 1981 to abide by its provisions pending the conclusion of new agreements. By mid-1986, there were signs that the United States might abandon this commitment.

(5) Destruction or dismantling of weapons

All of the agreements in Table 2 established restraints or prohibitions on the means of preparing or waging war or, in one case, consultative machinery regarding the implementation of agreements (no. 10); but only three agreements in the Table provided for actual *dis*armament, the destruction or dismantling of weapons or the diversion of military materials to peaceful purposes – the convention on bacteriological (biological) and toxin weapons (no. 7) by which states undertook to 'destroy' or to 'divert to peaceful purposes' the specified agents, and SALT I and SALT II (nos 8 and 17) which required both super-powers to dismantle some weapons.

If the last quarter of a century is any guide, many agreements to limit or ban weapons restrain states from doing what they had no intention of doing anyway.

VERIFICATION AND COMPLIANCE

Most negotiated disarmament agreements are subject to verification. There are three kinds of verification:

(1) international, such as the safeguards procedures of the International Atomic Energy Agency or UN inspection of the zones of limited armaments on the Golan Heights between Israel and Syria;

(2) regional, as under the 1954 Protocol to the Brussels Treaty whereby the German Federal Republic undertook not to manufacture atomic, biological, or chemical weapons on its territory, or the Treaty of Tlatelolco on the denuclearisation of Latin America;

(3) bilateral, as under various agreements between the super-powers on nuclear weapons.

Treaties which ban the use or first use of weapons, but not manufacture or deployment (such as the Geneva Protocol of 1925 banning the use of poisons and germs in war), do not provide verification procedures.

Any verification which relies on fallible machines or potentially lazy or disloyal human beings can never be 100% foolproof, so what is aimed at is verification sufficiently effective as to make cheating an irrational option. On-site inspection could improve the effectiveness of other systems of verification, but many states (especially, perhaps, those under Communist rule) are hesitant to allow foreigners to have access to sensitive military installations or security zones. There is, in any case, a fuzzy grey area between the illicit gathering of intelligence and the legitimate monitoring of arms control agreements.

The main methods of verification, used singly or in conjunction, are as follows:

1. On-site inspection

The Antarctic Treaty (no. 1) permits the parties to send observers to all areas of Antarctica at all times. The Outer Space Treaty (no. 3) provides for observation of stations, installations, equipment, and space vehicles 'on a basis of reciprocity' and of the flight of space objects 'on a basis of equality'. The Sea-bed Treaty (no. 6) allows unrestricted verification 'to promote the objectives of and insure compliance with' the Treaty. The Treaty on the denuclearisation of Latin America and the Treaty on peaceful nuclear explosions (nos 4 and 14) provide for selective but not unrestricted on-site inspection, and the nuclear Non-Proliferation Treaty (no. 5) provides for both regular on-site inspection and the use of unmanned instrumentation. There has been much discussion and negotiation about on-site inspection of putative bans on underground nuclear tests and the production of chemical weapons.

2. National technical means

These means are provided for in the threshold test ban treaty, the Treaty on peaceful nuclear explosions, the Interim Agreement on Strategic Arms and the Anti-Ballistic Missile Treaty and Protocol

(SALT I), and the 1979 treaty on strategic arms (SALT II) which has not yet been ratified by the United States (nos 8, 9, 11, 12, 14, and 17). Under SALT I and SALT II, the parties agreed not to conceal measures which might impede verification by the other party, and not to interfere with the other's national technical means. National technical means are not prohibited in other treaties, including the Antarctic and Partial Test Ban Treaties (nos 1 and 2). National technical means comprise photo-reconnaissance, radar, seismic detectors, signal interception, and other long-distance technologies.

3. Consultation

The two super-powers have established a Standing Consultative Commission (no. 10) to 'promote the objectives and implementation' of agreements and treaties on strategic arms and anti-ballistic systems (nos 8, 9, 11, and 17), and the treaty on peaceful nuclear explosions (no. 14) also provides for a Joint Consultative Commission to promote the objectives and implementation of the Treaty and to develop co-operation. Other agreements providing for consultation and the exchange of information are the Antarctic Treaty, the Treaty on the denuclearisation of Latin America, the Sea-bed Treaty, the Biological Weapons Convention, the Threshold Test Ban, the Convention banning environmental modification, and the agreement on the moon and other celestial bodies (nos 1, 4, 6, 7, 12, 15, and 18).

Many arms control agreements in addition to verification procedures contain one or more provisions for dealing with ambiguous activities or alleged breaches. These provisions may simply be for consultations: the Treaty of Tlatelolco for keeping nuclear weapons out of Latin America (no. 4) provides that a conference of all the parties may make appropriate recommendations in the event of non-compliance, and the Convention to ban biological weapons (no. 7) provides for consultation and co-operation 'through appropriate international procedures within the framework of the United Nations' in solving 'any problems which may arise ... '.

The Convention banning environmental modification (no. 15) provides for fact-finding if it is alleged that a party is in breach of its obligations. The Partial Test Ban, the nuclear Non-Proliferation Treaty, the Sea-bed Treaty, the biological weapons Convention, and the Threshold Test Ban (nos 2, 5, 6, 7, and 12) contain express provisions for withdrawal if 'extraordinary events ... have jeopardized the supreme interests' of a party. The Treaty of Tlatelolco (no. 4) provides for withdrawal if circumstances have arisen or may arise which affect the supreme national interests of a party or the peace and security of one or more parties. The Outer Space Treaty (no. 3) provides for withdrawal after one year's notice in writing. Some treaties provide for more than one procedure for dealing with alleged violations.

ALLEGED VIOLATIONS

In a series of reports in 1984–6, the Reagan Administration alleged that the Soviet Union has violated the Partial and Threshold Test Bans, the Interim Agreement on strategic arms and the ABM Treaty (SALT I), the 1979 Treaty on strategic arms (SALT II), and the Convention on biological weapons (nos 2, 7, 8, 9, 12, and 17). The United States had not ratified the Threshold Test Ban or SALT II.

One of the difficulties of assessing compliance is that some of the terms in the agreements are imprecise. The Interim Agreement on strategic arms (SALT I) (no. 8) prohibited the conversion of certain old missile launchers into launchers for 'heavy' missiles, and yet the two parties attached to the Agreement inconsistent declarations about the meaning of 'heavy'. Under the ABM Treaty (no. 9) the parties agreed not to deploy radars for early warning of strategic ballistic missile attack except at locations along the periphery of its national territory and oriented outwards, but how is it possible to know whether a radar is for early warning and battle management or for the tracking of peaceful space vehicles? Under SALT II, the parties agreed not to encode telemetric signals in missile tests in such a way as to impede verification by the other party, leaving plenty of scope for disagreement as to the criteria for determining when the use of code would impede verification. The ban on deployment of particular missiles under SALT II does not make it clear whether the storage of obsolete missiles represents deployment or not. SALT II contains several imprecise terms: 'systems for rapid reload of ICBM launchers' (what is the duration of 'rapid'?), 'new type of light ICBM' (how define 'new'?), 'no significant increase' (when is an increase 'significant'?).

President Reagan's report of 23 December 1985 is headed 'Soviet Non-compliance with Arms Control Agreements,[8] but many of the alleged breaches refer to 'ambiguities', 'uncertainties', 'evidence … insufficient fully to assess compliance', 'potential violation', 'may be preparing …'. There are also a number of unqualified allegations of non-compliance or of likely non-compliance with legal obligations or political commitments, of which the most serious relates to the siting, orientation, and capability of the phased-array radar at Krasnojarsk. President Reagan concluded that there was 'a pattern of Soviet non-compliance ... of increasing importance and serious concern' which had enabled the Soviet Union to register military gains.

The Soviet Union has firmly denied US allegations of non-compliance and has complained of US violations. According to the Soviet Union, the hardening of silos for MIRVed *Minuteman* III missiles violates the article in the SALT I Interim Agreement (no. 8) which prohibits deliberate attempts to impede the other side's national means of verification. The Soviet Union alleges that the US space-tracking radar at Shemya in the Aleutian Islands and the *Pave Paws* phased-array radars being constructed in the continental United States could be used for ABM tracking, and that these installations and the upgrading of the radars at Fylingdales Moor (England), Thule (Greenland), and Clear (Alaska) violate the ABM Treaty (no. 9). The Soviet Union also claims that some US underground nuclear tests have been in excess of 150 kilotons, and that radioactive debris has vented into Mexico and Canada, in contravention of the Threshold Test Ban (no. 12). The Soviet Union also alleges that the deployment of *Tomahawk* cruise missiles in Europe is inconsistent with the ban on cruise missiles with a range exceeding 600 kilometres contained in the Protocol to the SALT II Treaty (no. 17).[9]

It must be tempting for both states to go up to, and perhaps even beyond, the margins of what is permissible, as much to test the other side's capability to detect violations as to gain immediate military advantage from non-compliance. If this is done too blatantly, or too crudely, or too often, public opinion will conclude that arms control is a dangerous exercise which should be eschewed by prudent governments.

In any case, the preceding summary of what has been achieved may give a more hopeful impression than the situation warrants, for a great deal remains to be done if arms races are to be effectively curbed. The main near-nuclear powers have not become parties to the Non-Proliferation Treaty. China and France have not acceded to the partial test ban or agreed to respect the limits in the Threshold Test Ban, and there is at present no restriction at all on testing nuclear weapons underground so long as the yield does not exceed 150 kilotons. Although progress has been made in keeping nuclear weapons out of

Latin America, France has not yet ratified Protocol I to respect the denuclearisation provisions in territories for which it is responsible in the region, and no significant progress has been made to keep Africa, the Middle East, or South Asia free of nuclear weapons. There is still no agreement to ban the production, transfer, or deployment of chemical weapons, and there is no international control on transfers of conventional arms. The vertical proliferation of nuclear weapons has continued, and there is no agreement to prohibit their use or first use, comparable to the Geneva Protocol of 1925 which bans the use in war of bacteriological (biological) and chemical weapons. Proposals for a nuclear freeze, for a ban on anti-satellite activities, or for the demilitarisation of the Indian Ocean have made virtually no progress. The possibility of limiting military budgets has been helpfully elucidated, but no agreement is in sight.

On many of the issues which divide NATO and the Warsaw Pact, the Soviet positions have in recent years seemed more forthcoming than those of the United States. President Reagan and some of his close advisors had for long had a deep suspicion of Soviet intentions, a conviction that previous Administrations had shamefully neglected US defences, and a belief that arms control agreements are a snare and a delusion. Pressure from allies of the United States rather than the reasonableness of Soviet proposals induced the Reagan Administration to modify its initial hard stance on some disarmament issues, but not enough to impress uncommitted opinion. Reagan's Strategic Defence Initiative (Star Wars) had aroused anxieties about the likely militarisation of space and the destablisation of the strategic balance rather than hopes that future generations would escape from the nuclear threat and so live in peace.

On one crucial issue, nevertheless, the Soviet Union has apparently been unwilling to meet Western requirements. The reluctance of the Soviet side to accept unfettered on-site inspection, coupled with the conjecture that some Soviet acts had been in breach of international agreements, had fuelled the suspicions of Western arms control sceptics.

While it is nonsense to assert that nuclear weapons, and nuclear weapons alone, have kept the peace, the central strategic balance has been more stable and robust than even the most optimistic analysts predicted thirty-five years ago. But if perchance mutual deterrence should fail and nuclear weapons should be used in combat, it is unlikely that the war could be kept limited. It is almost certain that escalation would take place in quite a short period of time either because of a deliberate decision on one side or both or because of accidental or unauthorised use.

It is true that no state beyond the first five has claimed to possess nuclear weapons since the NPT (Non-Proliferation Treaty) was finalised almost twenty years ago. While not denying the utility of the NPT and the export guidelines of the London Club, I would stress that it has not been possible to induce a single near-nuclear country to stop the drive to acquire nuclear weapons. Each potential nuclear-weapon power uses much the same arguments for acquiring a nuclear-weapons capability as Britain has used for maintaining one.

The Soviet Union deploys chemical weapons, and the United States has threatened to build up its own stocks, especially of binary shells (weapons containing two chemicals of relatively low toxicity which mix while the munition is being delivered to the target so as to produce a nerve gas or other super-toxic agent). A medium-sized industrialised nuclear-weapons power like Britain or France is likely to devote about 5 per cent of the gross national product to defence, but there are at least nine countries, most of them rather poor, that spend more than twice that proportion (Ethiopia, Guyana, Iran, Jordan, Lebanon, Mongolia, North Yemen, Saudia Arabia, and Syria), two which spend more than 20 per cent (Israel and Oman), and one which spends more than 30 per cent (Iraq). Yet all attempts to control the trade in conventional arms have been frustrated by the opposition of recipients. It should not be forgotten in this connexion that there have been more than one hundred and fifty 'small' wars since 1945, mainly in the Third World.

The never-ending competition in the development of weapons shows how an arms race acquires a momentum of its own. The technical experts feel impelled to transform each new theoretical possibility into an actuality, and decide afterwards what its military justification should be. Each side, on the basis of intelligence which may be incomplete or faulty, over-reacts to the supposed developments on the other side. Both the United States and the Soviet Union, wishing to diversify their military capabilities, and insuring against a technological breakthrough by the other, have acquired a massive strategic 'overkill' capacity.

It is sometimes said that as a country acquires a nuclear capability, so its leaders inevitably develop an enhanced sense of international responsibility. If a direct connection between the two processes were proved beyond all doubt, then the NPT would seem to be an unmitigated disaster, since it denies to the vast majority of countries a sure means of achieving an enhanced sense of international responsibility.

The superpowers cannot use their nuclear strength for day-to-day political purposes. Power is the ability to persuade others to behave in ways they had not intended, but the excessive power which the nuclear states believe to be necessary for deterrence is, one hopes, unusable. The paradox is that nuclear weapons are not there to be used, but to deter their use by others.

Although the central strategic balance is relatively stable, the nuclear powers realise that deterrence alone is not enough: they have to face the possibility that deterrence may fail, whether by accident, miscalculation, or sheer lunacy. In a multilateral alliance, who should decide when deterrence has failed, and what should be a prudent response? How can the risks of escalation be minimised?

Nuclear strategy has acquired an esoteric intellectual frame-work and jargon of its own, but the possibility of nuclear war is too serious a matter to be left to the pundits in the think-tanks. The ordinary citizen is entitled to basic information about the nuclear weapons now available, and the implications of using them, and he is entitled to decide in time of peace on any limits within which he wishes his government to operate in the event that deterrence should fail. A crucial moral question is whether there are any circumstances in which a civilised government would be right actually to use stràtegic offensive nuclear weapons. Simply to ask the question may be thought to weaken the credibility of deterrence, but if it is a proper question for governments to ask and answer in private (which it surely is), it is difficult to maintain that it is an improper question for ordinary citizens to ask and try to answer in public.

For myself, I can only say that I cannot alter the fact that nuclear weapons cannot be disinvented. I consider that the security of mankind requires their immediate control and ultimate abolition. I believe that to the extent that Britain has influence, it should be to insist that such weapons shall never be used against enemy cities or civilian areas, whatever the provocation. The resolution of the UN General Assembly condemning the use of nuclear weapons (see Appendix 4) may not have been legally binding, but I find its main thrust morally persuasive.

6 In Obedience to Conscience

I have often thought that one of the less attractive traits of various professional bodies and institutions is the deeply ingrained suspicion and outright hostility which can exist towards anything unorthodox or unconventional. I suppose it is inevitable that something which is different should arouse strong feelings on the part of the majority whose conventional wisdom is being challenged ... . I suppose, too, that human nature is such that we are frequently prevented from seeing that what is taken for today's unorthodoxy is probably going to be tomorrow's convention. Perhaps we just have to accept it is God's will that the unorthodox individual is doomed to years of frustration, ridicule and failure in order to act out his role in the scheme of things, until his day arrives and mankind is ready to receive his message: a message which he probably finds hard to explain, but which he knows comes from a far deeper source than conscious thought.

Prince Charles, 1982

It is, I think, obvious that resort to armed conflict involves a number of contradictions.

PROMISE AND PERFORMANCE

One clear contradiction is that between the obligations of states under international law, including the obligations of UN Membership, and the way states behave in practice. All the world's major sovereign states except Switzerland and the two Koreas are Members of the United Nations, and there are three main conditions of Membership: to be a state, to be 'peace-loving', and to be 'able and willing' to carry out in good faith the obligations contained in the UN Charter (Arts 2(2) and 4(1)). Among the obligations of UN Membership are to settle international disputes peacefully and without endangering international peace and security (Arts 2(3) and 33(1)) and, obversely, to refrain from the threat or use of force against the territorial integrity or political independence of any state (Art. 2(4)).

It is common knowledge that there have been more than 150 wars since the United Nations was founded. Some of these wars were wholly internal, conflicts between the armed forces of a state and dissident

156

armed forces or other organised armed groups, such as the Greek Civil War of 1945–9. Some were conflicts between two governmental authorities within one nation, as in the first phase of the Korean War which began on 25 June 1950. Some were internal wars but with major external assistance to one or more sides, such as the conflict in Cyprus in 1974 or that in the Lebanon since 1976. But having eliminated the doubtful or ambiguous cases, one is left with a core of more than one hundred inter-state wars, of which that between Iraq and Iran is the most notable at the time of writing.

It is stated explicitly in the UN Charter that the Charter does not impair the inherent right of individual or collective self-defence (1) if an armed attack occurs, and (2) until the Security Council has taken the necessary measures to maintain peace and security (Art. 51). When states resort to armed force or other coercive action, the first line of diplomatic defence tends to be the claim that they were acting in self-defence. When Israel complained in the 1950s that Egypt was interfering with transit through the Suez Canal, Egypt argued that self-preservation, which it equated with self-defence, was a national duty, and citing the self-defence provision of the UN Charter as the justification for the Egyptian blockade. 'Egypt was and still is the victim of aggression', claimed Egypt with questionable plausibility.[1] Similarly, when Israel attacked Arab airfields on 5 June 1967, the Israeli ambassador in New York told the Security Council with equal implausibility that Egyptian forces had 'moved against Israel' and that Israeli forces were 'now engaged in repelling the Egyptian forces.'[2] Turning to more recent times, it is noteworthy that when Libya and the United States were at loggerheads about Libyan terrorism and US retribution in March–April 1986, both parties claimed to be exercising self-defence under Article 51 of the UN Charter.[3] The plea of self-defence clearly covers a multitude of sins.

In order to plug whatever leaks there may be in the UN Charter, the General Assembly has adopted resolutions on the threat or use of force (Appendices 2, 5, 6, 8, 10, and 11) and on what constitutes aggression (Appendices 3 and 13). The process of drafting and debating such resolutions was doubtless educative for the participants, but more radical steps are needed if states are really to fulfil in good faith their obligations under the UN Charter. It is now an axiom of international law that a person who commits an act which constitutes a crime under international law is responsible therefor and liable to punishment. The world now needs a court or tribunal, paralleling the existing Court at the Hague, before which could be brought persons accused of major international crimes, including those violations of the UN Charter which were defined at Nürnberg as crimes against peace.

THE NECESSITIES OF WAR AND THE CLAIMS OF HUMANITY

If, in spite of the commitments which states have entered into, wars still occur, what can be done on an international basis to minimise human suffering? Was the International Law Commission right in 1949 when it refused to codify the laws of war on the ground that such an action would seem to show lack of confidence in the capacity of the United Nations to keep the peace? Do the Hague and Geneva Conventions legitimise violence, as was the view of the notable peace-worker, Gräfin Bertha von Suttner, or do they reinforce humanity, as the Red Cross movement has intended? Do efforts to bring aid to war victims have the unintended effect of making war more acceptable? Which should have higher priority: efforts to abolish war or efforts to make war more humane?

For pacifists, the main task has not been the drawing up of guidelines regarding the just use of armed force, since they believe that resort to armed force nearly always creates more problems than it solves. For them, the main problem has been whether the renunciation of armed force is compatible with responsible citizenship in a substantially non-pacifist world. Is pacifism a vocation for the few, analogous to the vocation of celibacy, a commitment and testimony to another way of life; or is it a doctrine which can be translated into workable policies which could be put before the electorate as practicable alternatives to those present policies which depend, in the last resort, on willingness to threaten or use military power?

Max Weber distinguished between an ethic of responsibility and an ethic of ultimate ends, which seem to be 'two fundamentally differing and irreconcilably opposed maxims'. An ethic of responsibility takes account of 'the average deficiencies of people', and it must be willing to pay the price of using morally dubious means 'or at least dangerous ones'. The person who engages in politics encounters ethical paradoxes and must face the consequences of what may become of himself under the impact of those paradoxes. Whoever uses violent means for whatever ends – 'and every politician does' – must take account of the consequences of violence. Indeed, it is when we come to the legitimising of violence that we face the most acute ethical problem of politics, for underneath an ethic of responsibility there lurk 'the diabolic forces … in all violence.' The person who seeks salvation should not pursue it along the avenue of politics, for the tasks of politics 'can only be solved by violence'.

The believer in an ethic of ultimate ends also feels responsible, but only for seeing that the flame of pure intention is not quenched. The demands of the Sermon on the Mount imply a law of absolute imperatives. Weber held that an ethic of ultimate ends must reject all action that employs morally dubious or dangerous means.

Politics is made with the head, claimed Weber, but certainly not with the head alone. A person following an ethic of responsibility may in the end reach a point where he says: 'Here I stand; I can do no other.' That is something 'genuinely human and moving'. Anyone who is not spiritually dead must realise the possibility of finding himself in that position. So in reality the two ethics are not absolute contrasts but supplements 'which only in unison constitute a genuine man'.[4]

This was an issue which I often discussed with George Orwell in 1944–5, but he remained firmly of the view that 'pacifism refuses to face the problem of government' and that pacifists always think of themselves as 'people who will never be in a position of control, which is why I call them irresponsible.'[5]

Non-pacifists will doubtless continue to look to some version of the Just War doctrine to provide guidelines regarding the just use of armed force. Admittedly, the doctrine has been more elegant in theory than useful in practice. The fact that the principles of proportion and non-combatant immunity are increasingly difficult to apply in practice is not, in itself, a reason for renouncing them.

The dilemma for pacifist and non-pacifist alike has been well stated by Sir Laurens van der Post: 'To me the most urgent problem of our time is the problem of discovering a way of overcoming evil without becoming another form of evil in the process.'[6]

For the Red Cross movement and those other humanitarians who want to subject armed force to moral and legal controls, the issue is not simply whether to include work for peace among the aims: that is taken for granted. The problem is whether the peace effort should be restricted to the proclamation of pious generalities, which would certainly be otiose, or should include detailed plans for a more peaceful world, such as the advocacy of general and complete disarmament or universal respect for human rights, which would probably be divisive.

The Red Cross movement has striven to pursue a middle course, but leaning slightly to the platitudinous side. Henry Dunant, who, along with Gustave Moynier, is generally regarded as the inspirer of the Red Cross idea, was always sympathetic to the pacifist idea but he did not interest himself in the peace *movement* until he was almost 70 years of age, when he made contact by letter with the Gräfin von Suttner.

Dunant had been born into a patrician Geneva family in 1828. He was a puzzling character: philanthropist, internationalist, reformer, visionary, unsuccessful businessman, always effervescing with novel ideas, but over-credulous and a poor judge of other people. Having witnessed the carnage at the battle of Solferino in 1859, Dunant wrote his *Un Souvenir de Solférino*,[7] which led in a short time to the foundation of the International Committee for the relief of wounded in time of war, with Dunant as secretary, which later was to become the International Committee of the Red Cross. Dunant's draft for the charter of the international Red Cross movement stated that each national committee would be authorised 'to compensate ... for the inadequacies of the official medical services of armies ... '. This was too much for the British War Office: perhaps over-sensitive after Florence Nightingale's revelations about medical deficiencies in Crimea, the British representative claimed that his country's medical services were perfectly well able to cope without foreign guidance. If there were shortcomings in other countries, they should examine what Britain had done. Britain was officially opposed to any action which might detract from national responsibility. Dunant's draft charter was tactfully amended so as to provide that, should the need arise, each national committee would 'assist the army medical services by every means in its power.'[8]

Dunant was tireless in touring the European capitals to urge the formation of national relief committees for victims of war, often disregarding advice or even instructions from his colleagues in Geneva. In 1867, disaster struck, when a bank in Geneva of which Dunant was a director went bankrupt, and the court found that Dunant had 'knowingly deceived his colleagues'. The International Committee severed all ties with Dunant. Within a few years, he had disappeared from view. Ill and poverty-stricken, Dunant eventually reached the Swiss village of Heiden, about 8 miles east of St Gallen, where he entered the town hospital. He was so poor that he had to stay in bed while his clothes were laundered. He wrote his memoirs in simple exercise books, denouncing states and churches and other official institutions. He wanted to be 'a disciple of Christ as in the 1st century, nothing more.' In 1895, 28 years after the bankruptcy, a passing journalist met him by chance in a public park and discovered his identity. The following year, on Dunant's 68th birthday, messages of congratulation descended on him from all parts of Europe. In 1897, shortly after his 69th birthday, he finally took the decisive step of joining the Society of the Friends of Peace.

Scholars may argue about the morality or legality of war, but wars do in fact take place, and states engaged in armed conflict are bound by the laws and customs of war. The Nürnberg Tribunal held that the rules of land warfare expressed in the Hague Convention of 1907 were in 1939 recognised by all civilised nations and were declaratory of the laws and customs of war (Appendix 1(b)). The US manual of military law states that 'the general principles' of the Geneva POW Convention of 1929 'have been held declaratory of the customary law of war to which states are subject.'[9] The position of the ICRC is that the minimum principles of humanitarian law found in the Conventions and Protocols are valid at all times, in all places, and under all circumstances.[10]

Situations may arise during armed conflict for which there are no express provisions in the Hague Conventions and the Geneva Conventions and Protocols. War has been transformed by technology since the adoption of the Hague Conventions in 1899 and 1907, and some matters which were traditionally part of the Hague law governing the conduct of military operations are now covered by the Geneva law for the protection of war victims.

The delegates who assembled in the Hague in 1899 and 1907 were not able to devise rules covering all the circumstances which might arise in practice, though they did hope that it would be possible at a later stage to prepare a more complete code of the laws of war. On the other hand, they did not intend that unforeseen cases should be left to the arbitrary judgement of military commanders. They therefore agreed on 20 June 1899, after heated debate, that the gaps should be covered by a declaration devised by the Russian jurist F. F. Martens.

Fedor Fedorovich Martens was a familiar figure at international conferences on humanitarian law, a Russian Privy Counsellor while only in his twenties, legal expert of the Imperial Foreign Ministry, and eventually to become a member of the Permanent Court of Arbitration. Because of his passionate commitment to the idea of international arbitration, Martens was widely known as the Chief Justice of Christendom or, in Britain, as the Lord Chancellor of Europe.[11]

Martens was born in Estonia in 1845 into a poor Lutheran family.

When he was ten years old he went to an orphan school in St Petersburg, then took a law degree, and in 1868 entered the Imperial Foreign Ministry. He joined the Orthodox Church and adopted a Russian name. In 1871 he became lecturer in international law at the Imperial Law School, and in 1873 he was appointed to the chair of international law at the university of St Petersburg. He was a staunch Russian patriot who, according to Arthur Nussbaum, 'considered it his professional duty ... to defend and back up the policies of his government at any price.' Legal argument enabled him to render his pleas for Russian claims 'more impressive or more palatable'. T. E. Holland makes the same point but in more charitable language: Martens was 'a faithful exponent of the humane theories of his Imperial masters; so much so that his arguments sometimes suggested rather the diplomatist ... than the jurist ... '.

Martens was present at the abortive gathering in Brussels in 1874 on humanitarian law. He was twice appointed vice-president of the Institute of International Law, was an honorary member of the French Academy of Moral and Political Science, a corresponding member of the British Academy, and an honorary doctor of Oxford, Cambridge, and Yale. He was a prolific writer and editor. During the first Hague Conference in 1899 he chaired the commission on the laws and customs of war on land: in 1907, he chaired the commission on naval questions, and the relative failure of that commission was certainly not the fault of Martens, for he always strove for acceptable compromises. He was in favour of making arbitral awards binding on the parties, and he spoke vigorously in defence of commissions of inquiry as a means for the peaceful settlement of international disputes. He always spoke extemporaneously and without notes: in later life, he was crippled with gout. He died in 1909 in the course of a train journey from Estonia to St Petersburg.

A clause from the declaration drafted by Martens is to be found in the preamble to the Hague Conventions of 1899 and 1907 on the laws and customs of war on land, and is reproduced in the Geneva Conventions and Protocols and other humanitarian instruments. How the Martens declaration came to be drafted in 1899 is recorded by Frederick Holls, a member of the US delegation; James Scott Brown gives the text of the vital clause in his massive 1,500-page study of the Hague Conferences but, strangely, makes no mention of the author.

Discussion on the laws and customs of land warfare at the 1899 Conference was based on three documents: the code drawn up in 1863 in the United States by Francis Lieber, the Brussels Declaration of

1874 (which never entered into force), and the Oxford Manual prepared by a committee of the Institute of International Law, of which Martens was a member.

When the Hague Conference came to consider who should be entitled to benefit from the laws and customs of war, the basis of discussion was Article 9 of the Brussels Declaration, which lists four conditions for combatant status.

The British War Office was firmly opposed to *any* international code on the laws and customs of war; 'but an undertaking may be given that His Majesty's Government will consider the question of issuing instructions on these subjects for the general guidance of British forces.' Some delegates in the Hague found the four Brussels conditions for combatant status too restrictive, and the British delegate proposed the following amendment:

> Nothing in this chapter shall be construed as diminishing or denying the right belonging to the people of an invaded country to fulfil their duty of opposing the invaders by the most energetic patriotic resistance, and by all permitted means.

The Belgian delegate took the same line: too great a limitation on belligerent status 'would practically mean the abolition of patriotism'. The first duty of every citizen was to defend his own country, and national uprisings against invaders formed the grandest episodes of history. The Dutch delegate, on the other hand, pointed out that 'operations on the part of an undrilled population against an army had become more and more hopeless'. The Swiss delegate proposed an amendment to prohibit reprisals against 'any population which has openly taken arms to resist the invasion of its territory' (*Levée en Masse*). The German delegate commented that much had been said on the subject of humanity, but it was time to remember that soldiers too were human beings. Exhausted soldiers who had engaged in heavy combat and long marches had a right to be sure that apparently peaceable inhabitants would not suddenly prove to be wild and merciless enemies. While he would vote for a compromise text in a spirit of conciliation, 'my concessions must cease; it is absolutely impossible for me to go one step further … '.

It was in this situation of apparent deadlock that Martens introduced the declaration which forms the epigraph of chapter 4; the British and Swiss amendments were withdrawn; and the Martens declaration was adopted unanimously. The crux of the Martens clause is as follows:

> Until a more complete code of the laws of war has been issued, the

high contracting Parties deem it expedient to declare that, in cases
not included in the Regulations adopted by them, the inhabitants
and the belligerents remain under the protection and the rule of the
principles of the law of nations, as they result from the usages
established among civilized peoples, from the laws of humanity, and
the dictates of the public conscience.

The main responsibility for maintaining and improving international
humanitarian law now rests with the International Committee of the
Red Cross, but its responsibility is not exclusive; the UN and regional
agencies, in the work to secure universal respect for and observance of
human rights, have a parallel role. Arms control and disarmament,
whether by express agreement, tacit understanding, or unilateral
initiative, are also required. In the long run, however, there is no
substitute for an informed, alert, and enlightened public opinion.

It is obvious that those who are actually engaged in armed conflict
should respect the humanitarian codes, but how should they act if
confronted with a contradiction between the claims of humanity and
military necessity? The preamble to the Hague Conventions, for
example, refers to the hope of diminishing the evils of war 'as far as
military requirements permit', and one of the Hague rules declares it
'especially forbidden' to destroy or seize the enemy's property unless
such action is 'imperatively demanded by the necessities of war' (Art.
23(g)). What weight should be given to the claims of humanity and to
military necessity?

Military necessity is defined in the US manual of military law as
those measures which are indispensable for securing the complete
submission of the enemy as soon as possible but which are not
forbidden by international law; the plea of military necessity cannot be
used as a defence for acts forbidden by the laws of war.[12] The British
manual of military law makes it clear that military necessity is not a
defence to crime.[13]

This was made clear in one of the war crimes trials in Hamburg after
the second world war. The defence argued that the principles
underlying the Hague Conventions had to be adjusted to the
necessities of war, that because the comprehensive character of total
war had implications which were not generally foreseen when the
Hague regulations were drafted, the principles of those regulations
could no longer be regarded as absolute or unconditional but must be
modified if not suspended in the light of military necessity. It was

claimed by the defence that the laws of war have grown out of the practice and experience of warfare, and that these laws of war are merely usages arising from military practice. War is not a legal but a political act, it was argued, and the usages of war cease to be binding when they interfere with the effective prosecution of the war. The decision when military necessity would justify disregard of the usages of war must be left to the discretion of the military commander concerned.

The British military court rejected the argument that the principles underlying the Hague Convention have to be adjusted to the necessities of war. Referring to the preamble to the Convention, the court held that the Hague rules themselves 'have already made allowance for military necessity. Military necessity has already been taken into consideration in the framing of these laws'. The court also rejected the plea of superior orders, while admitting that an officer receiving an order from his superior to commit a wrongful act is placed in a position of extreme difficulty.

The accused was found guilty of some but not all of the charges and sentenced to imprisonment for eighteen years, subsequently reduced to twelve years.[14]

DETERRING WAR AND CONDITIONAL INTENTIONS

Some nuclear deterrers have reservations about attempts to subject war to legal or moral restraints, for they believe that deterrence depends on the conditional intention to perform deeds which would be unspeakably macabre if committed. For them, the more appalling the conditionally-intended act, the greater the deterrent effect, and consequently the less likely the need to perform it.

I have not encountered any convincing ethical justification for this position, but one can see how it has come to be held. The enormously destructive power of the other side's nuclear weapons has meant that the two super-powers are 'condemned to suicide or coexistence', as Raymond Aron has put it.[15]

It would be easier to find an ethical justification for the idea of making war as terrible as possible if technical mistakes could be certainly prevented and if all rulers were invariably rational, but history unquestionably shows that mistakes do occur and that rulers sometimes act in ways contrary to their own interests. It is not inconceivable that mutual deterrence might one day fail, and the greater the number of nuclear-weapon states, the greater the risk of failure. Moreover, the more horrible the acts conditionally intended or threatened in time of peace, the more horrific would the consequences likely to be if deterrence should indeed fail.

Moreover, anger and hatred have led to military excesses. I do not accept that aggression is an ineradicable human drive, a 'universal trait of the social life of humans'.[16] But Konrad Lorenz has shown that human beings do have characteristics which make them dangerous creatures – in particular, lack of natural weapons, and lack of strong inhibitions against injuring their own kind. And humans become more of a danger as their capacity to injure, kill, and destroy by 'unnatural' means increases.[17]

It is because of the temptation to lose control in the heat of battle that professional military men pay heed to the obligations of the Martens clause, for there has always been an unwritten code of chivalry and magnanimity in war, often based on the expectation of reciprocity. One of the earlier documented examples of military magnanimity dates from about 1000 BC. The warrior David had developed an intense friendship with Jonathan, whom we would now call a royal prince for he was a son of king Saul of Israel. David was anointed by the prophet Samuel and became an armour-bearer to king Saul, whom he entertained by playing the harp. In time, Saul became very attached to David and, because of his military prowess, gave him an important military command. As a result, David became a popular hero, for the people shouted 'Saul hath slain his thousands, and David his ten thousands.' David's growing popularity and his intimacy with Jonathan began to arouse Saul's jealousy.

David falls in love with Saul's daughter Michal. Saul agrees to the betrothal but, instead of demanding a dowry, he incites David to make war on the Philistines and return with 100 enemy foreskins. David returns with 200.

Saul now encourages Jonathan to kill David, but Jonathan pleads for David's life because David has not sinned against Saul, 'and because his works have been to thee-ward very good.' In spite of Jonathan's plea, Saul tries to kill David but fails.

Jonathan warns David of the danger to his life, so David hides, leaving a pillow in his bed. When Saul's emissaries arrive, Michal says that David is sick. 'And when the messengers were come in, behold, there was an image in the bed, with a pillow of goat's hair ... '. David manages to flee.

Saul, furious with Jonathan, tries to kill him with a javelin, but

Jonathan escapes. David collects a band of 400 followers, an alienated group of outlaws composed of 'every one that was in distress, and every one that was in debt, and every one that was discontented ... '. They take refuge in the Cave of Adullam. Saul sets out to find David with an army of 3000 men. David moves to the wilderness near Ein Gedi on the Dead Sea, and then by chance he comes across Saul in a cave. David cuts off part of Saul's robe but does him no harm, so that Saul says, 'Thou art more righteous than I: for thou hast rewarded me good, whereas I have rewarded thee evil.' All the same, Saul's antagonism continues.

Some time later, David finds Saul asleep in a ditch. One of David's companions urges him to kill the king, but David refuses: 'The Lord forbid that I should stretch forth mine hand against ... the Lord's anointed.' David leaves, taking with him Saul's spear and water jar. When Saul wakes up, he realises that David has been magnanimous a second time, so he decides to patch up the quarrel: 'return, my son David: for I will no more do thee harm ... behold, I have played the fool, and have erred exceedingly.'

Jonathan is killed in battle, and Saul finally takes his own life, leading to David's well-known lament, 'How are the mighty fallen ... '.[18]

This story, no doubt based on real events, combines brutality and generosity in much the same way as war has done down the ages. In our day, however, we have to operate within internationally-agreed codes, and major violations of these codes may constitute war crimes. A person who commits an act which is a crime under international law is responsible therefor and liable to punishment. That is the first principle of the Nürnberg process.

NATIONAL CONSENSUS AND PERSONAL CONSCIENCE

Before the nineteenth century, those in Britain who objected on grounds of conscience to direct participation in war, or preparation for war, simply did other things. It was, in a sense, a non-issue. Britain had not been invaded for more than seven hundred years, and Britain's wars were always fought somewhere else. War was of immediate interest to a few politicians and to men in the armed forces, but its impact for ordinary people was marginal, pretty well limited to increased taxes and the occasional appearance of press gangs. Samuel Pepys, as surveyor-general of victualling, was about as close to the

Anglo-Dutch war of 1665–7 as it was possible for a civilian to be. He was, moreover, intensely inquisitive about all aspects of the conduct of war, but he never once mentions in his diary what the war was about. For civilians like Pepys, war was a calamity like the Fire of London or the Plague, something to be endured with patience and fortitude.

The War of American Independence (the American Revolution) was probably the last major war which most ordinary British people could disregard most of the time. The political objectors to the war were regarded as a nuisance by the king and his ministers, but not as traitors or cowards, and those in the armed forces who opposed the war or its methods simply asked to be assigned elsewhere.

Take the case of admiral Augustus (later Viscount) Keppel. He strongly condemned the war and so begged to be excused from serving in the Western hemisphere. He was, however, quite willing to serve with the Channel fleet against France. After an engagement near Brest in 1778, he was tried by court-martial on charges of misconduct but was acquitted. In 1782, he was appointed First Lord of the Admiralty.[19]

Or consider another military opponent of the war, Jeffrey Amherst, after whom Amherst College was named. Amherst, who became a peer in 1776, had had a distinguished military career in North America. He was a man of great humanity and probity, tolerating no graft or looting, and avoiding billeting his troops on unwelcoming households except in situations of dire emergency. He was reluctant to fight against the American colonists, and his name was considered as a possible conciliator. He declined the over-all command in North America in 1778 and was then appointed commander-in-chief in Great Britain. He was created field marshal in 1796.[20]

Other opponents of the war adopted a more surprising expedient and tried to combine high military commands with conciliation towards the American colonists. The most notable of these were the Howe brothers, Richard and William, both of whom sat in the House of Commons while continuing on active service. Richard, who became an Irish peer in 1758, was a vice-admiral at the time of the American war and commanded the fleet in North America. Sir William, who was to inherit the Irish viscountcy after Richard had been made a British peer, held the rank of lieutenant-general and was appointed commander-in-chief in North America.

The stance of the Howe brothers was that to demand the unconditional surrender of the colonists would lead to determined resistance, forcing Britain to conquer one of its own colonies and thereafter leaving the colonists sullen and ungovernable. Two British

Quakers, David Barclay and Dr John Fothergill, had already been in touch with Benjamin Franklin about a negotiated settlement, but Franklin's plan of conciliation demanded too much of Britain. Richard Howe made contact with Franklin in the hope of moderating his plan of conciliation, even raising with Franklin the possibility of a joint peace mission, while at the same time suggesting to British ministers that he be sent to America to explore a peaceful settlement. Meanwhile, his brother William was trying to secure a senior military command which would enable him to negotiate directly with the colonists.[21]

These efforts at conciliation were unavailing, and the Howe brothers were given high commands in America, where they were soon making friendly gestures and taking new peace initiatives. When general George Washington complained that American prisoners were being badly treated, William Howe let it be known that he utterly disapproved of all infringements of human rights. Richard Howe was most reluctant to enforce a coastal blockade so long as the freedom of American ships to engage in ordinary subsistence activities was not materially abused. His aim was 'to encourage and cultivate all amicable correspondence' with the colonists, and thus gain their confidence and goodwill. Both Howes took a strong stand against looting, which was a special problem with the Hessian mercenaries. The Howes also resisted attempts to organise raids on the New England coast.

The Howes made repeated attempts to negotiate with the colonists, and the politicians at home regarded them as half-hearted about prosecuting the war. King George III complained that their leniency was really cruelty, for it encouraged the colonists to keep up a hopeless struggle. In the end, Richard Howe asked to be relieved of his command and William announced that he intended to retire.

The character of warfare was to change radically in the next two centuries. Goethe dates the transition precisely as 20 September 1792. This was the date of the battle between Austria–Prussia and France at Valmy in Marne, the opening engagement of the French revolutionary wars. Goethe experienced for himself the stress of battle. At dusk, he gathered with the soldiers and, as was his custom, said something to enliven and amuse the troops.

> From this place and from this day forth commences a new era in the world's history, and you can all say that you were present at its birth.[22]

From then onwards, war in the Western world increasingly engaged whole societies and not just politicians and military professionals. With the spread of education and the introduction of democratic govern-ment, all adult citizens had views as to the justice of the wars in which their countries were engaged, and on acceptable terms for peace. Amateur strategists in pubs and wine cellars pronounced dogmatically on the conduct of military operations. Hardly a family in the belligerent countries in the first world war was untouched by death or injury. Patriotism had become a national virtue, and opposition to a particular war was ascribed to disloyalty or, for males of military age, to selfishness or cowardice.

British people of my generation were brought up to regard love of country and bravery in its defence as prime values. Patriotism was inculcated at home and school: indeed, at my school it was the supreme virtue. Armistice Day, the only weekday which was a whole holiday, was observed with great solemnity. When the king visited the school, he wore military uniform and his inspection of the Officers Training Corps (OTC) was the most important event of the day. It was compulsory for all boys to serve in the OTC, though one maverick refused on grounds of conscience. There was a large board in the school hall with the names of those masters and boys who had been killed during the first world war, under the inscription *Dulce et decorum est pro patria mori*. On one memorable Speech Day, after we had sung 'Fight the good fight', a bishop assured us that service in the armed forces was the most Christian vocation open to us, more virtuous even than becoming a schoolmaster or taking holy orders: we then sang 'Onward, Christian soldiers'. Patriotism shaded into nationalism, nationalism into chauvinism, and chauvinism into xenophobia.

British people of this sort, and doubtless their counterparts in other countries, were not brought up to love their country right or wrong, for it was taken for granted that their country would always be right, and it was inconceivable that there would ever be a contradiction between loyalty to nation and obedience to conscience. Such a conflict might arise in enemy or potential enemy countries, but not on our side. And the more democratic the system of government, the greater was the obligation to respect the national consensus.

Yet for a few people, the choice between national loyalty and obedience to conscience has been a real one, and there have always been some in the twentieth century who have refused to take a combatant role in wars they considered unjust. I do not have in mind those absolute pacifists who, for reasons of conscience, reject *all* use of armed force, whatever the consequences for themselves and others;

nor those, like Bertrand Russell, who engage in civil disobedience in order to gain publicity for minority views;[23] nor those, like some British and French fascists in the second world war, who want the enemy to win. I have in mind, rather, those who have no moral objection to the limited and discriminate use of armed force, and who desire no publicity for their own conscientious stands, and who have no particular sympathy for the enemy's society or war aims, but who become objectors or even draft dodgers because they believe that the goals or methods of their own side in a particular war are offensive to an informed conscience – those Portugese, for example, who refused to fight in colonial wars in Africa, or those non-pacifist Americans who regarded the Viet Nam war as a moral disaster, or those white South Africans who now consider that a statutory system of racial discrimination is indefensible. A few Germans, both pacifists and non-pacifists, resisted the Nazi tyranny and refused to take part in the struggle to impose it on unwilling people, but in their cases nearly always at great cost. Some, like Dietrich Bonhoeffer, are now well known: others were quiet heroes like my own father-in-law, a German Quaker, who was incarcerated in the Buchenwald concentration camp. The Nazi indictment, which we treasure in our family, stated that he had a politically negative attitude to the National Socialist state (*politisch ablehnende Haltung gegenüber dem nat. soc. Staat*), especially by his pacifist convictions and friendliness towards Jews (*seine pazifistische und judenfrendliche Haltung*).[24]

The German heroes and heroines of the resistance suffered for their convictions. We in Britain are privileged to live in a democracy, and we should not lightly decide that loyalty to personal conscience should take precedence over the obligations of citizenship, especially when the very values of democratic society are at risk. The law in Britain during the second world war provided that those who had genuine conscientious objections to military service should be granted exemption, either unconditionally or on condition of performing an alternative form of service. What more could the community be reasonably asked to do, it might be asked, to respect the consciences of those unwilling to undertake combatant service in a war against a régime which was so blatantly anti-humanitarian?

The Nürnberg Tribunal held that a person who commits a crime under international law is not relieved of responsibility by the plea that the international crime of which he is accused is not an offence under internal law, nor that he acted as head of state or responsible government official or in accordance with superior orders. These are important principles, even though the prosecutors and judges at Nürnberg were from the victors and the defendants from the vanquished. 'When I refuse to obey an unjust law,' wrote Alexis de Tocqueville, 'I do not contest the right which the majority has of commanding, but I simply appeal from the sovereignty of the people to the sovereignty of mankind.'[25]

It is evident that those preparing for or engaged in armed conflict, even in a subordinate role, now have to consult international law as well as their own consciences. Indeed, it is stipulated in the Geneva Conventions that in order to be sure of POW status if captured, combatants have to conduct military operations in accordance with the laws and customs of war.

This places a heavy responsibility on those who perform military service as well as on those who give political directions, and it is a task that has become more onerous with the invention of nuclear weapons and other weapons of mass destruction. And it is unquestionably difficult to take moral decisions in the midst of battle or when national survival is at stake: 'as anyone who has studied what actually happens on a battlefield quickly grasps, the place is in effect a moral no man's land ... '.[26]

Reinhold Niebuhr held that 'group relations can never be as ethical as those which characterise individual relations',[27] but Pope John XXIII was satisfied with no less. 'The same moral law, which governs the relations between individual human beings, serves also to regulate the relations of political Communities with one another.'[28] That is why the Martens clause places such confidence in the usages established among civilised peoples, the laws of humanity, and the dictates of the public conscience.

It has been my experience that ordinary people in Britain *do* understand that it is in normal circumstances immoral to obey an immoral command, but they consider that this right or duty should be exercised with exceptional caution after one has taken an oath of allegiance or undertaken a commitment of loyalty, and especially in time of war when national values are at stake.

All the same, people *do* consult their own consciences about the just use of force. A few members of the armed forces in the Netherlands, for example, have asked not to be assigned to tasks connected with nuclear weapons, and a few scientists and engineers have declined to work on nuclear or biological weapons for reasons of conscience. One such was Leo Szilard, who was one of the first scientists to discern the awesome moral and political implications of the atom bomb research on which he was engaged. When he learned from Niels Bohr that German scientists were working on nuclear fission, Szilard immediately set to work to see whether uranium could sustain a chain reaction. He later worked with Enrico Fermi: Fermi wanted to publicise their findings, but Szilard was opposed to this course and in the end he persuaded Einstein to write to president Roosevelt about the destructive potential of nuclear fission. In a memorandum written as early as 1942, Szilard urged that more thought should be given to 'the ultimate political necessities' which would arise from the work on the atomic bomb: 'We cannot have peace in a world in which various sovereign nations have atomic bombs in the possession of their armies ... '.[29] Szilard once told his friend Hans Bethe that he was thinking of keeping a diary: 'I don't intend to publish it; I am merely going to record the facts for the information of God.' 'Don't you think God knows the facts?' Bethe asked. 'Yes,' said Szilard. 'He knows the facts, but He does not know *this version of the facts.*' This is doubtless why the documentary record of Szilard's life is sub-titled *his version of the facts.*[30]

Michael Bess has written that Szilard 'did as much as any other single person to bring nuclear weapons into existence ... [but] he worked even harder to rid the planet of them.' Szilard realised that many scientists did not understand what would be the long-term consequences of their research. 'Well,' Robert Oppenheimer said to him one day 'this is a weapon which has no military significance. It will make a big bang – a very big bang – but it is not a weapon which is useful in war.'

In 1945, when the atom bomb had been tested but not yet used, Szilard began to organise his fellow-scientists in a movement against using the bomb. He thought a petition was unlikely to have a decisive influence on the course of events, but 'I personally feel that it would be a matter of importance if a large number of scientists who have worked in this field went clearly and unmistakably on record as to their opposition on moral grounds to the use of these bombs in the present phase of the war.' In a perceptive address a few weeks after the two bombs had been dropped on Japan, Szilard foresaw clearly the doctrine of deterrence: 'Perhaps we are resolved not to use them [nuclear weapons] but think that the mere possession of them will impress other countries ... '. But possession alone was not enough: ' ... these bombs will be of no earthly use to us unless we are actually determined to go to war if necessary.' He did not believe that a situation of mutual deterrence, in which both the United States and the Soviet Union have large stockpiles of atomic bombs, could be durable. He believed in 1945 that the only hope lay in world government, but he put the chance of achieving this at only 10 per cent. This was not a very high chance, 'but ... we have to base our thinking and acting entirely on this narrow margin of hope.'

Gradually Szilard came to understand that world government was not on the agenda, and so he switched to less ambitious goals: international control of nuclear weapons, phased disarmament, the creation of zones from which nuclear weapons or all weapons would be excluded, mutual inspection to assure compliance, a UN security force, the strengthening of international law, personal contacts among scientists. He always insisted that nuclear wars would not be limited and could not be won. A disarmed peace would undoubtedly be risky, but so was an armed peace.

Szilard started corresponding with world leaders, including Khrushchev, and he was an active though unpredictable participant in the Pugwash movement, an international effort of scientists designed to prevent nuclear war, which first met in the home of Cyrus Eaton, a wealthy businessman, in the Nova Scotian village of Pugwash. Szilard's journey, according to Michael Bess, was 'solitary and uphill', but he never wavered from his commitment to 'a continually receding ideal'. His fertile brain went on producing imaginative and novel ideas – 'a bewildering array of alternatives.' In my last conversation with him in 1959, he advanced the idea, which he admitted was 'a little fantastic', of locating the US and Soviet chiefs of staff in each other's capitals. He pointed out that civilians in cities in the two countries were already 'atom-bomb hostages', and this was supposed to exert a deterrent effect. Why not go a logical step further and locate the decision-makers from both sides in places which would inevitably be targets for their own bombs if mutual deterrence should fail? What could be more deterring than that? This was not advanced as a solution for all time, but talking about it forced people to think: he wanted to give human beings a breathing spell in which to build a saner world.

Another scientist who worked on the atom bomb in the Manhattan Project and then withdrew for conscientious reasons when he realised what was at stake was Joseph Rotblat. The discovery of the fission of uranium in 1939 was known among the international community of physicists, and Rotblat soon realised that a chain reaction would release a vast amount of energy in a short period of time, resulting in an explosion of a different order of magnitude from conventional chemical explosives. When he read in a German journal about the possibility of nuclear explosives, Rotblat found a rationale for working on nuclear weapons.

> I convinced myself that the only way to stop the Germans from using [an atomic bomb] against us would be if we too had the bomb and threatened to retaliate. My scenario never envisaged that we should use it, not even against the Germans. We needed the bomb for the sole purpose of making sure that it would not be used by them ... .

After conducting experiments which established the feasibility of the bomb, Rotblat realised that to translate a theory about a nuclear explosion into a weapon would require an enormous technological effort, and in due course he found himself in the Manhattan Project at Los Alamos.[31]

In 1944, Rotblat happened to be present at a conversation between General Leslie Groves, the director of the Manhattan Project, and Professor (later Sir) James Chadwick, a senior British scientist. Groves mentioned quite casually (and most improperly, one might add) that the real purpose of making the bomb was to 'subdue' the Soviet Union. Rotblat was shocked that a responsible American could contemplate using the atomic bomb 'against the people who were making extreme sacrifices ... ', especially 'at a time when thousands of Russians were dying every day on the Eastern Front'.

When Rotblat heard at the end of 1944 that the Germans had abandoned their atom bomb research, he left the Manhattan Project and spent the rest of his career working in medical physics. He was one of the founders of the Pugwash movement, was for many years its secretary-general, and is now chairman of the British group.

Rotblat has reviewed the motives of those who have worked on nuclear weapons. For some, it was primarily a matter of ending the war quickly and so saving allied lives. Others thought that work on weapons would advance their careers. For others, it was pure and simple scientific curiosity. Rotblat himself is not an absolute pacifist, but he told me recently that he regards scientific work on weapons of mass destruction as an abuse of professional integrity.

Consider also the case of William Douglas Home, playwright and brother of Lord Home of the Hirsel. Home was not an absolute pacifist, so that when he was called up for military service in 1940, he wrote to the Labour Exchange to say that, as no tribunal would exempt him from military service, he was prepared to be conscripted.

> I did not feel able to claim 'religious' objection (though my estimate of the Gospels inevitably led me towards such a state of mind)

because, rightly or wrongly, I assumed that if a man is to be a religious objector to war, he must be a good man, in the sense that he keeps all the commandments ... .

Not surprisingly, the Labour Exchange had more pressing tasks than to reply to this letter. When Home was selected for training as an officer, he told the colonel that he had political reservations about the war because of the absence of peace aims. 'Oh, to hell with politics!' the colonel replied. 'You're in the Army now, you bloody fool.' Home noted that few people were touched with doubt, so that the story of his military life would make many people sick.

In the first place, they will not tolerate the thought that any man has the right to think for himself when his country is at war. Secondly, they will assert that, even if he does have disquieting thoughts, he should keep them to himself.

Lord Home thought that his brother William was 'a genuine conscientious objector'.[32]

Home served as an officer in a tank regiment until the evening before an assault on Le Havre, when the colonel wanted to appoint him as liaison officer. The German general had asked to be allowed to evacuate civilians, and Home considered that the request should have been met.

I knew, as I had known at other times since 1939, that I must voice my protest or else curse myself for evermore ... . Faced with what I conceived to be an immoral order, I must either obey it and abandon what I had conceived to be the humanitarian fight that I had waged so long ... or I must disobey it and face the unknown fate that would be mine.

The following dialogue ensued.

'No', I said.
'Do what you're told, Home.'
'No', I said again.
'Why not?' he asked me, angrily.
'Because we haven't let out the civilians.'
'That's no concern of yours.'
'I disagree.'
...
'All right, Home. Go and look after the transport.'
'No sir, I'm afraid not. I'm not taking part at all.'

Home was court-martialled ('they could do nothing else', he wrote to his parents), was cashiered and sentenced to one year's hard labour, which he served (no doubt with remission) in Wormwood Scrubs and then at Wakefield. 'I was a prisoner – a tired, confused, bewildered prisoner, but, for the first time in the war, I had a conscience clear as day.' He found that Wormwood Scrubs shared, to an almost unbearable degree, 'the cold impersonal austerity of any public lavatory'. Anyone who wishes to gain some idea of the adverse effect which prison *décor* has on the morale of prisoners, he wrote, should spend a couple of hours contemplating the 'chilly, shiny, dampish interior of such an architectural abortion as the gentlemen's lavatory in Piccadilly Circus'. When his parents visited him in prison, his father, invariably courteous, made a point of going to the governor's house to thank him for his hospitality to their son.

A second example is even more surprising, for it concerns a simple peasant on the other side, Franz Jägerstätter.

Jägerstätter was born out of wedlock in the remote Austrian village of St Radegund in 1907. He had a normal Catholic upbringing in a peasant family, though as a youth he was said to have been rather wild. He considered joining a religious order, but the village priest advised against this. In 1936 he married a woman from a nearby village, and they spent their honeymoon in Rome. About this time, he seems to have had a deep religious experience. He worshipped regularly at the village church, receiving the sacrament daily, and he served as sexton. The Jägerstätters had three daughters.[33]

Jägerstätter belonged to no political organisation, but he had a fundamental moral objection to the Nazi ideology and was the only man in St Radegund to vote against the Anschluss in 1938. He refused all government hand-outs because he considered the source tainted. He was called up for military service in February 1943, but was determined not to fight for the Nazi régime. He was imprisoned, first in Linz and then in Berlin, and was beheaded on 9 August 1943. He was 36 years old. The prison chaplain arranged for his body to be cremated, but the ashes were given a ceremonial burial in St Radegund after the war.

Jägerstätter reached a kind of pacifist position entirely on his own. He was a 'simple, untutored peasant' from 'a remote and isolated rural village'. He was highly respected by the village priest, but all the clergy with whom he came in contact advised him against going through with his conscientious objection to fighting for the Nazi régime, as did his defence lawyer. The prison chaplain told him that, as a private citizen, he had no responsibility for the acts and policies of the government. All of his spiritual counsellors

> advised him that the order of priority, as far as his personal obligations and responsibilities were concerned, began with his duties as husband and father and loyal citizen; that he had neither the competence, the information, nor the right to challenge the secular ruler as to the justice or injustice of the war in which he had been ordered to serve.

At one stage, Jägerstätter toyed with the idea of performing non-combatant service in a medical unit but finally decided against this. His lawyer assured him that he would never be called on to bear arms if he would withdraw his refusal to serve, but he was unshakable.

All who met Jägerstätter were impressed with his firm Christian commitment and his mental balance. One commented that he was 'clear and logical in his arguments ... '. 'I definitely prefer to relinquish my rights under the Third Reich [wrote Jägerstätter] and thus make sure of deserving the rights granted under the Kingdom of God.' Christians are to obey secular rulers, he wrote, but only to the extent that they do not order us to do evil, for we must obey God rather than men. 'I do not believe that Christ ever said that one must obey ... rulers when they command something that is actually wicked.' He preferred to do his fighting with the word of God and not with arms in an unjust war. Is it not more Christian, he asked, to offer oneself as a victim rather than to commit murder, to kill those who want to live and have a right to live?

He was careful not to criticise the bishops and priests for thinking differently: 'They, too, are men like us, made of flesh and blood ... much more sorely tempted by the evil enemy than the rest of us.' Maybe they had been too poorly prepared to take up this struggle between life and death. 'This is why we should not make it harder for our spiritual leaders ... by making accusations against them. Let us pray for them instead ... '.

When the village came to erect a war memorial after the war, Jägerstätter's name was included under a special inscription, *seinem Gewissen folgend*, in obedience to conscience.

Appendices

1. JUDGMENT OF THE NÜRNBERG TRIBUNAL, 1946

(a) crimes against peace

In the opinion of the Tribunal, the solemn renunciation of war as an instrument of national policy necessarily involves the proposition that such a war is illegal in international law; and that those who plan and wage such a war, with its inevitable and terrible consequences, are committing a crime in so doing. War for the solution of international controversies undertaken as an instrument of national policy certainly includes a war of aggression, and such a war is therefore outlawed by the Pact [of Paris of 1928] ...

(b) war crimes

In the opinion of the Tribunal the rules of land warfare expressed in the [Hague] Convention [of 1907 on land warfare] undoubtedly represented an advance over existing international law at the time of their adoption. But the convention expressly stated that it was an attempt 'to revise the general laws and customs of war', which it thus recognized to be then existing, but by 1939 these rules laid down in the Convention were recognized by all civilized nations, and were regarded as being declaratory of the laws and customs of war ...

2. ESSENTIALS OF PEACE (GA RES. 290, 1949)

The General Assembly ...
Calls upon every nation:
2. *To refrain* from threatening or using force contrary to the Charter;
3. *To refrain* from any threats or acts, direct or indirect, aimed at impairing the freedom, independence or integrity of any State, or at fomenting civil strife and subverting the will of the people in any State ...

3. PEACE THROUGH DEEDS (GA RES. 380, 1950)

The General Assembly ...
Solemnly reaffirms that, whatever the weapons used, any aggression, whether committed openly, or by fomenting civil strife in the interest of a foreign Power, or otherwise, is the gravest of all crimes against peace and security throughout the world ...

4. USE OF NUCLEAR AND THERMONUCLEAR WEAPONS (GA RES. 1653, 1961)

The General Assembly,
...

Gravely concerned that, while negotiations on disarmament have not so far achieved satisfactory results, the armaments race, particularly in the nuclear and thermo-nuclear fields, has reached a dangerous stage requiring all possible precautionary measures to protect humanity and civilization from the hazard of nuclear and thermo-nuclear catastrophe,

Recalling that the use of weapons of mass destruction, causing unnecessary human suffering, was in the past prohibited, as being contrary to the laws of humanity and to the principles of international law, by international declarations and binding agreements, such as the Declaration of St. Petersburg of 1868, the Declaration of the Brussels Conference of 1874, the Conventions of The Hague Peace Conferences of 1899 and 1907, and the Geneva Protocol of 1925, to which the majority of nations are still parties,

Considering that the use of nuclear and thermo-nuclear weapons would bring about indiscriminate suffering and destruction to mankind and civilization to an even greater extent than the use of those weapons declared by the aforementioned international declarations and agreements to be contrary to the laws of humanity and a crime under international law,

Believing that the use of weapons of mass destruction, such as nuclear and thermo-nuclear weapons, is a direct negation of the high ideals and objectives which the United Nations has been established to achieve through the protection of succeeding generations from the scourge of war and through the preservation and promotion of their cultures,

1. *Declares* that:
(*a*) The use of nuclear and thermo-nuclear weapons is contrary to the spirit, letter and aims of the United Nations and, as such, a direct violation of the Charter of the United Nations;
(*b*) The use of nuclear and thermo-nuclear weapons would exceed even the scope of war and cause indiscriminate suffering and destruction to mankind and civilization and, as such, is contrary to the rules of international law and to the laws of humanity;
(*c*) The use of nuclear and thermo-nuclear weapons is a war directed not against an enemy or enemies alone but also against mankind in general, since the peoples of the world not involved in such a war will be subjected to all the evils generated by the use of such weapons;
(*d*) Any State using nuclear and thermo-nuclear weapons is to be considered as violating the Charter of the United Nations, as acting contrary to the laws of humanity and as committing a crime against mankind and civilization;
...

5. INTERVENTION IN DOMESTIC AFFAIRS (GA RES. 2131, 1965)
...

1. No State has the right to intervene, directly or indirectly, for any reason whatever, in the internal or external affairs of any other State. Consequently,

armed intervention and all other forms of interference or attempted threats against the personality of the State or against its political, economic and cultural elements, are condemned.

2. No State may use or encourage the use of economic, political or any other type of measures to coerce another State in order to obtain from it the subordination of the exercise of its sovereign rights or to secure from it advantages of any kind. Also, no State shall organize, assist, foment, finance, incite or tolerate subversive, terrorist or armed activities directed towards the violent overthrow of the régime of another State, or interfere in civil strife in another State.

3. The use of force to deprive peoples of their national identity constitutes a violation of their inalienable rights and of the principle of non-intervention.
...

6. THREAT OR USE OF FORCE (GA RES. 2160, 1966)

The General Assembly ... Reaffirms, that:
(a) States shall strictly observe, in their international relations, the prohibition of the threat or use of force against the territorial integrity or political independence of any State, or in any other manner inconsistent with the purposes of the United Nations. Accordingly, armed attack by one State against another or the use of force in any other form contrary to the Charter of the United Nations constitutes a violation of international law giving rise to international responsibility;

(b) Any forcible action, direct or indirect, which deprives peoples under foreign domination of their right to self-determination and freedom and independence and of their right to determine freely their political status and pursue their economic, social and cultural development constitutes a violation of the Charter of the United Nations. Accordingly, the use of force to deprive peoples of their national identity ... constitutes a violation of their inalienable rights and of the principle of non-intervention;
...

7. USE OF CHEMICAL AND BACTERIOLOGICAL WEAPONS (GA RES. 2162B, 1966)

The General Assembly,
Guided by the principles of the Charter of the United Nations and of international law,

Considering that weapons of mass destruction constitute a danger to all mankind and are incompatible with the accepted norms of civilization,

Affirming that the strict observance of the rules of international law on the conduct of warfare is in the interest of maintaining these standards of civilization,

Recalling that the Geneva Protocol for the Prohibition of the Use in War of Asphyxiating, Poisonous or Other Gases, and of Bacteriological Methods of

Warfare, of 17 June 1925, has been signed and adopted and is recognized by
many States,
...

1. *Calls for* strict observance by all States of the principles and objectives of
the Protocol for the Prohibition of the Use in War of Asphyxiating, Poisonous
or Other Gases, and of Bacteriological Methods of Warfare, signed at Geneva
on 17 June 1925, and condemns all actions contrary to those objectives;
2. *Invites* all States to accede to the Geneva Protocol of 17 June 1925.

8. THREAT OR USE OF FORCE (GA RES. 2625, 1970)

...

Every State has the duty to refrain in its international relations from the
threat or use of force against the territorial integrity or political independence
of any State, or in any other manner inconsistent with the purposes of the
United Nations. Such a threat or use of force constitutes a violation of
international law and the Charter of the United Nations and shall never be
employed as a means of settling international issues.

A war of aggression constitutes a crime against the peace, for which there is
responsibility under international law.

In accordance with the purposes and principles of the United Nations,
States have the duty to refrain from propaganda for wars of aggression.

Every State has the duty to refrain from the threat or use of force to violate
the existing international boundaries of another State or as a means of solving
international disputes, including territorial disputes and problems concerning
frontiers of States.

Every State likewise has the duty to refrain from the threat or use of force to
violate international lines of demarcation, such as armistice lines, established
by or pursuant to an international agreement to which it is a party or which it is
otherwise bound to respect. Nothing in the foregoing shall be construed as
prejudicing the positions of the parties concerned with regard to the status and
effects of such lines under their special régimes or as affecting their
temporary character.

States have a duty to refrain from acts of reprisal involving the use of force.

Every State has the duty to refrain from any forcible action which deprives
peoples referred to in the elaboration of the principle of equal rights and
self-determination of their right to self-determination and freedom and
independence.

Every State has the duty to refrain from organizing or encouraging the
organization of irregular forces or armed bands, including mercenaries, for
incursion into the territory of another State.

Every State has the duty to refrain from organizing, instigating, assisting or
participating in acts of civil strife or terrorist acts in another State or
acquiescing in organized activities within its territory directed towards the
commission of such acts, when the acts referred to in the present paragraph
involve a threat or use of force.

The territory of a State shall not be the object of military occupation
resulting from the use of force in contravention of the provisions of the
Charter. The territory of a State shall not be the object of acquisition by

another State resulting from the threat or use of force. No territorial acquisition resulting from the threat or use of force shall be recognized as legal. Nothing in the foregoing shall be construed as affecting:

(a) Provisions of the Charter or any international agreement prior to the Charter régime and valid under international law; or

(b) The powers of the Security Council under the Charter.

All States shall pursue in good faith negotiations for the early conclusion of a universal treaty on general and complete disarmament under effective international control and strive to adopt appropriate measures to reduce international tensions and strengthen confidence among States.

All States shall comply in good faith with their obligations under the generally recognized principles and rules of international law with respect to the maintenance of international peace and security, and shall endeavour to make the United Nations security system based upon the Charter more effective.

Nothing in the foregoing paragraphs shall be construed as enlarging or diminishing in any way the scope of the provisions of the Charter concerning cases in which the use of force is lawful.

9. BASIC PRINCIPLES FOR THE PROTECTION OF CIVILIANS (GA RES. 2675, 1970)

1. Fundamental human rights, as accepted in international law and laid down in international instruments, continue to apply fully in situations of armed conflict.

2. In the conduct of military operations during armed conflicts, a distinction must be made at all times between persons actively taking part in the hostilities and civilian populations.

3. In the conduct of military operations, every effort should be made to spare civilian populations from the ravages of war, and all necessary precautions should be taken to avoid injury, loss or damage to civilian populations.

4. Civilian populations as such should not be the object of military operations.

5. Dwellings and other installations that are used only by civilian populations should not be the object of military operations.

6. Places or areas designated for the sole protection of civilians, such as hospital zones or similar refuges, should not be the object of military operations.

7. Civilian populations, or individual members thereof, should not be the object of reprisals, forcible transfers or other assaults on their integrity.

8. The provision of international relief to civilian populations is in conformity with the humanitarian principles of the Charter of the United Nations, the Universal Declaration of Human Rights and other international instruments in the field of human rights ...

10. INTERNATIONAL SECURITY (GA RES. 2734, 1970)

The General Assembly,

Solemnly reaffirms that every State has the duty to refrain from the threat or use of force against the territorial integrity and political independence of any other State, and that the territory of a State shall not be the object of military occupation resulting from the use of force in contravention of the provisions of the Charter, that the territory of a State shall not be the object of acquisition by another State resulting from the threat or use of force, that no territorial acquisition resulting from the threat or use of force shall be recognized as legal and that every State has the duty to refrain from organizing, instigating, assisting or participating in acts of civil strife or terrorist acts in another State ...

11. THREAT OR USE OF FORCE (GA RES. 2936, 1972)

The General Assembly,
...
Noting with concern that the use of force in various forms is still occurring in violation of the Charter,

Bearing in mind that the threat of the use of nuclear weapons continues to exist,

Guided by the desire of all peoples to eliminate war and above all to prevent a nuclear disaster,

Reaffirming, in accordance with Article 51 of the Charter, the inalienable right of States to self-defence against armed attack,

Mindful of the principle of the inadmissibility of acquisition of territory by force and the inherent right of States to recover such territories by all the means at their disposal,

Reaffirming its recognition of the legitimacy of the struggle of colonial peoples for their freedom by all appropriate means at their disposal,
...
Believing that renunciation of the use or threat of force and prohibition of the use of nuclear weapons should be fully observed as a law of international life,

1. *Solemnly declares*, on behalf of the States Members of the Organization, their renunciation of the use or threat of force in all its forms and manifestations in international relations, in accordance with the Charter of the United Nations, and the permanent prohibition of the use of nuclear weapons;
...

12. MEMORANDUM ON INCENDIARY WEAPONS, 11 JULY 1973

1. The UN report on 'Napalm and other incendiary weapons and all aspects of their possible use' (A/8803) was produced by a group of government experts. It surveys the development of incendiary weapons, from the dreaded Greek Fire reported by the Crusaders to the relatively unreliable battlefield weapons of the first world war, and up to modern incendiary weapons which

are highly effective for incapacitating enemy personnel and as area weapons. Estimates of the relative effectiveness of incendiary weapons compared with other weapons are largely based on experience during the second world war.

2. The UN experts make three points about the medical effects of incendiaries. First, these weapons cause especially intense pain. Secondly, there is a high death rate among casualties. Thirdly, casualties from developing countries suffer more than those from developed countries because of shortage of medical facilities, widespread malnutrition, chronic anaemias, and other deficiencies.

3. The experts point out that weapons containing napalm or phosphorus differ from other incendiaries in that particles of these agents adhere to surfaces while burning. The use of napalm and phosphorus incendiary weapons against personnel is thus likely to violate the ban on 'unnecessary suffering' contained in Art. 23(e) of the Regulations attached to the Hague Convention of 1907, which is now part of general international law.

4. There are three theoretical routes to possible limitation or prohibition: via the Law of the Hague, which governs the conduct of military operations; via the Law of Geneva (the Red Cross conventions), which is designed to secure humanitarian protection of those taking no direct part in the fighting; or by an arms control agreement.

5. The last comprehensive revision of the Hague Law was in 1907. If it is to have real value, it obviously must be brought up to date; but it is not at present a realistic route.

6. The two more promising possibilities are through the arms control machinery of the UN, or at the Diplomatic Conference to review the Red Cross conventions, due to meet in Switzerland in 1974.

7. Deliberate and direct attacks on non-combatants with *any* weapons are contrary to international law. This law has often been flouted, but the violator never questions the law; he justifies his violation by reference to a prior illegality by the enemy or some similar reasoning. The law on this point has been reaffirmed recently by the General Assembly and the International Red Cross Conference. It is a finely balanced question whether the rule of 'no deliberate and direct attacks on non-combatants' would be strengthened or weakened by its reaffirmation in an international agreement dealing only with incendiary weapons.

8. An international agreement designed to prevent 'unnecessary suffering' to combatants would deal primarily with incendiary weapons containing napalm or phosphorus. The question would then arise: are there adequate means to deter violations?

9. The main deterrent against violations of the Geneva Protocol's ban on using chemical weapons in war is the threat of reprisals. No system of ensuring compliance with arms control agreements can be entirely foolproof, but the international community can probably do better now than it did in 1925.

(i)   The parties to a ban on using those incendiary weapons defined in the agreement could be required to incorporate a standard form of wording into their manuals of military law.

(ii) Any agreement could reaffirm the Nürnberg principle that individual violators are responsible for their own acts and that the plea of 'superior orders' is no defence. Violators would be liable for prosecution as war criminals, preferably before an international criminal court.

(iii) Major violations would almost certainly be publicized through the mass media and would expose the violator to the condemnation of world opinion. In addition, there could be a complaints procedure similar to that contained in Article VI of the recent Biological Weapons Convention.
(iv) The ultimate deterrent would presumably be the threat of reprisal action. This would have to be subject to strict safeguards, laid down in the agreement. For example:
(a) Only properly authorized persons may decide to resort to reprisals;
(b) Such resort may only be in response to an enemy violation, and should be officially and publicly announced as such;
(c) The reprisal should be proportionate to the violation, and should cease when the violation stops.
10. I conclude with three points. First, an international ban on the more horrific uses of incendiary weapons is desirable on humanitarian grounds. Secondly, such a ban, while difficult to achieve, is within the realms of possibility. Thirdly, the present time of no major conflict is unusually propitious to conclude such an agreement.

S. D. B.

13. DEFINITION OF AGGRESSION (GA RES. 3314, 1974)

The General Assembly,
Basing itself on the fact that one of the fundamental purposes of the United Nations is to maintain international peace and security and to take effective collective measures for the prevention and removal of threats to the peace, and for the suppression of acts of aggression or other breaches of the peace,
Recalling that the Security Council, in accordance with Article 39 of the Charter of the United Nations, shall determine the existence of any threat to the peace, breach of the peace or act of aggression and shall make recommendations, or decide what measures shall be taken in accordance with Articles 41 and 42, to maintain or restore international peace and security.
Recalling also the duty of States under the Charter to settle their international disputes by peaceful means in order not to endanger international peace, security and justice,
Bearing in mind that nothing in this Definition shall be interpreted as in any way affecting the scope of the provisions of the Charter with respect to the functions and powers of the organs of the United Nations,
Considering also that, since aggression is the most serious and dangerous form of the illegal use of force, being fraught, in the conditions created by the existence of all types of weapons of mass destruction, with the possible threat of a world conflict and all its catastrophic consequences, aggression should be defined at the present stage,
Reaffirming the duty of States not to use armed force to deprive peoples of their right to self-determination, freedom and independence, or to disrupt territorial integrity,
Reaffirming also that the territory of a State shall not be violated by being the object, even temporarily, of military occupation or of other measures of force taken by another State in contravention of the Charter, and that it shall

not be the object of acquisition by another State resulting from such measures or the threat thereof,

...

Convinced that the adoption of a definition of aggression ought to have the effect of deterring a potential aggressor, would simplify the determination of acts of aggression and the implementation of measures to suppress them and would also facilitate the protection of the rights and lawful interests of, and the rendering of assistance to, the victim,

Believing that, although the question whether an act of aggression has been committed must be considered in the light of all the circumstances of each particular case, it is nevertheless desirable to formulate basic principles as guidance for such determination,

Adopts the following Definition of Aggression:

Article 1

Aggression is the use of armed force by a State against the sovereignty, territorial integrity or political independence of another State, or in any other manner inconsistent with the Charter of the United Nations, as set out in this Definition.

Explanatory note: In this Definition the term 'State':

(*a*) Is used without prejudice to questions of recognition or to whether a State is a member of the United Nations;

(*b*) Includes the concept of a 'group of States' where appropriate.

Article 2

The first use of armed force by a State in contravention of the Charter shall constitute *prima facie* evidence of an act of aggression although the Security Council may, in conformity with the Charter, conclude that a determination that an act of aggression has been committed would not be justified in the light of other relevant circumstances, including the fact that the acts concerned or their consequences are not of sufficient gravity.

Article 3

Any of the following acts, regardless of a declaration of war, shall, subject to and in accordance with the provisions of article 2, qualify as an act of aggression:

(*a*) The invasion or attack by the armed forces of a State of the territory of another State, or any military occupation, however temporary, resulting from such invasion or attack, or any annexation by the use of force of the territory of another State or part thereof;

(*b*) Bombardment by the armed forces of a State against the territory of another State or the use of any weapons by a State against the territory of another State;

(*c*) The blockade of the ports or coasts of a State by the armed forces of another State;

(*d*) An attack by the armed forces of a State on the land, sea or air forces, or marine and air fleets of another State;

(*e*) The use of armed forces of one State which are within the territory of another State with the agreement of the receiving State, in contravention of the conditions provided for in the agreement or any extension of their presence in such territory beyond the termination of the agreement;

(*f*) The action of a State in allowing its territory, which it has placed at the disposal of another State, to be used by that other State for perpetrating an act of aggression against a third State;

(g) The sending by or on behalf of a State of armed bands, groups, irregulars or mercenaries, which carry out acts of armed force against another State of such gravity as to amount to the acts listed above, or its substantial involvement therein.

Article 4

The acts enumerated above are not exhaustive and the Security Council may determine that other acts constitute aggression under the provisions of the Charter.

Article 5

1. No consideration of whatever nature, whether political, economic, military or otherwise, may serve as a justification for aggression.

2. A war of aggression is a crime against international peace. Aggression gives rise to international responsibility.

3. No territorial acquisition or special advantage resulting from aggression is or shall be recognized as lawful.

Article 6

Nothing in this Definition shall be construed as in any way enlarging or diminishing the scope of the Charter, including its provisions concerning cases in which the use of force is lawful.

Article 7

Nothing in this Definition, and in particular article 3, could in any way prejudice the right to self-determination, freedom and independence, as derived from the Charter, of peoples forcibly deprived of that right and referred to in the Declaration on Principles of International Law concerning Friendly Relations and Co-operation among States in accordance with the Charter of the United Nations, particularly peoples under colonial and racist régimes or other forms of alien domination; nor the right of these peoples to struggle to that end and to seek and receive support, in accordance with the principles of the Charter and in conformity with the above-mentioned Declaration.

Article 8

In their interpretation and application the above provisions are interrelated and each provision should be construed in the context of the other provisions.

14. PROTECTION OF WOMEN AND CHILDREN IN ARMED CONFLICTS (GA RES. 3318, 1974)

1. Attacks and bombings on the civilian population, inflicting incalculable suffering, especially on women and children, who are the most vulnerable members of the population, shall be prohibited, and such acts shall be condemned.

2. The use of chemical and bacteriological weapons in the course of military operations constitutes one of the most flagrant violations of the Geneva Protocol of 1925, the Geneva Conventions of 1949 and the principles of international humanitarian law and inflict heavy losses on

civilian populations, including defenceless women and children, and shall be severely condemned.

All States shall abide fully by their obligations under the Geneva Protocol of 1925 and the Geneva Conventions of 1949, as well as other instruments of international law relative to respect for human rights in armed conflicts, which offer important guarantees for the protection of women and children.

4. All efforts shall be made by States involved in armed conflicts, military operations in foreign territories and in territories still under colonial domination to spare women and children from the ravages of war. All the necessary steps shall be taken to ensure the prohibition of measures such as persecution, torture, punitive measures, degrading treatment and violence, particularly against that part of the civilian population that consists of women and children.

5. All forms of repression and cruel and inhuman treatment of women and children, including imprisonment, torture, shooting, mass arrests, collective punishment, destruction of dwellings and forcible eviction, committed by belligerents in the course of military operations or in occupied territories shall be considered criminal.

6. Women and children belonging to the civilian population and finding themselves in circumstances of emergency and armed conflict in the struggle for peace, self-determination, national liberation and independence, or who live in occupied territories, shall not be deprived of shelter, food, medical aid or other inalienable rights, in accordance with the provisions of the Universal Declaration of Human Rights, the International Covenant on Civil and Political Rights, the International Covenant on Economic, Social and Cultural Rights, the Declaration of the Rights of the Child or other instruments of international law.

15. DOCUMENTS ISSUED BY THE ICRC, 1978

(a) Fundamental rules of international humanitarian law

1. Persons *hors de combat* and those who do not take a direct part in hostilities are entitled to respect for their lives and physical and moral integrity. They shall in all circumstances be protected and treated humanely without any adverse distinction.

2. It is forbidden to kill or injure an enemy who surrenders or who is *hors de combat*.

3. The wounded and sick shall be collected and cared for by the party to the conflict which has them in its power. Protection also covers medical personnel, establishments, transports and *matériel*. The emblem of the red cross (red crescent) is the sign of such protection and must be respected.

4. Captured combatants and civilians under the authority of an adverse party are entitled to respect for their lives, dignity, personal rights and convictions. They shall be protected against all acts of violence and reprisals. They shall have the right to correspond with their families and to receive relief.

5. Everyone shall be entitled to benefit from fundamental judicial guarantees. No one shall be held responsible for an act he has not committed. No one

shall be subjected to physical or mental torture, corporal punishment or cruel or degrading treatment.

6. Parties to a conflict and members of their armed forces do not have an unlimited choice of methods and means of warfare. It is prohibited to employ weapons or methods of warfare of a nature to cause unnecessary losses or excessive suffering.

7. Parties to a conflict shall at all times distinguish between the civilian population and combatants in order to spare civilian population and property. Neither the civilian population as such nor civilian persons shall be the object of attack. Attacks shall be directed solely against military objectives.

(b) The soldier's rules

1. Be a disciplined soldier. Disobedience of the laws of war dishonours your army and yourself and causes unnecessary suffering; far from weakening the enemy's will to fight, it often strengthens it.
2. Fight only enemy combatants and attack only military objectives.
3. Destroy no more than your mission requires.
4. Do not fight enemies who are *hors de combat* or who surrender. Disarm them and hand them over to your superior.
5. Collect and care for the wounded and sick, be they friend or foe.
6. Treat all civilians and all enemies in your power with humanity.
7. Prisoners of war must be treated humanely and are bound to give only information about their identity. No physical or mental torture of prisoners of war is permitted.
8. Do not take hostages.
9. Abstain from all acts of vengeance.
10. Respect all persons and objects bearing the emblem of the Red Cross, Red Crescent, Red Lion-and-Sun, the white flag of truce or emblems designating cultural property.
11. Respect other people's property. Looting is prohibited.
12. Endeavour to prevent any breach of the above rules. Report any violation to your superior. Any breach of the laws of war is punishable.

16. NUCLEAR WEAPONS (COMMENT OF THE HUMAN RIGHTS COMMITTEE, 1984)

1. In its general comment 6(16) adopted at its 378th meeting, on 27 July 1982, the Human Rights Committee observed that the right to life enunciated in the first paragraph of article 6 of the International Covenant on Civil and Political Rights is the supreme right from which no derogation is permitted even in time of public emergency. The same right to life is enshrined in article 3 of the Universal Declaration of Human Rights adopted by the General Assembly of the United Nations on 10 December 1948. It is basic to all human rights.

2. In its previous general comment, the Committee also observed that it is

the supreme duty of States to prevent wars. War and other acts of mass violence continue to be a scourge of humanity and take the lives of thousands of innocent human beings every year.

3. While remaining deeply concerned by the toll of human life taken by conventional weapons in armed conflicts, the Committee has noted that, during successive sessions of the General Assembly, representatives from all geographical regions have expressed their growing concern at the development and proliferation of increasingly awesome weapons of mass destruction, which not only threaten human life but also absorb resources that could otherwise be used for vital economic and social purposes, particularly for the benefit of developing countries, and thereby for promoting and securing the enjoyment of human rights for all.

4. The Committee associates itself with this concern. It is evident that the designing, testing, manufacture, possession and deployment of nuclear weapons are among the greatest threats to the right to life which confront mankind today. This threat is compounded by the danger that the actual use of such weapons may be brought about, not only in the event of war, but even through human or mechanical error or failure.

5. Furthermore, the very existence and gravity of this threat generate a climate of suspicion and fear between States, which is in itself antagonistic to the promotion of universal respect for and observance of human rights and fundamental freedoms in accordance with the Charter of the United Nations and the International Covenants on Human Rights.

6. The production, testing, possession, deployment and use of nuclear weapons should be prohibited and recognized as crimes against humanity.

7. The Committee accordingly, in the interest of mankind, calls upon all States, whether Parties to the Covenant or not, to take urgent steps, unilaterally and by agreement, to rid the world of this menace.

Notes and References

INTRODUCTION

1. Carl H. Builder and Morlie H. Graubard, *The International Law of Armed Conflict: Implications for the Concept of Assured Destruction* (Rand Corp., ref. R-2804-FF, 1982) pp. iii, v, vii, ix, x, 40, 47–8; see also Arthur Selwyn Miller and Martin Feinrider (eds), *Nuclear Weapons and Law* (Westport and London: Greenwood, 1984).
2. St Petersburg Declaration; Hague Regulations of 1899 and 1907, Art. 23(g).
3. Preamble to the Hague Conventions; Nürnberg Charter, Art. 6(b); First Geneva Convention, Art. 50; Second Geneva Convention, Art. 51; Fourth Geneva Convention, Art. 147; Hague Convention on Cultural Property, Art. 4(2).
4. First Geneva Convention, Art. 8; Second Geneva Convention, Arts 8, 28; Third Geneva Convention, Art. 126; Fourth Geneva Convention, Arts 53, 143; Hague Convention on Cultural Property, Art. 11(2); Additional Protocol I, Arts 54(5), 62(1), 67(4), 71(3); Additional Protocol II, Art. 17(1).
5. Preamble to the Hague Conventions.
6. Ibid.; First Geneva Convention, Art. 63; Second Geneva Convention, Art. 62; Third Geneva Convention, Art. 142; Fourth Geneva Convention, Art. 158; Additional Protocol I, Art. 1(2); Additional Protocol II, Preamble; Convention on indiscriminate or excessively injurious weapons, Preamble.

1. THE JUST WAR IN CHRISTIAN ETHICS

1. C. John Cadoux, *The early Christian attitude to war* (London: Headley Bros, 1919) pp. 149–54.
2. F. Homes Dudden, *Life and Times of St Ambrose* (Oxford: Clarendon Press, 1935) pp. 497, 499.
3. *Summa Theologica, II/II*, Question 40, art. 1.
4. Ibid., Question 64, art. 7.
5. James Finn (ed.), *Protest: Pacificism and Politics* (New York: Council on Religion and International Affairs, 1968) p. 421.
6. Vitoria's *De Indis et de iure belli relectiones*, section 37, English translation by J. P. Bate, edited by E. Nys (Carnegie Endowment for International Peace, 1917) p. 179 of the English translation.
7. William V. O'Brien, *Nuclear War, Deterrence and Morality* (New York: Newman Press, 1967) pp. 31, 57, 81–3, 85; Richard Shelly Hartigan, 'Noncombatant Immunity: Reflections on its Origins and Present Status', *Review of Politics*, 29, 2 (April 1967) pp. 204–20; see also Hartigan's articles 'Saint Augustine on War and Killing: the Problem of the

Innocent', *Journal of Historical Ideas*, XXVII, 2 (April–June 1966) pp. 195–204, and 'Noncombatant Immunity: its Scope and Development', *Continuum*, II, 3 (Autumn 1965) pp. 300–14.

8. Walter M. Abbott (ed.), *Documents of Vatican II* (New York: America Press, 1966) 'Pastoral Constitution of the Church in the Modern World' (*Gaudium et Spes*) art. 80 (p. 294).

9. See my article 'Some reflexions on the use of force', *Friends Quarterly*, 16, 6 (April 1969) p. 261.

10. Ronald C. D. Jasper, *George Bell, Bishop of Chichester* (Oxford: Oxford University Press, 1967) pp. 261–4, 276–9. Harold Nicolson was so outraged when a cleric claimed that the bombing of Cologne was a Christian act that he wrote in his diary: 'I wish the clergy would keep their mouths shut about the war. It is none of their business' (11 June 1942).

11. See his seminal article 'The morality of obliteration bombing', *Theological Studies* V, 3 (September 1944) pp. 261–309.

12. Paul Ramsey, *War and the Christian Conscience: how shall modern war be conducted justly?* (Durham, N. C.: Duke University Press, 1961; paperback edn, 1970).

13. 'Christian Churches and Nuclear Weapons', *Disarmament: a periodic review by the United Nations*, VI, 3 (Autumn/Winter 1983) pp. 8–17.

14. *The Church and the Bomb* (London: Hodder & Stoughton, 1985); 'How we wrote "The Church and the Bomb"', *Crucible*, 22nd year (October–December 1983) pp. 177–84; 'Myths about "The Church and the Bomb"', *Friends Quarterly*, 23, 3 (July 1983) pp. 150–7.

15. The text of the letter was first published in Washington, D.C., in *Origins*, 13, 1 (May 1983). The British edition, published by the Catholic Truth Society and SPCK in 1983, has numbered paragraphs and I have quoted from this version.

16. *The era of atomic power* (London: SCM Press, 1946) p. 50.

17. *The Collected essays, journalism and letters of George Orwell*, II, *My Country, Right or Left, 1940–1943*, edited by Sonia Orwell and Ian Angus (Harmondsworth: Penguin Books, in association with Secker & Warburg, 1970) p. 437.

18. 'Thoughts on Hunger Strikes', *New Blackfriars*, 62, 733–4 (July–August 1981) p. 307.

2. THE JUST WAR IN INTERNATIONAL LAW

1. An English translation by F. W. Kelsey and others was published in 1925 by the Carnegie Endowment for International Peace in the series 'Classics of International Law', and reprinted in 1964 by Oceana Publications, New York (Wildy & Sons, London). The three volumes comprise an Introduction by the editor of the series, a Dedication and Prologue by the author, the main work, an Appendix, and the author's 'Notes on the Epistle of Paul to Philemon'. The work itself is divided into 56 chapters, 935 numbered sections, and many thousand numbered paragraphs. As the pages of the three volumes are numbered consecutively, I cite the page numbers in parenthesis, rather than volume, chapter, section and

paragraph numbers. The English translation of the Prologue only was published as a pamphlet in the United States by Bobbs-Merrill in 1957.

2. 'The Morality of Obliteration Bombing', *Theological Studies*, V, 3 (September 1944) p. 281.

3. Frits Kalshoven, *Belligerent Reprisals* [Leiden: Sijthoff, 1971] pp. 163–6, 168, 170, 175.

4. The Charter and Judgment of the Nürnberg Tribunal: memorandum by the UN Secretary-General (UN doc. A/CN.4/5, 3 March 1949, pp. 1–86); General Assembly Official Records, 5th session, Supplement no. 12, A/1316, paras 98–127 (para. nos and footnotes omitted).

5. UN docs. A/7720, 20 November 1969, paras 122–7; A/8052, 18 September 1970, para. 110 (both mimeo.).

3. HUMAN RIGHTS IN ARMED CONFLICT

1. General Assembly Official Records, 4th session, Supplement no. 10, A/925, para. 18.

2. The main reports of the UN Secretariat on human rights in armed conflict were as follows: A/7720, 20 November 1969; A/8052, 18 September 1970; A/8370, and Add. 1, 2 September and 5 October 1971; A/8438, 29 September 1971; A/8781, 20 September 1972, and Corr. 1, 11 October 1972; A/8803, 9 October 1972, and Corr. 1, 19 October 1972; A/9073, 9 July 1973; A/9123, 19 September 1972, and Corr. 1, 2 October 1972, and Adds 1 & 2, 8 November and 21 November 1973; A/9215 (2 vols), 7 November 1973; A/9643, 22 July 1974; A/9669 and Add. 1, 12 September and 19 November 1974; A/10147, 1 August 1975; A/10195 and Add. 1, 5 September and 11 November 1975; A/31/163, 18 August 1976; A/32/144, 15 August 1977 (all mimeo.).

3. On demilitarised sanctuaries, see also my *How wars end* (Oxford: Clarendon Press, 1982) I, pp. 230–5, 250–5.

4. UN doc. A/9123/Add. 1, 8 November 1973 (mimeo.).

5. UN doc. A/7495 and Add. 1, 28 May 1969 (both mimeo.).

6. General Assembly Official Records, 25th session, Annexes, Agenda item 101, p. 2, A/8164.

7. UN doc. A/8089, 26 October 1970 (mimeo.), para. 53.

8. UN docs E/CN.4/1016, 20 January 1970, para. 9, and A/8089, 26 October 1970, para. 11 (both mimeo.).

9. UN doc. E/CN.4/1016/Add. 2, 11 February 1970, pp. 2–6 (mimeo.).

10. The reports of the Special Committee have been issued as UN documents as follows: A/8089, 26 October 1970; A/8389 and Corrs 1 & 2, 5 October, 15 October and 10 December 1971; A/8389/Add. 1 and Corrs, 9 December and 18 December 1971; A/8828, 9 October 1972; A/9148 and Add. 1, 25 October and 20 November 1973; A/9817, 4 November 1974; A/10272, 27 October 1975; A/31/218, 1 October 1976; A/32/284, 27 October 1977; A/33/356, 13 November 1978; A/34/631, 13 November 1979; A/35/425, 6

October 1980; A/36/579, 26 October 1981; A/37/485, 20 October 1982; A/38/409, 14 October 1983; A/39/591, 29 October 1984; A/40/702, 4 October 1985; A/41/680, 20 October 1986.
11. General Assembly Official Records, 25th session Annexes, Agenda item 101, A/8237.
12. The mandate derives from General Assembly resolutions 2443, 2546, 2727, 2851, 3005, 3092B, 3240A and C, 3525A and C, 31/106C and D, 32/91B and C, 33/113C, 34/90A, 35/122C, 36/147C, 37/88C, 38/79D, 39/95D, and 40/161D.
13. See my *The making of resolution 242* (Dordrecht: Nijhoff, 1985).

4. INTERNATIONAL HUMANITARIAN LAW

1. Donald Greene (ed.), *The Oxford Authors: Samuel Johnson* (Oxford: Oxford University Press, 1984) pp. 547–8.
2. The usual method of citing the Conventions is to give first the number of the Convention in roman numerals, and then the article number(s).
3. *The Hague Conventions of 1899 (II) and 1907 (IV), respecting the Laws and Customs of War on Land* (Washington, D.C.: Carnegie Endowment for International Peace, 1915) pamphlet no. 5. In summarising the Conventions, I have used the translation of the 1907 text, and this is the version included in *Documents on the Laws of War*, edited by Adam Roberts and Richard Guelff (Oxford: Clarendon Press, 1982) pp. 43–59.
4. *The Law of Land Warfare* (Washington, D.C.: US Department of the Army, 1956) FM27-10, p. i.
5. In the Table of Contents of the British Manual of Military Law, the Convention is incorrectly ascribed to Geneva (p. xxiii).
6. *The Law of War on Land* (London: HMSO, 1958) paras 109, n. 1, and 110, n. 1.
7. *Social Contract* (1762) chapter IV in *Social Contract: essays by Locke, Hume and Rousseau* (Oxford: Oxford University Press, 1947, World's classics) p. 251.
8. Draft rules for the limitation of the dangers incurred by the civilian population in time of war, 2nd edn (Geneva: ICRC, 1958) pp. 46–50.
9. The italicised words were not in the 1899 Convention.
10. *The Law of Land Warfare* (Washington D.C.: US Department of the Army, 1956) FM27-10, para. 497a; see also *The Law of War on Land*, being part III of the British Manual of Military Law (London: HMSO, 1958) paras 642–9.
11. UN docs A/7720, 20 November 1969, para. 203, and A/8052, 18 September 1970, para. 42(c) (both mimeo.).
12. General Assembly Official Records, 23rd session, Agenda item 87, A/7326, para. 119.
13. Security Council Official Records, 11th year, Supplement for April–June 1956, pp. 40–1, paras 40, 44–6 of S/3596.
14. Reaffirmation and Development of the Laws and Customs applicable in Armed Conflicts: report submitted to the 21st International Conference of the Red Cross (Geneva: ICRC, 1969) pp. 83–7.

15. E. S. Colbert, *Retaliation in International Law* (New York: King's Crown Press, 1948) p. 200; Frits Kalshoven, *Belligerent Reprisals* (Leiden: Sijthoff, 1971) pp. 375, 377.
16. *Nuremberg and Vietnam: an American Tragedy* (Chicago: Quadrangle, 1970; a New York Times book distributed by Random House) p. 54.
17. Wording of Geneva Protocol of 1925 in square brackets.
18. I am indebted to David Carlton for this information. The file containing the minute is in the Public Record Office, ref. W 13568 in FO 371/14974.
19. The text of the vetoed proposals is given in my *Voting in the Security Council* (Bloomington: Indiana University Press, 1969) pp. 175–7.
20. *The Law of War on Land* (London: HMSO, 1958) paras 107 n. 1(b), 113; *The Law of Land Warfare* (Washington, D.C., US Department of the Army, 1956) para. 35.
21. Jean Pictet, *The Red Cross and Peace* (Geneva: ICRC, 1951) p. 10; *Reaffirmation and Development of the Laws and Customs applicable in Armed Conflicts*: report submitted to the 21st International Conference of the Red Cross (Geneva: ICRC, 1969) p. 11; Pictet, *The Red Cross as a Factor in World Peace*: report of a round table conference held at the Hague, 28 August 1967 (Geneva: ICRC, 1968) p. 9.
22. Shabtai Rosenne, 'The Red Cross, Red Crescent, Red Lion and Sun and the Red Shield of David', *Israel Yearbook on Human Rights*, 5 (1975) pp. 9–54. Iran formerly used as an emblem the Red Lion and Sun.
23. As note 30.
24. For text of the vetoed proposals, see my *Voting in the Security Council* (Bloomington: Indiana University Press, 1969) pp. 175–6, 188.
25. See my *How wars end* (Oxford: Clarendon Press, 1982) II, pp. 175–6; see also *Hospital Localities and Safety Zones* (Geneva: ICRC, 1952).
26. 'Nonmilitary areas in UN Practice', *American Journal of International Law*, 74, 3 (July 1980) p. 505.
27. *International Review of the Red Cross* (March–April 1981) pp. 76–83.
28. See 'The Security Council', chapter 7, in Philip Alston (ed.), *Making and Breaking Human Rights: a critical appraisal of the United Nations' record* (Oxford: Oxford University Press, 1987).
29. *Conflit de Corée: recueil de documents* (Geneva: ICRC, 1952) I, pp. 42–3, 165–8 (docs 55, 223); II, pp. 13–14, 29–40, 90–1, 107, (docs 322, 351, 408, 434); Security Council Official Records, 7th year, Special Supplement no. 3, pp. 19–21, S/2541; 9th year, Supplement for January–March 1954, p. 42, S/3185.
30. The main sources for this episode are as follows: GAOR, 18th session, Supplement no. 2, A/5502, pp. 6–8; SCOR, 17th year, Supplement for October–December 1962, pp. 168, 174–81, S/5197, S/5210, S/5214; 18th year, Supplement for January–March 1963, pp. 85–90, S/5227, S/5228, S/5230; U Thant, *View from the UN* (London: David & Charles, 1978) pp. 155–8, 161–94, 460–9; Annual Report of the ICRC for 1962, pp. 31–4; *A Paul Ruegger*, privately printed (Riehen, Basel: A. Schudel & Co., 1977) pp. 158–62.
31. *International Review of the Red Cross* (August and September 1970) pp. 424–59, 484–511; UN doc. A/8089, 26 October 1970 (mimeo.), paras 51–2, 149.

32. See, for example, Yoram Dinstein, 'The International Law of Belligerent Occupation and Human Rights', *Israel Yearbook on Human Rights*, 8 (1978) p. 107.

5. DISARMAMENT

1. But see my article 'An ethical basis for the regulation of weapons', *Crucible* (January 1974) pp. 13–18.
2. UN doc. A/35/392, 12 September 1980 (mimeo.) paras 259–60,
3. UN doc. A/6858, 10 October 1967 (mimeo.), paras 1, 14, 40, 42, 45, 80–1.
4. UN doc. A/35/392, 12 September 1980 (mimeo.), paras 9, 67, 143, 356, 493, 498.
5. 21 December 1957, pp. 1058–9.
6. The text of these and other agreements is given in Josef Goldblat, *Agreements for Arms Control: a critical survey* (London: Taylor & Francis, 1982) for the Stockholm International Peace Research Institute.
7. Fascinating inside accounts of the negotiations between the super-powers on strategic arms, from an American point of view, include John Newhouse, *Cold Dawn* (New York: Holt, Rinehart & Winston, 1973); Henry Kissinger, *White House Years* (Boston: Little, Brown, 1979) pp. 147–50, 195–225, 534–51, 810–23, 1128–31, 1216–46; Strobe Talbot, *Endgame* (New York: Harper & Row, 1979); Gerard Smith, *Doubletalk* (New York: Doubleday, 1980); Strobe Talbot, *Deadly Gambits* (New York: Knopf, 1984; London: Pan paperback, 1985).
8. *Special Reports* nos 122 and 136 (Washington, D.C.: US State Department, 1985).
9. 'The United States violates its international commitments', *Soviet News*, 1 February 1984, pp. 35–6.

6. IN OBEDIENCE TO CONSCIENCE

1. SCOR, 6th year, 549th mtg (26 July 1951), para. 78; 550th mtg (1 August 1951), paras 33, 36–40, 42; 553rd mtg (16 August 1951), para. 60; 9th year, 661st mtg (12 March 1954) paras 69–73. In view of the importance of the issues raised in this chapter, I am citing sources where possible.
2. SCOR, 22nd year, 1347th mtg (5 June 1967), para. 4.
3. UN docs A/41/231, 24 March 1986, S/17938, 25 March 1986; S/17983, 12 April 1986; S/17986, 14 April 1986; S/17990, 14 April 1986; S/PV.2668, 26 March 1986, pp. 21–2; S/PV.2673, 14 April 1986, pp. 13–15; S/PV.2674, 15 April 1986, p. 10 (all mimeo.).
4. Max Weber, 'Politics as a vocation' (speech at Munich University in 1918), in H. H. Gerth and C. Wright Mills (eds), *From Max Weber: essays in sociology* (London: Routledge & Kegan Paul, 1948) pp. 120–6.
5. *Collected Essays, Journalism and Letters of George Orwell*, edited by Sonia Orwell and Ian Angus (Harmondsworth: Penguin, 1970) II, pp. 136.

6. Letter to *The Times*, 23 November 1970.
7. (Washington, D.C.: American Red Cross, 1959) English translation of the first French edition, 1862.
8. Pierre Boissier, *From Solferino to Tsushima* (Geneva: Henry Dunant Institute, 1985) pp. 58, 74, 80, 89, 203–4, 353–5.
9. FM27-10, p. i.
10. Jean Pictet, *Development and Principles of International Humanitarian Law* (Dordrecht: Nijhoff; Geneva: Henry Dunant Institute, 1985) p. 86.
11. Information about Martens has been derived from the following sources: Frederick W. Holls, *The Peace Conference at the Hague and its bearing on international law and policy* (London: Macmillan, 1900) pp. 135–8, 141–2, 145, 151, 161–2, 169, 206–10, 251–2, 285, 287–90, 314, 321; James Scott Brown, *The Hague Peace Conference of 1899 and 1907* (Baltimore: Johns Hopkins Press, 1909) I, pp. 47, 73, 203, 281, II, pp. 63, 78, 81, 115, 134, 162, 174, 433, 525–6, 528; *American Journal of International Law*, 3, 4 (October 1909) pp. 983–5; T. E. Holland, 'Frederic de Martens', *Journal of the Society of Comparative Legislation*, X (1909) pp. 10–12; Andrew Dickson White, *Autobiography* (New York: Century, 1914) II pp. 264–6, 270, 283, 285–6, 292, 320–1, 328, 335, 336; G. P. Gooch and Harold Temperley (eds), *British Documents on the Origins of the War, 1898–1914* (London: HMSO, I, 1927; VIII, 1932) I, p. 226 (doc. 276); VIII, pp. 201, 207–14 (docs 173, 178–80, 182–3), 230 (ed. note), 225 (doc. 292); Arthur Nussbaum, 'Frederic de Martens: representative Tsarist writer on International Law', *Nordisk Tidsskrift for International Ret og Jus Gentium* (1952) pp. 51–66; Pierre Boissier, *From Solferino to Tsushima: history of the International Committee of the Red Cross* (Geneva: Henry Dunant Institute, 1985) pp. 311, 339–40, 358, 366, 369, 376, 383.
12. FM27-10, para. 3.
13. British Manual of Military Law, para. 633, note 1(c).
14. H. Lauterpacht (ed.), *Annual Digest and Reports of Public International Law Cases, 1949* (London: Butterworth, 1955) case 192, pp. 509–25.
15. *On War* (New York and London: Norton, 1968) p. 5.
16. Stanislav Andreski, 'Origins of War', in J. D. Carthy and F. J. Ebling (eds), *Natural History of Aggression* (London & New York: Academic Press, 1964) p. 129.
17. *On Aggression* (London: Methuen paperback, 1967) p. 207.
18. The story can be found in the first book of Samuel, chapters 16–26.
19. Thomas Keppel, *Life of Augustus, Viscount Keppel* (London: Henry Colburn, 1842) I, p. 409; II, pp. 1–2, 7, 10–11, 87, 103–8, 182–3.
20. J. C. Long, *Lord Jeffrey Amherst: a soldier of the king* (New York: Macmillan, 1933) pp. 120–1, 125–6, 137–8, 143, 223, 237–8, 243, 324.
21. Ira D. Gruber, *The Howe Brothers and the American Revolution* (New York: Norton, 1972, for the Institute of Early American History and Culture) pp. 52–5, 58, 62, 90, 95, 103, 142–3, 145, 151, 156–7, 159, 184, 194, 204–5, 208–9, 243, 261, 326, 339, 355, 359–60.
22. J. W. von Goethe, *Campaign in France in the year 1792*, trans. Robert Farie (London: Chapman & Hall, 1849) pp. 79–81.

23. *Autobiography, III, 1944–1967* (London: Allen & Unwin, 1969) p. 115.
24. Indictment of Leohnard Friedrich, Bad Pyrmont, 15 September 1942.
25. *Democracy in America*, 1835, chapter XV.
26. John Keegan in the *Times Literary Supplement*, 15 November 1985, p. 1286.
27. *Moral Man and Immoral Society* (New York and London: Charles Scribner's Sons, 1932) p. 83.
28. *Pacem in terris*, 1963, para. 80.
29. Prime Minister Clement Attlee made the same point when he wrote to President Truman that if mankind continued to make the atomic bomb without changing the political relationship of states, 'sooner or later these bombs will be used for mutual annihilation' (25 September 1945).
30. Spencer R. Weart and Gertrude Weiss Szilard, *Leo Szilard: his version of the facts* (Cambridge, Mass. and London: MIT Press, 1978) pp. 154, 185, 210, 234–5; Freeman Dyson, *Disturbing the Universe* (New York and London: Harper & Row, 1979) pp. ix, 52, 102, 130; Michael Bess, 'Leo Szilard: scientist, activist, visionary', *Bulletin of the Atomic Scientists*, 41, 11 (December 1985) pp. 11–18.
31. 'Leaving the bomb project', *Bulletin of the Atomic Scientists*, special anniversary issue (August 1985) pp. 16–19.
32. William Douglas Home, *Half-term report* (London: Longman, 1954) pp. 37–8, 104–5, 108–22, 130–1, 134–5, 139, 162–4, 170–3, 178–209; *Mr. Home pronounced Hume* (London: Collins, 1979) pp. 51–9; *Sins of Commission* (Salisbury: Michael Russell, 1985) pp. 10–11, 60–1, 65, 72–3; Lord Home, *The Way the Wind Blows* (London: Collins, 1976) p. 85.
33. Gordon C. Zahn, *In Solitary Witness, The Life and Death of Franz Jägerstätter* (London: Chapman, 1966; New York: Holt, Rinehart & Winston, 1964) pp. 3–4, 57–8, 64, 76, 80, 86, 88, 92, 96, 105, 107, 111, 126, 144, 161, 215, 220, 234–5; (paperback edition published by the Liturgical Press, Collegeville); Zahn, *Franz Jäegerstäetter: martyr for conscience* (Erie, Pa., Benet Press, no date but circa 1984).

Bibliography

Bailey, Sydney D., *Christian Perspectives on Nuclear Weapons*, second edn (London: British Council of Churches, 1984).
——, *Peaceful settlement of international disputes*, third edn (New York: UN Institute for Training and Research, 1970).
Best, Geoffrey, *Humanity in Warfare: The Modern History of the International Law of Armed Conflict* (London: Weidenfeld & Nicolson, 1980).
Boissier, Pierre, *From Solferino to Tsushima: history of the International Committee of the Red Cross* (Geneva: Henry Dunant Institute, 1985).
Bonhoeffer, Dietrich, *Ethics*, trans. Neville Horton Smith, ed. Eberhard Bethge (London: SCM Press, 1955; paperback edn, Fontana Library, 1964).
Brownlie, Ian, *International law and the use of force by states* (Oxford: Clarendon Press, 1963).
Bugnion, François, *The emblem of the Red Cross: a brief history* (Geneva: ICRC, 1977).
Builder, Carl H. and Morlie H. Graubard, *The International Law of Armed Conflict: Implications for the Concept of Assured Destruction* (Santa Monica, Ca.: Rand, 1982 (R-2804-FF)).
Caedel, Martin, *Pacifism in Britain, 1914–1945: the defining of faith* (Oxford: Clarendon Press, 1980).
'Challenge of Peace: God's promise and our response', first published in *Origins*, 13, 1 (May 1983); British edn, Catholic Truth Society and SPCK, 1983.
Church and the Bomb: nuclear weapons and Christian conscience, report of a working party (London: Hodder and Stoughton, 1985).
Common Security, report of the Palme Commission (London: Pan, 1982).
Comprehensive Study on Nuclear Weapons, report of an expert group: UN doc. A/35/392, 12 September 1980 (mimeo.).
Delessert, Christiane Shields, *Release and repatriation of prisoners of war at the end of hostilities …* (Zurich: Schulthess Polygraphischer, 1977).
Dunant, Henry, *Un Souvenir de Solférino*, first published 1862: (Berne: Swiss Red Cross, 1979; English translation, Washington, D.C.: American National Red Cross, 1959).
Durand, André, *From Sarajevo to Hiroshima: history of the International Committee of the Red Cross* (Geneva: Henry Dunant Institute, 1984).
Epstein, William, *The last chance* (New York: Free Press; London: Collier Macmillan, 1976).
Forsythe, David P., *Humanitarian Politics: The International Committee of the Red Cross* (Baltimore and London: Johns Hopkins University Press, 1977).
Fotion, N., and Elfstrom, G., *Military ethics: guidelines for peace and war* (London: Routledge & Kegan Paul, 1986).
Freedman, Lawrence, *Britain and nuclear weapons* (London: Macmillan, 1980, for the Royal Institute of International Affairs).
Freymond, Jacques, *Guerres, Révolutions, Croix-Rouge: Réflexions sur la rôle du Comité Internationale de la Croix-Rouge* (Geneva: Institut Universitaire de Hautes Études Internationales, 1976).

Glasstone, Samuel and Philip J. Dolan (eds), *The Effects of Nuclear Weapons*, third edn (Washington, D.C.: U.S. Government Printing Office, 1977).

Goldblat, Jozef, *Agreements for Arms Control: a critical survey* (London: Taylor and Francis, 1982, for the Stockholm International Peace Research Institute).

Greenspan, Morris, *The Modern Law of Land Warfare* (Berkeley and Los Angeles: University of California Press, 1959).

Grotius, Hugo, *De jure belli ac pacis*, English translation, (Washington, D.C.: Carnegie Endowment for International Peace, 1925) 3 vols; reprinted (New York: Oceana; London: Wildy, 1964).

Higgins, Rosalyn, *The development of international law through the political organs of the United Nations* (London: Oxford University Press, 1963, under the auspices of the Royal Institute of International Affairs).

Hospital Localities and Safety Zones (Geneva: ICRC, 1952).

Howard, Michael (ed.), *Restraints on war: Studies in the limitation of armed conflict* (Oxford: Oxford University Press, 1979).

Human Rights in Armed Conflict, reports of the UN Secretary-General: UN docs. A/7720, 20 November 1969; A/8052, 18 September 1970; and A/9215 (2 vols), 7 November 1973 (all mimeo.).

International Red Cross Handbook, 12th edn (Geneva: ICRC, 1983).

Kalshoven, Frits, *Belligerent Reprisals* (Leiden: Sijthoff, 1971).

——, *The Law of Warfare* (Leiden: Sijthoff, 1973).

Kenny, Anthony, *The logic of deterrence* (London: Firethorn, 1985).

Krass, Allan S., *Verification: how much is enough?* (London and Philadelphia: Taylor and Francis, 1985, for the Stockholm International Peace Research Institute).

Law of War on Land, being part III of the *Manual of Military Law* (London: HMSO, 1958 and subsequent amendments).

Lord McNair and A. D. Watts, *The legal effects of war* (Cambridge: Cambridge University Press, 1966).

Martin, David A., *Pacifism: an historical and sociological study* (London: Routledge and Kegan Paul, 1965).

Mayer, Peter (ed.), *The Pacifist Conscience* (New York: Holt, Rinehart and Winston; London: Rupert Hart-Davis; paperback edn, Pelican Books, 1966).

Moreillon, Jacques, *Le Comité international de la Croix-Rouge et la protection des détenus politiques* (Geneva: Henry Dunant Institute and l'Age d'Homme, 1973).

Niebuhr, Reinhold, *An Interpretation of Christian Ethics* (New York: Meridian Books, 1956).

Nye, Joseph S., *Nuclear Ethics* (London: Collier Macmillan; New York: Free Press, 1986).

Paskins, Barrie, and Michael Dockrill, *The Ethics of War* (London: Duckworth, 1979).

Pictet, Jean (general ed.), *Commentary on the Geneva Conventions of 12 August 1949*, 4 vols, (Geneva: ICRC, 1952–60).

——, *Humanitarian Law and the Protection of War Victims* (Leiden: Sijthoff, 1973).

Pictet, Jean, *Development and Principles of International Humanitarian Law* (Geneva: ICRC, 1985).

Ramsey, Paul, *War and the Christian Conscience: how shall modern war be conducted justly?* (Durham, N. C.: Duke University Press, 1961).

Roberts, Adam, and Richard Guelff (eds), *Documents on the laws of war* (Oxford: Clarendon Press, 1982).

Rosas, Allan, *The Legal Status of Prisoners of War: A Study in International Humanitarian Law Applicable in Armed Conflicts* (Helsinki: Suomalainen Tiedeakatemia, 1976).

Rosenblad, Esbjörn, *International Humanitarian Law of Armed Conflict: some aspects of the principle of distinction and related problems* (Geneva: Henry Dunant Institute, 1979).

Schindler, D. and J. Toman (eds), *The Laws of Armed Conflict* (Leiden: Sijthoff, 1973).

Schweitzer, Albert, *Civilization and Ethics* (London: Unwin Books, in association with Adam and Charles Black, 1961).

Sims, Nicholas A., *Approaches to disarmament*, second edn (London: Quaker Peace and Service, 1979).

Stone, Julius, *Legal Controls of International Conflict: a treatise on the dynamics of disputes- and war-law*, second edn (London: Stevens, 1959).

Tillich, Paul, *Morality and beyond* (London: Routledge & Kegan Paul, 1964, paperback edn, Fontana Library, 1969).

Unilateral Nuclear Disarmament Measures, report of an expert group: UN doc. A/39/516, 5 October 1984 (mimeo.).

Verzijl, J. H. W., *International Law in Historical Perspective, part IX-A, The Laws of War* (Alphen aan den Rijn, Netherlands: Sijthoff and Noordhoff, 1978).

Walzer, Michael, *Just and Unjust Wars: a moral argument with historical illustrations* (New York: Basic Books, 1977; London: Penguin, 1980).

Willemin, Georges, and Roger Heacock, under the direction of Jacques Freymond, *The International Committee of the Red Cross* (The Hague: Nijhoff, 1984).

Wright, Quincy, *A Study of War* (Chicago, Ill.: University of Chicago Press, 1942) 2 vols.

Index

Edited by

VINCENZO TRAVERSA

Racconti di Alberto Moravia

IRVINGTON PUBLISHERS INC., New York

First Irvington Edition 1979
Copyright © 1968 By Meredith Corporation

All rights reserved. No part of this book may be reproduced in
any manner whatever, including information storage or re-
trieval, in whole or in part (except for brief quotations in critical
articles or reviews), without written permission from the
publisher. For information, write to Irvington Publishers, Inc.,
551 Fifth Avenue, New York, New York 10017.

"Inverno di malato," "L'equivoco," and "Ritorno al mare"
are reprinted from *I racconti,* Copyright 1952 by Soc. An. Ed.
Valentino Bompiani & C., Via Senato N. 16, Milano.

"Il tacchino di Natale," "Una strana malattia," and "Primo
rapporto sulla terra dell' 'inviato speciale' della luna," are reprinted from *L'epidemia,* Copyright © 1956 by Casa Ed. Valentino Bompiani & C., S.p.A., Via Senato N. 16, Milano.

"La contrafigura," "Il camionista," and "Romolo e Remo"
are reprinted from *Racconti romani,* © 1963 by Casa Ed. Valentino Bompiani, Via Pisacane 26, Milano.

"Lo scimpanzè," "Non è il momento," and "Ci vorrebbe
Ugo" are reprinted from *Nuovi racconti romani,* © 1963 Casa
Ed. Valentino Bompiani, Via Senato 16, Milano.

"Hai dormito," "Passare il tempo," and "La vita è una
giungla" are reprinted from *L'automa,* © 1963 Casa Ed. Valentino Bompiani, Via Senato 16, Milano.

Library of Congress Cataloging in Publication Data

Moravia, Alberto, 1907-
    Racconti di Alberto Moravia.
    Reprint of the 1968 ed. published by Appleton-Century-
Crofts, New York.
    I. Traversa, Vincenzo Paolo, 1923-
II. Title.
PQ4829.O62R28   1979   458'.6'421   79-18466
ISBN 0-89197-368-0

Printed in the United States of America

PREFACE

The present selection of short stories by Alberto Moravia (1907-) has been devised as a textbook to enable students to become acquainted in their second year of Italian language with the narrative style and some of the main themes of the author.

Rather than merely following an order of increasing linguistic difficulty, we have tried to arrange the stories in such a way as to present various situations and characters representing, at least in part, the "reality" of Moravia's world, ranging from the easy-to-grasp structures of the first stories to the stylistic and psychological complexities of *Inverno di malato* and *Ritorno al mare*. The teacher, therefore, is advised to follow the order given in the table of contents and to use the exercises to stimulate the use of Italian in discussing and analyzing the material.

The exercises have been prepared by following as closely as possible the vocabulary and the idiomatic expressions of the stories. The grammatical items included in the exercises will give the teacher the opportunity of reviewing in a short time the grammar which is normally learned during the first year. The absence of passages for translation is prompted by the belief that both the work in class and the assignments at home should be entirely in Italian. The footnotes below the text are intended to clarify difficult idioms and grammatical structures.

In conclusion, we would like to assure the reader that in no way do we consider this a complete, comprehensive selection of Moravia's vast short story production. Thus, to those who wish to

know more, we suggest the titles of the books from which we
have chosen the stories edited in this reader: *L'epidemia* (1944),
I racconti (1952), *Racconti romani* (1954), *Nuovi racconti
romani* (1959), and *L'automa* (1963), all of which have been
published by Valentino Bompiani of Milano.

CONTENTS

INTRODUCTION

Alberto Moravia (originally Alberto Pincherle) was born in Rome
in 1907. As the writer himself reveals in a biographical note, his
father, an architect and painter, had literary tastes that led him
mainly to the works of Goldoni, Shakespeare, and Molière as well
as to the Spanish and French playwrights. 'Thus,' said Moravia, 'the
first books I read were dramas and comedies, and I believe that this
[preparation] has exerted a great influence on my literary works,
bringing me into the habit, from the very beginning, of considering men as well-defined characters, provided with a destiny [which
is] completely capable of being realized.' [1]

His parents had envisaged a diplomatic career for him and
had entrusted him to the care of several governesses from whom
he learned French, English, and German. His youth, however,
was marred by a serious, lingering illness that not only prevented
him from attending school regularly but had the effect of pre-
cociously developing his power of insight. In Moravia's words:
'. . . when I was about nine years old I became seriously ill and
had to give up my studies. Since then, until I reached the age of
seventeen, with short intervals of a year or a few months of false
recoveries, I was always ill . . . on the whole I spent five years

---

[1] This and the following autobiographical notes were taken from
Ines Scaramucci, *Alberto Moravia* (Milano: Marzorati, 1963).

in bed, the last two in a mountain sanatorium at Cortina d'Ampezzo.' If, on one hand, his forced immobility prevented him from acquiring the normal experience of direct, daily contacts with people of his age, on the other hand, he had plenty of time to read. He subscribed to the largest Italian circulating library, the Viesseux Library of Florence, and received four or five books a week. He would read everything available, in Italian, in French, or in English. His approach was to read systematically the works of a writer until he was sure he had gone through all of his books.

During those critical, formative years, Moravia's natural penchant for the narrative art manifested itself very strongly through spontaneous outbursts of imagination: 'Since the age of six or seven I became engrossed in telling myself long and confused adventures of imaginary characters. Especially during my vacations, I would walk through the fields, or I would stretch out on a couch, feet up and head down, in a room of the villa and speak to myself. I do not recall precisely the contents of these solitary narrations; I think they dealt with adventures, dangers, and violent and unreal facts. I remember very well, however, that I would resume my narration every day from the precise point I had stopped it the day before.'

The seemingly endless time he had to spend away from his family, mostly in the company of ill people in the peculiar atmosphere of the sanatorium where normal life takes on a different cast and the people take on different values, was to heighten his natural sensitivity and to leave a definite mark on his works. 'I suppose,' he wrote, 'that the experience of the sanatorium has been very important. . . . When I left the sanatorium, in the autumn of 1925, I was healed only in that specific illness of mine. . . .' It will not be difficult to prove the truth of this statement after studying the character of Girolamo in 'Inverno di malato,' to mention only one instance.

The other important factor in Moravia's life was Fascism. Apart from its political organization, Moravia could never accept the stifling, obtuse control of all intellectual thought. He avoided that 'boring, stuffy ambiance' by working for several newspapers during extended travels abroad. He began by contributing to the *Gazzetta del Popolo* and the *Stampa* of Turin. Curzio Malaparte, the author of *Kaputt, Maledetti Toscani, Benedetti Italiani,* and the highly controversial *La pelle,* had been editor-in-chief of the *Stampa* since 1929. A journalist by profession and an experienced traveler, Malaparte understood Moravia's longing for new ideas and for a different political environment and gave him an assignment to London for several months between 1930 and 1931. Shortly before this time, Moravia published an unflattering and pessimistic portrayal of some aspects of the Italian bourgeoisie in *Gli indifferenti,* a portrayal that almost brought him to blows with Fascist authorities. When he returned from a trip to Mexico and the United States, Moravia found all of Italy enthusiastic over the recent victory against Ethiopia. He was in the Piazza Venezia when the proclamation of the Italian Empire was made by Mussolini and was struck as never before with the enormous crowd and its sincere enthusiasm. In spite of its victories, or perhaps because of them, Fascism was becoming more and more boring and suffocating. Some time afterwards he left for China. Many years later, in 1956 and 1957, Curzio Malaparte also was to spend several months in China. Malaparte had been in a clinic there, returning to Rome shortly before his death.

At the beginning of the Second World War, Moravia was at Capri where he lived with his wife Elsa Morante, a very well-known novelist whom he had married in 1941. The war became more and more unfavorable for Italy. The Gran Consiglio del Fascismo gave a vote of no-confidence to Mussolini, forcing him to resign on July 25, 1943. In those tragic days, Moravia published in a Roman newspaper articles whose nature, unequivocally anti-dictatorial, compelled him to take shelter in the countryside of Latium. This was after Fascist rule was re-established with the creation, on September 13, 1943, of the short-lived Republic of Salò. What all these events meant in the writer's life is synthesized in this statement: 'I attribute great importance to my illness and

Fascism—because of my illness and Fascism I had to withstand and do things that I would have never withstood or done otherwise. Our character is shaped by those things we are forced to do, not by those we decide to do of our own will.'

In the years that followed, Moravia's literary works have been produced in a steady, extremely abundant rate and have secured him a prominent place in contemporary literature. At present he lives in Rome and devotes his attention to fiction, journalism, and the direction of the periodical *Nuovi Argomenti*.

It has been said that Moravia's themes are inspired by a sort of anger against life itself as well as an anger against men, society, and his own existence. These are, in fact, the characteristics a reader finds in his books which most strikingly set Moravia apart from traditional Italian narrative. Moravia's art deals with human instincts and feelings in a direct, merciless manner. On opening his books, we should be prepared to discover new, unsuspected aspects of our essence; we should be prepared for a stark, harsh, almost hopeless reality. This is Moravia's vision of human life. It is a vision of a society that has reached the ultimate level of impotency, indifference, and moral decay. Many critics see Moravia as an unperturbed analyst of the morality of society, and they have discovered in his extended writing many resemblances to Boccaccio, Dostoevski, Freud, the French naturalists, and the Italian 'veristi.'

From his first novel, *Gli indifferenti,* published in 1929 when he was only twenty-two, to *La noia* (1960) and *L'attenzione* (1965), Moravia's themes are centered around the discovery and development of both intellectual and sexual awareness. *Gli indifferenti* in particular portrays, as the title suggests, the indifference or inability of some members of the bourgeoisie to become actively interested in moral values. Love, hatred, indignation, and ambition are emotions that the characters can visualize and discuss but can never feel. It is a slow, relentless descent into emptiness and apathy, where reality loses its consistency and the absurd is chosen to replace it. Michele, the most disoriented character in the book, will always long for a moment of vitality and truth, for that spark of energy that will enable him to right the abnormal situations which engulf his family and himself. 'Come doveva essere bello il mondo' he thinks in an ironic regret, 'quando un marito tradito poteva gridare a sua moglie: Moglie scellerata; paga con la vita il fio delle tue colpe, e, quel ch'è più forte, pensar tali parole, e poi avventarsi, ammazzare mogli, amanti, parenti e tutti quanti, e restare senza punizione e senza rimorso: quando al *pensiero* seguiva *l'azione:* ti odio, e zac! un colpo di pugnale... quando *non si pensava tanto,* e il primo impulso era sempre quello buono; quando la vita non era come ora *ridicola,* ma tragica, e si moriva *veramente,* e si uccideva, e si odiava, e si amava *sul serio,* e si versavano *vere* lacrime per *vere* sciagure, e tutti gli uomini erano fatti di carne e ossa ed *attaccati alla realtà* come alberi alla terra.' [2]

The closer one observes these characters the better one sees them writhe in the grip of a sinister fate, itself a part of the decline of an epoch and the moral fiber of its society.

Le ambizioni sbagliate, Agostino, Il disprezzo, and other, more recent novels repropose Moravia's thesis that the search for and discovery of a sexual reality is the only motivation that leads to action. But even in these cases, it appears that the action is hampered by a constant, sterile introspection, by a relentless, cerebral activity that limits or utterly prevents the fulfillment of the act of love. Moravia is not, however, a writer of the negative. Rather, his efforts are an attempt to bring into full view, in an almost surgical process, the worst he sees in mankind. It is, possibly, a form of moralizing, as some critics have suggested, brought about with a detached, cold irony. It may also represent a reaction against the loneliness and isolation which so deeply affect the souls of his characters.

Concerning this problem, particular attention should be de-

---

[2] Alberto Moravia, *Gli indifferenti* (Milano: Bompiani, 1960), p. 233 (italics mine).

voted to another novel, *Il conformista,* published in 1951. Here
we find several of Moravia's typical themes such as the troubled,
anguished years of adolescence, the necessity of the individual
to identify himself with the group or a political regime and the
conjugal experience.

Marcello, the young protagonist, discovers in himself a sense
of guilt after a progression of destructive fits of anger—first against
some flowers, then against the lizards living in his garden and a cat,
and finally in the imaginary killing of a young neighbor, Roberto,
a murder 'non eseguito' but 'pensato e voluto...e tuttora eseguibile
e, forse, inevitabile.' He considers himself abnormal and, in
order to break loose from this obsession, he tries to provoke, without success, an act of punishment from his parents. In a rapid
succession of seemingly inescapable events, Marcello, derided in his
classroom and on the streets by his schoolmates, is rescued one day
by Lino, a homosexual, who tries to seduce him by promising him
a revolver. The weapon, which Marcello intended to show to
his mocking persecutors to prove his manliness, will be used against
Lino whose demands had become unbearable for the boy. The
fact of his having killed Lino separates Marcello more and more
from the other boys.

Seventeen years later we find Marcello in a library, turning
the pages of a newspaper published after the day of the murder.
He has gone to that place 'per vedere...quale sentimento gli ispirasse
la conferma della morte di Lino. Da questo sentimento, come
aveva pensato, avrebbe giudicato se egli era ancora il ragazzo di
un tempo, *ossessionato dalla propria fatale anormalità o l'uomo
nuovo del tutto normale,* che aveva in seguito voluto essere ed era
convinto che era.' [3] Shortly after, he goes with Giulia on his honeymoon trip which coincides with a secret mission of a political
nature on behalf of the Fascist government. He joined the party
not so much from conviction but for the 'normality' he had hoped

[3] Alberto Moravia, *Il conformista* (Milano: Bompiani, 1951), p. 86
(italics mine).

to acquire by doing what most people of his age had been doing. The reason for his physical union with Giulia was equally functional—'per potersi dire, almeno una volta: Sono stato un uomo simile a tutti gli altri uomini...ho amato, mi sono congiunto ad una donna e ho generato un altro uomo.' [4]

But while one witnesses Marcello going through the disturbing experiences in Paris at 'La cravatte noire,' a meeting place for lesbians, the killing of Quadri (the objective of his mission), the fall of the Fascist regime and the encounter with Lino (who survived in spite of his being wounded), one realizes that the desperate attempts to bridge the gulf of his estrangement could never alter an altogether immutable condition.

A cross-section of Moravia's numerous short stories is both a revealing and an essential experience for the understanding of his literary value. The majority of the stories portrays individuals, situations, and ideas of the common people. Here we are seldom confronted with complicated psychological problems, as in the novels, partly because of the shorter length and also because of the nature and structure of the stories. In his short stories Moravia relies on the quick effects of intuition. His brief, precise impressions follow one another like the frames of a cinematographic sequence and give the reader a glance at the many scenes that constitute, in Carlo Bo's words, a 'sottomondo.'

In these works Moravia is perfectly at ease; his acumen, his ability to synthesize a situation in a few lines and a character in a few strong, original adjectives combined with an evident tendency for the dramatic form leave a delightful, durable impression in the reader's mind. Observe, for example, Gloria in 'Lo scimpanzè.' The lines of her face are 'grossi e un po' brutali' and 'venivano fuori senza rimedio, come nudi.' Her nose 'senza essere brutto non era bello, un po' a forma di gnocco. E la bocca come di

[4] *Ibid.*, p. 206.

8   *Introduction*

negra...carica di rossetto, che luccicava.' ⁵ Agata, the girl in 'La controfigura,' wants to become a star because 'il cinema è una forza più forte di qualsiasi forza...' The day of her interview she appears to Gino 'enigmatica.' In order to look more interesting she had shaved her eyebrows so thoroughly that 'pareva avesse gli occhi gonfi.' Unfortunately her nose 'a manico di bricco non aveva potuto raddrizzarlo.' Later, after the interview with the director, she walks 'dritta e dignitosa, con le sue belle gambe storte.' It should be noted, incidentally, that Moravia possesses a unique, plastic fashion of describing a woman's body. Whether detailed and long or sketchy and impressionistic, the descriptions he makes on this subject represent unequivocally the search for truth and the discovery of 'reality.' The fullness of the breasts, 'attraverso un cellophane si potevano vedere i robusti reggipetti...color rosa carico' ('La vita è una giungla'), or 'un petto che si drizzava, aguzzo, proprio velenoso' ('Il camionista'), the firmness of Lorenzo's wife's legs, 'robuste e persino pesanti' which 'tendevano fortemente' her dress 'comunicando alla stoffa quasi la morbidezza, il calore e il peso della carne ('Ritorno al mare') seem to have a catalytic function in the attempt of the male self-assertion, rather than a purely esthetic reason.

The male characters, on the other hand, are dominated by their urges or their environment. This situation, in one instance, assumes unreal proportions as in the case of Gigi who is persecuted by a sentence ('Non è il momento') which, in rapid succession, is used in the most disparate circumstances with the result that the protagonist is left in a state of stupor and frustration. In 'Il tacchino di Natale' Policarpi-Curcio, a man of humble origin, unrefined but hardworking, is a great financial success yet he is duped by a cunning 'turkey' who seduces his daughter and plays havoc with the peace of his family.

Another case is offered by Ernesto ('Passare il tempo') who

---

⁵ Alberto Moravia, *Nuovi racconti romani* (Milano: Bompiani, 1963), pp. 30, 31.

cannot decide what to do during the two hours of an unexpected delay. His laborious searching for a purely physical activity that leaves the mind totally at rest leads him to the verge of absurdity: 'se veramente non avesse fatto niente, il tempo sarebbe stato sospeso, almeno per quanto lo riguardava, e le due ore...non soltanto sarebbero sembrate eterne ma lo sarebbero state davvero. Lui sarebbe uscito fuori del tempo, per assoluta impossibilità di farlo passare.' [6] While debating with himself, the solution comes to save him from terror in the words of Alina, the girl he had been waiting for. He should have simply thought of her. She, in her turn, had thought of him during the delay and time had passed with no difficulty.

The situation in 'Ritorno al mare' presents once more the problem of man's loneliness but in an unusually touching perspective. Moravia's cold irony seems to abate and a real participation in his character's destiny is accompanied by a constant feeling of sympathy that pervades the whole story. The main theme is represented by Lorenzo's belated and futile wish to win the affection of his frivolous, bored wife. As the story develops, the faults of the two characters reveal themselves during the brief, dramatic trip to the beach near Rome. But while Lorenzo, in an awkward, untimely confession of his mistakes implicitly condemns them and asks the woman's understanding, she, on the other hand, has already reached the decision to leave him, and, left untouched by her husband's anguish, refuses his love. The scene is set first among the splintered ruins of a restaurant by the sea and then along the beach crossed in all directions by barbed wire. Lorenzo's 'return to the sea' is thus preceded by a plea for indulgence in the moment of distress, when all the ideas he had believed in have collapsed leaving him empty and unprotected. He had been a high ranking Fascist official and after the war humiliation had come from his enemies and his own wife. For him, therefore, his experience is a sudden awakening from the unstable world of authority which

---

[6] Alberto Moravia, *L'automa* (Milano: Bompiani, 1963), p. 245.

had carried away his ambition and had prevented him from placing
in the right perspective the more durable values of life as a normal
man and husband. To be sure, there is no reason for his finding, at
the end, that consolation and understanding which he had been
unable to offer; but what moves us is knowing that he is quite aware
of his end while a faint hope, despair, hunger, and desire surge
in him 'come se lui non fosse stato più che un corpo esanime e
senza volontà e le voglie gli fossero cresciute addosso allo stesso
modo che crescono addosso ai morti i peli della barba.' [7]

His spiritiual crisis without solution, his wife suddenly gone
away, most certainly forever, Lorenzo's peace arrives with death
through the magic fascination of the sea in which his subconscious
mind had seen a symbol of perpetuating power, an everlasting re-
generation of youthful hopes, the image of a primeval innocence.

Alberto Moravia's works have been widely translated and are
universally known and acclaimed. The reason for his success,
as in the case of many a controversial writer, are not easily defined. What he expresses in his art, however, is something that
belongs to our experience and our feelings. It may be the immediate awareness of the problems of the present time, a certain
malaise in a moment of confused and changing beliefs or a universal anguish stemming from the human condition. Whatever
the reasons, Moravia's lesson is intelligible and meaningful for
our minds and this achievement, we are inclined to believe, is
also his main contribution as a man of letters.

---

[7] Alberto Moravia, *I racconti* (Milano: Bompiani, 1952), p. 607.

Major works of Alberto Moravia

Gli indifferenti Milano, 1929
Le ambizioni sbagliate Milano, 1935
La bella vita Lanciano, 1935
L'imbroglio Milano, 1937
I sogni del pigro Milano, 1940
La mascherata Milano, 1941
L'amante infelice Milano, 1943
Agostino Milano, 1944
L'epidemia, Racconti surrealisti e satirici Roma, 1944
Due cortigiane — Serata di Don Giovanni Roma, 1945
La romana Milano, 1947
La disubbidienza Milano, 1948
L'amore coniugale e altri racconti Milano, 1949
Il conformista Milano, 1951
I racconti Milano, 1952
Racconti romani Milano, 1954
Il disprezzo Milano, 1954
La ciociara Milano, 1957
Teatro Milano, 1958
Nuovi racconti romani Milano, 1959
La noia Milano, 1960
L'automa Milano, 1963
L'uomo come fine e altri saggi Milano, 1964
L'attenzione Milano, 1965
Una cosa è una cosa Milano, 1967

Racconti di Alberto Moravia

Non è il momento

Quel che sia ridere voi non potete saperlo se non conoscete Paolino, un amico mio delle ore piccole. Adesso Paolino non lo vedo più tanto, proprio per via[1] della sua risata; ma non posso negare che qualche volta, tra tanti musoni e fanatici che non sorridono mai, non mi venga la nostalgia di lui. Paolino è un ragazzòtto della mia età, piccoletto, con la fronte bassa, il naso schiacciato e tutto il peso del viso sulla mascella e intorno la bocca. Paolino ci ha[2] una mascella grande, quadrata, con la scucchia in fuori, che pare la pala di una scavatrice meccanica, di quelle che infornano mezza collina e poi si chiudono e girano e si riaprono sul camion e lo riempiono di colpo per metà. La bocca, poi, ce l'ha grandissima,

---

[1] *per via* because of, through
[2] *ci ha* [a pleonastic construction] has

da un orecchio all'altro, simile alla fenditura di un salvadanaio.
Io non so che ci abbia Paolino nella testa; probabilmente una mac-
chinetta delicata, a scatto, per ridere; perchè gli basta un nonnulla
per spalancare quella sua bocca enorme e smascellarsi dalle risate.
Dopo la risata, Paolino non diventa serio come tutti quanti;
continua ad avere la risata sul viso come un cielo continua ad essere
rosso dopo che il sole è andato sotto: gli occhi gli piangono, la
bocca gli rimane aperta, il viso è tutto scarlatto, congestionato e
stranito. Paolino, insomma, ride come mangiano certi affamati:
con frenesia, con furore. E bisogna dire che la sua vita sia fatta
tutta di risate perchè lui, ricordando questo o quest'altro avvenimento del passato, non manca mai di dire: 'Ti ricordi le risate?'
oppure: 'Ah le risate che ci facemmo'; proprio come un morto di
fame il quale ricorda una per una le poche vere mangiate che ha
fatto in vita sua.
    Basta, Paolino non ero davvero il tipo da chiedergli di accom-
pagnarmi, la sera della Befana, a piazza Navona; ma non trovai
che lui. A piazza Navona, quella sera, io non ci andavo, come
tanti, per far cagnara,³ bensì con uno scopo preciso: abbandonato
senza ragione da Iole, nell'impossibilità di trovarla a casa o dal
parrucchiere dove lei lavorava come manicure, perchè sempre lei
faceva in modo di sfuggirmi, sapendo che quella sera sarebbe
andata a piazza Navona, avevo deciso di cercarla lì, affrontarla, e
magari farle fare una brutta figura. Già, perchè io non sono come
Paolino e non rido se non quando c'è veramente da ridere, che
avviene di rado, e per me la vita è una cosa seria e ci tengo⁴ alla
dignità e, insomma, se una donna non mi vuol più bene, ha da
dirmelo chiaro e tondo⁵ e non svicolare ed evitarmi e mettermi
nella necessità di appostarla. Perciò, glielo dissi, a Paolino, già in
piazza Zanardelli: 'Tu ce lo sai perchè stasera vado a piazza
Navona. Non per strombettare e far cagnara. Perciò non mi
seccare con le tue risate.' 'E chi ride?' disse lui già ridendo, la

³ *far cagnara* merry-making, frolicking
⁴ *ci tengo* I care about
⁵ *chiaro e tondo* frankly, openly

faccia imporporata, gli occhi pieni di lagrime. 'Tu, ridi,' gli risposi duro, 'piantala.' [6] Lui si fece serio, con visibile sforzo però; e così ci avviammo verso la piazza.

Appena entrato, compresi subito il mio errore: prima di tutto di cercare Iole in mezzo a quella folla; e poi di averci portato Paolino. Lui, infatti, alla prima bancarella, volle comprarsi un fischietto che faceva un verso proprio sguaiato e un cappello di paglia con il tubo e la pompetta che, a premerla, faceva rizzare un saltaleone sulla cupola. Gli domandai irritato: 'Ma perchè tanta vogiia di fare il pagliaccio?' E lui, sganasciandosi dalle risate: 'Eh, di Befane ce n'è una sola all'anno.' Proprio in quel momento, guarda caso, vidi Iole ferma di fronte alla baracca del tiro a segno elettronico, a poca distanza dalla fontana centrale. Dissi a Paolino: 'Mò,[7] mi raccomando, piantala con le risate'; e mi avvicinai.

Iole è una di quelle bionde ossigenate, color platino, come vanno adesso, con il viso da morta per via della cipria pallida, le labbra scolorite e gli occhi dipinti di nero intorno intorno.[8] Vestita di un cappottino rosso, si stringeva ad un americano che conoscevo di vista, un certo Riccardo, il quale, ormai, sospettavo di essere la ragione principale del suo raffreddamento. Lui era in giacca a vento a scacchi verdi e neri, il sedere di fuori, la testa rossa, coi capelli tagliati corti, alla Marlon Brando, chiusa in una calottina di pelliccia. Un pezzo di giovanotto, se vogliamo, soprattutto a petto a [9] me che sono piuttosto piccolo; ma con un difettuccio non lieve: una bocca che pareva uno squarcio informe con la quale, lui, mentre parlava, ti spruzzava la saliva in faccia.

Lui aveva imbracciato un fucile, un piede avanti, il viso sul calcio, l'occhio al mirino; e Iole, da brava ragazzetta cui piacciono gli uomini forzuti, l'ammirava mentre lui sparava all'orso di latta che va a spasso per un bosco di latta, inseguito da un cane di latta, e colpiva, via via, sempre nel cerchio del bersaglio, così che l'orso

---

[6] *piantala* stop it
[7] *mò* now [dial.]
[8] *intorno intorno* around
[9] *a petto a* compared with

non faceva a tempo a fare le sue capriole. Bravo tiratore, non discuto; mai io ci avevo altro da fare che ammirare la sua perizia. Mi avvicinai, serio, e dissi a Iole, tirandola per la manica: "Buona sera. Senti un po', debbo dirti due parole.' Intanto, però, Paolino,
5 distruggeva tutto l'effetto della mia serietà, gridando, tra le risate: 'Iole, non conosci Gigi? Permetti che te lo presento?'
Lei si voltò alle mie parole e mi squadrò come se non mi avesse mai visto nè conosciuto; poi disse: 'Ma Gigi, non è il momento'; indicando con gli occhi l'americano. Insistetti: 'Ma io debbo
10 parlarti.' Sapevo che quello, invece, era il momento; se non l'avessi colto, non si sarebbe ripresentato mai più. L'americano, che doveva averci sentito, si voltò ad un tratto e disse ridendo: 'Gigi, non è il momento'; quindi mi passò il fucile: 'Provi un po' lei, vediamo.'
Presi meccanicamente il fucile e sparai qualche colpo, senza
15 colpire l'orso, però, perchè le mani mi tremavano dal nervoso. Allora buttai il fucile sul banco e dissi risolutamente: 'Insomma, tu hai da sentirmi perchè io ho da parlarti. Vieni, andiamo'; e l'acchiappai per un braccio. Sgarbata, con arie di gran signora offesa, lei si tirò indietro e ripetè, secca secca: [10] 'Ma se ti ho
20 detto che non è il momento.' Intanto dietro di me sentivo Paolino che rideva e ripeteva: 'Gigi, non è il momento.'
Insomma, mi canzonavano; nero, incapace di staccarmi da Iole che adesso si era messa a sparare anche lei, finsi di osservare il tiro: non ne azzeccava uno. L'americano, bonaccione, trasse dalla
25 tasca della giacca a vento un pacchetto di sigarette e me le offrì: 'Sigaretta?' Rifiutai dicendo: 'Io non sono venuto qui per fumare, ma per parlare con la signorina.' E lui, scuotendo l'indice, scherzoso: 'Parlare con la signorina? Ma non è il momento.'
Intanto Iole si era stufata di tirare all'orso ed era passata alla
30 baracca accanto, quella del tiro a segno alla pallina di celluloide che salta in cima allo zampillo d'acqua. Ricominciarono a sparare; anche qui l'americano faceva centro ogni volta; e io, tutto sconvolto, impotente ormai a controllarmi, riprovai a tirare Iole per la manica

---

[10] *secca secca*   in a curt manner

dicendole sottovoce: 'Due parole sole. Poi ti lascio e non mi vedi mai più.' Ma lei, che ormai pareva farlo apposta, mi rispose, alzando le spalle: 'Più tardi. Lo vedi che adesso non è il momento.' Paolino afferrò a volo la frase, come una palla, e gridò, con quanto fiato aveva: "Gigi, non è il momento.' ⁵

Proprio allora, un gruppo di quei giovinastri sfrenati, che vanno a piazza Navona per far chiasso e prendere in giro ¹¹ i passanti, ci stavano addosso strombettando e fischiando. Udire la frase di Paolino e riprenderla a gran voce, come un ritornello, tenendosi per mano e facendoci intorno il girotondo, fu tutta una cosa sola. ¹⁰ Eccoci dunque nel mezzo di una sarabanda di scalmanati che urlava in coro: 'Gigi, non è il momento.' Paolino, naturalmente, dal convulso delle risate, quasi rotolava a terra; anche l'americano rideva; persino Iole, benchè stizzita, non poteva trattenere un sorriso; soltanto io, serio, scuro, le braccia incrociate, aspettavo a ¹⁵ piè fermo che la cagnara si esaurisse. Come Dio volle, alla fine, sempre urlando: 'Gigi, non è il momento,' quei giovanotti si incolonnarono, tenendosi per i fianchi, uno dietro l'altro, e si allontanarono tra le proteste generali. L'americano guardò l'orologio e disse: 'È il momento di andare a mangiare qualche cosa. ²⁰ Venite anche voi.' Malvolentieri, li seguii in una trattoria, lì accanto.

A pianterreno non c'era posto: la gente, fitta fitta, gremiva i tavoli di fronte ai piatti e ai mezzi litri. L'oste ci venne incontro e, vedendoci perplessi, disse: 'Ci ho la saletta al secondo piano. C'è il ²⁵ pranzo sociale dei tranvieri, ma a voi non vi fa niente, no?' Paolino, ormai scatenato, rispose: 'Il pranzo sociale, la notte della Befana? Ma non è il momento.' L'oste lo guardò brutto, un attimo, quindi ci precedette su per la scala, al secondo piano.

Era una sala bassa, dove si erano addensati tutto il fumo ³⁰ e il puzzo di fritto della sala a pianterreno. Sotto il soffitto che, alzando la mano, si poteva toccare, c'era una grande tavola a ferro di cavallo, di soli uomini, tutti omaccioni di mezza età, i

---

¹¹ *prendere in giro*   to make fun of

tranvieri, che si mangiavano il loro pranzo sociale. Alla prima
occhiata li giudicai sbronzi: sulla tavola i litri, i mezzi litri e i
fiaschi non si contavano. L'oste ci apparecchiò un tavolino in un
angolo e quindi ordinammo, tutta roba greve, romanesca, rigatoni
con la pagliata, coda alla vaccinara, abbacchio, porchetta. Cioè
ordinarono, perchè io, che dal nervoso mi sentivo addirittura
nauseato, dissi: 'Per me una cicoria in brodo.' Paolino subito gridò,
sganasciandosi dalle risate: 'Una cicoria in brodo la notte della
Befana? Ma Gigi, non è il momento.' Insomma, ricominciavano.
Non c'è niente di peggio di quando una frase cretina si pianta nel
cervello come un chiodo. Quella frase: 'Gigi, non è il momento,'
adesso me la ripetevano ad ogni occasione tutti e tre: l'americano
da vero americano bonaccione, senza capirla, quasi affettuosamente;
Paolino con malignità concentrata, smascellandosi dalle risate; Iole
con fastidio, quasi a dire: 'Tu ci sei, esisti? Ma Gigi, non è il
momento.' Ed era inutile protestare perchè quella frase serviva
anche a rispondere alle mie proteste. Dicevo, per esempio:
'Piantatela o se no, parola,[12] finisce che vi prendo a pugni.'[13] E
loro: 'A pugni? Ma Gigi, non è il momento.' Oppure calmissimo,
incominciavo: 'Lo sapete voi che siete?' e loro, interrompendomi:
'Non dircelo Gigi, non è il momento.' Era proprio uno sfinimento;
e io ci sformavo; e non serviva neppure che io stessi zitto perchè,
allora, loro mi stuzzicavano dicendo: 'Perchè così triste e così
silenzioso? Ma Gigi, non è il momento.'

Portarono le vivande e loro mangiarono ma io quasi non toccai
cibo perchè come ho detto, non avevo fame, benchè loro mi
canzonassero dicendo: 'Gigi, non hai fame? Ma non è il momento.'
Intanto, lì vicino, il pranzo sociale si avvicinava alla fine. Ecco
che si leva uno dei tranvieri, un pezzo d'uomo con la faccia rossa
e i baffi neri, alzando in alto il bicchiere. Subito, per tutto il ferro
di cavallo, gridarono: 'Zitti, zitti'; e anche noi facemmo silenzio e
guardammo. Quell'omaccione in una mano teneva il bicchiere e

---

[12] *parola*   upon my word (of honor)
[13] *vi prendo a pugni*   I'll sock you

nell'altra un foglio di carta. Disse, imbrogliandosi nelle parole perchè ci aveva la lingua grossa dal molto vino bevuto: 'E adesso cari amici, amici belli, vi chiedo di far silenzio perchè vorrei leggervi una mia modesta, ma sincera poesia in onore del pranzo sociale.' Paolino che stava a sentirlo, con la faccia tutta imporporata dalle risate, non si sa come saltò su,[14] allora: 'Una poesia? Ma non è il momento.'

Il poeta che stava avvicinando il foglio agli occhi si voltò subito come una vipera, dicendo: 'Ohò, che dici a noi?' Ora quello era invece proprio il momento, tanto per adoperare questa frase maledetta, di far silenzio e abbozzare[15] perchè quelli erano venti e noialtri quattro e quelli erano sbronzi e per giunta ignoranti e non potevano certo capire lo scherzo. Purtroppo, però, anche l'americano era sbronzo, ormai. Così lui venne di rincalzo a Paolino, urlando come un ossesso: 'Sicuro, a voi: non è il momento.'

Quello che avvenne poi ve lo potete facilmente immaginare. Il poeta e quattro altri dei più forzuti e più ubbriachi tosto ci vennero incontro, minacciosi, gridando: 'Ma chi siete? Ma che volete?' Poi vidi Paolino andar giù con tutta la seggiola per via di uno spintone che il poeta gli aveva dato in cima al petto; gli altri quattro aggredirono l'americano e me che non c'entravo. Intanto dal tavolo a ferro di cavallo si levavano urla feroci: 'Schifosi, che vogliono questi schifosi? Buttateli giù per la scala'; e Iole spaventata, gridava: 'Aiuto, si ammazzano, aiuto.'

Dal pianterreno arrivarono di corsa i camerieri, l'oste, qualche avventore e si gettarono in mezzo cercando di dividerci. Adesso tutta la tavolata dei tranvieri era in piedi urlando: 'Schifosi, schifosi'; il poeta perdeva sangue dal naso; l'americano si era fatto brutto e tirava pugni all'impazzata; io mi divincolavo tra due tranvieri che mi prendevano a botte in testa; e quel disgraziato di Paolino, rannicchiato sotto il tavolo, continuava a gridare: 'Non è il momento.'

---

[14] *saltò su* broke in suddenly to say
[15] *abozzare* to stop, to leave off

Insomma, finì che a spinte, a urli e a pacche, fummo tutti e quattro cacciati dalla trattoria. Come ci ritrovammo, malconci, in quel fracasso di piazza Navona, Iole si attaccò al braccio dell'americano il quale filò direttamente verso piazza Zanardelli. Qui li aspettava un macchinone lungo, mezzo verde e mezzo giallo; e loro fecero per salirci. Col coraggio della disperazione, mi attaccai allora al braccio di Iole dicendole: 'Senti, ora basta, de riffe o de raffe [16] devi ascoltarmi.' Questa volta lei volle essere ragionevole: 'Ma Gigi, renditi conto, non è possibile adesso, non è...' esitò e quindi finì con una smorfia di dispetto, quasi suo malgrado, 'non è il momento.' L'americano era già salito e accese il motore. Salì anche lei; l'americano si voltò e, scuotendo l'indice, disse per l'ultima volta, scherzoso: 'Gigi, non è il momento.' Quindi la macchina partì come un razzo lasciandoci noi due, Paolino ed io, in mezzo alla piazza deserta.

Mi voltai imbestialito, contro Paolino; e senza dir nulla l'acchiappai per il bavero della giacca. Lui ripeteva: 'Non è il momento, Gigi, non è il momento,' e cercava di liberarsi. Ci separarono a gran fatica alcuni passanti e due guardie accorse al tafferuglio. Ma sapete che disse una delle guardie? 'Vi pare questo il momento di menarvi? [17] La notte della Befana? Vergogna, ragazzacci, e adesso circolate.' Così anche la guardia, senza rendersene conto, mi canzonava.[18] Ma, insomma, quando sarà il momento?

---

[16] *de riffe o de raffe*   one way or other
[17] *menarvi*   to fight each other
[18] *mi canzonava*   was making fun of me

Primo rapporto sulla terra dell''inviato speciale' della luna

Strano paese. È abitato da due razze ben distinte, sia moralmente, sia, fino ad un certo punto, fisicamente: la razza degli uomini chiamati ricchi e quella degli uomini chiamati poveri. Il significato di queste due parole, ricchi e poveri, è oscuro e la nostra imperfetta conoscenza della lingua del paese non ci ha permesso di accertarlo. Ma le nostre informazioni vengono in grandissima parte dai ricchi, assai più dei poveri abbordabili, ciarlieri e ospitali.

Dicono dunque i ricchi che i poveri sono una gente venuta da non si sa dove, che si stabilì nel paese in tempi immemorabili e che da allora non ha fatto che proliferare, sempre mantenendo inalterato il suo spiacevole carattere. Nessuno, conosciuto questo carattere, potrebbe non deplorarlo e dar torto ai ricchi. I poveri, prima di tutto, non amano la pulizia e la bellezza. I loro vestiti sono sudici e rattoppati, le loro case squallide, le loro masserizie logore e brutte. Ma per una strana perversione del gusto essi sembrano preferire gli stracci ai panni nuovi, le case popolari alle ville e ai palazzi, i mobili di poco prezzo a quelli di marca.[1]

Chi infatti, domandano i ricchi, potrebbe affermare di aver mai visto un povero ben vestito e alloggiato in una bella casa, tra suppellettili di lusso?

Non basta. I poveri non amano la cultura. È molto difficile vedere un povero con un libro in mano, o in un museo, o seduto ad ascoltare un concerto. I poveri nulla sanno delle arti e scambiano tranquillamente un'oleografia con un quadro di maestro,[2] una statuina di Lucca con un Prassitele, una canzonetta volgare con un preludio di Bach. Se dipendesse da loro, le Muse, questa consolazione degli uomini, avrebbero da tempo disertato il mondo. I divertimenti dei poveri, spiegano i ricchi, sono quanto di più rozzo si possa immaginare: bicchierate, ballonzoli, partite di bocce o di pallone, pugilati e altri simili svaghi. Gli è che i poveri preferiscono l'ignoranza alla cultura, affermano i ricchi.

Ancora: i poveri odiano la natura. Alla bella stagione i ricchi sogliono andarsene di qua e di là, al mare, in campagna, in montagna. Godono delle belle acque azzurre, dell'aria pura, delle solitudini alpestri; ritemprano gli animi e i corpi. Ma i poveri non vogliono uscire a nessun costo[3] dai loro fetidi quartieri cittadini. Il variare delle stagioni li lascia indifferenti; non sentono il bisogno di mitigare il freddo col caldo e il caldo col freddo; preferiscono al mare le vasche municipali, alla campagna i rognosi prati della periferia, e ai monti le terrazze delle loro case. Ora, domandano i ricchi, come si fa a non amare la natura?

E almeno i poveri in città facessero vita di società. Nient'affatto; essi non sembrano conoscere altro luogo di riunione che le cosiddette fabbriche. Figuratevi che queste fabbriche sono quanto di più lugubre si possa immaginare: sinistri vascelli di cemento e di

---

[1] *di marca*   first quality
[2] *quadro di maestro*   an original painting
[3] *a nessun costo*   in no case, on no account

vetro, popolati di macchine fragorose, fumosi, sudici, gelati d'inverno e ardenti d'estate.

Altri poveri, addirittura, non vivono in città ma nella solitudine delle campagne. Loro sola occupazione e, bisogna credere, loro solo svago: rivoltare con rozzi e pesanti strumenti di ferro le zolle 5 della terra, dall'alba al tramonto, in tutte le stagioni, sotto il solleone come sotto la pioggia. E pensare, dicono i ricchi, che ci sarebbero tante altre cose da fare a questo mondo e tanto più intelligenti e più dilettose.

Altri poveri, poi, anche più stravaganti, antepongono al sole le 10 tenebre e al cielo le viscere della terra. Si inabissano in gallerie profondissime e lì, al buio, si dilettano di estrarre pietre. Questi luoghi sotterranei sono chiamati miniere. A nessun ricco verrebbe mai in mente di scendere in una miniera.

Tutto ciò i poveri designano con il termine di lavoro, altro 15 vocabolo di significato, per noi, misterioso e indecifrabile. I poveri sono tanto affezionati a questo loro lavoro che, ove per qualche motivo che non abbiamo potuto appurare, le fabbriche rimangano chiuse e le miniere inattive, protestano, gridano e minacciano tumulti e violenze. Chi ci capisce nulla, dicono i ricchi, non 20 sarebbe più facile e più piacevole riunirsi in qualche comodo salotto, in qualche circolo decoroso?

Non parliamo della cucina dei poveri. Non esistono per loro i deliziosi manicaretti, i vini vecchi, i dolci squisiti. Essi preferiscono di gran lunga [4] rozzi cibi quali i fagioli, le cipolle, le rape, le 25 patate, l'aglio, il pan secco. Quelle rare volte che si adattano a mangiare carne e pesce, state pur certi che sceglieranno infallibilmente il pesce più tiglioso, la carne più dura. Il vino non gli [5] piace che agro o annacquato. Non amano le primizie e aspettano a mangiare i piselli quando sono farinosi, i carciofi quando sono 30

---

[4] *di gran lunga*   by far
[5] *gli*   [colloq. m. sing., indirect personal pronoun used with the meaning of *loro*]

stopposi, gli asparagi quando sono legnosi. Impossibile, insomma, fargli apprezzare la gioia della tavola.

E che dire del tabacco dei poveri? Disdegnano, gli sciocchi, i delicati prodotti dell'Oriente o quelli più sapidi dell'America e ⁵ fumano certa robaccia nera, acre, che fa tossire e non dà alcun piacere. Un buon sigaro Avana, una leggera sigaretta turca, non dicono nulla ai poveri. Altra stranezza dei poveri: la salute non gli preme. Che altro si dovrebbe pensare, infatti, vedendo la noncuranza con la quale si ¹⁰ espongono alle intemperie e la negligenza che, una volta malati, pongono nel curarsi? Non comprano medicine, non vanno in sanatorio, neanche accettano di starsene a letto quei giorni o quei mesi che sono necessari.

I ricchi spiegano che i poveri trascurano la salute per quella ¹⁵ loro assurda passione di non mancare un solo giorno nelle fabbriche, nelle miniere e nei campi. È incomprensibile, ma tant'è: la ragione è questa.

Non si finirebbe mai di parlare dei poveri e del loro attaccamento ad abitudini nocive, rozze, stravaganti. Piuttosto sarà più interes- ²⁰ sante esaminare i motivi di così anormale condotta.

I ricchi ci informano che studi approfonditi sulla razza dei poveri sono stati fatti in tutti i tempi. Grosso modo,⁶ gli studiosi si dividono in due categorie: coloro che attribuiscono il carattere dei poveri ad una perversità, per così dire, volontaria, e pensano ²⁵ che si potrebbe correggerli e trasformarli; e coloro che affermano non esservi rimedio, perchè quel carattere è innato. I primi consigliano un'attiva predicazione e opera di persuasione; i secondi, più scettici, soltanto delle misure di polizia. Questi ultimi sembrano aver ragione perchè fin adesso tutte le prediche sui vantaggi della ³⁰ pulizia, della bellezza, del lusso, della cultura e dell'ozio, non hanno sortito ⁷ alcun risultato.

Anzi, nonostante le cure che i ricchi si prendono dei poveri,

---

⁶ *grosso modo*   roughly (speaking)
⁷ *non hanno sortito*   have not produced

questi, assai ingrati, non amano i ricchi. Bisogna però riconoscere
che i ricchi non sempre riescono a nascondere la loro ripugnanza
per il modo di vivere dei poveri.

Come sempre, nei nostri viaggi, abbiamo voluto sentire anche
l'altra campana.[8] Così abbiamo interrogato i poveri. Non è stato   5
facile, vista la loro ignoranza di qualsiasi lingua che non sia quella
del paese. Però, alla fine, siamo riusciti ad ottenere questa straor-
dinaria risposta: la ragione della differenza tra loro e i ricchi è
una sola: e cioè che i ricchi posseggono una cosa chiamata denaro,
la quale, invece, fa quasi sempre difetto[9] ai poveri.   10
Abbiamo voluto vedere che cosa fosse questo denaro capace
di produrre diversità così enormi. E abbiamo scoperto che si
tratta per lo più di foglietti di carta colorata o di pezzetti di
metallo di forma tonda.

Data la ben nota inclinazione dei poveri a nascondere la verità,   15
dubitiamo che questo cosiddetto denaro sia la causa determinante
di così strani effetti.

E perciò ripetiamo: strano paese.

---

[8] *sentire . . . campana* to hear the other party, the other side of the
question
[9] *fare difetto* to lack, to be lacking

Lo scimpanzè

Inverno romano. Scendevo giù per il viale di Villa Borghese che porta al Museo e intanto pioveva a dirotto.[1] Ma si poteva vedere ogni goccia venir giù rigando di bianco il cielo nero, per via del sole che risplendeva chiaro in fondo ai boschetti, tra le nuvole che scappavano d'ogni parte, luminose. Pioveva e c'era il sole; se non avessi saputo che era gennaio, avrei pensato che fosse marzo, tanto l'aria era dolce e l'erba, nei sottoboschi, alta, folta e verde. Pioveva a stecche d'ombrello e il sole risplendeva che pareva d'oro e quell'erba, sotto gli alberi, si beveva egualmente la pioggia e il sole. Tutto ad un tratto mi sentii felice, con una gran forza nelle gambe, come se fossi stato un grillo gigantesco, da potere con un salto salire in cima al tetto del Museo che si vedeva in fondo al

---

[1] *pioveva a dirotto* it was pouring

viale con la sua bella facciata gialla; e feci davvero il salto aprendo
la bocca verso il cielo e una goccia di pioggia mi cadde dritta nella
bocca e mi parve che mi ubbriacasse come se fosse stato un sorso
di liquore e pensai: 'Ci ho vent'anni...e ho ancora da vivere questa
vita tanto bella almeno altri quaranta o cinquant'anni...viva la vita.'   5
A destra del viale, in cima ad una collinetta, vidi due o tre cavalli
grossi e pasciuti con dei ragazzi ben vestiti in sella che aspettavano
la fine della pioggia riparati sotto i lecci e non so perchè quei
cavalli mi parvero tanto belli e pensai ancora: 'Sono proprio felice.'
Intanto, quasi senza accorgermene, avevo cominciato a canterellare   10
una canzonetta alla moda; e mi ricordai ad un tratto del titolo di
un film che avevo visto tempo addietro: cantando sotto la pioggia.

Forse ero felice perchè andavo al mio primo appuntamento con
Gloria, la cassiera di un bar dalle parti di piazza della Regina dove
io lavoravo come meccanico in un garage. Questa Gloria l'avevo   15
accostata al buio, assistendo nel bar alla televisione; e prima le avevo
sfiorato il braccio con il braccio, e poi, facendomi coraggio,[2] le
avevo messo la mano sulla mano; e così, finita la televisione, le
avevo fissato un appuntamento per giovedì che era il giorno in
cui la padrona le dava il cambio alla cassa del bar. Oggi era giovedì,   20
io andavo all'appuntamento e mi sentivo felice.

La sola preoccupazione era che ci avevo pochi soldi. Sono cose
che succedono quando si ha vent'anni e si è meccanici in un garage.
Tanto pochi da non potere offrire a Gloria che una visita al giardino
zoologico e poi, tutt'al più,[3] un espresso, in piedi, in un bar. Niente   25
cinema, perchè i cinema dalle parti di via Veneto sono cari; a
maggior ragione, niente ballo in una sala, anche fosse quella del
Quadraro. Ma io ci ho la passione[4] degli animali e mi illudevo
che anche Gloria ce l'avesse. E poi contavo sul sentimento: se
questo c'è, che importano i soldi? Tra questi pensieri ero giunto al   30
Museo che era il luogo dell'appuntamento. Mi misi al riparo della
pioggia, sotto un cornicione, e aspettai.

---

[2] *facendomi coraggio*   summoning up my courage
[3] *tutt'al più*   at the most
[4] *ho la passione*   I adore, I am fond of

Finalmente, ecco Gloria arrivare da uno di quei viali deserti, sotto la pioggia, riparandosi con l'ombrellino. Non so perché dal modo come era acconciata compresi subito il mio errore: quella non era la ragazza che ci voleva per me. Era tutta infronzolata, con un cappotto nuovo, rosso, e un vestito di seta verde bottiglia; aveva una nuova acconciatura ai capelli così che quasi quasi non la riconobbi. Di solito li portava lisci e sciolti ai due lati del viso. Adesso, invece, li aveva tutti raccolti in cima al capo in tanti riccetti, e i tratti del viso che lei aveva grossi e un po' brutali venivano fuori senza rimedio, come nudi. Mi colpì il naso che, senza essere brutto, non era bello, un po' a forma di gnocco. E la bocca come di negra, di espressione schifiltosa, carica di rossetto, che luccicava. Mi disse, appena ci fummo salutati: 'Ci voleva anche la pioggia, auffa.[5] Beh,[6] dove andiamo? Perchè non andiamo al cinema, qui accanto, a via Veneto?'

Risposi: 'Bel divertimento. Stare insieme al buio in un cinema e poi, finito il film, salutarsi e buonanotte.' 'Allora andiamo a ballare.' 'Io non so ballare.' 'Non sai ballare? E che aspetti a imparare? Povera me, sono cascata bene.[7] E dove vogliamo andare allora? A sederci su una panchina?'

Incominciai: 'Ci sarebbe lo zoo...' Ma lei, subito, storcendo la bocca: 'Come le serve e i militari in libera uscita.[8] Grazie tanto, me ne torno a casa.' E fece il gesto di andarsene. Allora dissi, quasi sperando, in fondo, che se ne andasse davvero: 'E va bene, arrivederci.' Lei questa volta ebbe paura che la lasciassi: 'E va bene, andiamoci pure, pazienza.'

Così, scendemmo verso lo zoo, per un viale deserto, sotto la pioggia. Gloria ci veniva malvolentieri, si capiva persino dal modo di camminare, dispettoso e strascicato. Giungiamo alle porte dello zoo, non c'era un cane[9] o meglio c'era soltanto l'uomo dei

---

[5] *auffa*   expression of boredom or displeasure
[6] *beh*   good! well?
[7] *sono cascata bene*   I struck it lucky
[8] *in libera uscita*   on pass
[9] *non c'era un cane*   there was not a soul

palloncini di gomma colorata, riparato sotto un albero. Prendo due biglietti, compro pure due sacchetti di nocciline e ne do uno a Gloria. Lei fa: [10] 'Che roba è questa?' 'È per le scimmie.' 'Beh, dagliele tu, non posso soffrire [11] le scimmie.'

Entrammo e lei si diresse verso il recinto degli elefanti. Ce n'era uno, enorme, con la pelle grigia tutta cascante come se gli fosse stata troppo larga, la fronte appoggiata contro le sbarre. Dissi, già contento: 'Lo vedi, l'elefante.' E lei, sgarbata: 'Già, l'elefante, che c'è di speciale?'

L'elefante, simpatico, ci guardava fisso con i suoi occhietti intelligenti; allora mi chinai, strappai da terra un pugno d'erba e lo diedi a Gloria dicendole: 'Prova un po' a dargliela.' Lei non voleva, poi accettò di malagrazia. L'elefante stese la proboscide, prese l'erba dalla mano di Gloria, arrotolò indietro lento lento la proboscide e si mise l'erba in bocca. Gloria non potè fare a meno di gridare: 'Guarda, mangia, mangia,' con gioia; e io, per un momento, sperai che ci prendesse gusto.[12] Ma lei subito si pentì: 'Ecco che mi sono sporcata le mani di terra...guarda,' e si pulì la mano con schifo, sul mio impermeabile. Passammo dall'elefante al rinoceronte il quale era proprio brutto, con quel corno tra gli occhi, e stava fermo come un monumento, tutto luccicante di pioggia. Dissi a Gloria: 'È brutto ma non ne ha colpa. Sotto tutto quel po' po' di corazza [13] ci ha un carattere buono: non mangia che erba.' Ma Gloria disse, dispettosa: 'Che ci trovi di interessante? Sembra tutto ricucito come un pallone di football.' E tirò via [14] entrando nella casa dell'ippopotamo.

Ci faceva buio,[15] nella casa, e in un angolo c'erano tante balle di fieno e dietro le sbarre si indovinava una grande vasca di acqua nera e tranquilla: l'ippopotamo non si vedeva. 'Non c'è, andiamo,'

---

[10] *lei fa*   she says
[11] *non posso soffrire*   I can't stand, I can't bear
[12] *sperai . . . gusto*   I hoped she would take a liking for it
[13] *sotto . . . corazza*   under all that heavy armor
[14] *tirò via*   went on
[15] *faceva buio*   it was dark

disse Gloria sempre dispettosa; e uscì di corsa. Io ero rimasto
indietro e, proprio, in quel momento, ecco emergere dall'acqua
come due cornetti luccicanti, gli occhi dell'ippopotamo, e poi
un po' di groppa simile ad una cotica nera e quindi tutta la testa.
5   Poveretto, era lento perchè era tanto grosso e ci aveva messo un
po' di tempo a venir fuori dell'acqua, ma adesso voleva farsi
vedere, buono buono, e anzi, ecco, spalancava la bocca, enorme,
tutta foderata di carne, con certi denti gialli e corti piantati di
traverso e la lingua che pareva un cuscino di carne rosa. Chiamai,
10 pieno di gioia: 'Gloria, Gloria, è venuto fuori.' Ma sì, fatica
sprecata, lei era già lontana, dalla parte degli orsi bruni.
     Questi stavano accucciati dietro le sbarre, buttati in terra, con
gli zamponi pelosi pieni di unghioni sotto le guance, dormendo
in santa pace; [16] e Gloria non volle neppure guardarli perchè, disse,
15 a lei gli orsi gli ricordavano lo scendiletto, appunto, di pelle d'orso
di una sua vecchia zia. Insomma era proprio sgarbata e lo faceva
apposta,[17] si vedeva. E più lo fu di fronte alle gazzelle, tanto
carucce, con quelle gambe sottili, quegli occhi neri e belli e quelle
corna tutte arrotolate: 'Capre, che sono venuta a vedere le capre?'
20 Contavo sui felini, come sarebbe a dire tigri, leoni, pantere e
simili. In una gabbia c'erano due tigri proprio magnifiche che pas-
seggiavano incrociandosi l'una con l'altra, senza posa, e ogni tanto
guardavano a noialtri, con gli occhioni inviperiti e gialli tra le tante
striscie gialle e nere. Gloria concesse a mezza bocca [18] che erano
25 belle e stavamo appunto ammirandole quando ci fu un fuggi
fuggi [19] generale di quei pochi visitatori verso un'altra gabbia: il
pasto dei leoni. Dissi a Gloria: 'Presto, corriamo a vedere'; e
lei questa volta si lasciò trascinare ma per sfortuna inciampò e
tutto ad un tratto gridò con voce lamentosa: 'Povera me, mi sono
30 rotto un tacco.' Era vero, nella corsa aveva messo un piede in

---

[16] *in santa pace*   peacefully
[17] *lo faceva apposta*   she was doing it intentionally
[18] *a mezza bocca*   reluctantly
[19] *fuggi fuggi*   a headlong flight

fallo [20] e si era rotto il tacco di una scarpa. 'Queste scarpe, lo so io quanto mi sono costate; e adesso chi me le ripaga,' incominciò a piagnucolare, tastando il tacco, e io intanto le stavo accosto, fremendo, e dalla gabbia dei leoni veniva un finimondo di ruggiti e poi non si sentì più nulla: il meglio del pasto era finito. Infatti quando, lei zoppicando appoggiata al mio braccio e io sorreggendola, ci arrivammo, non c'era quasi più niente da vedere: i leoni stavano accucciati negli angoli più scuri, con i testoni biondi chinati a rosicchiare qualche costola spolpata di cavallo. Gloria disse: 'Puzzano, però'; e questo fu tutto quello che trovò da dire su quei tre leoni tanto belli, da stare un'ora a guardarli senza fiato.

Adesso ero anch'io di malumore. L'avrei ammazzata, parola.[21] Arrivammo alle montagnole dove ci sono gli orsi e le foche del Polo Nord. Gli orsi stavano qua e là , rimminchioniti, con i loro pelliccioni bianchi: uno si era messo a zampe per aria, e si strofinava il dorso, come se avesse avuto il prurito; un altro dondolava la testa su e giù, con aria così tonta che mi fece ridere. Ma Gloria commentò: 'Altri scendiletti.' A me piacevano anche le foche: nuotavano felici, due a due, come se avessero ballato, saltavano senza gambe e senza braccia sui finti lastroni di ghiaccio, divincolando il corpo nero e luccicante, poi si tuffavano di nuovo nell' acqua. Ma Gloria mi trascinò via dicendo: 'La sola foca che m'interessa è quella delle scarpe e delle borsette.'

Insomma non gliene andava bene una. Volli, a questo punto, farle capire che ero stufo e, dopo le foche, presi direttamente per un viale verso l'uscita. Lei capì e si aggrappò al mio braccio domandando: 'Dove andiamo?' 'Usciamo.' 'E le scimmie, non le vediamo le scimmie?' 'No, le vediamo un'altra volta.' 'Ma che, ce l'hai con me?'[22] 'Sì, mi hai stufato,' E lei allora, tutta vezzosa: 'Su, non avertene a male.[23] Lo sai che ieri ti ho pensato?' 'E che

---

[20] *aveva . . . in fallo* she had taken a wrong step
[21] *parola* on my word; I swear
[22] *ce l'hai con me?* are you angry with me?
[23] *non avertene a male* don't take offense at it

hai pensato?' 'Niente, ti ho pensato, ecco tutto. Beh, vieni, andiamo a vedere le scimmie.'

Ecco i gabbioni delle scimmie. Ce n'erano di piccole assai, ma con la coda lunga che loro si prendevano in mano spulciandola
5 svelte svelte e guardandoci intanto con le faccette tristi; altre più grandi, con il sedere che pareva tutto un mazzo di melanzane violette, e la testa di cane. Adesso Gloria voleva dimostrarmi che a lei le scimmie piacevano; ma lo faceva con un tale sforzo che quasi quasi l'avrei preferita sgarbata come prima. Tanto che le dissi:
10 'Ma piantala. Si vede lontano un miglio che a te le bestie non ti interessano.' E lei: 'Lo vedi come sei, sempre scontento. Mi piacciono, sì, mi piacciono moltissimo, ma non posso ballare dalla gioia. Dammi quelle noccioline.' Intanto aveva ricominciato a piovere, fino fino, controluce al sole che risplendeva chiaro dietro
15 le palme dello zoo.

Eravamo adesso davanti la gabbia degli scimpanzè. Uno di questi scimpanzè, grande come un ragazzo, con tutto il pelo bruno arruffato, stava in un cantuccio mangiando una banana come una persona, cioè con le mani, a morsetti piccoli, dopo aver tirato via,
20 con garbo e educazione, la buccia; un altro era salito sopra l'altalena e andava su e giù, ritto in piedi, e non si capiva perchè lo facesse, tanto era serio. Accanto a noi c'erano due giovanotti, uno magro e alto a uno piccolo e grasso che ridevano commentando i gesti e le smorfie delle scimmie.
25 Lo scimpanzè che stava sull'altalena discese e si accostò alle sbarre, ritto in piedi. Allungava la bocca, nera fuori e rosa dentro, come per parlare e faceva un mugolio strano; intanto si grattava la pancia là dove il pelo era meno fitto. Gloria gli stese la mano con una nocciolina ma lo scimpanzè manco se ne accorse. Gloria disse:
30 'Ma si può sapere che ci ha? [24] Non gli piacciono le noccioline?' Lo scimpanzè fece una specie di fischio, si allontanò, curvo e come affaticato, verso il fondo della gabbia, quindi si rivoltò ad un tratto,

---

[24] *ma si può sapere che ci ha?*   I wonder what's wrong with it?

raccattò una manciata di non so che sudiciume dal pavimento,
prese la rincorsa e ce la gettò in faccia.

La sola colpita fu Gloria: io le stavo dietro e quei due giovanotti furono lesti a saltare da parte. Tutto avvenne in un attimo:
Gloria si guardò il bel cappotto rosso schizzato da capo a fondo, ⁵
quei due giovanotti scoppiarono in una risata, Gloria gridò:
'Maledetto lo zoo e maledette queste bestiacce' e corse via singhioz-
zando. Provai a seguirla ma lei mi avvertì: 'Non avvicinarti.
Lasciami. Lasciami stare;' ²⁵ e io allora, piano piano, rallentai il
passo e alla fine mi fermai. Gloria infilò l'uscita e scomparve. ¹⁰
Intanto, sul cielo nero, era apparso un grande arcobaleno di
tutti i colori, benchè piovesse ancora. Mi avviai anch'io fuori dello
zoo e poi risalii il viale e mi ritrovai in quello stesso luogo dove, un
paio d'ore prima, mi ero sentito così contento. Adesso invece ero
smosciato ²⁶ e triste e Villa Borghese mi pareva la solita Villa ¹⁵
Borghese di tutti i giorni e quella stessa pioggia che prima mi aveva
fatto tanto piacere e me la sarei bevuta, adesso mi infastidiva. Ah,
perchè le donne hanno il potere di rendere felici, e non lo sanno,
e rovinano ogni cosa con il loro pessimo carattere?

---

²⁵ *lasciami stare*   leave me alone
²⁶ *smosciato*   fed up

La vita è una giungla

Dopo le espansioni della sera avanti, nel locale notturno dove aveva conosciuto le due ragazze, la voce al telefono sembrò a Girolamo, in maniera inspiegabile, restia e quasi ostile: 'A colazione? Vuole che andiamo fuori a colazione con questo caldo?'

'Ma ieri sera eravamo restati d'accordo che stamani avremmo fatto colazione insieme.'

'Si dicono tante cose la sera, dopo aver bevuto un poco.'

'Veramente, se lei ricorda, fu proprio lei a raccomandarmi di telefonare per la colazione.'

'Fui io? Si vede che ero ubriaca.'

'Insomma, cosa vuole fare?'

'Aspetti un momento.'

Girolamo udì i tacchi della ragazza allontanarsi sul pavimento e poi udì un rumore di discussione concitata e sgradevole; ma non

distinse le parole. Quindi, ecco di nuovo la voce: 'Venga tra
un'ora.'

'Viene lei sola?'

'Non se ne parla neppure. Viene anche la mia amica.'

Assai malcontento, domandandosi se non fosse il caso di trovare 5
un pretesto e liberarsi dell'impegno, Girolamo passò quell'ora
correndo in macchina da un viale periferico all'altro, all'ombra dei
grandi platani carichi di fogliame estivo. Le due ragazze abitavano
ai Parioli; come si fermò davanti alla loro casa, fu meravigliato dal
lusso moderno della facciata, tutta vetri e marmi: all'apparenza gli 10
erano sembrate di modesta condizione, forse due impiegate. Ma
una volta entrato nell'ingresso, scoprì che l'appartamento stava nel
seminterrato. Discese la scala, al buio trovò la porta e suonò. La
solita voce sgarbata gli gridò dall'interno che andasse ad aspettare
in strada. Girolamo pensò che le ragazze probabilmente dispone- 15
vano di una sola stanza e che questa stanza era in gran disordine.
Risalì la scala e andò a sedersi nell'automobile, di fronte al portone.

Aspettò un pezzo,[1] sotto il sole che arroventava la carrozzeria;
finalmente, eccole. Erano assai diverse: una piccola, graziosa e
più giovane; l'altra grande, brutta e più vecchia; ma avevano in 20
comune la stessa cipria cadaverica sulle facce pallide, lo stesso
mortuario cerchio di tintura nera intorno agli occhi, lo stesso rossetto anemico, color mucosa, sulle labbra. Anche i vestiti erano
simili: due gonnelle verdi, in forma di tulipani e due camicette
diafane, rigide e trasparenti attraverso le quali, come attraverso 25
un cellophane, si potevano vedere i robusti reggipetti, ben tirati e
aderenti, color rosa carico. I capelli di ambedue erano di un biondo
paglierino che contrastava con gli occhi e le sopracciglia nere. Si
avvicinarono e la più piccola mise la faccia allo sportello e disse:
'Andiamo pure a colazione. Ma l'avverto che abbiamo da fare[2] tra 30
mezz'ora, tre quarti d'ora al massimo.'

Girolamo disse, seccato: 'Che fretta.'

---

[1] *aspettò un pezzo*   he waited for a long time
[2] *abbiamo da fare*   we'll be busy

'Mi dispiace, ma o le va bene così, oppure torniamo a casa.'

Chiedendosi il perchè di quella villania, quasi più incuriosito che offeso, Girolamo le portò velocemente ad una trattoria non lontana dal Ponte Milvio. Ma come entrarono nel giardino, videro una quantità di tavole vuote, all'ombra rada e calda delle acacie. 'Non c'è nessuno,' disse Girolamo 'è Ferragosto,[3] si capisce. Volete restare qui oppure volete che proviamo altrove?'

La più piccola rispose sgarbatamente 'Non siamo venute per farci vedere ma per mangiare. Restiamo pure qui.'

Sedettero, venne il cameriere, la più piccola prese a leggere [4] la lista: 'Aragosta. Posso ordinare dell'aragosta?'

Girolamo disse, stupefatto: 'Ma si capisce, che domanda.'

'Non si sa mai. Ha contato i suoi soldi prima di invitarci?'

Il cameriere, il taccuino in mano, aspettava, paziente, con l'aria di chi conosce queste situazioni e non si stupisce. Girolamo disse ridendo ma, in fondo, irritato: 'Ho contato i miei soldi: vada per l'aragosta.'

'Allora aragosta,' disse il cameriere. 'E come vino?'

La più piccola domandò di nuovo: 'Posso ordinare una bottiglia di vino? Oppure debbo prendere il vino sciolto?'

'Può ordinare quello che vuole,' disse Girolamo annoiato.

La più grande disse: 'Non si arrabbi, lo facciamo per lei. Tante volte ci invitano e poi non hanno abbastanza soldi.'

Il cameriere se ne andò; la più piccola domandò rudemente: 'A proposito non so neppure come si chiama, lei.'

'Mi chiami Girolamo.'

'Non mi piace Girolamo, mi fa pensare a girarrosto.'

'E voi come vi chiamate?'

'Lei si chiama Cloti,' disse la più grande, 'e io Maia.'

'Ma sono due diminutivi, non è vero?'

'Sì lei si chiama Clotilde e io Marianna.'

Girolamo domandò a Cloti: 'Che diminutivo suggerisce per me?'

---

[3] *Ferragosto*   August holidays
[4] *prese a leggere*   began to read

'Nessuno,' rispose la ragazza bruscamente.

'Eppure in qualche modo dovrà pur chiamarmi. E visto che Girolamo non le piace...'

Cloti rispose: 'Cosa vuole che la chiami? Se fra mezz'ora ci lasceremo e non ci vedremo mai più?'   5

'Ne è sicura?'

'Oh, sicurissima.'

Arrivò il cameriere; e presero a mangiare in silenzio l'aragosta, guardando ai tavoli vuoti sui quali, ogni tanto, dai rami delle acacie, venivano a svolazzare e posarsi certi grossi passeri in cerca di   10 briciole. Girolamo osservava di sfuggita [5] Cloti e si confermava nell'idea che era molto graziosa e che gli piaceva. Aveva un volto camuso, con gli occhi neri, lucidi e un po' a fior di pelle; il naso era minuscolo e sfuggente, con le narici scoperte; la bocca l'aveva capricciosa, imbronciata, carnosa, con il labbro inferiore ripiegato   15 sul mento quasi inesistente. Questa testa era posata su un collo bellissimo, tondo, bianco, liscio e forte. Girolamo disse alla fine:

'Lei lo sa che ha degli occhi molto belli?'

Cloti rispose, ringhiosa: 'È inutile che lei mi faccia dei complimenti. Si ricordi: non sono pane per i suoi denti.'   20

'E per i denti di chi, allora?'

'Non sono cose che la riguardano.'

Girolamo si voltò verso Maia: 'Può farmi un piacere?'

L'amica aveva una faccia paffuta e circolare, dalla quale, come il becco di un uccello, sporgeva un lungo naso appuntito. Domandò: 'Che piacere vuole che le faccia?'   25

'Dica alla sua amica di essere un po' più gentile.'

L'amica si voltò e pronunziò, proprio come un pappagallo: 'Cloti, hai sentito? Perchè non sei più gentile?'

'Avete voluto che venissi a colazione, sono venuta. Ma non   30 chiedetemi di più.'

'Ma Cloti...'

'Oh, lasciami in pace.'

---

[5] *di sfuggita* quickly

Girolamo disse con un sospiro: 'Parliamo d'altro. Come mai ancora in città sotto Ferragosto? Non andate in villeggiatura?' Cloti rispose: 'E lei? Anche lei, perchè non è partito?'
'Mi piace Roma d'estate.'
⁵ 'Guarda, anche a noi piace Roma d'estate.'
'Siamo impiegate,' spiegò Maia, 'andremo in ferie soltanto alla fine del mese.'
'Dove lavorate?'
Cloti intervenne subito: 'Che gliene importa? Le chiedo forse
¹⁰ io dove lei lavora?'
'Se me lo chiedesse, glielo direi.'
'Ma io non glielo chiedo, non m'interessa.'
'Ma Cloti,' disse Girolamo affettuosamente, 'si può sapere perchè ce l'ha con me?' ⁶ Tese una mano attraverso la tavola e la
¹⁵ posò sulla mano piccola, un po' gonfia, graziosa della ragazza. Subito Cloti tirò via la mano gridando: 'Non mi tocchi.'
'Ma che le prende, Cloti, che ha?'
'E poi non mi chiami Cloti.'
'E come debbo chiamarla?'
²⁰ 'Mi chiami signorina Clotilde.'
'Oh, insomma,' disse Girolamo perdendo la pazienza, 'se non voleva venire, poteva dirlo. Ma una volta che ha accettato, ha il dovere di essere almeno educata.'
'Il dovere? Lei è matto. Perchè il dovere? Forse perchè lei mi
²⁵ offre la colazione?'
'Ma Cloti,' disse l'amica.
'Sta' zitta tu,' gridò Cloti, 'sei stata tu a farmi accettare quest'assurdo invito. Anzi, visto che sei stata tu, restaci tu con lui. Io me ne vado. Arrivederci, arrivederci.' Si levò e, passando in
³⁰ fretta tra i tavoli, si allontanò verso il cancello.
'Adesso,' disse Girolamo appena Cloti fu scomparsa, 'lei deve farmi il piacere di spiegarmi il contegno, a dir poco incomprensibile della sua amica.'

---

⁶ *ce l'ha con me*   you are angry with me

La vide scuotere la testa: 'La colpa è mia che ho insistito perchè accettasse. Lei non voleva venire.'

'Ma perchè non voleva venire.'

'Non si offenda. Perchè non vuole più perdere tempo con dei tipi squattrinati.'

'Ma io,' disse Girolamo profondamente stupito, 'io non sono squattrinato.'

'Lei non è squattrinato?'

'No, non sono affatto squattrinato.'

'Strano, Cloti aveva questa impressione. E anch'io, non si offenda, l'avrei giurato.'

'Ma che cosa ve l'aveva fatto pensare?'

'Così, tutto l'insieme.'

Girolamo stette zitto un momento e poi riprese: 'Ma visto che Cloti ha queste idee sugli uomini, perchè, prima di trattarmi in quel modo, non si è informata, non me l'ha chiesto? Le avrei detto la verità, che non sono squattrinato, così lei sarebbe stata gentile e saremmo stati bene insieme.'

'Lei deve scusarla. È la paura.'

'Ma paura di che?'

'Paura di capitare con uno dei soliti spiantati. Lei deve capirci: siamo due ragazze povere, che meraviglia che cerchiamo di conoscere degli uomini che abbiano dei mezzi?'

'Sì, ma almeno informatevi.'

'La vita è una giungla,' disse la ragazza filosoficamente. 'Cloti cerca di difendersi, ecco tutto. Lei fa presto a ragionare; [7] ma chi ha paura non ragiona.'

Girolamo non disse più niente. Il cameriere portò il conto e Girolamo pagò. La ragazza disse, alla fine: 'Se vuole, domani possiamo andare al mare. Parlerò io a Cloti.'

---

[7] *lei fa presto a ragionare* it's easy to reason

Girolamo disse: 'Non credo che potremo andarci.'

'Ma perchè, è offeso?'

'No, ma adesso la paura l'avete fatta venire a me.'

'Ma paura di che?'

'La vita è una giungla,' disse Girolamo alzandosi.

La contrafigura

Dopo un anno che facevamo l'amore,[1] Agata ed io, mi accorsi che, pian piano, lei si raffreddava e diradava gli incontri. Fu proprio come un fuoco che si spegne: da prima non ve ne accorgete, poi, improvvisamente, non c'è più che cenere e tizzi neri e vi sentite gelati. In principio furono cose leggere: mezze parole, silenzi, sguardi. Poi le scuse: raffreddori, impegni, la madre da aiutare nelle faccende di casa, la scuola di dattilografia. Finalmente l'impuntualità e la fretta: arrivare agli appuntamenti magari con un'ora di ritardo e andarsene con un pretesto dopo un quarto d'ora. Intanto mi parlava in tono impaziente come se le cose che dicevo fossero sempre di troppo;[2] e qualche volta mi sembrò perfino

---

[1] *facevamo l'amore* · we had been in love
[2] *di troppo* superfluous

che al contatto della mano o allo sfioramento delle labbra, si tirasse
indietro.   Ora, siccome ci soffrivo, e, d'altra parte, mi accorgevo
che, sebbene lei mi trattasse ormai malissimo, io ero sempre
innamorato allo stesso modo, e quel piacere che prima provavo a
sentirle dire: 'Ti voglio tanto bene,' [3] adesso lo avevo identico
se appena pronunziava a labbra strette: 'Addio Gino;' una volta,
incontrandoci a piazzale Flaminio, mi decisi e le dissi bruscamente:
'Parliamoci chiaro: tu, per me, non senti più nulla.' Ci credereste?
si mise a ridere e rispose: 'Aho, ma sei duro...volevo vedere quanto
ci avresti messo [4]...l'hai capito finalmente.' Restai a bocca aperta,
senza fiato; poi feci un giro su me stesso, come un fantoccio, e
mi allontanai. Ma, fatti pochi passi, mi voltai: speravo che mi
richiamasse. Era salita, invece, sulla pedana della fermata del
tram e lì aspettava, calma, serena. Me ne andai.

      Adesso, vedendo le cose a distanza, posso anche riderci sopra;
ma allora ero innamorato e l'amore mi faceva travedere. Passai dei
brutti giorni: sentivo che l'amavo e avrei voluto non amarla più;
e per non amarla più cercavo di ricordarmi soprattutto i suoi difetti.
Mi dicevo: 'Ha le gambe storte e cammina male...ha le mani
brutte...rispetto al corpo, ha la testa troppo grossa...di passabile
non ha che gli occhi e la bocca: ma è pallida, anzi gialla di
carnagione, coi capelli crespi e opachi e il naso in forma di manico
di bricco, all'insù e largo alla base.' Fatica sprecata: mentre
pensavo queste cose, mi accorgevo che quelle gambe, quelle mani,
quei capelli, quel naso mi piacevano e che, forse forse, mi piacevano
appunto perchè erano brutti. Allora pensavo: 'È bugiarda,
ignorante e con un cervello di canarino, vanitosa, interessata,
civetta.' E subito dopo scoprivo che questi suoi difetti li avevo
nel sangue e mi eccitavano la fantasia. Insomma, quando tutto
era stato detto, mi rendevo conto che non avevo cessato di amarla.

      Decisi di non farmi vivo per un mese almeno, pensando, a torto,
che, non vedendomi più, mi avrebbe cercato. Ma non ebbi la

---

[3] *ti voglio tanto bene*   I love you very much
[4] *quanto . . . messo*   it would take you

forza di tener parola e, dopo una settimana, una mattina presto, entrai in un bar di piazza Flaminio e le telefonai. Fu lei a rispondere e, prim'ancora che aprissi bocca, mi fissò lì per lì un appuntamento, quella mattina stessa. Uscii dal bar, attraversai il piazzale, andai dal fioraio sotto le mura e comperai un mazzo di violette. Erano le ⁵ nove, l'appuntamento era per le dieci. Col mio mazzo di violette in mano, presi a camminare in su e in giù sulla pedana, fingendo di aspettare la circolare.⁵ Il tram veniva, la gente saliva, poi il tram ripartiva e io restavo a terra. Poco dopo la pedana si affollava di nuovo e io fingevo di nuovo di aspettare il tram, tra gente nuova ¹⁰ che non sapeva che aspettavo il tram bensì Agata. Attesi così quell'ora che dovevo attendere, e poi attesi ancora dieci minuti che non dovevo attendere, e allora fui sicuro che non sarebbe più venuta. Dieci minuti di ritardo non erano molti, specie trattandosi di una donna: ma io sapevo di certo che non sarebbe venuta, come ¹⁵ si sa di certo, in certi giorni sereni, che scoppierà un temporale: era per l'aria. Non sarebbe venuta e infatti non venne. Per esserne del tutto sicuro, aspettai ancora mezz'ora e poi ancora un quarto d'ora, e poi cinque minuti e poi contai fino a sessanta e poi aspettai altri cinque minuti per fare un'ora oltre quella fissata. Finalmente, ²⁰ andai alla fontana sotto le mura e gettai il mazzo delle violette nell'acqua sporca. Il fioraio aspettò che mi fossi allontanato e ripescò il mazzo.

Si sa come vanno queste faccende: si comincia col perdere piede; ⁶ dopo la prima sciocchezza se ne fa un'altra e poi un'altra ²⁵ ancora; e poi non se ne azzecca più una ⁷ e si sbagliano tutte. Quel pomeriggio stesso mi venne il dubbio che Agata non avesse capito il luogo dell'appuntamento e le telefonai. Buono buono, le domandai: 'Agata, perchè non sei venuta? Forse non mi ero spiegato bene.' Lei rispose subito: 'Ti eri spiegato benissimo.' 'E allora ³⁰

⁵ *la circolare* [a streetcar route in Rome. In this case, however, the word is used for the streetcar itself.]
⁶ *si comincia col perdere piede* one begins by losing ground
⁷ *non se ne azzecca più una* one is no longer successful in his attempts

perchè non sei venuta?' 'Perchè non ne avevo voglia.' [8] Anche
questa volta rimasi senza parola: riattaccai pian piano il ricevitore
e me ne andai.

Un altro si sarebbe dato per vinto.[9] Ma io l'amavo e desideravo
5   tanto esserne amato che persino se mi avesse dato una coltellata
avrei potuto pensare che non era la coltellata definitiva o addirittura
che me l'aveva data per amore e non per odio. L'amore certo
non mi faceva vedere quel che non c'era; ma mi faceva sperare
che tra le tante specie di amori ci fosse anche questo: di una donna
10 che non viene agli appuntamenti, che risponde male, che disprezza
e se ne infischia. Così, il giorno dopo, a punto di orologio,[10] le
telefonai di nuovo. Questa volta mi mandò la sorellina a dirmi
che non c'era; ma il telefono, come sapevo, era nella sala da pranzo
e udii benissimo la voce di lei che dava l'imbeccata [11] alla bambina.
15 Allora persi del tutto la testa e incominciai a telefonarle a tutte
l'ore: durante i pasti, la mattina presto, la sera tardi: non c'era mai.
Adesso, al momento di entrare nella cabina .telefonica mi veniva
quasi la nausea: però formavo lo stesso qu... maledetto numero. A
.forza di telefonate e di attese tra una telefonata e l'altra, la mia
20 vita era diventata un pasticcio, una poltiglia senza capo nè coda: io
lo sentivo, ma non potevo farci niente e continuavo ad impanta-
narmi sempre più. Da ultimo, disperato, pensai di appostarmi,
presto, la mattina, davanti a casa sua. Aspettai un paio d'ore,
vergognandomi, perchè non c'erano pedane di tram, poi lei apparve
25 sotto il portone, mi vide e tornò indietro. Passarono ancora due
ore: mi insospettii, feci una perlustrazione e scoprii che il palazzo
aveva due ingressi. Rinunziai agli appostamenti.

Ero così disperato che anche il fatto di trovar lavoro dopo mesi
di disoccupazione, non mi recò alcun sollievo. Sono nato per fare
30 l'attore, su questo tutti sono d'accordo; ma un difetto di pronunzia

---

[8] *non ne avevo voglia*   I didn't feel like it
[9] *si sarebbe dato per vinto*   would have given up
[10] *a punto di orologio*   at the right time
[11] *dava l'imbeccata*   was suggesting the answer

che mi fa mangiare le parole e mi spinge la saliva tra le labbra, mi impedirà di far mai altro che la comparsa. Questa volta però non ero neppure comparsa: ero controfigura. In un filmettino stupido, da quattro soldi,[12] dovevo prendere il posto dell'attor giovane nei momenti in cui voltava le spalle. L'attore che dovevo   5
sostituire era in tutto e per tutto [13] simile a me: stessa statura, stessi capelli, stesse spalle, stesso modo di camminare. A lui, però, le parole non si bagnavano di saliva e così lui, in quel film, prendeva un milione e io poche migliaia. Controfigura, insomma; come dire: uomo di paglia, pupazzo, sosia di occasione.   10

Stando in teatro a rodermi e ad annoiarmi, il più del tempo senza far nulla, in un angolo buio fuori della luce dei riflettori, mi venne fatto di pensare [14] ad un trucco per rivedere Agata. Sapevo che anche lei, come tutti, tirava al [15] cinema, sperando, chissà perchè, un giorno, di diventare attrice. Soltanto, lei, neppure la   15
comparsa le facevano fare: secondo me era negata. Così, pensai che se fossi riuscito a gettarle l'amo [16] del cinema, avrebbe abboccato [17] senza fallo. Il regista era un tipo brusco, che tirava soltanto ai soldi e non faceva piaceri a nessuno. Ma l'aiuto-regista, che conoscevo da un pezzo, era un giovanotto simpatico, della mia età.   20
Lo presi a parte al ristorante del teatro e gli chiesi il favore. Si mise a ridere e poi mi battè la mano sulla spalla e disse che me lo avrebbe fatto.

Agata, naturalmente, aveva mandato ai produttori di quel film fotografie in pose diverse, indirizzo, numero del telefono. Il giorno   25
fissato, di buon mattino, l'aiuto-regista le fece telefonare che si presentasse in teatro dentro due ore: avevano bisogno di lei. Il cinema è una forza più forte di qualsiasi forza: se, poniamo, un re avesse invitato Agata a presentarsi alla reggia, lei magari ci avrebbe

---

[12] *da quattro soldi*   of little (artistic) value
[13] *in tutto e per tutto*   in all respects
[14] *mi venne fatto di pensare*   I happened to think
[15] *tirava al*   was aspiring towards
[16] *gettarle l'amo*   to lure her
[17] *avrebbe abboccato*   she would have fallen for it

pensato su; ma il portieraccio della casa di produzione che le diceva
di passare al teatro, bastava a farla accorrere a qualsiasi ora. Quel
mattino mi appostai nell'anticamera, tra le tante comparse e la-
voranti del cinema che aspettavano; e, infatti, all'ora fissata, eccola
apparire. Erano ormai due mesi che non la vedevo e, sul momento,
quasi non la riconobbi. I capelli, che aveva castani e sparsi sulle
spalle, adesso erano rossi e tirati su, in un nodo, in cima alla testa,
in modo da lasciar scoperte le orecchie e il collo. Si era depilata le
sopracciglia con tanto accanimento che pareva che avesse gli occhi
gonfi. Atteggiava la bocca ad una smorfia enigmatica. Purtroppo
il naso a manico di bricco non aveva potuto raddrizzarlo. Mi colpì
il vestito: una giacca larga, rosso fiamma, nuova, con il bavero
rialzato dietro la nuca, e una gonna nera, dritta. Al risvolto aveva
un 'clip' in forma di vascello con le vele spiegate, di metallo
giallo; sotto il braccio stringeva una borsa che pareva di serpente:
forse era vero e chissà quanti sacrifici aveva fatto per comprarla.
Entrò dignitosa, lenta, distante: come se in quell'anticamera piena
di gente simile a lei avesse temuto di sporcarsi. Andò all'usciere
e gli disse a bassa voce non so che cosa. Quello, da vero villano,
rispose senza alzare gli occhi dal giornale che stava leggendo:
'Si metta un po' qua...verrà il suo turno.' Lei si voltò e allora mi
vide. L'ammirai in quel momento: mi fece un saluto da lontano e
andò a sedersi nell'angolo opposto al mio, come se non ci conoscessi-
mo che di vista.

Mi faceva pena [18] adesso, vedendo come si era vestita, preparata, lisciata, azzimata, e quanto si credeva,[19] per quella chiamata
falsa della casa di produzione. Mi rendevo conto che era stata
un crudeltà attirarla con quel pretesto; e tuttavia non potevo fare
a meno di esserne contento: finalmente la rivedevo. Così
aspettammo un pezzo, nell'anticamera affollata, piena di gente
che camminava in su e in giù, chiacchierando e fumando. Lei ogni
tanto apriva la borsetta, si guardava nello specchio, ritoccava un

[18] *mi faceva pena*   I felt pity for her
[19] *quanto si credeva*   how highly she thought of herself

ricciolo, si ridava il rosso sulle labbra, la cipria sul naso. Aveva accavallato le gambe che, mentre stava seduta, potevano anche sembrare belle. Non mi guardò mai, neppure una sola volta: e sì che [20] io, invece, non staccavo gli occhi da lei.

Alla fine venne la sua volta; [21] andò dentro la stanza dell'aiuto- regista e ci rimase forse due minuti; quindi ne uscì sempre con la stessa superbia. Il patto era che l'aiuto-regista doveva guardare alle fotografie e poi dirle: 'Signorina, può darsi che presto avremo bisogno di lei...si tenga preparata, una di queste mattine la chia- miamo.' Nient'altro. Ma per lei era abbastanza. Da quella povera ragazza che era quando era entrata, ecco che usciva già cambiata, nella sua fantasia, in stellina o addirittura stella.

Mi levai anch'io e la seguii, per i corridoi lunghi e nudi. Cam- minava senza fretta, dritta e dignitosa, con le sue belle gambe storte. Esitò un momento all'incrocio dei corridoi, poi imboccò l'anticamera e uscì nella strada. I teatri si trovano alla periferia, lungo uno stradone mezzo di campagna e mezzo di città: da una parte c'erano i campi, pieni di sole in quel mattino di ottobre; dall' altra i palazzoni popolari, alti come torri, pieni di finestre e di panni stesi ad asciugare. Lei camminava piano lungo i palazzi; e io feci presto a raggiungerla. Chiamai, trafelato: 'Agata...'

Mi guardò e poi pronunziò a fior di labbra,[22] quasi senza voltarsi: 'Ciao, Gino...'

Dissi, tutto in una volta, come un solo lamento: 'Agata, perchè non vuoi vedermi?...ti voglio tanto bene...perchè non mi vuoi bene...Agata vediamoci.'

'Ora mi vedi,' fece lei stringendosi nelle spalle.

Dissi: 'Agata, vuoi sposarmi?'

'Non ci penso neanche,' rispose, sempre camminando.

'Perchè?'

Per tutta risposta, domandò: 'Che fai adesso?'

---

[20] *e sì che*   and yet
[21] *venne la sua volta*   her turn came
[22] *a fior di labbra*   from the corner of her mouth

'Faccio la controfigura, ma...'

'Perchè ti ostini a voler fare l'attore,' continuò cattiva, "non lo sai che non ci sei tagliato? [23]...fai la controfigura e vorresti sposarmi...ma che, mi prendi per scema?'

5 'Agata...' esclamai disperato, e feci per prenderla per un braccio. Si svincolò subito con una violenza che mi offese. Persi la testa e gridai: 'Controfigura è sempre meglio che nulla...che ti credi? che stamattina ti hanno telefonato sul serio? sono io che ti ho fatto chiamare dall'aiuto-regista, per vederti...a te, cara mia, non ti

10 faranno mai far niente, neppure i rumori di fondo.' [24]

Subito mi pentii di aver parlato ma ormai era troppo tardi. Capii dal suo contegno che mi credeva; e capii pure che con quelle parole avevo distrutto ogni speranza di riaverla. Non disse nulla, non si fermò, non cambiò colore, non mi guardò: continuò a cam-

15 minare piano, calma, la borsa sotto il braccio. Pentito, incominciai a correrle a fianco, supplicandola di perdonarmi: ma lei, questa volta, fece come se io non ci fossi stato. Tirò dritta,[25] senza fretta, per la strada deserta, tra i campi e i palazzi popolari. Finalmente, vedendo che non mi dava retta,[26] mi fermai in mezzo al marcia-

20 piede, a guardarla, mentre si allontanava. La delusione doveva essere stata terribile per lei; ma non trapelava se non nel modo di camminare. Prima era stato soddisfatto, pavoneggiante; adesso era soltanto malinconico. Lo si capiva da come muoveva le gambe e teneva la testa un po' inclinata verso la spalla. Mi fece pena e

25 mi parve a un tratto di non averla mai amata tanto. Aprii la bocca come per chiamare: 'Agata'; ma, in quello stesso momento, lei svoltò e scomparve. E io rimasi con la bocca spalancata sulla prima *a* di Agata, davanti la strada deserta.

---

[23] *non ci sei tagliato*   you are not cut out for it
[24] *i rumori di fondo*   background noise
[25] *tirò dritta*   she kept on going
[26] *non mi dava retta*   she was not paying any attention to me

L'equivoco

Tale Urati, meccanico, dopo essere stato cameriere per una diecina di giorni in una villa, era rimasto con l'idea fissa di entrarci di soppiatto [1] una notte e far man bassa [2] su quanti oggetti di valore vi si trovavano. L'Urati era incensurato, ma quei dieci giorni di servizio l'avevano, come egli stesso si esprimeva, fatto ricredere. C'era lì dentro, egli pensava, di che viver comodi e senza lavorare per qualche anno. Egli si confidò con un semplice e rozzo suo compagno a nome Lopresto. L'Urati, cittadino, aveva tutto del borghese; e finchè non gli si vedevano le mani callose e sformate con le unghie spezzate e nere, si poteva anche scambiarlo per uno studente o un giovane impiegato. Anzi, il viso fine e bruno, dal naso

---

[1] *di soppiatto* furtively
[2] *far man bassa* to steal

dritto e dai baffi concisi, rammentava molto quello di un celebre
attore cinematografico. Il Lopresto, invece, era campagnuolo
e non le mani soltanto aveva rozze e informi ma anche il viso;
sul quale, in qualsiasi circostanza, permaneva l'espressione attonita
e tarda di chi sia avvezzo al lavoro manuale e poco a riflettere.
L'Urati disse al Lopresto che c'era da diventare ricchi senza fatica
e senza pericolo; e gli espose il suo piano. L'Urati aveva già molto
ascendente sul Lopresto. Non gli ci volle molto, con una parlantina
perentoria e disinvolta, a convincere o meglio a stordire il compagno. Il quale, fatte due o tre obbiezioni ridicole e lontanissime
dall'argomento, davanti alla canzonatura dell'Urati si arrese quasi
subito e accettò.

La villa dove aveva servito l'Urati stava in cima ad un poggio
solitario, in una zona collinosa ai margini di un sobborgo elegante.
L'Urati, poco coraggioso nonostante le vanterie con le quali aveva
abbagliato il Lopresto, oltre che dalla gran copia di oggetti preziosi
sparsi nei salotti, era attratto a tentare l'impresa dal fatto che nella
villa non si trovavano che donne: la vecchia padrona di casa, sua
figlia e due domestiche. L'Urati che conosceva le abitudini di
queste donne, disse al compagno che potevano andarci a colpo
sicuro [3] dopo la mezzanotte: a quell'ora tutti dormivano. L'Urati
aveva conservato la chiave della porta; essi sarebbero entrati,
avrebbero svaligiato le sale del pianterreno e se ne sarebbero andati
del tutto inavvertiti. Ora l'Urati si sbagliava. Da un mese la
villa era stata venduta. E non apparteneva più a quella vecchia
signora bensì a certo Sangiorgio, mercante.

Il Sangiorgio, uomo tozzo e largo di spalle come un gorilla, con
una faccia badiale gialla e piatta su cui ricadevano in lunghe ciocche
aguzze certi lisci capelli neri senza forza e come di morto, era
uomo placido soltanto in apparenza. In realtà soggiaceva una o
due volte ogni anno a furie spaventose [4] di collera omicida durante

---

[3] *a colpo sicuro*   with no risk
[4] *soggiaceva . . . a furie spaventose*   was subjected . . . to frighten-
ing fits of rage

le quali, perso il lume degli occhi,[5] si sentiva irresistibilmente
inclinato a commettere atti irreparabili. Il Sangiorgio conosceva
perfettamente questa sua fatalità e ne aveva una terribile paura.

Ma a parte questa specie di maledizione, il Sangiorgio non
soltanto era buono e onesto ma anche naturalmente portato ai   5
sentimenti gentili. Gli piacevano a tal punto i bambini che andava
apposta nei giardini pubblici, nelle ore di sole, per vederli giuo-
care; e senza tregua rimuginava da anni il sogno ormai meticoloso
di una moglie che lo amasse e che egli potesse colmare di doni e di
carezze. Di quei bambini, di questa moglie, egli provava un acuto,   10
lamentoso bisogno. E per converso[6] cresceva in lui l'insofferenza
della solitudine. Egli era ricco e la ricchezza si accresceva ogni
giorno: ma perchè lavorava, per chi? Spinto da tutte queste
necessità, il Sangiorgio che non conosceva che uomini d'affari e
soltanto per via d'affari, finì per sposare la figlia di un suo contabile   15
a nome Gilda. Bionda e delicata, di carattere tranquillo, ella
pareva avere tutte le qualità che il Sangiorgio attribuiva alla moglie
dei suoi sogni. Il Sangiorgio, semplice e digiuno di[7] complicazioni
psicologiche, aveva creduto, sposandosi, che la ragazza l'amasse.
O per lo meno che col tempo l'avrebbe amato. Pur con il suo   20
disperato bisogno di affetto, il Sangiorgio nulla capiva del carattere
femminile; e nel matrimonio ragionava un po' come negli affari.
Aveva pagato, c'era il contratto, dunque la moglie era sua. Ma
Gilda, la sera stessa delle nozze, come furono giunti in quella villa
che egli aveva acquistato apposta per lei, gli dichiarò senza ambagi   25
che ella non l'amava e l'aveva sposato unicamente per togliersi di
casa.[8] Lui, Gilda soggiunse, doveva apprezzare questa sua lealtà; e
non volere strapparle con la forza quelle dimostrazioni anche le
più superficiali di affetto coniugale che ella era risolutissima a non
concedergli mai. Sarebbe stata, ella concluse, una compagna per lui,   30

---

[5] *perso il lume degli occhi*   flying in a fit of anger
[6] *per converso*   on the other hand
[7] *digiuno di*   knowing nothing about
[8] *togliersi di casa*   to get away from her family

una collaboratrice, un'amica, ma una moglie mai. La ragazza, forse
esaltata dalla lettura dei romanzi, credeva in buona fede che il
Sangiorgio avrebbe accolto queste dichiarazioni se non con compiacimento, per lo meno con comprensione; e che avrebbe ammirato il
5 suo coraggio e la sua dirittura molto più che non si sarebbe sentito
deluso nelle sue aspirazioni e nei suoi desideri. Come sempre
avviene quando si è infatuati di una propria idea e non ci si accorge
di quanto di offensivo vi sia in essa per gli altri, ella dimenticava
che il Sangiorgio non l'aveva sposata per procurarsi soltanto una
10 dama di compagnia. Il Sangiorgio, del resto, non solo non apprezzò
affatto questa tardiva e improvvisa sincerità ma non credette una
sola parola di quello che gli disse la ragazza. Diffidente per natura,
pensò che Gilda l'avesse ingannato per altri motivi che quelli che
diceva; che ella, insomma, avesse fin da prima delle nozze un
15 amante a cui, nonostante il matrimonio, intendeva rimanere fedele.
    Crudelmente deluso, avvelenato dai sospetti, dopo una scena
violenta durante la quale si guardò tuttavia dal manifestare la
propria gelosia, egli annunziò a Gilda che, visto che ella la
intendeva in questo modo, lui avrebbe ripreso da quella sera stessa
20 la vecchia vita di un tempo; e, intanto, il giorno dopo sarebbe
partito alla volta di ⁹ M. dove lo aspettava un certo affare che per
via delle nozze aveva rimandato. Il Sangiorgio non aveva alcuna
intenzione di intraprendere quel lungo viaggio. Era convinto che
la moglie avrebbe approfittato della sua assenza per farsi venire
25 in casa l'amante; e voleva sorprenderli.
    Partì dunque il Sangiorgio, o meglio finse di partire la sera dopo
quella sua prima, squallida notte di nozze; e al momento di partire
ebbe il primo accesso del suo furore. Alla moglie che lo accompagnava alla porta, chiese un bacio; ma Gilda glielo rifiutò
30 ricordandogli, come ella disse, con caparbia e puerile meticolosità, i
loro patti. Il Sangiorgio che non voleva saperne di patti e dopo
essere stato truffato si vedeva ora anche beffato, la guardò scuro
stringendo i denti: quindi se ne andò in silenzio.

---

⁹ *alla volta di* for

Il Sangiorgio si recò in un cinema del quartiere e vi passò la serata. Mentre guardava, senza vederlo, lo schermo, il suo furore andava crescendo. E cresceva proprio nei rari momenti in cui si accorgeva di interessarsi suo malgrado al film. In quei momenti il Sangiorgio si ribellava ad ogni propria possibile indifferenza di fronte al tradimento della moglie e forniva alla sua rabbia nuova materia per divampare. Come chi, pur di scaldarsi, butti nel fuoco ogni volta che lo vede vacillare e decrescere tutto quel che di combustibile gli cada sottomano, fino ai mobili di casa. Quando uscì dal cinema il Sangiorgio si accorse di aver lasciato i guanti nella poltrona. Tornò indietro e chiese di potere ricercarli. Ma sia che qualcuno li avesse già presi, sia che la maschera non gli illuminasse bene il luogo, i guanti non ,urono ritrovati. Questo incidente, e, forse, ancor più, il fatto di non potersi impedire, nelle circostanze in cui si trovava, dal prenderlo a cuore, mandarono al colmo il miserabile e accanito furore del Sangiorgio. A piedi, egli si avviò per le strade deserte del sobborgo verso casa.

Era una notte d'inverno, freddissima, spazzata da un vento pungente. La luna, al colmo del suo fulgore, splendeva bianca nel cielo sereno. In certi tratti, la luce lunare era così forte che si vedevano i colori, il verde delle finestre, il rosso dei mattoni, seppure velati di gelo notturno. Ma al Sangiorgio questo straordinario plenilunio che durava ormai da più di una settimana accrebbe, invece di placarlo, il furore. Il vento gli agghiacciava le mani senza guanti e le ginocchia, egli pensava, assurdamente, che quella luna così splendente dovesse scaldare come il sole e d'istinto si portava nella strada là dove la luce lunare pareva più fulgida. Ma il freddo per questo non cessava e allora il Sangiorgio si sentiva ancora di più infuriare. Tra questi accessi d'ira e di acuta infelicità, giunse ai piedi del poggio sul quale sorgeva la villa.

Contro quel cielo trasparente, la villa gli apparve tutta nera con una sola finestra al secondo piano che splendeva di luce gialla. Era la finestra della moglie e il Sangiorgio per un istante pensò che i propri sospetti fossero infondati. Ma proprio nel momento in cui formulava questo pensiero, ecco, ad un tratto, un rettangolo

giallo accendersi improvvisamente a pianterreno là dove si trovava
la porta di casa. Il Sangiorgio vide in questo rettangolo disegnarsi
una figura nera la quale fece il gesto di chi chiama. E infatti di
lì ad un momento, altra figura nera uscì dall'ombra che spandeva
la facciata della villa ed entrò a sua volta. Il rettangolo di luce si
spense. Ma subito dopo una finestra si illuminò a pianterreno
nel punto dove si trovava il salotto.

Il Sangiorgio in un primo momento aveva sospettato della moglie
sperando tuttavia in fondo all'anima che non fosse vero; poi,
scorgendo quel solo lume acceso al secondo piano, aveva pensato
che la moglie gli fosse fedele, ma nello stesso tempo aveva sperato
che ella non lo fosse perchè così ormai voleva il suo furore. Ora,
vedendo la porta aprirsi e la moglie chiamare un uomo in casa, fu
atterrito. Egli aveva sì sospettato; ma un sospetto che si faccia
ad un tratto realtà pare cosa tutta nuova e quella previsione non
fa che aggiungerci un che di diabolico, come di un miracolo alla
rovescia. Tutto ad un tratto, parve al Sangiorgio di scoprire come
per la prima volta l'efferatezza della moglie.

La strada che portava al poggio saliva a zig-zag con quattro
comode rampe. Le rampe erano collegate tra di loro da scorciatoie
in forma di scalinate. Il Sangiorgio, ansimante e fuori di sè,[10]
prese a salire quei faticosi gradini, nel chiaro di luna che li
illuminava.

Il Sangiorgio credeva di aver scoperto la moglie che tutta trepidante di adultera gioia chiamava in casa l'amante. In realtà non
aveva veduto che l'Urati il quale, entrato di soppiatto e constatato
che la villa era immersa nel sonno, aveva chiamato il suo compagno
rimasto fuori a far da palo.[11]

L'Urati, fatto entrare il Lopresto nell'atrio e chiusa la porta,
rimase per un momento incerto. Quello era infatti l'atrio della villa
in cui aveva servito. Ecco il pavimento di mosaico lucido, ecco le
quattro colonne, due per lato, di marmo grigio e rosso con i capitelli

---

[10] *fuori di sè*   beside himself
[11] *far da palo*   to act as a lookout

cremosi, ecco, in fondo, la spirale di bianchi gradini della scala che avvolgendosi su se stessa saliva al secondo piano. Ma dove erano andati a finire[12] i seggioloni, le poltrone e i tavoli, che prima si trovavano nell'atrio? E poi, come mai a quell'ora, contro ogni abitudine della casa, atrio e scala erano illuminati? L'Urati finì per pensare che la padrona avesse fatto qualche cambiamento e disse al compagno di seguirlo. Egli sapeva che nel salotto c'erano una gran quantità di ninnoli e di oggetti preziosi sparsi sui tavolini. Accanto al salotto c'era la sala da pranzo con i piatti e le posate d'argento. L'Urati contava di svaligiare quelle due sole stanze e poi andarsene.

Ma grande fu la sua meraviglia, poiché ebbe acceso il lampadario del salotto, trovando quella stanza un tempo affollata di suppellettili, trasformata in una specie di gelata sala di museo. Il Sangiorgio, nella sua fretta di sposarsi, era andato a comprare da un negoziante di mobili una di quelle stanze complete che si vedono talvolta nelle vetrine; e tale e quale l'aveva fatta trasportare nella sua villa. Era un salotto Luigi quindici; e il Sangiorgio non aveva fatto a tempo ad aggiungervi neppure il minimo ninnolo da quando ve l'avevano scaricato i facchini della fabbrica. Tutto quell'oro era altrettanto disabitato e deserto là dentro che nella bottega. Anzi di più, perchè nella vetrina, stando allo stretto, in qualche modo i mobili parevano animarsi, qui invece disseminati sul pavimento nudo, contro le bianche pareti disadorne, stavano ciascuno per conto suo; a distanze tali l'uno dall'altro da escludere che nessuno mai ci si fosse seduto e ci avesse conversato.

L'Urati dal primo sguardo capì quel che era accaduto; e che tutta quella falsa ricchezza di riccioli di legno dorato, di specchi in cornice, di stoffe sottese, non gli avrebbe permesso di portare via neppure uno spillo. In tono deluso disse al Lopresto, abbagliato da tutte quelle dorature, che la casa aveva certamente cambiato proprietario. Ma se non c'era nulla a portata di mano,[13] era meglio non insistere e andarsene via.

---

[12] *dove erano andati a finire*   what had become of

[13] *a portata di mano*   within reach

Ma la sala da pranzo riserbava all'Urati maggiore sorpresa. Cominciò che, girato l'interruttore, la luce non si accese. Allora, entrato un poco nella sala, l'Urati fregò uno zolfanello. A quella fiammella tremolante la sala apparve del tutto vuota. Schizzi di calce macchiavano il pavimento, i muri sembravano imbiancati di fresco, in un canto si vedeva tutto l'armamentario di un imbianchino: latte piene di vernice, pennelli, scatole, e una scala a pioli appoggiata contro la parete. Lo zolfanello si spense ripiombando nelle tenebre la stanza. 'Proviamo un po' il secondo piano,' disse l'Urati assai sconcertato.

Ma il Lopresto che, passato il primo sbalordimento delle chiacchiere dell'Urati, non aveva fatto in seguito che risvegliarsi e constatare sempre più la gravità dell'impresa in cui si era cacciato, disse improvvisamente che non voleva salire al piano superiore, e che l'avrebbe aspettato quaggiù nel salotto. Il suo tono era rozzamente fermo e disperato; come se avesse ad un tratto compreso a che cosa l'avesse trascinato il compagno e lealmente preferisse non rimproverarlo ma semmai prendersela con se stesso. Per un momento, ritti ambedue nello spicchio di luce che si spandeva dal salotto sul pavimento macchiato e polveroso della sala da pranzo, contrastarono a bassa voce. Il Lopresto si rifiutava di seguire l'Urati; e l'Urati cercava di convincerlo a non abbandonarlo. Finalmente, visti vani i sarcasmi come le preghiere, gli ordini come gli insulti, l'Urati, assai contrariato, disse che ci sarebbe andato da solo.

Cautamente, in punta di piedi,[14] l'Urati salì la scala, e giunto nell'anticamera sulla quale davano tutte le stanze del secondo piano, esitò per un momento. Tutti quegli usci apparivano serrati fuorchè uno socchiuso; e per la fessura si vedeva che la stanza era buia. L'Urati ci andò con risolutezza, accese francamente la luce e la prima cosa che gli cadde sotto gli occhi fu un tavolino da notte dal piano di marmo grigio sul quale brillava un largo e piatto portasigarette d'oro. In quella stanza, assai piccola, ammobiliata

---

[14] *in punta di piedi* on tiptoe

con suppellettili di fortuna, dormiva il Sangiorgio in attesa del-
l'arredamento definitivo. L'Urati intascò il portasigarette, spense la
luce e tornò nell'anticamera.

Adesso l'Urati, imbaldanzito dal rinvenimento del portasigarette,
pensava che la casa fosse del tutto disabitata. Egli attraversò   5
l'anticamera e andò all'uscio opposto, là dove sapeva che c'era un
guardaroba. Con grande lentezza, procurando di non far rumore,
l'Urati disserrò l'uscio, entrò e accese la luce.

Scoprì che la stanza era rimasta nelle stesse condizioni di quando
aveva servito nella villa: tutta foderata di armadi a muro dalle   10
imposte laccate di bianco. Un tavolo, come allora, occupava il
centro della stanza. Un ferro da stiro elettrico stava sul tavolo ma
la presa era staccata.

Gli occhi dell'Urati andarono subito all'altro uscio dello stanzino
e vide allora che era socchiuso e che una luce trapelava per la   15
fessura. L'Urati spense in fretta il lume del guardaroba e andò a
mettere l'occhio a quella fessura.

Vide una camera da letto completamente arredata e, quel che
era più importante, con tutti i segni di essere abitata. Il letto, basso
e gonfio, aveva le coperte rovesciate; vi si scorgeva una camicia   20
da donna, di velo rosa, stesa con le braccia aperte sul guanciale.
Indumenti si vedevano sulle seggiole. Presso il letto, una toletta
sormontata da una psiche era ingombra di scatole e di boccette.

L'Urati era così sicuro del fatto suo [15] che dimenticò ad un tratto
i motivi per i quali si era introdotto nella villa e non pensò più   25
che a spiare la donna che abitava quella camera. Le donne erano
la passione dominante dell'Urati; soprattutto per soddisfare le
molte necessità in cui lo metteva questa passione, egli si era risolto
a rubare. All'Urati non parve vero di poter spiare qualche bella
e giovane donna nel cuore della sua intimità.   30

Di lì a poco l'uscio della stanza da bagno si aprì e Gilda entrò
apparendo subito nello spazio visuale dell'Urati. Gilda indossava
una leggera vestaglia azzurra, la quale, molto lunga e ampia, le

---

[15] *era . . . suo*   was so self-confident

strascicava dietro come un manto regale. La vestaglia era aperta e
Gilda appariva senza veste nè gonna, i piedi nelle scarpe dal tacco
alto, le gambe dinoccolate calzate di seta fino a mezza coscia, il
corpo vestito di un trasparente velo azzurro che metteva una
mortale freddezza su quella sua carne bianca e magra. Ella aveva
sciolto i capelli che di giorno portava ravvolti attorno al capo.
Questi capelli di un biondo metallico sparsi sulle spalle e increspati
in mille onde minute, facevano una massa compatta d'oro. Il viso
di Gilda ne spuntava [16] con una fronte sporgente e infantile, tondi
occhi cilestri, naso sottile, bocca molto carnosa e rossa; frigido e
sdegnoso di solito, in quel momento lo ravvivava un'espressione
di vanità. Ella si avvicinò alla psiche e, volgendo le spalle all'Urati,
si guardò. Per un momento stette come incerta, quindi sollevando
i capelli con una mano assunse un atteggiamento neghittoso con
le anche e le lunghe gambe; quale hanno spesso i manichini delle
case di mode presentando qualche vestito; e rimase immobile.
L'Urati che si aspettava qualche altro gesto, magari più intimo,
fu deluso. Gilda si guardava tra attonita e compunta, e tanto pareva
bastarle. In realtà quello a cui assisteva l'Urati era una specie
di rito che si ripeteva ogni sera. Altri prima di coricarsi prega, o
legge o fantastica. Gilda invece passava mezz'ora, un'ora davanti
lo specchio, con l'aria di scrutarsi e di riflettere; ma, in effetti, non
pensando nulla e sprofondando in uno stupore senza fondo. Gilda
non era curiosa che di se stessa e avrebbe passato davanti allo
specchio la vita intera.

L'Urati aspettò qualche momento che la donna si smuovesse dalla
sua contemplazione; quindi, vedendo che non accadeva nulla,
decise di andarsene via. Il portasigarette era un bottino sufficiente,
avrebbe potuto andar peggio. L'Urati si tolse dalla fessura e, in
punta di piedi com'era venuto, uscì nell'anticamera e si avviò per la
scala. Era così preoccupato di quello che faceva che non guardò
giù nell'atrio se non quando fu a metà dei gradini. Allora vide il
Sangiorgio che sbucava dal salotto.

---

[16] *ne spuntava*   protruded

Tanta fu la sorpresa dell'Urati che per una volta perse la testa e si slanciò di nuovo verso il secondo piano senza preoccuparsi di non far rumore. Quando, dopo due o tre gradini, si accorse che i suoi passi risuonavano forte nel silenzio della villa, era già troppo tardi. Il Sangiorgio l'aveva udito e lo inseguiva. 5

L'Urati non sapendo dove cacciarsi, corse a rifugiarsi nel guardaroba. Qui, sforzato dalla necessità e dall'urgenza del pericolo che lo minacciava, ebbe un'idea che gli parve buona. L'Urati si disse che un ladro va in prigione. Invece un amante sorpreso se la cava con una fuga precipitosa. Inoltre si denuncia il ladro, non 10 l'amante. Parve all'Urati che se avesse finto di essere l'amante di quella donna intravvista nella camera attigua, avrebbe potuto salvarsi.

Questo piano era in tutto rispondente al carattere e ai gusti dell'Urati più furbo e vano che coraggioso. Gilda, nonostante l'ansietà 15 del momento, gli era piaciuta; questa finzione era una specie di rivalsa per non avere potuto impadronirsi di lei come del portasigarette. Ma non c'era un istante da perdere. L'Urati che aveva già lasciato il soprabito fuori della villa, si tolse la giacca e, sollevando un lembo del tappeto, la buttò sotto la tavola. L'Urati 20 pensava che un amante dovesse farsi trovare con gli abiti in disordine, come si vede nei film; quelle maniche di camicia, a suo vedere, erano l'amore. Aveva appena finito questo travestimento, che il Sangiorgio entrò nel guardaroba.

L'Urati aveva avuto cura di chiudere l'uscio che dava nella 25 camera di Gilda. E così la poveretta non potè udire la menzogna che doveva confermare il Sangiorgio nei suoi sospetti. Il Sangiorgio vide un giovane bruno, avvenente, senza giacca. E subito pensando che fosse quello che sospettava, gli si gettò addosso. L'Urati che non si aspettava questo assalto, si buttò da parte e, fatto il giro della 30 tavola, fronteggiò il Sangiorgio. Ambedue, ansimanti, non avevano detto parola.

L'Urati, sempre badando ai gesti che faceva il Sangiorgio, incominciò a supplicarlo che lo lasciasse andare. L'Urati più abile in finzione che in furti, prese apposta un tono supplichevole, 35

querulo, e al tempo stesso misterioso e indeciso. Come di ragazzo
di buona famiglia che trovandosi in un impiccio non sa se debba,
per salvarsi, sacrificare l'onore della donna amata. Egli non era
un ladro, ripetè più volte, era soltanto una persona che si trovava
per caso nella villa. L'Urati che non era neppur sicuro che il
Sangiorgio fosse il marito della donna intravista, voleva così tastare
prima il terreno.[17] Ma tutto ad un tratto il Sangiorgio ruppe quel
silenzio minaccioso e disse con voce profonda e bassa che non gli
avrebbe fatto nulla: voleva soltanto sapere da quanto tempo. L'Urati
capì l'errore del marito e una gran gioia gli si allargò in petto:
era salvo. Assumendo un tono vergognoso e reticente, rispose
che erano ormai già sette mesi. L'Urati ormai sicuro del fatto
suo e che cominciava a divertirsi voleva aggiungere che però lui
doveva promettergli di non torcere neppure un capello[18] alla
moglie. Ma non fece in tempo perchè il Sangiorgio, senza più
curarsi di lui, si slanciò verso l'uscio della camera da letto, l'aprì e
scomparve.

Gilda che non aveva udito nulla, dopo essersi ben bene spec-
chiata, era tornata nello stanzino da bagno per prendere certa crema
di cui si ungeva il viso ogni sera prima di coricarsi. Ora, con il
barattolo in mano, la vestaglia aperta su quel suo magro corpo
di fanciulla, ella rientrava nella camera. Grande fu la sua meraviglia vedendo il marito che credeva in viaggio, seduto sulla sponda
del letto, le mani sulle ginocchia e gli occhi fissi nel vuoto.

'Tu qui, o come mai?' ella disse con accento di calmo stupore.
Questa tranquillità convinse definitivamente il Sangiorgio di avere
a che fare con una donna di raffinata e mostruosa falsità. Era il
tono della perfetta innocenza; in tutto simile per chi sospetta, a
quello della più efferata colpevolezza. Il Sangiorgio decise di
mostrarsi addirittura più calmo di lei; seppure con intenti e in
direzione tutta diversa.

Senza muoversi, il Sangiorgio domandò con voce appena intel-

---

[17] *tastare prima il terreno*   to explore the ground first
[18] *non torcere neppure un capello*   not to touch a hair

ligibile se la sua presenza la stupisse. Intanto la guardava; e vedendola per la prima volta in vita sua così discinta pensava che quel corpo leggiadro era stato poc'anzi tra le braccia di un altro. Ma Gilda vide quello sguardo e con un gesto caparbio e evidente chiuse la vestaglia. Poco mancò, nonostante il suo proposito di restar calmo, che questo gesto facesse scoppiare il compresso furore del Sangiorgio. Ma si contenne e ripetè con voce più chiara la sua domanda: forse la stupiva di vederlo così presto di ritorno.

Gilda pensava che il marito fosse geloso e per questo fosse tornato indietro. Ma non penetrava il furore del Sangiorgio; nel quale continuava, come in passato, a non vedere che un poveruomo inoffensivo e noioso. Rispose che comprendeva benissimo i motivi del suo ritorno e più che altro si stupiva che egli potesse pensare a certe cose. Ella gliel'aveva già detto e tornava a ripeterglielo: voleva essere la sua compagna e niente di più. Ma per ottenere questo egli doveva aver fiducia in lei. Tutto ciò, standosene in piedi davanti la psiche e spalmandosi con le quattro dita la crema sulla faccia. La vestaglia, non più trattenuta, si era di nuovo aperta.

Il Sangiorgio ripetè con voce profonda: 'Ah la compagna...' e restò per un momento silenzioso. 'Compagna mia e amante di un altro,' soggiunse dopo un momento. Ma la voce strangolata non riuscì neppure ad articolare il sarcasmo.

Gilda levò le spalle. E gli disse che se doveva parlare in questo modo, era meglio che se ne andasse. Del resto l'aveva avvertito: egli non doveva capitarle in camera sua senza prima bussare; e, comunque, mai di notte.

Questo fu troppo per il Sangiorgio. Egli si alzò in piedi e afferrata la moglie per un braccio le domandò chi fosse, in tal caso, l'uomo che aveva nascosto nel guardaroba. Gilda ripetè la frase con meraviglia e fece un gesto come per dire che il marito era pazzo. Soggiunse con malgarbo che la lasciasse. Queste parole vennero proferite con reale ripugnanza. Prima ancora che potesse rendersi conto di quello che era accaduto, ella si ritrovò supina sul letto col Sangiorgio sopra, ansimante, che le stringeva il collo. Gilda ebbe paura e, tutto ad un tratto, con voce infantile, invocò la madre. Ma il Sangiorgio, staccando le sillabe, lentamente, le disse che doveva prepararsi a morire. Gilda sbarrò gli occhi e prese a dibattersi. Il Sangiorgio allora spinse quel viso sotto il guanciale.

Il Sangiorgio, come si riebbe, restò per un momento addosso alla moglie ansimando e guardando al guanciale sotto il quale il bel volto aveva ormai cessato di vivere. Quindi, pian piano, si levò in piedi e andò alla finestra.

Non sapeva neppur lui quel che volesse fare. Ma gli venne un senso di panico e di follia guardando intorno per la stanza tranquilla, con tutti i lumi accesi e i vestiti della moglie sparsi sulle seggiole. Quasi gli parve che l'aria fosse affollata di voci sommesse che sussurravano fitte, e che aprendo la finestra quella foltezza di maligni mormorii si sarebbe dileguata fuori, nella notte.

Come si fu affacciato alla finestra, il Sangiorgio sentì con sollievo che la sua mente, la quale durante il delitto si era ammutolita come un meccanismo inceppato, ricominciava a riflettere. Egli si disse che aveva fatto opera di giustizia e non aveva da pentirsene. Con stupore, scoprì il Sangiorgio di odiare la moglie anche ora che la sapeva morta.

Il Sangiorgio pensò a tutti quei suoi lontani sogni di farsi una famiglia, di vivere in pace con una moglie che l'amasse; e si prese il viso tra le mani. Ora l'odio svaniva in compassione di sè e anche della moglie. A bassa voce, le dita sulla bocca, il Sangiorgio incominciò a parlare come se Gilda fosse ancora viva e avesse potuto udirlo. 'Perchè hai fatto questo? avremmo potuto essere così felici.'

Stava tra questi pensieri quando prima uno, poi due colpi di arma da fuoco rimbombarono nella notte destando gli echi della valle sottostante. I colpi erano vicini; al Sangiorgio, non sapeva neppur lui perchè, venne ad un tratto una speranza. Si tolse dalla finestra e corse fuori della camera.

Come giunse a pianterreno, risuonò improvvisamente il campanello della porta. Sempre con l'istinto di salvarsi, il Sangiorgio andò alla porta e la spalancò, trovandosi faccia a faccia [19] con una guardia, la quale, egli lo vide subito, pareva più turbata di lui.

Il Sangiorgio non ebbe il tempo di parlare perchè la guardia levò per aria un astuccio d'oro in cui il Sangiorgio riconobbe uno dei regali di nozze, e gli chiese con voce ansante se fosse suo. Allora, nello stesso tempo, comprese il Sangiorgio l'abbaglio che aveva preso e il modo che doveva tenere per salvarsi.

La guardia che pareva più ansiosa di scolparsi che di accusare, disse, volgendosi verso qualcuno, sul piazzale: 'Ecco, vedi.' Il Sangiorgio si affacciò e scorse una seconda guardia che teneva per il braccio un uomo che non aveva mai visto. Ma in terra, ai piedi del muro della villa, giaceva rannicchiato, nero nella bianca luce lunare, un altro uomo nel quale il Sangiorgio riconobbe subito quello del guardaroba. Era infatti in maniche di camicia; la giacca gli stava buttata allato.

La guardia disse concitata che aveva voluto lottare e nella lotta era rimasto ucciso. Il Sangiorgio ebbe in quel momento un sincero spasimo di dolore. E gridò che quello era l'assassino della moglie sua. Egli pensava alla menzogna dell'Urati, non alla propria salvezza.

Ma alla guardia conveniva scoprire che l'ucciso oltre che un ladro era anche un assassino. E senza per tempo in mezzo,[20] entrò nella villa seguito dal compagno che teneva per il braccio il Lopresto.

Come furono nella camera da letto, il Sangiorgio si buttò in ginocchio presso il letto e, presa una mano della morta, se la mise contro gli occhi. Il Sangiorgio credeva di dover fare questo atto per meglio confermare la propria innocenza. Ma ad un tratto incominciò a piangere. Così era stato tutto un inganno, pensava. Egli capiva tutto, ora: l'innocenza della moglie, il proprio abbaglio, la malvagità inconsapevole dell'Urati. E provava un senso fermo

---

[19] *faccia a faccia*   face to face
[20] *senza . . . mezzo*   without delay

e ammirato di desolazione. Come a scoprire una persecuzione ingegnosa, oscura che non gli aveva lasciato tregua finchè non l'aveva visto perduto.

Intanto la casa si riempiva di gente. Il Sangiorgio senza sapere come fosse accaduto, si ritrovò ad un tratto seduto in una delle poltrone dorate del salotto. Attraverso l'uscio aperto vedeva nell'atrio un viavai di persone, borghesi e guardie. Verso l'alba, alcuni suoi parenti vennero e lo portarono via a casa loro. Gettatosi tutto vestito sopra un letto, in una stanza buia, il Sangiorgio si addormentò e sognò che era innocente. Ma verso mezzogiorno si destò e si accorse che era tuttora quel Sangiorgio che aveva ucciso la moglie. Sebbene fosse ormai sicuro che la colpa era stata addossata al morto Urati.

A tavola, quello stesso giorno, i parenti parlavano sottovoce e ostentavano un gran rispetto per lui. 'L'oliera a Tino...ripassate al signor Sangiorgio...vuoi ancora di questo arrosto?' Dopo il pranzo, la moglie di quel parente lo prese a parte [21] e gli disse che doveva ora pensare a rifarsi una nuova vita. Il Sangiorgio rispose che così avrebbe fatto. Ma pensava che la sua vita ormai non avrebbe più potuto essere nè vecchia nè nuova. Il Sangiorgio, poco dopo il pranzo, si congedò dalla famiglia.

---

[21] *lo prese a parte*   took him aside

Il tacchino di Natale

Quando, il giorno di Natale, il commerciante Policarpi-Curcio si
sentì dire per telefono dalla moglie che rincasasse puntualmente
perchè c'era il tacchino, si rallegrò molto giacchè, con gli anni, al-
l'infuori di quella della gola [1] non gli era rimasta altra passione.[1]
Grande però fu la sua meraviglia allorchè, giunto a casa verso il
mezzogiorno, trovò il tacchino non già in cucina, infilato nello
spiedo e in atto di girare lentamente sopra un fuoco di carbonella,
bensì in salotto. Il tacchino, vestito con una eleganza un po'
vecchiotta,[2] di una giacca nera dai risvolti di seta, di un paio di
pantaloni a quadretti pepe e sale e di un gilé di panno grigio coi

[1] *gola* [literally] throat; *passione della gola* a strong liking for
good food

[2] *un po' vecchiotta* rather old-fashioned

bottoni di osso, conversava con la figlia del Curcio. Tanta fu la sorpresa del Curcio di trovarlo in un atteggiamento e in un luogo così insoliti, che dopo le presentazioni, cogliendo un momento di silenzio, non potè fare a meno di chinarsi in avanti e di proferire con cortesia ma anche con fermezza: 'Scusate signore...non vorrei errare...ma...ma mi sembra che il vostro posto non dovrebbe essere qui...ripeto...non vorrei errare...ma il vostro posto dovrebbe essere...' Stava per aggiungere 'nella pentola,' quando la moglie che, come ella stessa si esprimeva, conosceva i suoi polli,[3] gli camminò sopra un piede; e il Curcio, che sapeva per antica esperienza quel che significasse questo atto, tacque. La moglie poi gli fece cenno [4] e, trascinatolo fuori del salotto, gli disse con voce bassa e concitata che, per carità, non rovinasse ogni cosa. Il tacchino era nobile, ricco e influente; un buon partito [5] insomma; e già mostrava un interesse particolare e visibilissimo per Rosetta; voleva forse egli, con le sue stupide osservazioni, mandare a monte [6] il matrimonio che già pareva profilarsi? Il Curcio si scusò con la moglie e giurò che non avrebbe più aperto bocca.[7] Quanto al tacchino, la domanda dell'incauto ospite non aveva sortito altro effetto che di fargli prendere il monocolo e squadrare bene bene il malcapitato. Poi era tornato subito a conversare con la figlia del Curcio.

'Si ha un bel dire' [8] pensava poco dopo il Curcio a tavola, mentre la moglie si prodigava in cortesie verso il tacchino 'ma ad un tipo di quel genere lì, piuttosto che augurarsi che sposi la figlia, si vorrebbe tirargli il collo.' Il Curcio era soprattutto irritato dall'aria di superiorità e di accondiscendenza che assumeva il tacchino ogni

---

[3] *che . . . conosceva i suoi polli* [The obvious play on the word *polli* (poultry, chicken) cannot be rendered in English. The expression means:] who knew whom she had to deal with

[4] *gli fece cenno* gave him a sign

[5] *un buon partito* a suitable match (as a husband)

[6] *mandare a monte* to cause something to fail

[7] *non . . . bocca* he wouldn't have said one more word

[8] *si ha un bel dire* it's no use talking about it

volta che gli rivolgeva la parola. Il Curcio sapeva bene di venire, come si dice, dal nulla,[9] e che i suoi modi non erano così levigati come la moglie e la figlia avrebbero desiderato. Ma lui aveva lavorato tutta la vita e aveva guadagnato dei bei baiocchi, questo era il motivo per il quale non aveva potuto curare la propria educazione. Il tacchino invece, con tutto il suo sussiego, non avrebbe potuto dire lo stesso. Belle maniere, certo, aria da gran signore, ma in fin dei conti,[10] il Curcio l'avrebbe giurato, poca sostanza. Altro fatto che dava ai nervi al Curcio era la maniera con la quale, dopo aver detto qualcosa di spiritoso o di profondo, il tacchino tirava indietro il capo, ficcando il becco e i bargigli nella cravatta nera a plastron e gonfiando il petto sotto il gilé. Infine il tacchino parlava alla moglie con la stessa scelta accurata di parole e la stessa modulata preziosità di accento che se si fosse rivolto ad una duchessa. Ma il Curcio imbestialiva perchè gli pareva di ravvisare non sapeva che ironia in questo rispetto eccessivo. 'Alla pentola' pensava 'alla pentola...'

Del resto questa antipatia del Curcio era più che compensata dalla infatuazione delle due donne, madre e figlia, per il tacchino. La moglie del Curcio e Rosetta pendevano addirittura dalle labbra, o meglio, dai bargigli del tacchino; il quale le affascinava con racconti mai uditi di feste, di svaghi, di viaggi, di successi mondani. La familiarità rispettosa di un tacchino come quello che era stato a tu per tu[11] con il gran mondo, lusingava la madre. Quanto a Rosetta ella arrossiva, impallidiva, tremava e volgeva al tacchino sguardi, ora supplichevoli, ora infiammati, ora languidi, ora spauriti. Il fatto si era che fin dall'inizio del convito il piede del tacchino, calzato di un antiquato ma elegante stivaletto di camoscio grigio coi bottoni di madreperla, non aveva cessato un sol minuto di tartassare la scarpetta della ragazza.

Partito il tacchino ci fu una discussione violentissima tra il

---

[9] *venire . . . dal nulla*   to come from the gutter
[10] *in fin dei conti*   after all
[11] *a tu per tu*   intimate with

Curcio e la moglie. Il Curcio diceva che era l'ora di finirla con questi elegantoni sofisticati e snobistici i quali poi, si sa, nascondono sotto la loro superbia una quantità di magagne. Lui aveva lavorato tutta la vita e non si sentiva affatto inferiore a tutti i tacchini di questo mondo. La moglie rispondeva che questo suo furore era inutile; il tacchino non aveva mai affermato di essergli superiore; quale tarantola l'aveva morso?[12] Quanto a Rosetta, andata a dormire come era solito ogni giorno dopo colazione, ella già sognava il tacchino. Lo vedeva inclinato su di lei che giaceva supina, i vanni delle ali intorno ai suoi omeri, il becco sulle sue labbra semiaperte. Il tacchino la guarda accigliato, e si gonfia, si gonfia riempiendo la stanza delle sue penne grige; ma con tutto che sia immenso, pare leggero, al petto di Rosetta. La quale sospira nel sonno e mormora 'caro tacchino.'

I giorni seguenti, nonostante l'antipatia crescente e visibile del Curcio, il tacchino si insediò addirittura nella casa. Veniva a pranzo; e poi, andato in salotto con la figlia, vi rimaneva fino all'ora di cena. I due erano ormai, disse la moglie al Curcio, fidanzati. Sebbene, per motivi di famiglia, il tacchino si opponesse a che si facesse per ora l'annunzio ufficiale. 'Bel genero' brontolava il Curcio 'datemi un brav'uomo lavoratore, semplice, di buon cuore, ma un tacchino...' Il Curcio, rincasando, poteva vedere, attraverso i vetri dell'uscio del salotto, la vezzosa testa della figlia accanto a quella vana, feroce e stupida del tacchino. Egli pensava che forse quelle manine così bianche e piccole accarezzavano quei rossi e rugosi bargigli e la sua antipatia cresceva.

Intanto, però, pur continuando a corteggiare Rosetta, il tacchino non si decideva a chiederne la mano.[13] Anche la madre cominciava ad essere inquieta. Se era un tacchino serio, ella disse alla fine alla figlia, doveva presentarsi ai genitori e chiederla in moglie. Rosetta a queste parole guardò spaventata la madre e non disse nulla. In realtà il tacchino era riuscito fin dai primi giorni a strappare gli

---

[12] *quale tarantola l'aveva morso?* why was he becoming so upset?
[13] *chiederne la mano* to propose to her

estremi favori alla povera ragazza. La quale ora, non meno della madre, era ansiosa che il tacchino regolarizzasse, come si dice, la sua posizione.

Uno di quei giorni Rosetta accolse il tacchino nel salotto con un fiume di lagrime. Ella non poteva più vivere in questo modo, balbettava tra i singhiozzi, mentendo a se stessa e ai genitori. Il tacchino misurava a grandi passi [14] il salotto, le penne tutte arruffate fuori del colletto, il becco semiaperto e infuriato, gli occhi iniettati di sangue. Finalmente disse che ella poteva togliersi dalla testa che lui la sposasse.[15] Piuttosto, se voleva, poteva fuggire con lui all'estero. Quella notte stessa, o mai più. Rosetta, dopo molte esitazioni, finì per acconsentire.

Quella notte il Curcio che soffriva d'insonnia si levò per andare a prendere una boccata d'aria alla finestra. Era una notte d'estate, con la luna al colmo dello splendore. I Curcio abitavano in un villino. Affacciatosi alla finestra senza far rumore nè accendere lumi per non destare la moglie, la prima cosa che il Curcio vide fu l'ombra gigantesca del tacchino, eretta la testa dal collo gonfio, il becco bitorzoluto rivolto in alto, riflessa chiaramente sulla parete della villa inondata di bianca luce lunare. Egli abbassò gli occhi e fece appena in tempo [16] a scorgere la figlia capitombolare da una finestra del primo piano tra le braccia del tacchino. Il quale, caricatala sulle spalle come un fagotto con una forza che nessuno avrebbe sospettato, rapidamente se la portava via verso il cancello. Il Curcio destò la moglie, corse a prendere un vecchio fucile da caccia. Ma, sceso che fu, non trovò più alcuna traccia dei due fuggiaschi.

Il giorno dopo il Curcio andò a sporgere regolare denunzia [17] per rapimento. Ma nei commissariati nessuno gli credette. Un tacchino, dicevano, come è possibile che un tacchino abbia rapito

---

[14] *misurava a grandi passi* was taking long strides
[15] *poteva . . . sposasse* she could get the idea of his marrying her out of her head
[16] *fece appena in tempo* had barely the time
[17] *sporgere . . . denunzia* to report (to the police)

vostra figlia. I tacchini stanno nella stia. Del resto la figlia era maggiorenne e non c'era nulla da fare.

Ma saltarono fuori le magagne del tacchino, egualmente. Si scoprì che era sposato e con prole. Si scoprì ancora che non era nè nobile nè ricco, bensì soltanto un ex cameriere scacciato da più luoghi per furto. Il Curcio trionfava seppure pieno di bile.[18] La moglie non faceva che piangere e invocava la figlia.

Andò a finire con il solito ricatto; e il Curcio dovette sborsare molti di quei suoi 'bei baiocchi' così faticosamente guadagnati per riavere in casa la figlia disonorata. Questo avvenne in dicembre. Il giorno di Natale la moglie telefonò al Curcio che non ritardasse a rincasare perchè c'era il tacchino; soggiungendo a scanso di equivoci [19] che si trattava di [20] persona molto seria che dimostrava una visibile inclinazione per Rosetta. Non era, insomma, un tacchino come quello dell'anno scorso, di questo ci si poteva fidare. 'Ecco come sono le donne' pensò il Curcio. Ma si ripromise questa volta di spalancare bene gli occhi. E di non lasciarsi abbagliare dalle false apparenze e dai vani discorsi di qualsiasi anche altolocato tacchino o gallinaccio.

---

[18] *pieno di bile*   at the height of his anger
[19] *a scanso di equivoci*   in order to avoid any misunderstanding
[20] *si trattava di*   it was

Romolo e Remo

L'urgenza della fame non si può paragonare a quella degli altri bisogni. Provatevi a dire ad alta voce: 'Mi serve [1] un paio di scarpe...mi serve un pettine...mi serve un fazzoletto,' tacete un momento per rifiatare, e poi dite: 'Mi serve un pranzo,' e sentirete subito la differenza. Per qualsiasi cosa potete pensarci su, cercare, scegliere, magari rinunciarci, ma il momento che confessate a voi stesso che vi serve un pranzo, non avete più tempo da perdere. Dovete trovare il pranzo, se no [2] morite di fame. Il cinque ottobre di quest'anno, a mezzogiorno, a piazza Colonna, sedetti sulla ringhiera della fontana e dissi a me stesso: 'Mi serve un pranzo.' Da terra dove, durante questa riflessione, volgevo gli occhi, levai

---

[1] *mi serve* I need
[2] *se no* otherwise, or else

gli sguardi al traffico del Corso e lo vidi tutto annebbiato e tremolante: non mangiavo da più di un giorno e, si sa, la prima cosa che succede quando si ha fame è di vedere le cose affamate, cioè vacillanti e deboli come se fossero esse stesse, appunto, ad aver fame. Poi pensai che dovevo trovare questo pranzo, e pensai che se aspettavo ancora non avrei più avuto la forza neppure di pensarci, e cominciai a riflettere sulla maniera di trovarlo al più presto. Purtroppo, quando si ha fretta non si pensa nulla di buono. Le idee che mi venivano in mente non erano idee ma sogni: 'Salgo in un tram...borseggio un tale...scappo'; oppure: 'Entro in un negozio, vado alla cassa, afferro il morto [3]...scappo.' Mi venne quasi il panico e pensai: 'Perduto per perduto, tanto vale [4] che mi faccia arrestare per oltraggio alla forza pubblica...in questura una minestra me la danno sempre.' In quel momento un ragazzo, accanto a me, ne chiamò un altro: 'Romolo.' Allora, a quel grido, mi ricordai di un altro Romolo che era stato con me sotto le armi. [5] Avevo avuto, allora, la debolezza di raccontargli qualche bugia: che al paese ero benestante mentre non sono nato in alcun paese bensì presso Roma, a Prima Porta. Ma, adesso, quella debolezza mi faceva comodo. [6] Romolo aveva aperto una trattoria dalle parti del Pantheon. Ci sarei andato e avrei mangiato il pranzo di cui avevo bisogno. Poi, al momento del conto, avrei tirato fuori l'amicizia, il servizio militare fatto insieme, i ricordi... Insomma, Romolo non mi avrebbe fatto arrestare.

Per prima cosa andai alla vetrina di un negozio e mi guardai in uno specchio. Per combinazione, [7] mi ero fatto la barba quella mattina con il rasoio e il sapone del padrone di casa, un usciere di tribunale che mi affittava un sottoscala. La camicia, senza essere proprio pulita, non era indecente: soltanto quattro giorni che la portavo. Il vestito, poi, grigio spinato, era come nuovo: me l'aveva

---

[3] *il morto*   the cash, the loot
[4] *tanto vale*   I had better, I might as well
[5] *sotto le armi*   in the military service
[6] *mi faceva comodo*   was convenient for me
[7] *per combinazione*   by chance

dato una buona signora il cui marito era stato mio capitano in
guerra. La cravatta, invece, era sfilacciata, una cravatta rossa che
avrà avuto dieci anni. Rialzai il colletto e rifeci il nodo in modo
che la cravatta, adesso, aveva una parte lunghissima e una parte
corta. Nascosi la parte corta sotto quella lunga e abbottonai la
giacca fino al petto. Come mi mossi dallo specchio, forse per lo
sforzo di attenzione con cui mi ero guardato, la testa mi girò e
andai a sbattere contro una guardia ferma sull'angolo del marciapiede. 'Guarda dove vai,' disse, 'che sei ubriaco?' Avrei voluto
rispondergli: 'Sì, ubriaco di appetito.' Con passo vacillante mi
diressi verso il Pantheon.

Sapevo l'indirizzo, ma quando lo trovai non ci credevo. Era
una porticina in fondo a un vicolo cieco,[8] a due passi da quattro
o cinque pattumiere colme. L'insegna color sangue di bue portava
scritto: 'Trattoria, cucina casalinga'; la vetrina anch'essa dipinta
di rosso conteneva in tutto e per tutto [9] una mela. Dico una mela
e non scherzo. Cominciai a capire, ma ormai ero lanciato ed
entrai. Una volta dentro, capii tutto e la fame per un momento
mi si raddoppiò di smarrimento. Però mi feci coraggio e andai a
sedermi a uno qualsiasi dei quattro o cinque tavoli, nella stanzuccia
deserta e in penombra.

Una stoffetta sporca, dietro il banco, nascondeva la porta che
dava sulla cucina.[10] Picchiai con il pugno sul tavolo: 'Cameriere!'
Subito ci fu un movimento in cucina, la stoffetta si alzò, apparve e
scomparve una faccia in cui riconobbi l'amico Romolo. Aspettai
un momento, picchiai di nuovo. Questa volta lui si precipitò di
fuori abbottonandosi in fretta una giacca bianca tutta sfrittellata
e sformata. Mi venne incontro con un 'comandi' premuroso, pieno
di speranza, che mi strinse il cuore. Ma ormai ero nel ballo e
bisognava ballare. Dissi: 'Vorrei mangiare.' Lui incominciò a
spolverare il tavolo con uno straccio, poi si fermò e disse guardandomi: 'Ma tu sei Remo...'

---

[8] *vicolo cieco*   blind alley
[9] *in tutto e per tutto*   all in all
[10] *dava sulla cucina*   opened on to the kitchen

'Ah, mi riconosci,' feci, con un sorriso.

'E come se ti riconosco...non eravamo insieme sotto le armi? Non ci chiamavano Romolo e Remo e la Lupa per via di quella ragazza che corteggiavamo insieme?' Insomma: i ricordi. Si vedeva che lui tirava fuori i ricordi non perchè mi fosse affezionato ma perchè ero un cliente. Anzi, visto che nella trattoria non c'era nessuno, *il* cliente. Di clienti doveva averne pochi e anche i ricordi potevano servire a farmi buona accoglienza.

Mi diede alla fine una manata sulla spalla: 'Vecchio Remo,' poi si voltò verso la cucina e chiamò: 'Loreta.' La stoffa si alzò e apparve una donnetta corpulenta, in grembiale, con la faccia scontenta e diffidente. Lui disse, indicandomi: 'Questo è Remo di cui ti ho tanto parlato.' Lei mi fece un mezzo sorriso e un gesto di saluto; dietro di lei si affacciavano i figli, un maschietto e una bambina. Romolo continuò: 'Bravo, bravo... proprio bravo.' Ripeteva: 'Bravo' come un pappagallo: era chiaro che aspettava che ordinassi il pranzo. Dissi: 'Romolo, sono di passaggio a Roma [11]... faccio il viaggiatore di commercio...siccome devo mangiare in qualche luogo, ho pensato: "Perchè non andrei a mangiare dall'amico Romolo?" '

'Bravo' disse lui, 'allora che facciamo di buono: spaghetti?'

'Si capisce.' [12]

'Spaghetti al burro e parmigiano...ci vuole meno a farli e sono più leggeri...e poi che facciamo? Una buona bistecca? Due fettine di vitella? Una bella lombatina? Una scaloppina al burro?'

Erano tutte cose semplici, avrei potuto cucinarle da me, su un fornello a spirito. Dissi, per crudeltà 'Abbacchio...ne hai abbacchio?'

'Quanto mi rincresce...lo facciamo per la sera.'

'E va bene...allora un filetto con l'uovo sopra...alla Bismarck.'

'Alla Bismarck, sicuro...con patate?'

'Con insalata.'

---

[11] *sono di passaggio a Roma*   I am passing through Rome
[12] *si capisce*   of course, naturally

'Sì, con insalata...e un litro, asciutto, no?'

'Asciutto.'

Ripetendo: 'Asciutto,' se ne andò in cucina e mi lasciò solo al tavolino. La testa continuava a girarmi dalla debolezza, sentivo che facevo una gran cattiva azione; però, quasi quasi, mi faceva piacere di compierla. La fame rende crudeli: Romolo era forse più affamato di me e io, in fondo, ci avevo gusto.[13] Intanto, in cucina, tutta la famiglia confabulava: udivo lui che parlava a bassa voce, pressante, ansioso; la moglie che rispondeva, malcontenta. Finalmente, la stoffa si rialzò e i due figli scapparono fuori, dirigendosi in fretta verso l'uscita. Capii che Romolo, forse, non aveva in trattoria neppure il pane. Nel momento che la stoffa si rialzò, intravvidi la moglie che, ritta davanti il fornello, rianimava con la ventola il fuoco quasi spento. Lui, poi, uscì dalla cucina e venne a sedersi davanti a me, al tavolino.

Veniva a tenermi compagnia per guadagnar tempo e permettere ai figli di tornare con la spesa. Sempre per crudeltà, domandai: 'Ti sei fatto un localetto proprio carino...beh, come va?'

Lui rispose, abbassando il capo: 'Bene, va bene...si capisce c'è la crisi...oggi, poi, è lunedì...ma di solito, qui non si circola.'

'Ti sei messo a posto,[14] eh.'

Mi guardò prima di rispondere. Aveva la faccia grassa, tonda, proprio da oste, ma pallida, disperata e con la barba lunga. Disse: 'Anche tu ti sei messo a posto.'

Risposi, negligente: 'Non posso lamentarmi...le mie cento, centocinquantamila lire al mese le faccio sempre...lavoro duro, però.'

'Mai come il nostro.'

'Eh, che sarà...voialtri osti state sul velluto: la gente può fare a meno di tutto ma mangiare deve...scommetto che ci hai anche i soldi da parte.'

Questa volta tacque, limitandosi a sorridere: un sorriso proprio straziante, che mi fece pietà. Disse finalmente, come ram-

---

[13] *ci avevo gusto*   I was glad of it
[14] *Ti sei messo a posto*   You have found your place

mentandosi: 'Vecchio Remo...ti ricordi di quando eravamo insieme
a Gaeta?' Insomma voleva i ricordi perchè si vergognava di mentire
e anche perchè, forse, quello era stato il momento migliore della
sua vita. Questa volta mi fece troppa compassione e lo accontentai
5 dicendogli che ricordavo. Subito si rianimò e prese a parlare,
dandomi ogni tanto delle manate sulle spalle, perfino ridendo.
Rientrò il maschietto reggendo con le due mani, in punta di piedi,
come se fosse stato il Santissimo, un litro colmo. Romolo mi versò
da bere e versò anche a se stesso, appena l'ebbi invitato. Col vino
10 diventò ancor più loquace, si vede che anche lui era digiuno. Così
chiacchierando e bevendo, passarono un venti minuti, e poi, come
in sogno, vidi rientrare anche la bambina. Poverina: reggeva con
le braccine, contro il petto, un fagotto in cui c'era un po' di tutto:
il pacchetto giallo della bistecca, l'involtino di carta di gior-
15 nale dell'uovo, lo sfilatino avvolto in velina marrone, il burro
e il formaggio chiusi in carta oliata, il mazzo verde dell'insalata e,
così mi parve, anche la bottiglietta dell'olio. Andò dritta alla
cucina, seria, contenta; e Romolo, mentre passava, si spostò sulla
seggiola in modo da nasconderla. Quindi si versò da bere e rico-
20 minciò coi ricordi. Intanto, in cucina, sentivo che la madre diceva
non so che alla figlia, e la figlia si scusava, rispondendo piano:
'Non ha voluto darmene di meno.' Insomma: miseria, completa,
assoluta, quasi quasi peggio della mia.
    Ma avevo fame e, quando la bambina mi portò il piatto degli
25 spaghetti, mi ci buttai sopra senza rimorso; anzi, la sensazione di
sbafare alle spalle di gente povera quanto me, mi diede maggiore
appetito. Romolo mi guardava mangiare quasi con individia, e non
potei fare a meno di pensare che anche lui, quegli spaghetti, doveva
permetterseli di rado. 'Vuoi provarli?' proposi. Scosse la testa
30 come per rifiutare, ma io ne presi una forchettata e gliela cacciai
in bocca. Disse: 'Sono buoni, non c'è che dire,' come parlando
a se stesso.
    Dopo gli spaghetti, la bambina mi portò il filetto con l'uovo
sopra e l'insalata, e Romolo, forse vergognandosi di stare a contarmi
35 i bocconi, tornò in cucina. Mangiai solo, e, mangiando, mi accorsi

che ero quasi ubbriaco dal mangiare. Eh, quanto è bello mangiare quando si ha fame. Mi cacciavo in bocca un pezzo di pane, ci versavo sopra un sorso di vino, masticavo, inghiottivo. Erano anni che non mangiavo tanto di gusto.

La bambina mi portò la frutta e io volli anche un pezzo di parmigiano da mangiare con la pera. Finito che ebbi di mangiare, mi sdraiai sulla seggiola, uno stecchino in bocca e tutta la famiglia uscì dalla cucina e venne a mettersi in piedi davanti a me, guardandomi come un oggetto prezioso. Romolo, forse per via che aveva bevuto, adesso era allegro e raccontava non so che avventura di donne di quando eravamo sotto le armi. Invece la moglie, il viso unto e sporco di una ditata di polvere di carbone, era proprio triste. Guardai i bambini: erano pallidi, denutriti, gli occhi più grandi della testa. Mi venne ad un tratto compassione e insieme rimorso. Tanto più che la moglie disse: 'Eh, di clienti come lei, ce ne vorrebbero almeno quattro o cinque a pasto...allora sì che potremmo respirare.'

'Perchè?' domandai facendo l'ingenuo 'non viene gente?'

'Qualcuno viene,' disse lei, 'soprattutto la sera...ma povera gente: portano il cartoccio, ordinano il vino, poca roba, un quarto, una foglietta...la mattina, poi, manco accendo il fuoco, tanto non viene nessuno.'

Non so perchè queste parole diedero sui nervi a Romolo. Disse: 'Aho, piantala con questo piagnisteo [15]...mi porti iettatura.' [16]

La moglie rispose subito: 'La iettatura la porti tu a noi...sei tu lo iettatore...tra me che sgobbo e mi affanno e tu che non fai niente e passi il tempo a ricordarti di quando eri soldato, lo iettatore chi è?'

Tutto questo se lo dicevano mentre io, mezzo intontito dal benessere, pensavo alla migliore maniera per cavarmela nella faccenda del conto. Poi, provvidenziale, ci fu uno scatto da parte di Romolo: alzò la mano e diede uno schiaffo alla moglie. Lei non

---

[15] *piantala con questo piagnisteo*   stop complaining
[16] *mi porti iettatura*   you bring me bad luck

esitò: corse alla cucina, ne riuscì con un coltello lungo e affilato, di quelli che servono ad affettare il prosciutto. Gridava: 'Ti ammazzo,' e gli corse incontro, il coltello alzato. Lui, atterrito, scappò per la trattoria, rovesciando i tavoli e le seggiole. La bambina intanto era scoppiata in pianto; il maschietto era andato anche lui in cucina e adesso brandiva un mattarello, non so se per difendere la madre o il padre. Capii che il momento era questo o mai più. Mi alzai, dicendo: 'Calma, che diamine...calma, calma'; e ripetendo: 'Calma, calma,' mi ritrovai fuori della trattoria, nel vicolo. Affrettai il passo, scantonai; a piazza del Pantheon ripresi il passo normale e mi avviai verso il Corso.

Passare il tempo

Nello stesso momento, risuonò il campanello della porta e squillò il telefono. Ernesto pensò che doveva prima di tutto correre ad aprire la porta perchè era la cosa più importante: erano infatti le tre e a quell'ora Alina, come tutti i giorni, sarebbe apparsa sulla soglia. Quanto al telefono, l'avrebbe lasciato squillare, forse non [5] avrebbe neppure risposto: certo era qualche seccatore o comunque qualche cosa di cui non gli importava niente,[1] poichè la sola cosa di cui veramente gli importasse, l'arrivo di Alina, era già avvenuta.

Pensò tutto questo correndo a precipizio dallo studio all'ingresso. Rovesciò uno sgabello sul quale stavano accatastati alcuni scartafacci [10] di ingegneria e, ansimante, mentre il telefono continuava a squillare, spalancò la porta.

---

[1] *qualche . . . niente* something that was of no interest to him

Ma sulla soglia non c'era Alina, bensì il garzone del bar, un ragazzotto dalle guance rosse e dalla testa rapata, con alcune bottiglie di liquori che aveva ordinato poco prima rientrando in casa: 'Le bottiglie.'

Il telefono continuava a squillare con una insistenza che parve ad un tratto ad Ernesto significativa. L'animo pieno di delusione e di presentimento, disse al ragazzo: 'Posa qui, grazie,' e corse al telefono. Ecco, infatti, la voce di Alina che disse subito: 'Finalmente.'

'Che c'è? Non mi dirai che non puoi venire.'

'Sì, o meglio, no. Non posso più venire alla stessa ora.'

Ernesto domandò con sollievo: 'E a che ora puoi venire?'

'Alle cinque. Tra due ore.'

'Ma perchè?' domandò Ernesto irritato, già dimentico del sollievo di poco prima.

'Ti spiegherò. Aspettami, ci vediamo tra due ore.'

'Ma che farò in queste due ore?'

'Hai tante cose da fare: leggi, ascolta la musica, lavora. Ciao, allora. A più tardi.'

Ernesto guardò il ricevitore, come se avesse voluto ancora dire qualche cosa; quindi lo posò e tornò nello studio. Alina aveva ragione, in fondo: aveva molte cose da fare. Andò, così, allo scaffale dei libri, ne tolse un romanzo che non aveva ancora letto; poi mise un disco di musica classica sul giradischi; infine sedette nella sola poltrona che c'era nello studio e, persino, calandosi sulle vecchie molle cigolanti, provò ad emettere un sospiro di soddisfazione, proprio come qualcuno che si accinga a passare un paio d'ore in maniera tranquilla, piacevole ed istruttiva.

Ma era un sospiro falso, come pensò quasi subito. Infatti si accorse che, mentre i suoi occhi seguivano meccanicamente le parole stampate sulla pagina, da sinistra a destra, la sua mente era altrove e non afferrava il senso di quello che tuttavia andava leggendo. D'altra parte, il suono del violino che si levava dal giradischi e si snodava e si attorcigliava per l'aria come un vegetale tropicale gonfio di linfa o come un serpente in amore, gli solleticava, sì, i

timpani ma non li oltrepassava, restando così mero rumore, senza
arrivare a diventare musica. Insistette ancora per un poco a leggere
e ad ascoltare; poi chiuse lentamente il libro e altrettanto lentamente
si alzò, andò al giradischi e fermò il disco.

Gli occhi gli caddero sul tavolo sul quale era solito [2] disegnare. 5
Gli venne in mente di seguire ancora una volta il consiglio di
Alina, a lavorare. Forse, pensò, il lavoro l'avrebbe impegnato più
della lettura della musica: c'era nel lavoro una partecipazione più
attiva e più rischiata che nello svago. Ma come ebbe acceso la
lampada sulla carta da disegno e si fu chinato sul tavolo, provò 10
una sensazione strana e spiacevole: di non essere più una sola
persona ma due: una era rimasta laggiù, nella poltrona; l'altra si
chinava sulla tavola da disegno. E quella che stava nella poltrona
era la più importante, la più vera; mentre quella che si chinava
sul tavolo non era che un cattivo attore il quale recitava male la 15
sua parte. Accese una sigaretta per darsi un contegno,[3] quindi
spense la lampada e si allontanò dalla tavola.

Gli venne in mente che per far passare il tempo gli conveniva
prima di tutto tenersi alla convenzione inscritta sul quadrante dell'-
orologio. I tempi della lettura, della musica, del lavoro erano tempi 20
psicologici, sentimentali, lunghi o corti secondo l'interesse del
momento. Ma il tempo dell'orologio, convenzionalmente diviso
in secondi e in minuti, era quello che era: un'occupazione che
si fosse regolata su quel tempo, sarebbe durata esattamente quanto
doveva durare. Soltanto che un'occupazione simile, la quale esclu- 25
deva ogni partecipazione da parte di chi vi si dedicava, doveva
essere completamente meccanica. Lui doveva dunque trasformarsi
in una macchina per far passare il tempo, abolendo qualsiasi attività
della mente, qualsiasi impulso del sentimento e riducendo la sua
presenza alla ripetizione di un gesto sempre eguale. 30

Girò gli occhi per lo studio affollato di roba in disordine, vide
un grosso pacco su una seggiola e ricordò che conteneva due libri

---

[2] *era solito* he used
[3] *per darsi un contegno* to strike an attitude

che aveva acquistato giorni addietro. Erano due libri francesi che riguardavano i suoi studi di ingegneria e rammentò che non erano rilegati e avevano i fogli intonsi. Andò a prendere il pacco, lo disfece; ed ecco, infatti, due libroni di settecento pagine l'uno.

5   I fogli erano piegati in modo che bisognava tagliarli non soltanto in cima ma anche sulla costa; la carta era così grossa che non si potevano tagliare le pagine quattro alla volta ma una sola. Sedette nella poltrona e fece un rapido calcolo: a quindici secondi per pagina voleva dire un minuto ogni quattro pagine cioè più di due ore

10 per libro. Ammettendo che quindici secondi erano troppi e riducendoli alla metà, si aveva tuttavia più di un'ora a libro. Cercò con gli occhi un tagliacarte, e ricordò che non ne possedeva. Allora prese sul tavolo da disegno una lama da barba di cui si serviva per fare la punta alle matite, tornò a sedersi e incominciò a tagliare

15 le pagine del primo libro. Non era facile, la lama troppo piccola e affilata ogni tanto andava fuori strada e squarciava la pagina; ogni tanto gli sfuggiva e si perdeva in fondo al libro. Tuttavia tagliò con calma, metodicamente per qualche minuto, provando quasi del piacere a far scorrere la lametta su su per il libro e

20 sentire la carta aprirsi come un fiore. Poi, ad un gesto falso, la lama uscì dal solco e tagliò via di netto mezza pagina. Ernesto si alzò, andò a cercare della carta gommata, ne strappò un pezzo della lunghezza della pagina e l'incollò. Ma come fece per riprendere l'operazione, si accorse che la lametta era scomparsa.

25 Adesso avrebbe potuto continuare con un coltello da cucina, con un cartone, con una matita; ma sentì che non aveva più voglia. Era vero: mentre aveva tagliato le pagine, la sua mente era stata assente, i suoi sentimenti avevano taciuto; ma sempre più aveva avvertito [4] nel braccio e nella mano una svogliatezza profonda, e,

30 insomma, c'era stato come una cattiva volontà muscolare nel suo corpo, la quale gli aveva fatto guardare con spavento alle centinaia di pagine che gli restavano ancora da tagliare. Prese i due libri e li andò a posare sullo scaffale, tra gli altri già tagliati e letti.

---

[4] *aveva avvertito*   had felt

Pensò che, tuttavia, la faccenda del tagliare le pagine non era probante. Tagliare le pagine di un libro appena comprato era una di quelle cose che, nei buoni momenti, si faceva con curiosità, impazienza, entusiasmo. Naturale quindi che, mancando l'avidità della lettura, intervenisse la svogliatezza. No, pensò ancora,   5
bisognava fare qualche cosa di assolutamente meccanico e assurdo, che non implicasse alcuna partecipazione, anche minima. Riflettè qualche minuto, affondato nella poltrona e poi si disse che un'azione completamente meccanica e assurda era difficile a trovarsi, appunto perchè l'uomo non è una macchina e non fa volentieri le cose   10
assurde. Poi improvvisamente, gli parve di avere trovato. Si alzò e uscì dallo studio.

Nella piccola cucina ingombra di stoviglie, presso la finestra, sul tavolino, c'era un grosso cartoccio di drogheria che aveva portato a casa quel giorno stesso. Era un cartoccio del peso di mezzo chilo,   15
pieno di caffè in chicchi: Ernesto era solito berne molto mentre lavorava. Un atto meccanico e assurdo, pensò guardando con speranza al cartoccio, avrebbe consistito nel contare uno a uno i chicchi di caffè e metterli dentro una scatola di metallo. Forse contare i chicchi, sia pure di un cartoccio del peso di mezzo chilo,   20
sarebbe stato una cosa più rapida che tagliare millequattrocento pagine intonse; ma in compenso sarebbe stato una cosa davvero del tutto meccanica e assurda. Del resto, una volta contati i chicchi, poteva fare molte altre cose dello stesso genere, per passare il tempo: per esempio ritagliare un giornale intero in tante   25
striscioline e le striscioline in tanti quadratini. Adesso che aveva scoperto la combinazione della meccanicità con l'assurdità, si accorgeva che c'erano infinite cose che si potevano fare con la ragionevole sicurezza che servissero a far passare il tempo.

Prese dunque una seggiola, sedette e rovesciò il cartoccio sulla   30
tavola. I chicchi si sparsero largamente, scivolando sulla superficie del marmo con le loro rotondità oleose e quindi continuando a svuotarsi il cartoccio, si ammucchiarono in una piccola piramide bruna. Ernesto prese una scatola rotonda di metallo che un tempo aveva contenuto dei biscotti, l'aprì e la pose a poca distanza dalla   35

piramide dei chicchi. Quindi raccolse il primo chicco, disse ad alta voce 'uno' e lo gettò nella scatola dove esso cadde con un tintinnio discreto. Continuò, così, a contare e gettare; i chicchi cadevano l'uno dopo l'altro nella scatola; le sue dita si erano fatte unte. Poi, improvvisamente, gli parve di vedersi tutto solo, seduto ad un tavolo da cucina, in atto di contare dei chicchi di caffè e pensò che era diventato pazzo. Questo pensiero della pazzia lo smontò [5] di colpo. Infatti: se una macchina fosse cosciente di essere una macchina, penserebbe certamente di essere pazza. E di conseguenza, cessando, appunto a causa di questo pensiero, di essere una macchina, rifiuterebbe di agire oltre da macchina. La scatola era ancora quasi vuota. Ernesto gettò ancora alcuni chicchi, ne sgranocchiò un paio, quindi si alzò e uscì dalla cucina.

Una volta di nuovo nello studio gli venne fatto di avere questo pensiero terrificante: forse le due ore non sarebbero mai passate, in quanto lui non poteva fare niente, assolutamente niente; e se veramente non avesse fatto niente, il tempo sarebbe stato sospeso, almeno per quanto lo riguardava, e le due ore, proprio come vuole il luogo comune in simili casi, non soltanto sarebbero sembrate eterne ma lo sarebbero state davvero. Lui sarebbe uscito fuori dal tempo, per assoluta impossibilità di farlo passare. Sull'altra sponda, Alina gli avrebbe teso le braccia, ma invano: il tempo che non passa, cioè l'eternità, li avrebbe divisi per sempre.

Si cacciò le mani nei capelli, atterrito. Poi, ad un tratto, udì il ben noto, inconfondibile colpo di campanello di Alina. Si precipitò ad aprire e, meraviglia, eccola ritta sulla soglia, sorridente: 'Sono in anticipo. Ho finito prima di quanto sperassi.'

'Ma che avevi da fare?'

'Figurati, una cosa insopportabile: stare in casa a sorvegliare l'idraulico che doveva aggiustarmi il bagno. Non finiva mai; poi, tutto ad un tratto, non so come, mi ha detto che aveva terminato e che se ne andava.'

'E che cosa hai fatto mentre aspettavi?'

---

[5] *lo smontò*   deflated him

'Mi pareva un'eternità. Ma poi ho trovato il modo di far passare benissimo il tempo. Indovina che cosa ho fatto?'

'Che cosa?'

'Ho pensato a te.'

Ernesto la seguì nello studio. Pur seguendola, si accorse che si domandava con stupore: 'Ed io, perchè non ho fatto lo stesso, perchè non ho pensato a lei?'

Ci vorrebbe Ugo

All'E.U.R., quella notte, in quel deserto di asfalti neri circondati di colonnati bianchi, Ugo forse per la stanchezza della visita alla mostra elettronica, mi fece uno sfogo: 'Io sono romano ma ce l'ho con [1] Roma, da qualche tempo. E lo sai perchè? Perchè a Roma le donne non pensano che all'interesse e chi ci ha i soldi si diverte e chi non ce li ha, si gratta.[2] E io ti dico così che sono stufo e che uno di questi giorni me ne vado al Venezuela.' Domandai, seccato: 'E al Venezuela che fai?' E lui: 'Faccio che laggiù ci ho mio fratello che ha l'officina e guadagna e la ragazze si sprecano, americane, e tutte le sere c'è una cosa nuova. Invece di stare a Roma, a

---

[1] *ce l'ho con* I have a grudge against
[2] *si gratta* is left out in the cold

perdere tempo, mi divertirei, ecco quello che farei.' Impermalito,
allora gli dissi: 'E tu vacci al Venezuela.'

Proprio in quel momento, davanti a noi, sul marciapiede, vidi
due ragazze che camminavano piano, come indecise. Erano tutte
e due della stessa statura e vestite nello stesso modo: camicetta
bianca e gonnella verde, forse due sorelle, come pensai. Una era
bionda, coi boccoli sparsi sulle spalle, e pareva la più formosa,
almeno a giudicare dalla schiena: l'altra, bruna, coi capelli tagliati
alla maschietta, più magra. Tutte e due, poi, alte e grandi, un po'
cavallone insomma, con le gambe lunghe e i fianchi larghi, sui
venticinque anni. Quindi la bionda disse con voce chiara, come
per concludere un discorso. 'Eh già, ci vorrebbe Ugo.'[3] Ed io allora,
non so come, allungai il passo e dissi con faccia tosta:[4] 'Ci
vorrebbe Ugo? Ma eccolo, Ugo.'

Ugo, rimasto indietro mi faceva intanto un cenno come per
dire 'Ma che sei matto?' Ormai, però, ero lanciato: anche perchè
volevo dimostrargli, una volta tanto, che le ragazze di Roma non
erano come lui le credeva; d'altra parte quelle due si erano fermate
e ci guardavano. Le guardai anch'io: la bionda aveva un volto di
bambola, ma volgare, con gli occhi celesti senza espressione, il naso
un po' rosso e la bocca spessa e lustra. La bruna aveva il volto più
lungo, pallido, gli occhi belli, un'aria smarrita, ansiosa. La bionda
disse, sgarbata: 'Ma voi chi vi conosce? Perchè entrate nei discorsi
nostri?'

Provai a dire scherzando: 'Avete detto che ci voleva Ugo e
questo, appunto, è Ugo.' La bionda squadrò Ugo, il quale, bruno
e snello com'è, proprio è un bel ragazzo, e poi disse: 'Ugo quello?
Si vede che non lo conoscete, Ugo.' E io allora: 'E che sarà mai?
Marlon Brando? James Dean? Si chiama Ugo anche lui, ecco tutto.
Scherzi a parte,[5] se volete si può andare insieme a bere qualche
cosa.' La bionda storse la bocca: 'Noi, veramente...' Ma la bruna

---

[3] *ci vorrebbe Ugo*   if Ugo were here
[4] *con faccia tosta*   brazenly
[5] *scherzi a parte*   seriously

disse ad un tratto, in fretta: 'Ma sì, andiamo, tanto, Ugo ormai non viene più, andiamo.'

Così si presentarono: la bionda si chiamava Fedora e la bruna Luciana. Erano sorelle, come avevo pensato, e ci dissero pure che erano tutte e due commesse in un negozio di profumeria del centro. Come mai si trovavano all'E.U.R. a quell'ora? La bionda spiegò: 'Dovevamo andare al Luna Park insieme con Ugo ma abbiamo fatto tardi per colpa di Luciana che non è mai pronta. E così eccoci in mezzo alla strada. Ugo non ci ha aspettate. Non aspetta mai, lui.' Dissi 'Vi ci portiamo noialtri al Luna Park.' E lei sgradevole: 'Ma ce li avete i soldi? Contateli, non si sa mai, il Luna Park costa caro.' A queste parole Ugo mi lanciò un'occhiata, come per dire: 'Lo vedi'; ma io finsi di non accorgermene.

Basta, entrammo nel Luna Park che ci apparve quasi deserto, sotto il fogliame basso degli alberi, con le baracche illuminate che parevano tanti negozi senza clienti. Per prima cosa la bionda, che era proprio antipatica, ci avvertì: 'Ugo ci aveva dato appuntamento alle nove. Se non lo trovavamo alle nove, disse che sarebbe ripassato alle dieci e mezzo. A quell'ora torniamo su, d'accordo?' Dissi a denti stretti: 'D'accordo.' La bionda concluse: 'Con Ugo non si scherza, è puntuale e vuole che anche gli altri siano puntuali.'

Questo Ugo mi cominciava a dare sui nervi; [6] ma non dissi nulla. Ecco, in una radura, il misuratore della forza, un martello che, a scagliarlo, faceva salire una specie di termometro. Ugo disse: 'Voglio provare.' La bionda osservò: 'Luciana, ti ricordi Ugo? Segnò il punto più alto.' Luciana, in maniera inaspettata, disse: 'E piantala col tuo Ugo.' La bionda ci rimase male [7] ma non disse nulla.

Ugo prese il martello e lasciò andare il colpo con tutte le sue forze: il termometro salì di poco: 'Eh, bisogna esser forti,' disse la bionda. 'Come Ugo?' domandai io, ironico. Dal martello passammo alla baracca del tiro a segno dei piatti, i quali, di cattiva

---

[6] *dare sui nervi*   to get on my nerves
[7] *rimase male*   was cross

terraglia, stavano allineati su certe mensole, sullo sfondo di una
lamiera di ferro che, ogni volta che si tirava la boccia, faceva un
rimbombo da non si dire. Ugo ci provò con quattro palle e non
ruppe che un piatto. Ci provò anche Luciana e fece cilecca.[8] La
bionda disse: 'Bisogna avere la mira buona... Dovevate vedere
Ugo.' L'uomo della baracca disse, asciutto: 'Cinquecento lire.'
Facemmo un salto, io ed Ugo, perchè tra tutti e due non ci avevamo
che tremila lire e io dissi: 'Con cinquecento lire ci compravamo un
servizio per sei, compresi i bicchieri.' La bionda disse sarcastica:
'Ve l'avevo detto di contare i soldi.'
  Dalla baracca dei piatti, andammo a quella dei palloncini. Ce
n'erano di ogni grandezza e colore, e ballavano, tentanti, su e giù,
in una specie di gabbia, sopra una corrente d'aria. Le pistole,
pesanti, dal calcio ricamato d'argento, ce le diede una donna
formosa, di mezza età, coperta di gioielli falsi. La bionda prese la
pistola, osservando intanto: 'Il suo amico e Luciana sono scom-
parsi... Non vorrei però che il suo amico si facesse delle illusioni:
Luciana ci ha il vizio di dare speranza agli uomini.' E io: 'E a lei
che gliene importa?' La bionda cominciò a sparare, pam, pam,
bucando quasi tutti i palloncini; poi disse: 'M'importa molto:
Luciana è di Ugo.'
  Finalmente Luciana ed Ugo spuntarono da un boschetto, un po'
trafelati, tenendosi per mano. 'Cretina,' disse la bionda, 'te ne vai
e mi pianti [9] con questo quì.' Luciana non disse niente; ma io
affrontai la bionda: 'Per piacere, ripeta: chi è questo qui?' 'Lei.'
'Io, per regola sua, mi chiamo Attilio, capito?' 'Basta, basta,' gridò
Luciana, 'andiamo alle montagne russe.' Così ci avviammo verso
le montagne russe, la bionda ed io avanti, Ugo e Luciana appresso.
Ma, voltandomi, vidi che Ugo e Luciana si tenevano per la vita,
proprio come due innamorati, e fui contento per Ugo.
  Giunti, però, alle montagne russe, la bionda dichiarò: 'Questa
volta lei viene con me,' indicando Ugo, 'e Luciana va con il signor

---

[8] *fece cilecca*   missed
[9] *mi pianti*   you leave me

Attilio.' Ubbidimmo e così mi trovai accanto a Luciana, sullo stesso sedile. Ci fu un fischio, un gemito di ferraglia, un lamento di musica, e poi la gondola cominciò a salire su per una china di ferro nero, tra le cime nere degli alberi. Dissi a Luciana, mentre la gondola saliva: 'Ma si può sapere che è questo Ugo per lei?' 'Il mio fidanzato.' 'E lei gli vuol bene?' 'Sì e no.' 'E allora?' 'E allora lui è così prepotente che non so resistergli.' 'Ma non preferirebbe un ragazzo simpatico come, per esempio, il mio amico?' 'Sì, lo preferirei...ma mia sorella non vuole.' 'Che c'entra sua sorella?' [10] 'Lei ha un carattere forte e io invece...e poi ci sono altre cose.' 'Per esempio?' 'Ugo ci aiuta...' 'I soldi però non sono tutto nella vita.' La gondola adesso precipitava in giù, quasi volando, e così lei, invece di rispondermi, tutto ad un tratto mi si buttò addosso, con le braccia al collo e il petto contro il petto, gridando: 'Uh, che paura,' e stringendosi forte contro di me. Mi ricordai quello che aveva detto la sorella: 'Luciana ci ha il vizio di dare speranza agli uomini'; e infatti come la gondola prese a risalire, lei disse, con voce bassa: 'Anche lei è simpatico.' Guardai davanti a me: Fedora e Ugo sedevano uno lontano dall'altra, immobili. Dissi a Luciana: 'Stia un po' composta...come loro.' Lei mi lanciò un'occhiata stupita e poi si tirò indietro. Intanto la gondola rallentava la corsa, si fermava con un ultimo lamento. La bionda saltò giù dicendo: 'Ho sete, andiamo al caffè, a bere qualche cosa.'

Prima di arrivare al caffè, Ugo mi prese a parte e mi disse: 'Guarda, che io sono rimasto in tutto con trecento lire.' 'E io con duecento.' Decidemmo lì per lì [11] che noi due non avremmo consumato e raggiungemmo le sorelle. Questionavano; e la bionda diceva, concludendo un suo rimprovero: 'Guarda che lo dico a Ugo.' Tutto ad un tratto mi sentii, come si dice, saltare la mosca

---

[10] *che . . . sorella?* What does your sister have to do with this?
[11] *lì per lì* on the spur of the moment

al naso [12] e sedetti, incominciando aggressivo: 'Beh, parliamo un po' di questo famoso Ugo.'

La bionda disse, seccata: 'Ma perchè? Che gliene importa?' Risposi: 'M'importa e basta... Dunque com'è Ugo?' La bionda disse alla bruna: 'Diglielo tu com'è.' Ma la bruna rispose: 'No, diglielo tu.' La bionda, annoiata, incominciò: 'Intanto è un bell'uomo...' 'Bell'uomo, Ugo,' esclamò la bruna, 'si vede che non l'hai mai guardato: basso, calvo, gli occhi loschi, le gambe corte.' La bionda finse di non avere udito e continuò: 'Poi è distinto, fine, un vero signore.' 'Ma se è un cafone numero uno,[13] un maleducato come ce ne sono pochi.' La bionda proseguì: 'E soprattutto è un uomo con il quale si sta bene...sempre allegro, pieno di trovate, spiritoso.' 'Sì, lo spirito di quelli che ti tolgono la seggiola di sotto e ti fanno cadere col sedere in terra.' Questa volta Fedora perse la pazienza: 'Ma allora, se non ti piace, perchè non glielo dici in faccia? Invece, quando stai con lui, fai la gattamorta.[14] Diglielo in faccia, abbi questo coraggio.' La bruna non rispose nulla.

Volli, a questo punto, riassumere: 'Beh, se ho capito bene, questo famoso Ugo è brutto, volgare, ignorante e maleducato. Dico bene?' Ma la bionda si offese: 'Non permetterò mai che un tizio qualsiasi parli cosí di un nostro amico. Andiamo, Luciana. E poi Ugo trappoco ripassa. Andiamo.' La bruna provò a ribellarsi: 'Ma no, restiamo qui; si sta bene.' La bionda si avvicinò alla sorella, e, senza parer di nulla, le diede un pizzico sul braccio, ma così forte che l'altra cacciò un gemito; sibilando nello stesso tempo: 'Su, cretina, vieni.' Restammo a bocca aperta,[15] Ugo ed io, vedendo questa volta la bruna alzarsi e seguire docilmente la sorella.

Dissi a Ugo: 'Seguiamole... Se insisti, Luciana viene via con te.' Incoraggiato da queste parole, lui si mise a correre e io gli venni

---

[12] *mi sentii . . . saltare la mosca al naso* I felt . . . I was losing my temper

[13] *un cafone numero uno* a first-rate boor

[14] *fai la gattamorta* you act like a hypocrite

[15] *restammo a bocca aperta* we were astonished

dietro. Raggiungemmo le due donne fuori del Luna Park, su quei marciapiedi desolati dell'E.U.R. Camminavano in fretta, la bionda stringeva la sorella per un braccio. Ugo, sempre correndo, gli fu a paro e acchiappò Luciana per l'altro braccio. 'Ahò,
5 tu vieni con me.' La bionda si rivoltò: 'Lasci stare mia sorella.' 'La lasci lei.' 'Io chiamo una guardia.' 'La chiami pure, vediamo.' Stiracchiata tra quei due, Luciana pareva indecisa, una volta di più. Disse alla fine: 'Fedora, che si fa? Ormai Ugo non viene più. Tu prendi l'autobus e io rimango ancora un poco con loro.' Proprio
10 in quel momento, in quel deserto di asfalti illuminati, tra tutte quelle colonne, si udì una voce enorme che andava avvicinandosi, una voce che sembrava parlare dentro un megafono. 'Eccolo Ugo,' disse la bionda con sollievo.

Sorpresi guardammo, e allora vedemmo spuntare, laggiù, in
15 fondo alla piazza dove c'è l'obelisco, una di quelle automobili che fanno la pubblicità ai dentifrici. Un'automobile in forma di tubetto gigantesco, con l'orifizio dalla parte del portabagagli e un serpente bianco di pasta che ne usciva, faceva il giro della carrozzeria e poi formava come un nodo sopra il parabrezza. Questa macchina
20 andava piano e urlava nella notte: 'Provate il dentifricio X. Denti d'avorio con il dentifricio X.' Io dissi, allora, sarcastico: 'Ah, questo è Ugo, e quella è la sua macchina.' La bionda rispose sprezzante: 'Sempre meglio quella macchina che nessuna come voialtri.' La macchina-tubetto si avvicinava senza fretta; la bionda
25 ci lasciò e le corse incontro.

Ugo disse a Luciana: 'Su, vieni, che aspetti?' Ma Luciana pareva indecisa. Intanto la bionda aveva raggiunto la macchina e parlava concitata, in piedi presso il finestrino. Ugo insistette: 'Ma se non gli vuoi bene, perchè non vieni via con me?' Ad un tratto, però,
30 avvenne un fatto imprevisto. L'altoparlante interruppe in tronco la frase pubblicitaria e cominciò ad urlare con quella sua voce enorme: 'Luciana non fare la cretina. Vieni qui. Luciana mi hai sentito? Luciana muoviti, altrimenti...'

A questa voce, Luciana, d'improvviso, diede un guizzo, disse
35 in fretta a Ugo: 'Telefonami domani a quel numero che ti ho dato,'

e corse via verso la macchina. Vedemmo le due sorelle infornarsi [16]
dentro il tubetto gigantesco; poi l'automobile ripartì lentamente
mentre l'altoparlante riprendeva ad urlare le frasi pubblicitarie.
Adesso eravamo di nuovo soli. 'Le telefonerai?' domandai a
Ugo. Lui disse: 'Mi sento scoraggiato. Davvero me ne andrei al
Venezuela.' E io: 'Ma che ti credi di trovarci al Venezuela? Un
tubetto di dentifricio più grande, un altoparlante più forte, ecco
quello che ci troveresti. Da' retta, telefonale, con le donne ci vuole
pazienza.' 'Sì, ci vuole pazienza,' disse lui un po' consolato. Così,
discorrendo, ci avviammo verso la fermata dell'autobus.

[16] *infornarsi* get into

Hai dormito

Il cancello di ferro era socchiuso; prima di entrare, la madre indicò al padre il cartello sul quale era scritto che i riscatti non si potevano fare che al mattino, tra le dieci e le dodici: 'Assurdo. E se uno ha l'abitudine come me, di alzarsi tardi la mattina, come fa?'

Girolamo non aspettò di udire la risposta del padre e svincolandosi dalla mano di lui, entrò per primo nel recinto del canile. Ecco lo spiazzo di cemento, di una bianchezza opaca; ecco la casa degli uffici, proprio di fronte al cancello, bassa e giallognola; ecco, a sinistra, le gabbie in cui si trovavano i cani padronali, in osservazione, e a destra le file delle celle in cui erano rinchiusi i cani randagi. Girolamo disse ansiosamente alla madre: 'Mamma, il grifone nero era nella cella numero sessanta.'

La madre non gli rispose; ma disse al padre: 'Bisogna cercare l'inserviente. Un biondino. Intanto noi guarderemo i cani.' Il padre accese una sigaretta e quindi si avviò verso la casa degli uffici. La madre prese per mano Girolamo e si diresse con lui verso le celle.

Il recinto era immerso in un silenzio completo, insieme pesante e sospeso, al quale il leggero odore ferino che era nell'aria pareva attribuire un significato di attesa angosciosa. Ma appena la madre e Girolamo si furono affacciati alla prima cella, subito un cane solo dapprima, poi due, poi tre, poi tutti quanti incominciarono a ululare. Girolamo notò che erano ululati molto diversi, come erano diversi i cani che li emettevano, dal guaito stridulo al latrato profondo; tuttavia gli sembrò che una sola nota accomunasse quelle voci discordanti: quella di una preghiera straziante e perfettamente consapevole. Pensò che tutti quei latrati erano per lui, e desiderò prendersi il cane che aveva scelto e andarsene al più presto. Ripetè di nuovo, tirando la mano alla madre: 'Mamma, il grifone è nella cella numero sessanta.'

'Eccola la cella numero sessanta,' disse la madre.

Girolamo si affacciò e guardò. Cinque giorni prima, quando erano venuti di pomeriggio, la cella era stata occupata da un piccolo cane nero e irsuto, con gli occhi di carbone e i denti candidi, di una vivacità smaniosa e patetica, il quale, appena Girolamo si era affacciato, gli si era precipitato incontro abbaiando e tendendogli la zampa attraverso le sbarre. Avevano deciso di prendere quel cane; ma gli era stato detto di tornare al mattino che era l'ora in cui si potevano fare i riscatti. Ora però la cella sembrava vuota; o meglio, proprio in fondo, Girolamo vide un piccolo volpino marrone, acciambellato, che lo guardava con occhi tristi e spenti, fremendo ogni tanto per tutto il corpo, come per un ricorrente tremito di ribrezzo. Girolamo disse con voce già disperata: 'Mamma, il grifone non c'è più.'

'L'avranno messo in un'altra cella,' disse la madre in tono evasivo, 'a meno che il padrone non sia venuto a riprenderselo. Adesso lo domanderemo all'inserviente.'

Il padre arrivò in questo momento, venendo dalla casa degli uffici: 'L'inserviente sarà qui trappoco.'

'Andiamo a vedere i cani, intanto.'

Noncuranti di Girolamo che avrebbe voluto aspettare l'inserviente presso la cella numero sessanta, i genitori presero a camminare esaminando i cani uno per uno. Girolamo, come in una
5 nebbia di amara incertezza, udì la madre che diceva al padre: 'L'altro giorno c'erano anche un paio di cani di razza. Un boxer e un bracco. Strano, eh, che cani simili capitino qui.'

Il padre rispose: 'Se li perdono. Oppure li abbandonano apposta. Molti sognano di abbandonare nello stesso modo qualche
10 persona che gli è di peso [1] e si sfogano coi cani.' [2]

I cani continuavano ad abbaiare disperatamente; e Girolamo si domandava se tra tutti quei latrati ci fosse anche quello del suo grifone. Il padre osservò a fior di labbra: [3] 'Lo sai...ho l'impressione che i bastardi facciano un guaito più doloroso dei cani di
15 razza pura.'

'E perchè?'

'Perchè si rendono conto [4] che non sono puri e che hanno meno probabilità di salvarsi.'

La madre alzò le spalle: 'Ma loro non lo sanno che cosa vuol
20 dire essere puri o bastardi. Sono gli uomini che fanno queste distinzioni.'

'No, lo sanno perchè vedono che sono trattati peggio e chi si vede trattato peggio dapprima pensa che sia colpa degli altri, poi, dàgli e dàgli, [5] finisce per pensare che sia colpa propria. S'intende
25 che esser bastardi non è in sè una colpa; ma lo diventa a causa del trattamento diverso.'

'Oh, eccoti con le tue solite sottigliezze.'

Si fermarono a caso davanti una cella. Un cane ancora cucciolo, buffo e brutto, pezzato di giallo e di bianco, con le zampe e la
30 testa enormi e il corpo minuscolo si precipitò sulla griglia e le-

---

[1] *gli è di peso*   who is a burden for them
[2] *si sfogano coi cani*   they vent their anger upon their dogs
[3] *a fior di labbra*   in a whisper
[4] *si rendono conto*   they realize
[5] *dàgli e dàgli*   by and by

vandosi in piedi cominciò a guaire in maniera molto espressiva, cercando nello stesso tempo di lambire la mano di Girolamo e di mettergli la zampa nella palma. La madre lesse ad alta voce sul cartellino segnaletico: 'Meticcio. Catturato in via delle Sette Chiese.' E quindi voltandosi verso il padre: 'Eccone uno, poveretto, che è proprio brutto. Ma dove sta via delle Sette Chiese?' 'Dalle parti di via Cristoforo Colombo.'

Il cane bastardo uggiolava e smaniava, cercando di introdurre la zampa nella mano di Girolamo, quasi avesse voluto stringere un patto di amicizia con lui. Girolamo gliela strinse alla fine; e il cane parve quasi un poco rassicurato. La madre domandò: 'Dicono che i bastardi siano più intelligenti dei cani di razza, sarà vero?'

'Non credo. È una voce messa in giro [6] dai cani di razza,' disse il padre un po' scherzosamente.

'E perchè?'

'Per svalutare l'intelligenza nei confronti di altre qualità come la bellezza, il fiuto, il coraggio e così via.'

Si fermarono davanti un'altra cella nella quale, grande come la cella e con l'aria di stare allo stretto, si trovava un lupo molto sciupato e forse vecchio, dal pelo ingiallito e rado, dagli occhi infelici, rossi e cattivi. Come Girolamo fece per avvicinarsi, il lupo si avventò con un ringhio, scoprendo i denti bianchi e aguzzi, quasi imbellito e ringiovanito di colpo dal suo scoppio di furore. Girolamo fece un salto indietro per la paura; ma nello stesso tempo, paragonando l'ululato così intelligente e così straziante del piccolo bastardo preso in via delle Sette Chiese con il ringhio ottuso del lupo, gli parve che quest'ultimo, il quale non aveva neppure la consolazione di capire quel che gli stava succedendo, destasse più compassione [7] del primo. La madre disse: 'Questo, sì, che è cattivo. Ma non avrà la rabbia?'

'No, se l'avesse non sarebbe qui. Protesta perchè l'hanno rinchiuso, ecco tutto.'

---

[6] *messa in giro*   spread
[7] *destasse più compassione*   inspired more pity

Girolamo guardava il lupo fissamente; ma gli pareva, interessandosi a lui, di distrarsi da una pena grave che gli opprimeva il cuore. Poi capì: era il pensiero del grifone che ancora non si era trovato. Domandò improvvisamente: 'E il grifone, mamma?'

5 'Lo sapremo, appena viene l'inserviente.'

Adesso si trovavano davanti una cella in cui c'era un piccolo cane da caccia bastardo, il quale giaceva sul fianco, respirando affannosamente e tremando. Girolamo sentì il cuore mancargli[8] e domandò: 'Ma che ha? Sta male?'

10 La madre riflettè e poi disse: 'Non sta male, soltanto è angosciato.'

'Perchè?'

'Non saresti anche tu angosciato se ti fossi perduto e ti avessero portato in un luogo straniero lontano dalla tua famiglia?'

15 'Ma il padrone verrà a cercarlo?'

'Sì, certo che verrà.'

Il padre disse: 'Eccolo, l'inserviente.'

Era un giovanotto dalla testa bionda e rapata, dal naso aguzzo e dagli occhi intensamente azzurri. Si avvicinò dondolandosi sulle

20 gambe e, a pochi passi, salutò. La madre disse: 'Siamo qui per quel piccolo grifone nero. Si ricorda?'

'Quale grifone?'

'Quello della cella numero sessanta,' disse Girolamo facendosi avanti.

25 'L'avevate visto nella cella numero sessanta?' disse il biondino con accento dialettale, strascicando la voce. 'Ma quello non c'è più.'

'Ecco, lo vedi, mamma,' gridò Girolamo.

La madre fece un cenno al ragazzo; quindi rivolta all'inserviente: 'Sono venuti a riprenderselo?'

30 'No, siccome erano passati i tre giorni regolamentari, più altri due giorni l'abbiamo...' il biondino parve cercare un termine eufemistico ma alla fine si rassegnò a dire la verità, 'l'abbiamo mandato alla camera a gas.'

---

[8] *sentì il cuore mancargli*   felt his heart break

'Ma avevamo detto che saremmo venuti a prenderlo.'

'Signora, lei l'aveva detto ma poi non si è fatta vedere. Il regolamento è quello.'

'Quanti ne eliminate alla settimana?' domandò a questo punto il padre avvicinandosi e offrendo al biondino il pacchetto delle sigarette. Il biondino ringraziò, prese una sigaretta che si mise dietro l'orecchio e rispose: 'Beh, dieci, quindici la settimana.'

Girolamo era rimasto incerto. Domandò alla fine alla madre, con ansietà profonda: 'Ma che cos'è la camera a gas?'

La madre esitò e poi disse seccamente, in tono didascalico: 'I cani randagi sono uccisi perchè possono diffondere la rabbia che è una terribile malattia. Allora vengono messi nella camera a gas dove muoiono senza soffrire.'

'Così il grifone è morto?'

Il padre mise una mano sulla spalla di Girolamo e disse: 'Ho paura di sì.'

Si avviarono verso l'uscita. La madre disse a Girolamo: 'Oggi non c'era alcun cane che avrei voluto avere. Ma uno di questi giorni ci torniamo e ne prendiamo uno. Va bene?'

Girolamo non disse niente. Adesso ricordava il bastardo che gli aveva messo la zampa nella mano; ma gli pareva che ormai non fosse più possibile salvare nè quello nè alcun altro cane. Tutto, come sentiva, era travolto da una confusione e da una noncuranza inspiegabili. Attraversarono la strada, andarono alla macchina. Il padre disse, aprendo lo sportello: 'Mi avete fatto perdere una mattinata con questa storia del cane. Ora debbo correre all'ufficio.'

Salirono e sedettero tutti e tre sul sedile anteriore. Improvvisamente Girolamo disse: 'Io lo sapevo, mamma, che bisognava andarci avant'ieri. E te l'ho detto, mamma. Sono venuto alla tua camera ieri e avant'ieri e te l'ho detto.'

Il tono del figlio parve sorprendere la madre che rispose un po' rigidamente: 'Tu sei venuto ma io non sono potuta uscire perchè ero stanca e avevo bisogno di riposare.'

'Ma perchè, mamma, non sei venuta, perchè?'

'Te l'ho detto. Perchè ho dormito.'

'Sì, hai dormito mamma, hai dormito.' Girolamo prese ad un tratto a singhiozzare così forte che il padre, il quale stava già avviando la macchina, frenò e disse: 'Su, non piangere. La settimana prossima la mamma te ne cercherà un altro.'

Girolamo ripetè ancora, con una voce forte che meravigliava lui stesso: 'Hai dormito, mamma, hai dormito, hai dormito.'

Il padre disse di nuovo, riaccendendo il motore: 'Su, non piangere. Un uomo non piange.' La madre osservò: 'Questo ragazzo non sta tanto bene da qualche tempo. È troppo nervoso.' La macchina partì.

Il camionista

Sono magro, nervoso, con le braccia sottili, le gambe lunghe e il ventre così piatto che i pantaloni mi cascano di dosso: [1] insomma sono proprio il contrario di quello che ci vuole [2] per essere un buon camionista. Guardate i camionisti: sono tutti pezzi d'uomini [3] con le spalle larghe, le braccia da facchini, il dorso e il ventre forti. Perchè il camionista si basa soprattutto sulle braccia, sulla schiena e sul ventre: le braccia per girare la ruota del volante che nei camion ha un diametro poco meno di un braccio, e certe volte, nelle svolte di montagna, deve farle fare il giro completo; la schiena per resistere alla fatica di star seduto ore e ore, sempre nella stessa

---

[1] *mi cascano di dosso*   hang loosely on me
[2] *ci vuole*   it takes
[3] *pezzi d'uomini*   well-built men

posizione, senza indolenzirsi nè irrigidirsi; finalmente il ventre per
star bene fermo, calato nel seggiolino, incastrato come un masso.
Questo per il fisico. Per il morale sono ancora meno adatto. Il
camionista non deve aver nervi, nè grilli per la testa,[4] nè nostalgie,
nè altri sentimenti delicati: la strada è esasperante e ammazzerebbe
un bue. E quanto alle donne, il camionista poco deve pensarci,
come il marinaio; altrimenti con quel continuo partire e ripartire,
diventerebbe matto. Ma io sono pieno di pensieri e di preoccupazioni; sono di temperamento malinconico; e mi piacciono le
donne.

Però, con tutto che [5] non fosse un mestiere per me, volli diventare
camionista e riuscii a farmi assumere da una ditta di trasporti.
Mi diedero per compagno un certo Palombi che era, si può dirlo,
un vero bruto. Proprio il camionista perfetto, non perchè i
camionisti non siano, spesso, intelligenti, ma lui aveva anche la
fortuna di esser stupido, così da formare un pezzo solo con il
camion. Con tutto che fosse un uomo sopra i trent'anni, gli era
rimasto qualche cosa del ragazzotto: una faccia spessa con le
guance abbottate, gli occhi piccoli sotto la fronte bassa, la bocca
tagliata come quella di un salvadanaio. Parlava poco, anzi niente,
e preferibilmente a grugniti. L'intelligenza gli si schiariva soltanto
quando si trattava di roba da mangiare.[6] Ricordo una volta che
entrammo, stanchi e affamati, in un'osteria di Itri, sulla via di
Napoli. Non c'erano che fagioli con le cotiche e io appena li toccai
perchè mi fanno male. Palombi divorò due scodelle colme; quindi,
tirandosi indietro sulla seggiola, mi guardò un momento, con
solennità, come se stesse per dirmi qualche cosa di importante.
Pronunziò, finalmente, passandosi una mano sulla pancia: 'Me ne
sarei mangiati altri quattro piatti.' Questo era il gran pensiero che
aveva messo tanto tempo ad esprimere.

Con questo compagno che pareva di legno, non vi dico se fui

---

[4] *grilli per la testa*   whims
[5] *con tutto che*   although
[6] *si trattava di roba da mangiare*   it was a question of food

contento quando incontrammo per la prima volta Italia. In quel tempo facevamo la Roma–Napoli,[7] portando la roba più diversa: laterizi, rottami di ferro, bobine di carta da giornale, legname, frutta e perfino, qualche volta, piccoli greggi di pecore che si spostavano da un pascolo all'altro. Italia ci fermò a Terracina chiedendoci di portarla a Roma. L'ordine era di non prendere su nessuno [8] ma, dopo averle dato un'occhiata, decidemmo che per quella volta l'ordine non valeva. Le accennammo di salire e lei saltò su tutta vispa dicendo: 'Viva la faccia dei camionisti che sono sempre gentili.'

Italia era una ragazza provocante: non c'era altra parola. Aveva il busto con la vita lunga da non credersi, e, in cima, un petto che si drizzava, aguzzo, proprio velenoso, sotto certe maglie attillate che le scendevano fino ai fianchi. Anche il collo aveva lungo, con una testa piccola e bruna e due grandi occhi verdi. Sotto quel busto tanto lungo, aveva gambe corte e storte, così da dare l'impressione che camminasse con le ginocchia piegate. Non era bella, insomma, ma meglio che bella; e n'ebbi la prova in quella prima gita, quando all'altezza di [9] Cisterna, mentre Palombi guidava, mi introdusse la mano nella mano e me la strinse forte, senza mai lasciarla fino a Velletri, dove diedi il cambio a Palombi. Era estate, verso le quattro del pomeriggio che è l'ora più calda, le nostre due mani scivolavano per il sudore ma lei, ogni tanto, mi lanciava un'occhiata con quei occhi verdi di zingara e a me pareva che la vita, dopo essere stata per tanto tempo nient'altro che una fettuccia di asfalto, tornasse a sorridermi. Avevo trovato quello che cercavo: una donna a cui pensare. Tra Cisterna e Velletri, Palombi si fermò e discese per andare a guardare le ruote e io ne approfittai per darle un bacio. A Velletri diedi volentieri il cambio a Palombi: una stretta di mano e un bacio, per quel giorno, mi bastavano.

Da allora, regolarmente, Italia, una e anche due volte alla setti-

---

[7] *facevamo la Roma-Napoli* we covered the Rome-Naples route
[8] *non prendere su nessuno* not to pick up any riders
[9] *all'altezza di* in the proximity of

mana, si fece portare da Roma a Terracina e ritorno. Ci aspettava la mattina, sempre con qualche pacco o valigia, presso le mura,
e poi, se guidava Palombi, mi stringeva la mano fino a Terracina.
Al nostro ritorno da Napoli, ci aspettava a Terracina, rimontava,
e ricominciava le strette di mano e anche, sebbene lei non volesse,
i baci di straforo,[10] quando Palombi non poteva vederci. Insomma,
mi innamorai sul serio, anche perchè era tanto tempo che non
volevo bene a una donna e non ero più abituato. A tal punto
che bastava adesso che lei mi guardasse in un certo modo e io
subito mi commuovevo come un bambino, fino alle lagrime. Erano
lagrime di dolcezza; ma a me parevano una debolezza indegna di
un uomo e mi sforzavo, senza riuscirci, di trattenerle. Quando
guidavo io, approfittando che Palombi dormiva, parlavamo sottovoce. Non ricordo niente di quello che dicevamo: segno che erano
cose da poco, scherzi, discorsi da innamorati. Ricordo, però, che il
tempo passava svelto: perfino la fettuccia di Terracina,[11] che di
solito non finisce mai, andava via come d'incanto. Io rallentavo
fino a trenta, a venti all'ora, facendomi passare quasi quasi anche
dai carretti: sempre, però, arrivava la fine e Italia smontava. Di
notte era anche meglio: il camion andava avanti quasi da solo, io
tenevo con una mano il volante e con l'altra cingevo la vita al-
l'Italia. Quando, in fondo al buio, si accendevano e spegnevano i
fari delle altre macchine, rispondendo ai segnali avrei voluto
comporre con le luci qualche parola che dicesse a tutti quanto fossi
felice. Per esempio: Io amo Italia e Italia ama me.

Palombi, o non si accorse di nulla oppure finse di non accorgersi.
Fatto sta che[12] non protestò nemmeno una sola volta contro quelle
gite così frequenti dell'Italia. Quando lei saliva, le faceva, come
saluto, un grugnito e poi si tirava da parte per farla sedere. Lei
stava sempre in mezzo, perchè io dovevo pur tenere d'occhio la
strada e avvertire Palombi, quando si trattava di sorpassare un'altra

---

[10] *di straforo*   furtive
[11] *la fettuccia di Terracina*   the Terracina straightaway route
[12] *fatto sta che*   the fact is that

macchina, che c'era via libera. Palombi non protestò neppure quando, infatuato, volli scrivere sul vetro del parabrise qualche cosa che riguardasse l'Italia. Ci pensai su e poi scrissi a lettere bianche: 'Viva l'Italia.' Ma Palombi, tanto era stupido, non si accorse del doppio senso se non quando certi camionisti, scherzando, ci domandarono come mai fossimo diventati così patriottici. Soltanto allora, mi guardò a bocca aperta e poi, abbozzando un sorriso, disse: 'Credono che sia l'Italia e invece è la ragazza...sei intelligente, l'hai trovata bene.'

Tutto questo andò avanti un paio di mesi o forse più. Uno di quei giorni, dopo aver lasciato Italia, al solito, a Terracina, giunti a Napoli, ricevemmo l'ordine di scaricare e tornare subito a Roma, senza pernottare. Mi dispiacque perchè l'appuntamento con l'Italia era per la mattina dopo; ma l'ordine era quello. Io presi il volante e Palombi incominciò subito a russare. Fina a Itri tutto andò bene, perchè la strada è piena di svolte e di notte, quando comincia la stanchezza, le svolte che fanno stare con gli occhi aperti, sono le amiche del camionista. Ma dopo Itri, tra quei boschetti di aranci di Fondi, mi venne sonno e, per scacciarlo, mi misi d'impegno a pensare all'Italia. Però, pur pensandoci, mi pareva che i pensieri mi si incrociassero sempre più fitti nella mente, come i rami di un bosco che sempre più infoltisce e, alla fine, diventa buio. Ad un tratto, ricordo che mi dissi: 'Per fortuna ho il pensiero di lei a tenermi sveglio...altrimenti mi sarei già addormentato.' E invece io già dormivo e questo pensiero non lo facevo da sveglio ma dormendo, ed era un pensiero che il sonno mi mandava per farmi dormire meglio e con più abbandono. Nello stesso tempo sentii il camion uscirmi dalla strada ed entrare nel fosso; e sentii, dietro, il fracasso e la botta del rimorchio che si rovesciava. Andavamo piano e così non ci facemmo male; ma, una volta discesi, vedemmo che il rimorchio si era capovolto con le ruote per aria e tutto il carico, pelli da concia, stava ammonticchiato nel fosso. Faceva buio, senza luna, ma con un cielo pieno di stelle. Eravamo, per fortuna, alle porte di Terracina: a destra avevamo il monte e a sinistra, oltre le vigne, il mare calmo e nero.

Palombi disse soltanto: 'L'hai fatta tonda'; [13] e poi, soggiungendo che dovevamo andare a Terracina a cercare aiuto, si avviò a piedi. Erano pochi passi, ma come fummo alla porta di Terracina, Palombi, che pensava sempre a mangiare, disse che aveva fame e siccome, prima che fosse arrivata la macchina di soccorso con la gru sarebbe passata qualche ora, tanto valeva andare [14] all'osteria. Così, entrati a Terracina, ci mettemmo alla ricerca di un locale. Ma era dopo mezzanotte e in quella piazza tonda tutta sforacchiata dai bombardamenti, non c'era che un caffè aperto, e per giunta, stava chiudendo. Prendemmo una straduccia che sembrava dirigersi verso il mare e, di lì a poco, vedemmo un lume con una insegna. Affrettammo il passo, pieni di speranza, era davvero un'osteria, ma la saracinesca era calata per metà, come se stesse per chiudere. Aveva le porte a vetri e la saracinesca lasciava scoperta una striscia di questi vetri, da poterci guardare dentro. 'Vuoi vedere che è chiusa,' disse Palombi e si chinò per guardare. Anch'io mi chinai. Allora scorgemmo una stanzaccia di osteria di paese, con pochi tavoli e il banco. Le seggiole erano posate capovolte sui tavoli, e Italia, armata di scopa, faceva svelta le pulizie, uno straccio intorno i fianchi. Dietro il banco, poi, proprio in fondo alla stanza, c'era un gobbo. Ne ho visti di gobbi, ma perfetto come quello, nessuno. Il viso incastrato tra le mani, la gobba più alta del capo, guardava fisso Italia con gli occhiacci neri e biliosi. Lei scopava svelta, poi il gobbo le disse non so che cosa, senza muoversi, e allora lei gli venne accanto, appoggiò la scopa al banco, gli mise un braccio intorno il collo e gli diede un bel bacio lungo. Quindi riprese la scopa, volteggiando per la stanza come se ballasse. Il gobbo discese dal banco nel mezzo dell'osteria: era un gobbo marino, con i sandali tripolini, i pantaloni di tela blu, da pescatore, rimboccati e la camiciola scollata alla robespierre. Si avvicinò alla porta, e

---

[13] *l'hai fatta tonda*   now you have done it
[14] *tanto valeva andare*   we might as well have gone

noi due ci tirammo indietro, come con lo stesso pensiero. Il gobbo
aprì la porta a vetri e dal di dentro tirò giù la saracinesca.
 Dissi, per nascondere il turbamento: 'Chi l'avrebbe mai detto?'
e Palombi rispose: 'Già,' con un'amarezza che mi sorprese. Andammo al garage, e poi passammo quella notte a raddrizzare il
camion e a ricaricare tutte quelle pelli. Ma all'alba, scendendo
verso Roma, per la prima volta, si può dire, da quando lo conoscevo,
Palombi cominciò a parlare: 'Hai visto quello che mi ha fatto
quella strega dell'Italia?'
 Dissi, istupidito: 'Che cosa?'
 'Dopo avermi fatto tante storie,' continuò lui lento e ottuso,
'che mi stringeva la mano tutto il tempo mentre andavamo su e
giù e io le avevo detto che volevo sposarla e, per così dire, eravamo
fidanzati, hai visto? Un gobbo.'
 Restai senza fiato e non dissi nulla. Palombi riprese: 'Le avevo
fatto tanti bei regali: i coralli, un fazzoletto di seta, le scarpe
lucide...dico la verità, le volevo bene e poi era proprio quello che ci
voleva per me, quella ragazza...ingrata e senza cuore: ecco quello
che è...'
 Continuò così un pezzo, lento e come parlando da solo, in quella
luce smorta dell'alba, mentre correvamo sferragliando incontro a
Roma. Così, non potei fare a meno di pensare, l'Italia per rispar-
miare i biglietti del treno, ci aveva ingannati tutti e due. Mi bruciava
di sentire parlare Palombi perchè diceva le stesse cose che avrei
potuto dire io, e poi perchè, in bocca a lui che quasi non sapeva
parlare, queste cose mi sembravano ridicole. Tanto che, ad un
tratto, gli dissi brutalmente: 'Ma lasciami un po' in pace con quella
sgrinfia...ho sonno.' Lui, poveretto, rispose: 'Certe cose, però,
fanno male'; e poi stette zitto fino a Roma.
 Poi, per molti mesi, fui sempre triste; la strada per me era
tornata quello che era prima: senza fine nè principio, nient'altro
che una fettuccia amara da ingoiare e risputare due volte al giorno.
Quello, però, che mi convinse a cambiare mestiere fu che Italia
aprì un'osteria proprio sulla strada di Napoli, all'insegna de 'Il

ritrovo dei camionisti.' Sì, bel ritrovo, da fare centinaia di chilo-
metri per frequentarlo. Naturalmente non ci fermammo mai, ma,
lo stesso, vedere Italia dietro il banco e il gobbo che le passava i
bicchieri e le bottiglie di birra, mi faceva male. Me ne andai. Il
camion con la scritta 'Viva l'Italia,' e Palombi al volante, è sempre
in giro.

Una strana malattia

Da quel lontanissimo paese giunsero un giorno due scienziati. Dicevano di andare in cerca di [1] un rimedio per una epidemia che vi era scoppiata. E infatti, appena arrivati, visitarono subito autorità mediche, ospedali, centri di studi. Richiesti, ad una riunione di nostri scienziati, di quale malattia si trattasse, uno di loro diede la seguente spiegazione:

'La malattia si manifesta bruscamente, senza il preavviso di febbri, malesseri o altri simili sintomi. Il fatto che essa si presenti come una modificazione radicale della visione della realtà, l'ha fatta chiamare malattia della realtà. In altre parole il malato si corica una sera vedendo il mondo com'è e si leva la mattina dopo [2]

---

[1] *andare in cerca di*   they were looking for
[2] *la mattina dopo*   the following morning

vedendolo come non è nè sarà mai. Egli entra allora nella prima
fase del morbo, che è chiamata dell'incredulità. Si stropiccia conti-
nuamente gli occhi, scuote il capo, si pizzica le cosce, si bagna la
fronte con l'acqua fredda, magari [3] si fa pungere o ferire: compie,
insomma, tutti gli atti di coloro che non credono ai propri occhi,
ritengono di sognare o di essere ebbri.

'La fase dell'incredulità dura a lungo. Il malato si corica ogni
sera sperando di ritrovare il giorno dopo, al risveglio, il solito
sguardo tranquillo, la solita visione pacifica delle cose. Dopo
qualche giorno, vedendo che la guarigione si fa aspettare, il malato
ricorre alle cure, palliativi, per lo più, [4] che la malattia ha fatto
sorgere come funghi.

'Ma come ho detto si tratta di palliativi quando non, addirittura,
di ciarlatanerie. Il malato riconosce ben presto che le cure sono
inutili, che la malattia segue il suo corso, e allora si abbandona
alla disperazione. Non lavora più, non ride più, non mangia più,
non si occupa più della famiglia, diserta gli amici, passa il giorno
sul letto tentando di dormire. Dice che, incubo per incubo,
preferisce quello del sonno a quelli della veglia. La fase della
disperazione è più lunga assai di quella dell'incredulità. Finalmente
il malato muore. Bisogna a questo punto osservare che muore
volentieri perchè la morte gli par nulla al confronto della malattia.
Ma anche la morte ha un suo carattere particolare. Proprio nel
momento in cui muore, il malato crede di guarire. Tutto ad un
tratto il viso gli si rischiara, gli occhi gli brillano, leva le mani
come per ringraziare il Cielo; e dopo un istante è morto.'

Quest'esposizione così precisa non soddisfece tuttavia i nostri
scienziati; i quali opposero allo straniero che egli aveva descritto
bensì i sintomi esterni della malattia; ma non aveva spiegato in che
cosa consistesse poi la malattia stessa, ossia quali fossero le modificazioni che essa portava nella visione della realtà.

Lo straniero pur riconoscendo la fondatezza di questa osserva-

---

[3] *magari*   perhaps
[4] *per lo più*   for the most part

zione, rispose che descrivere tali modificazioni non era poi così
semplice come dipingere i sintomi esterni della malattia; e questo
per la buona ragione che queste modificazioni erano veramente
mostruose e incredibili, paragonabili, per intenderci, alle allucinazioni di animali, di mostri e di presenze fantastiche che si verificano [5] durante il delirium tremens, negli alcoolizzati inguaribili.
Tanto è vero, soggiunse, che la malattia veniva chiamata alcoolismo
secco, volendosi così intendere che il malato subiva tutte le
conseguenze di una specie di intossicazione senza tuttavia aver
mai bevuto o comunque assorbito alcuna sostanza intossicante.

Tuttavia, pressato dalle domande, lo straniero riconobbe che in
questa specie di pazzia c'era, come dice Polonio, qualche metodo.
Ossia che, nonostante la gran varietà delle descrizioni dei malati,
esse potevano in qualche modo essere tutte riunite in un solo quadro
clinico non privo di logica e di una certa quale regolarità e prevedibilità. Gli fu chiesto di descrivere, a mo' d'esempio,[6] uno di
questi deliri; il che egli fece subito, di buona grazia e con grande
ricchezza di particolari.

Ma allora avvenne questo. Mentre lo straniero raccontava, i
nostri professori si guardavano in faccia stupiti e scandalizzati.
Perchè quelle che egli chiamava mostruose allucinazioni della
misteriosa malattia, altro non erano che gli aspetti familiari di
un mondo simile al nostro, anzi del nostro mondo stesso.

In altre parole la malattia consisteva in questo: il malato cessava
ad un tratto di vedere la realtà di quel paese e vedeva la nostra:
con gli stessi costumi, le stesse apparenze fisiche, le stesse caratteristiche. Per fare un solo esempio: il malato affermava talvolta
di scorgere in cielo stuoli di mostri rombanti, fatti in questo e
questo modo, dotati di queste e queste particolarità. 'Aeroplani'
non poterono fare a meno di pensare i nostri scienziati stupefatti.

Ma lo lasciarono parlare fino alla fine, cioè fino alla conclusione
di una pittura quanto mai precisa e vivace della nostra bella civiltà

---

[5] *si verificano* happen
[6] *a mo' d'esempio* by way of example

occidentale. Poi, come si fu taciuto, seguì per qualche minuto un profondo silenzio. Nessuno osava parlare, nessuno osava dire la verità. Finalmente uno dei più giovani arrischiò: 'La vostra descrizione della malattia è interessante...ma se siete venuti qui per cercare un rimedio, allora vi siete sbagliati di grosso.' [7] 'E perchè?' domandò lo straniero. 'Perchè?' lo scienziato si guardò intorno, vide che tutti lo incitavano con gli occhi e si fece coraggio. 'Perchè quella che voi chiamate malattia, qui è la normalità...e nessuno si sogna [8] di chiamarla malattia...tutti noi viviamo in una realtà identica a quella che, delirando, credono di vedere i vostri malati...Perciò o siamo noi i malati e allora dovremmo cercare anche noi un rimedio di cui però non sentiamo affatto la necessità...oppure il malato siete voi...e quei vostri malati sono sani.' Lo straniero non si scompose: 'Se fossero sani,' si limitò ad osservare, 'non morirebbero.' Nacque a questo punto una discussione ingarbugliatissima. Alcuni opinavano che bisognava ricoverare d'urgenza lo straniero in un manicomio; altri che era un mistificatore; altri ancora protestavano in nome della nostra civiltà così gloriosa e così positiva e, accusando lo straniero di lesa civiltà, ne invocavano [9] l'arresto immediato. Ma uno degli scienziati che non aveva ancora parlato, un vecchietto di grande esperienza, osservò: 'Qui stiamo facendo una confusione maledetta...invece di disputarci per sapere se quest'uomo è un pazzo, o un ciarlatano, o un criminale, domandiamogli piuttosto che cosa sia questa famosa realtà del suo paese...se non altro,' [10] soggiunse il vecchio non senza ironia, 'potremo arricchire le nostre conoscenze etnologiche...senza parlare della gloria che potrebbe venire ad uno di noi da una bella relazione col ghiotto [11] titolo: 'Alcoolismo secco. Siamo noi tutti degli alcoolizzati

---

[7] *vi siete sbagliati di grosso*   you have made a great mistake
[8] *si sogna*   dreams
[9] *invocavano*   demanded
[10] *se non altro*   at least
[11] *ghiotto*   attractive

senza saperlo? Così almeno ritiene il professor Z in viaggio di studi nel nostro paese.'

Ma le sorprese non erano finite. Alle domande ansiose dei nostri scienziati, lo straniero rispose che non aveva nulla da dire. Il suo paese era tanto diverso dal nostro, che, mancando qualsiasi termine di paragone, gli era assolutamente impossibile spiegare loro come fosse fatto.

'Ma un momento,' disse uno dei nostri scienziati, 'avrete almeno la stessa natura: alberi, fiumi, montagne, laghi...'

'Natura?' rispose l'altro. 'Forse l'abbiamo, ma io non me ne sono mai accorto.'

Altre simili domande ebbero tutte la stessa risposta. Apparve chiaro, alla fine, che lo straniero non soltanto veniva da un paese differente dal nostro ma anche vedeva il nostro in una maniera diversa da come lo vediamo noi.

Così la riunione finì senza approdare a nulla.[12] Val la pena[13] tuttavia di riferire la conclusione malinconica a cui pervenne lo straniero. Prima di andarsene disse che i malati, al suo paese, domandavano anche loro ansiosamente come fosse la realtà in cui avevano vissuto un tempo e alla quale aspiravano con tanta nostalgia. E che proprio nella impossibilità di spiegarglielo consisteva la gravità della malattia.

'Sarebbe come spiegare ai pazzi la maniera di essere savi,' egli finì, 'e voi sapete che questo è impossibile.'

---

[12] *senza approdare a nulla*   without coming to any conclusion
[13] *val la pena*   it may be worthwhile

Inverno di malato

Di solito, quando nevicava o pioveva, e, sospesa la cura del sole, i due malati avevano da [1] trascorrere nella cameretta intere giornate l'uno a fianco dell'altro, il Brambilla, per passare il tempo, si divertiva a tormentare il suo compagno più giovane, Girolamo. Il ragazzo era di famiglia una volta ricca e ora impoverita, e il Brambilla, viaggiatore di commercio [2] e figlio di un capomastro, l'aveva a poco a poco convinto, in otto mesi di convivenza forzata, che un'origine borghese o, comunque, non popolare [3] fosse poco meno che un disonore. 'Non sono mica [4] un signorino io,' diceva

---

[1] *avevano da*   had to
[2] *viaggiatore di commercio*   traveling salesman
[3] *popolare*   of the common people; of humble birth
[4] *non . . . mica*   [in a negative sentence] not at all; not in the least

per esempio sollevandosi sul letto e guardando con un disprezzo
ben recitato, con quei suoi occhi cilestri e falsi, il ragazzo mortificato, 'non sono mica stato tirato su nell'ovatta io...a quindici
anni già nei cantieri e mai un soldo in tasca e mio padre non era
un fannullone..., non possedeva nulla mio padre..., ma scarpe   5
grosse e cervello fino [5]... Venne a Milano che era muratore e ora
ha una ditta bene avviata... s'è fatto da sè mio padre...: che
abbiamo da rispondere a tutto questo...? Fatti ci vogliono, fatti e
non parole...'

Col busto fuor delle coltri, appoggiato sopra un gomito, il   10
ragazzo fissava quei suoi occhi sofferenti sull'uomo, la finzione gli
sfuggiva, era profondamente umiliato.

'Ma che colpa ha mio padre se è nato ricco?' domandava con
una voce tremante in cui si tradiva un'esasperazione antica.

'Colpevolissimo,' rispondeva il Brambilla nascondendo un mezzo   15
sorriso di crudele divertimento; 'colpevolissimo. Anch'io sono
nato per lo meno benestante,[6] ma non un sol momento ho pensato
di campare alle spalle di mio padre [7]... Lavoro, io!'

Convinto di aver torto, Girolamo non trovava nulla da rispondere e taceva; ma il Brambilla non per questo si placava, e   20
dopo il padre passava a beffarsi della sorella del ragazzo. Nei
primi tempi Girolamo aveva commesso l'imprudenza di mostrare
al suo compagno una fotografia di sua sorella, graziosa fanciulla
poco più che ventenne;[8] ne era fiero di questa sorella elegante,
maggiore di lui, e credeva, mostrandola al Brambilla, di esserne,   25
in certo senso, accresciuto nella stima dell'uomo. Ma questo
ingenuo calcolo dovette subito avverarsi sbagliato.

'E così?' domandava ogni tanto il viaggiatore di commercio 'come
va la sorellina?... Con chi fa all'amore in questo momento?'

---

[5] *scarpe grosse e cervello fino* [from *"Contadino, scarpe grosse e cervello fino,* a proverb meaning] a peasant is often more intelligent than he looks

[6] *benestante* well-to-do

[7] *campare alle spalle di mio padre* to live at my father's expense

[8] *ventenne* twenty years old

'Ma...non credo che mia sorella faccia all'amore...' opponeva Girolamo troppo intimidito per protestare con sicurezza.

L'altro scoppiava a ridere:

'Eh...che razza di storie [9] mi viene a raccontare! Ad un altro le vada a raccontare, non a me... Hanno tutte l'amante le ragazze come sua sorella...'

Una grande indignazione covava nell'anima del ragazzo: 'Mia sorella non ha amanti...,' avrebbe voluto gridare; ma tale era la sicurezza dell'uomo, così persuasiva l'atmosfera di umiliazione nella quale da otto mesi era immerso, che quasi dubitava della sua memoria; 'e se poi avesse veramente un amante?' si domandava.

'Hanno tutte un amante le ragazze come sua sorella!' continuava il Brambilla. 'Tengono gli occhi bassi, sono tutte contegnose, fanno le santarelle, ma appena papà e mammà hanno voltato le spalle, corrono dall'amante...eh, vada là [10]...sono anzi sicuro che sua sorella è una di quelle che si fanno meno pregare...con quegli occhi, quella bocca! Certo va nelle *garçonnières* sua sorella!'

'Perchè parlare così di una persona che non si conosce?' protestava allora Girolamo.

'Perchè?' rispondeva il Brambilla, 'ma perchè è vero... Io, per esempio, una ragazza come sua sorella non la sposerei neppure per tutto l'oro del mondo...; non si sposano le ragazze come sua sorella!'

Senza pensare all'assurdità di queste affermazioni, Girolamo si sentiva molto umiliato dall'ipotetico disprezzo del commesso viaggiatore, e spingeva una viltà non del tutto inconsapevole fino al punto di dire:

'Ma in compenso mia sorella le porterebbe la sua bellezza e la sua intelligenza.'

'Che m'importa,' lo interrompeva il Brambilla 'no, no...moglie e buoi dei paesi tuoi!' [11]

---

[9] *che razza di storie* what sort of a story

[10] *vada là* [expression of contempt or disappointment] go away

[11] *moglie e buoi dei paesi tuoi* [proverb] choose wives and cattle from your own village

Il ragazzo subiva queste umiliazioni senza quasi risentirle, a tal punto era immerso nella deprimente atmosfera del sanatorio. A queste crudeltà, il Brambilla aggiungeva un despotismo rallegrato e compiaciuto, al quale, del resto, Girolamo si sottoponeva con una buona volontà che era il risultato di una psicologia completa- [5] mente traviata [12] dalla malattia e dall'abbandono: oppresso dagli altri, Girolamo si riconosceva colpevole e volontariamente si univa al gruppo dei suoi oppressori. Gli succedeva il tal modo di provo-care i sarcasmi del suo compagno con frasi volutamente ingenue e goffe; non era raro che egli stesso cominciasse a parlare della sua [10] famiglia per il gusto non piacevole di vedersela bistrattare dal com-messo viaggiatore; oppure ostentava le sue manie di ragazzo ricco e viziato, inventava magari frivolezze mai conosciute, sicuro di provocare subito un'eco docile nell'ironia del Brambilla. Quest'ul-timo, d'altra parte, non indovinava mai queste tristi malizie e [15] abboccava immancabilmente all'amo.[13] Il repertorio dei tormenti, in un clima tanto favorevole, era diventato ben presto assai vario; uno dei procedimenti più usati dal Brambilla era quello di attirare sulla persona del ragazzo la familiarità e il disprezzo dei subordi-nati, infermieri o camerieri. Entrava, per esempio Joseph, un [20] robusto austriaco, infermiere patentato,[14] col quale il Brambilla era in ottimi rapporti:

'Ebbene, si figuri Joseph,' gli diceva il commesso viaggiatore, 'il signor Girolamo vuole per forza che io sposi sua sorella...che ne dice lei, Joseph?' [25]

'Dipende, signor Brambilla,' rispondeva l'ottuso austriaco ridendo d'intesa.

'Che ci sia qualcosa sotto?' [15] continuava l'altro. 'La signorina avrà commesso qualche peccatuccio, è incinta, e la mi si vuole ap-

---

[12] *traviata* distorted
[13] *abbaccava . . . all'amo* bit . . . at the hook
[14] *infermiere patentato* a male registered nurse
[15] *che ci sia qualcosa sotto?* there is more in this than meets the eye.

piccicare [16]... Questi borghesi sono terribili...che ne pensa lei, Joseph?'

'Eh, certo, il signor Girolamo avrà le sue ragioni,' rispondeva ridacchiando l'infermiere che, senza gli incoraggiamenti del Brambilla, non avrebbe mai osato prendersi beffa [17] di un malato. 'Non si dà niente per niente.'

'Ma non ho mai detto questo!' protestava a questo punto Girolamo.

'Eh, vada là...non fa che parlarmene tutto il santo giorno [18] e decantarmene le bellezze... Joseph, dica un po' lei, che penserebbe, al mio posto?'

'Eh signor Brambilla..., certo penserei molte cose.'

'Ma lei non l'ha vista la donna che mi si vuol far sposare,' diceva a questo punto il Brambilla; e poi rivolto a Girolamo: 'faccia vedere la fotografia della sorellina a Joseph..., su [19]...la tiri fuori.'

Il ragazzo esitava. 'Non so dov'è...' incominciava; al che il Brambilla: 'Su, non faccia l'imbecille [20]..., perchè Joseph non è un borghese come lei, si crede in diritto di disprezzarlo...ma sa lei che Joseph val mille volte più di lei?'

'Non ho mai pensato a disprezzare Joseph,' protestava il ragazzo; e, a malincuore, tendeva il ritratto della sorella all'infermiere; questi lo prendeva con le sue mani rosse e callose.

'Ebbene, che ne pensa, Joseph?' domandava il Brambilla. 'Crede che meriti un marito come me? Non le pare che sia piuttosto una di quelle ragazze con le quali...ehm! non so se mi spiego...ma che non si sposano?'

Era chiaro che l'infermiere, nonostante tali incoraggiamenti, esitava ad assumere nei riguardi del ragazzo quegli atteggiamenti ingiuriosi che il Brambilla desiderava; guardava Girolamo, il commesso viaggiatore, poi finalmente vincendo la più naturale tendenza

---

[16] *la mi si vuole appiccicare*   they want to force her on me
[17] *prendersi beffa* (*di qualcuno*)   to make a fool (of someone)
[18] *tutto il santo giorno*   all day long
[19] *su*   come on
[20] *non faccia l'imbecille*   don't be silly

al rispetto: 'Una bella signorina, signor Brambilla,' rispondeva, 'ma forse lei ha ragione...forse non sarà necessario sposarla...'

Queste familiarità riuscivano odiose al ragazzo; pure non era senza una certa civetteria, un certo esagerato pregare che egli chiedeva che gli venisse resa la fotografia: 5

'E ora che l'ha guardata,' pregava 'per piacere, signor Joseph, sia buono, mi renda la fotografia...'

Egli sapeva che in questo modo metteva se stesso e la sorella in quelle grosse mani dell'infermiere, ma gli pareva, con questa commedia della preghiera, di vendicarsi delle umiliazioni che quei 10 due gli infliggevano umiliandosi a sua volta, spontaneamente, e in maniera ancor più crudele. Il commesso e l'infermiere non scorgevano quanto di frivolo e falso fosse in queste ardenti suppliche; ci vedevano piuttosto una debolezza di adolescente delicato e viziato. 15

'Debbo rendergliela, signor Brambilla?' domandava l'austriaco sorridendo.

'Sì, me la renda...,' supplicava Girolamo.

'Gliela dia... gliela dia,' interveniva a questo punto il commesso viaggiatore, 'non sappiamo che farcene noi di sua sorella... abbiamo 20 di meglio...glielo dica lei, Joseph, che abbiamo di meglio...'

Questi giuochi, mentre non erano per il Brambilla che un passatempo qualsiasi, affondavano invece Girolamo, ogni giorno di più, in una nera atmosfera di umiliazione e di sofferenza. E, d'altra parte, così serrato era da parte sua l'impegno, così perdutamente 25 egli aderiva a questa realtà, che se qualcuno gli avesse allora domandato se soffriva, probabilmente avrebbe risposto di no; gli mancavano, per capire in quale miseria fosse ormai caduto, i termini di confronto, la visione esatta di quel che avrebbe dovuto essere la sua vita di ragazzo tra i coetanei e in famiglia; abituatosi, per 30 trapassi quasi insensibili, ad un'aria irrespirabile, ad una umiliazione ininterrotta, ad una assoluta mancanza di quelle attenzioni che prima, in famiglia, gli venivano prodigate, credeva di vivere normalmente, di essere lo stesso Girolamo di otto mesi prima. Ma l'artificiosità di questo suo stato d'animo si rivelava in certe 35 súbite [21] esasperazioni, in certe crisi di pianto, che lo prendevano, soprattutto di notte, mentre il Brambilla dormiva. Allora, sotto le coltri, con occhi pieni di lagrime, gli succedeva di desiderare acutamente le lontanissime carezze materne, o, per uno di quei pentimenti che mostrano l'inesistenza dei delitti di cui ci si pente,[22] di chiedere a bassa voce perdono a sua sorella per tutte quelle sue compiacenti viltà della giornata; poi, stanco, penetrava lentamente in quella specie di galleria sotterranea che era il suo sonno di malato. Neppure però il sonno gli dava pace, il suo letargo era popolato di sogni, gli pareva talvolta di piangere, di stare in ginocchio, di supplicare il Brambilla di perdonargli non sapeva quale misfatto; ma il Brambilla era implacabile e già lo spingeva riluttante e frenetico verso un misterioso supplizio, e inutilmente egli prometteva di essere docile, di piegarsi a qualsiasi bassezza,[23] di essere obbediente; quando qualche cosa di cupo travolgeva loro due e il sogno: nel cuor della notte [24] egli si destava, tremava per tutto il corpo, aveva la fronte bagnata di sudore. Ma poi si accorgeva che quel che l'aveva svegliato era la caduta pesante di un cumulo di neve fresca dal tetto del sanatorio sopra la terrazza; e ben presto tornava ad addormentarsi.

Al principio di gennaio nevicò parecchi giorni di seguito. Chiusi nella loro stanza, i due malati potevano vedere, di fuori, la neve cadere, formicolante e appena diagonale e così lenta che, a guardarla con attenzione, la vista finiva per ingannarsi e pareva che quel monotono turbinío piuttosto che cadere, salisse dalla terra verso il cielo. Dietro questa cortina opaca, quei fantasmi grigi e costernati erano gli abeti della foresta vicinissima; il gran silenzio che giungeva dall'esterno dava un'idea della fittezza e dell'estensione della nevicata. Ma se la neve per gli abitatori dei grandi alberghi, giù a valle, era gioia, spettacolo pittoresco, promessa di campi vergini per gli sci, per i malati era piuttosto quel che può essere una

---

21 *súbite*   sudden
22 *di cui ci si pente*   of which one repents
23 *bassezza*   base action
24 *nel cuor della notte*   in the middle of the night

mareggiata per i pescatori, un fatto noioso, un'interruzione sgradita, un ritardo alla guarigione; e nella stanza tutta ingombra dei due letti, dove la luce era accesa fin dal mattino e l'aria viziata della notte non se ne andava mai completamente, le ore passavano interminabili.

Il Brambilla, quando s'era stancato di canzonare Girolamo, di solito cominciava a narrare le sue avventure amorose. Nonostante incarnasse nell'aspetto fisico, coi suoi capelli biondi, i suoi occhi celesti e falsi, la sua faccia accesa, il perfetto tipo del commesso viaggiatore, pure, per un'illusione più che comune, si riteneva un finissimo seduttore. Per Girolamo poco più che diciassettenne e di tali faccende del tutto ignorante,[25] questo era un mondo completamente nuovo; così non dubitava di nulla, era tutto orecchi, e se il commesso viaggiatore gli avesse confidato di essere stato l'amante di una principessa, l'avrebbe senz'altro creduto. Del resto, con ogni probabilità, le storie del Brambilla, almeno nel complesso, erano vere; si trattava[26] quasi sempre di cameriere afferrate per i fianchi mentre rifacevano un letto; o di sartine portate a cena, poi al cinematografo e alfine in qualche albergo; oppure, più semplicemente di prostitute fermate in strada e abbandonate dopo due ore. Quel che invece certo non era vero, era la bellezza di queste donne, la passione che il Brambilla sapeva loro ispirare, e il disprezzo col quale le trattava. Ma, come s'è detto, Girolamo credeva tutto, la sua ammirazione per il commesso cresceva sempre più, segretamente gli invidiava quelle fortune, il Brambilla era ormai per lui il tipo ideale al quale con ogni sforzo egli doveva cercare di rassomigliare.

Qualche volta, durante queste narrazioni, entrava Joseph, appena uscito dalla camera delle operazioni, con le maniche rimboccate sopra le braccia nerborute, le mani sporche di gesso, e le forbici per tagliare gli apparecchi ortopedici pendenti fuor della tasca del càmice. S'appoggiava alla ringhiera del letto del Brambilla e stava

---

[25] *di tali . . . ignorante* completely unaware of these things
[26] *si trattava* it concerned

lì dieci minuti, un quarto d'ora, ascoltando, ogni tanto ridacchiando, spesso aggiungendo del suo. Anzi, un giorno, poichè il Brambilla ebbe finito, l'infermiere si voltò verso il ragazzo e disse:

'E lei, signor Girolamo, quando ci racconterà le sue avventure amorose?'

Sarebbe stato molto facile per il ragazzo dire la verità; 'non ho mai avuto alcuna avventura,' ma la vergogna di rivelare una tale deficienza, la paura di essere canzonato dal suo sarcastico compagno di stanza, gli impedirono una sincerità che gli pareva disonorevole, e gli ispirarono un atteggiamento misterioso e reticente che poteva lastiar supporre chissà quali sfrenati libertinaggi.

'Le mie avventure?' rispose arrossendo e non senza una specie di civetteria, 'non sono da raccontare le mie avventure.'

Il Brambilla appoggiato sopra il gomito lo guardava fissamente: 'Non faccia l'imbecille,' proruppe alla fine con irritazione, 'che avventure vuole avere avuto...? giusto con la balia quando era in fasce..., ma se è appena nato..., ma mi faccia il piacere...; e poi con quella faccia lì..., con quella faccia lì.'

'Perchè?' protestò debolmente il ragazzo: 'non crede che sia possibile che qualcun altro oltre lei possa avere avventure?'

'Chi lo dice?' rispose l'altro: 'per esempio, non dubito che Joseph abbia avuto anche più avventure di me... Non è vero, Joseph? glielo dica lei quel che ci vuole per certe malate,' e il Brambilla ammiccava all'infermiere che, tra confuso e goffo, rideva; 'ma lei no..., lei non è una persona seria come Joseph... Quando lei con quella faccia lì dice che ha avuto avventure fa ridere anche i polli [27]...; dica lei, Joseph, che avventure può aver avuto un signor Girolamo?'

L'infermiere che, nonostante gli adescamenti, s'era fin'ora limitato a prudenti ironie, questa volta non resistette ad una così facile tentazione:

'Lei, signor Brambilla,' disse sorridendo, 'ha dimenticato che il signor Girolamo ha conquistato il cuore della signorina Polly.'

---

[27] *fa ridere anche i polli*   you see fit to make a cat laugh

Era, questa della signorina Polly, una delle più abusate canzonature del Brambilla. La Polly era una ragazzetta inglese di poco più di quattordici anni, malata alla colonna vertebrale e ricoverata in prima classe dove ciascun degente aveva una stanza per sè. Girolamo aveva conosciuto questa bambina per via [28] della madre, che, desiderosa di distrarre la figlia, aveva stimato che il ragazzo, sia per l'età, sia per l'origine familiare, fosse il compagno più conveniente alla giovanissima inferma; e tale era la scarsità dei divertimenti nel sanatorio, che Girolamo, nonostante la differenza di età, aveva finito per prendere gusto [29] a queste visite e per aspettare quasi con ansietà i giorni fissati per gli incontri. Uscire non senza difficoltà dalla stanza, percorrere, sia pure dentro il letto, i corridoi oscuri del sanatorio, scendere fino al piano in quell'ascensore piacevolmente lento e angoscioso, fare un ingresso quasi trionfale in quell'altra stanza tanto più spaziosa della sua e dove tutte le cose, i fiori nei vasi, le fotografie, i libri, la carta delle pareti, persino la luce, per essergli nuove e inconsuete, gli parevano festive e immeritate; tutto questo, benchè non se lo confessasse, era per il ragazzo un godimento certo altrettanto intenso che quello che può provare un recluso movendo i primi passi fuori della sua prigione. Senonchè, ad un certo punto arrivò il Brambilla e tutto cambiò: bastarono poche canzonature, poche frasi come, per esempio: 'oggi il signor Girolamo scende all'asilo,' per far cessare questo innocente piacere. Girolamo si vergognò di questa sua amicizia, non trovò più alcun divertimento in quei giochi, in quelle conversazioni quasi puerili, e fu soltanto per un riguardo verso la madre della ragazzetta che non cessò affatto le sue visite.

Quella frase dell'infermiere non poteva dunque non ferire il ragazzo; il quale, però, sperimentando il suo nuovo sistema di difesa, rispose con una mollezza, con un rossore, con una confusione quasi femminili, che aggiungendo all'umiliazione inflittagli dall'austriaco un'umiliazione più forte, agivano da controveleno e

---

[28] *per via di*   because of, through
[29] *aveva . . . gusto*   had ended up by liking

parevano nel tempo stesso lasciare intendere che, in verità, almeno quel cuore aveva saputo conquistarlo.

Ma il Brambilla, tutto piegato sul fianco sinistro, lo guardava con la più brutta faccia di questo mondo, e non pareva convinto:

⁵   'Ma neppure quella, Joseph,' protestò alfine, 'neppure la signorina pollo o come si chiama... Aspetti che venga un inglese dall'Inghilterra, e vedrà come gli dà subito il benservito,³⁰ vedrà come se lo leva subito dai piedi il nostro Girolamo... Se glielo dico che non è buono a nulla.'

¹⁰   In questo momento la porta si aprì ed entrò la cameriera col vassoio delle cene; Joseph si ricordò che aveva da scendere nella stanza delle radiografie ed uscì. Per quella sera l'argomento della piccola inglese non fu più toccato.

Se avessero allora domandato al ragazzo quel che pensava del
¹⁵ Brambilla, avrebbe certo finito per riconoscere che non era davvero uomo da esser preso come modello; se gli avessero chiesto, fuor d'ogni questione d'affetto, chi stimava di più, suo padre o il Brambilla, la risposta non sarebbe stata dubbia; eppure, per una di quelle frequenti smentite che dà la sensibilità alla ragione, nono-
²⁰ stante la disistima in cui lo teneva, il ragazzo sentiva per il suo compagno di stanza una profonda attrazione, quale nessun'altra persona aveva mai saputo ispirargli. Avveniva così che amici della famiglia di Girolamo, gente elegante venuta in quel luogo di montagna per gli sports invernali, salissero fino al sanatorio, tutti
²⁵ impietositi dalla sensazione della propria bontà, dalla prospettiva di fare una buona azione, più che sicuri di essere ricevuti con entusiasmo; e si vedevano invece accolti con impazienza e freddezza da Girolamo nervoso ed evasivo, desideroso soprattutto di vederli partire presto e di andare a ritrovare il suo commesso viaggiatore,
³⁰ la sua stanza angusta, e i tormenti deliziosamente angosciosi ed abitudinari di quella conversazione senza pietà. Oppure era la madre di Girolamo, una piccola donna dal volto sciupato dal belletto e dai dispiaceri, dai movimenti rapidi e minuti, una donna

---

³⁰ *dà...il benservito*   dismiss . . . him

così piccola che pareva impossibile che Girolamo fosse suo figlio, e
lei stessa, non senza leziosaggine, se ne meravigliava continua-
mente. Era la madre del ragazzo che arrivava il giorno di Natale,
tutta impellicciata, le braccia cariche di regali, trattenendo a stento
le lacrime che le ispirava la vista del figlio, là, in fondo a quel suo
letto, sforzandosi di sorridere, di parere gaia; e Girolamo che
pochi mesi prima non avrebbe finito di baciare quel volto, quei
capelli, quel collo, ora si vergognava di abbracciare la donna
commossa, era imbarazzatissimo, silenzioso, quasi freddo, e mentre
con le mani respingeva macchinalmente da sè la madre, con gli
occhi non cessava di osservare il commesso viaggiatore, timoroso
di sembrargli ridicolo e nello stesso tempo molto preoccupato di
quel che potesse pensare di sua madre. Dopo due o tre giorni di
un soggiorno impacciato, freddo, e rattristato, con gran sollievo di
Girolamo, la donna partiva; egli tornava alla compagnia del commesso il quale, contro ogni previsione, non derideva il suo amore
filiale, bensì invece gli rimproverava d'essere senza cuore, disumano, d'aver trattato male sua madre: 'questi figli di borghesi!'
concludeva il Brambilla con disprezzo, 'non amano neppure i loro
genitori.' Allora, la stessa notte, per una di quelle reazioni tanto
più violente quanto più lunga e più forte è stata la compressione dei
sentimenti che le ha ispirate, un tale rimpianto della presenza ma-
terna assaliva ad un tratto il ragazzo, che il rumore dei suoi
singhiozzi e delle sue voci sommesse destava il Brambilla: 'ora non
si potrà stare in pace neppure la notte,' gli gridava costui dall'oscurità. Girolamo atterrito si raggomitolava sotto le coltri, tratteneva
persino il fiato, la paura gli faceva dimenticare il dolore, coll'animo
pieno di amarezza e di confusione finiva per addormentarsi.

Ma questa attrazione che il ragazzo provava per il Brambilla, non
andava senza un ardente desiderio di meritare la stima del commesso, di entrare, come per esempio Joseph, nel novero dei suoi
amici. Il disprezzo che il Brambilla ostentava per Girolamo pareva
soprattutto fondato sopra una pretesa inettitudine o ingenuità
del ragazzo: dimostrargli di non essere inetto nè ingenuo, d'essere
invece capace di quelle stesse prodezze di cui si vantava continua-

mente il commesso, d'essere, insomma, un uomo nè più nè meno
di Joseph, ed, ecco, subito, la stima acquistata, pensava ingenua-
mente Girolamo, ecco l'amicizia ottenuta.   Che, poi, qui non fosse
questione di stima o di amicizia, ma soltanto di crudele passatempo,
⁵ questo fatto tanto evidente sfuggiva completamente al ragazzo
che, a differenza del Brambilla e dell'austriaco, aderiva anima e
corpo a questa amara commedia.   Convinto di dovere smentire coi
fatti i sarcasmi del compagno di stanza, Girolamo cercò a lungo
un'occasione propizia; quell'accenno alla Polly, quella frase, 'se
¹⁰ glielo dico che non è buono a nulla,' gli suggerirono alfine l'idea
che cercava: per meritare la stima e l'amicizia del Brambilla, egli
avrebbe sedotto la ragazzina inglese.

S'era allora nel cuor dell'inverno, tutto pareva prestarsi a facili-
tare questo suo disegno.   Prima di tutto il tempo: ora nevicava, ora
¹⁵ pioveva, il cielo era sempre coperto da un fitto coltrone di nuvole
grige e basse, di conseguenza ogni cura solare era impossibile e i
malati dovevano restare ben chiusi nelle loro stanze; in secondo
luogo la madre della Polly, richiamata per affari in Inghilterra,
era partita già da qualche giorno, ottenendo però dal primario del
²⁰ sanatorio che, nonostante la sua assenza, Girolamo continuasse le
sue visite presso la figliuola.   Girolamo poteva dunque condurre a
compimento ³¹ il suo proposito con la sicurezza di non venire
scoperto o disturbato.

Questa decisione, se da un lato calmava quel suo bisogno di
²⁵ mettersi in buona luce presso il Brambilla, dall'altro però lo riempì
di un turbamento straordinario.   Non aveva mai toccato una donna,
era la prima volta che ci pensava e, benchè sapesse press'a poco
come doveva comportarsi, così grande era la sua timidezza che
dubitava di poter mai non pure sedurre, ma persino osar guardare
³⁰ con occhi non indifferenti e normali la sua piccola amica della prima
classe.

A queste preoccupazioni troppo naturali, se ne aggiungevano
altre di ordine morale.   Così la madre come la figlia non gli avevano

---

³¹ *condurre a compimento*   carry out

fatto che del bene, per le feste egli aveva ricevuto dei regali, c'era stato anzi tra la famiglia di Girolamo e la signora inglese uno scambio di lettere tutte piene di vicendevoli ringraziamenti. Girolamo capiva che, a parte il fatto che questa seduzione era già da sola una cattiva azione, lo era doppiamente in queste condizioni; gli balenò anche per la mente che, nel caso fosse stato scoperto, avrebbe messo se stesso e la propria famiglia nella posizione più imbarazzante. Ma queste esitazioni morali vennero vinte molto più facilmente che non quelle fisiche.

Girolamo provava difatti una specie di rancore per le due straniere, madre e figlia, ed ecco perchè: l'aveva prima di tutto offeso l'essere stato messo a pari con una bambina di quattordici anni; l'avevano poi urtato quell'atmosfera di famiglia, quella corrispondenza tra la donna e i suoi parenti; era stato alfine profondamente ferito dalle attenzioni pietose e quasi materne che, in quel luogo dove tutti si burlavano di lui, aveva avuto per lui la madre della Polly. 'Mi crede un povero piccolo malato,' era press'a poco il suo pensiero, 'un povero ragazzino, buono come il pane,[32] a cui bisogna fare del bene, portare cioccolatini e libri, e poi dirsi da sola: come sono buona...; ebbene, voglio mostrarle che non ho bisogno di nessuno, e che, all'opposto di lei, sono cattivo, anzi cattivissimo, e che perciò è meglio che non si occupi di me.' D'altra parte, c'era sempre stato in lui il sospetto che tutte quelle gentilezze fossero fatte per adescarlo a visitare la ragazzetta. 'Brambilla ha ragione,' pensava, 'se qui arrivasse un inglese...certo cesserebbe di occuparsi di me...'

Questi pensieri gli davano l'impressione d'essere molto malvagio, gli pareva d'essere decaduto completamente, senza remissione nè speranza. Fu anche per un rabbioso desiderio di nuove umiliazioni e nuove amarezze, che decise alfine di portare irrevocabilmente a termine i suoi propositi di seduzione.

Il giorno in cui doveva aver luogo la solita discesa di Girolamo al piano inferiore, l'alba stentò a spuntare sotto una nuvolaglia

---

[32] *buono come il pane* good and kind

bassa e gonfia che dava a tutto il paesaggio nevoso un aspetto di
attesa e di mortale immobilità.   Un'oscurità nera restò dalla notte
nelle stanze e nei corridoi del sanatorio; alla gialla luce della
lampada elettrica, subito dopo pranzo, il Brambilla e Girolamo, per
ingannare il tempo, incominciarono una partita a scacchi.

La scacchiera fu messa sopra una sedia tra i due letti; i malati,
sporgendosi fuori delle coltri, disposero i grossi pezzi, i re, le
regine, le torri, i cavalli, gli alfieri, che molte mani d'infermi
avevano resi lustri e levigati come i rosarii sgranati senza tregua
dalle dita delle pinzochere.   Di solito Girolamo giocava meglio
del Brambilla, ma quel giorno i suoi pensieri erano altrove,
un'ansietà, un malessere intollerabile l'opprimevano.   Quasi con
voluttà si fece vincere due volte di seguito dal Brambilla sogghi-
gnante e trionfante; ma un sarcasmo bene azzeccato destò in lui lo
spirito dell'emulazione; giocò a denti stretti una terza partita,
sforzandosi d'inventare combinazioni irresistibili, di studiare ogni
mossa dell'avversario, di vincere, insomma, a tutti i costi. Ma ad
un tratto s'accorse di stare per perdere daccapo, e, pieno di rabbia,
buttò per aria la scacchiera.   Questo gesto nervoso gli attirò una
furente filippica del Brambilla. Spaventato da quel che aveva fatto,
il ragazzo non staccava gli occhi dalla faccia del suo compagno,
con le mani faceva convulsi gesti di diniego e nello stesso tempo
tentava timidamente di rimettere a posto il giuoco disperso. Il
Brambilla, a cui non pareva vero di trovare una così facile occasione
per nuovi sarcasmi, raddoppiava la violenza...: a questo punto fu
bussato e Joseph entrò.

'Ordine di portare il signor Girolamo dalla signorina Polly,'
annunziò quasi militarmente strizzando l'occhio al Brambilla e
incominciando a spostare il letto del ragazzo.

'Ci siamo,' pensò Girolamo. Il malessere che la rabbia del giuoco
aveva scacciato, gli tornò; senza più occuparsi del Brambilla che gli
gridava: 'Vada..., vada dalla sua inglese,' s'abbandonò sopra i
cuscini, e per un istante chiuse gli occhi; quando li riaprì era già
fuori della porta, nel corridoio.

Il corridoio oscuro era disseminato di lampade accese; altri letti

candidi, coi loro pallidi malati supini e immobili sotto le coltri tanto
piatte da parere vuote, erano manovrati in quell'ombra da certe
robuste donne vestite di bianco; le rotelle di gomma rendevano un
loro sordo e angoscioso rumore strisciando sopra i tappeti di juta;
poi fu la volta dell'ascensore dalla discesa interminabile e ronzante,   5
con Joseph seduto in fondo al letto, nell'angusta cabina, come un
angelo custode di nuovo genere...; tutte queste cose erano note
al ragazzo, però, così irritata e tesa era la sua sensibilità che egli ne
soffriva in modo indicibile, come se fossero state nuove e spavento-
samente assurde.   10

Ma appena fu in quella stanza, e l'austriaco, disposto il suo letto
accanto a quello della ragazzetta, se ne fu andato, questa ansietà di
Girolamo a un tratto scomparve, ed egli si sentì fin troppo calmo.
La camera assai vasta era immersa in una penombra calda e grade-
vole, la lampada, fissata sopra i capezzali paralleli, illuminava le   15
loro due teste. I due letti, bianco quello di Girolamo, avvolto in
una coperta a scacchi colorati quello della fanciulla, si toccavano, e
questo contatto, per le possibilità impensate che forniva alla rea-
lizzazione del suo disegno, turbava non poco Girolamo. Intanto
s'era tirato alquanto fuori delle coltri, s'appoggiava anzi con un   20
braccio su quell'altro letto, e come se l'avesse vista per la prima
volta, pur domandandole in un suo goffo francese che cosa avesse
fatto negli ultimi giorni, esaminava con curiosità la fanciulla.

La Polly non mostrava più dei quattordici anni che aveva. Era
bionda, coi capelli saggiamente [33] tagliati all'altezza delle guance,   25
aveva occhi cilestri, un volto pieno di salute, roseo e bianco, e, pur
nella sua banalità, sarebbe stata graziosa, se non fosse stata una
leggera pinguedine derivata evidentemente dalla lunga infermità,
che le dava un aspetto pigro, addormentato e come sornione. Nulla
insomma di precoce era in lei, anche in un senso tutto inconsapevole   30
e fisico; semmai, all'opposto di Girolamo, la malattia pareva averla
intorpidita e quasi respinta in una ritardata infantilità.

Girolamo la guardava, non sapeva come incominciare, cercava di

---

[33] *saggiamente* properly

immaginare come avrebbe agito al suo posto il Brambilla. Abituato
dal commesso a considerare inetto ogni sentimentalismo, gli pareva
che incominciare con un 'ti amo,' che d'altra parte non aveva mai
proferito prima di allora, sarebbe stato ingenuo e soprattutto inutile.
⁵ Non che egli pensasse che bisognava essere cinici; ma, in buona
fede, credeva che la sola cosa meritevole di essere fatta in compagnia
di una donna fosse una certa quantità di atti sempre più audaci che
gradatamente dovevano portare alla completa seduzione. Fu dunque con l'aria più naturale di questo mondo che si decise alfine a
¹⁰ domandare alla piccola amica se avesse mai baciato o fosse mai
stata baciata da qualcuno.
La bambina accennò di no con la testa. Supina, col capo affondato
nel guanciale, guardava il ragazzo con due occhi tra stupiti e curiosi;
le coltri le coprivano a metà il petto grasso; sia per il calore eccessivo
¹⁵ della stanza, sia per un inconsapevole pudore, le guance le si erano
accese di un rossore intenso. Teneva un braccio, nudo fino al
gomito, girato intorno alla testa; e con le dita giuocava macchinalmente con una pupattola appesa alle sbarre del letto.
'È una cosa molto piacevole,' affermò nervosamente Girolamo.
²⁰ Ignaro di ogni preliminare e pieno di intenzioni troppo ardite,
questa frase gli parve oltremodo insipida. 'Vuoi che proviamo?'
soggiunse con sforzo. Evidentemente la ragazzetta non aveva
capito neppure di che cosa egli parlava, perchè ebbe un tenue
sorriso interrogativo; allora Girolamo si protese fuori del letto e
²⁵ la baciò sopra una guancia.
Quegli occhi cilestri lo fissavano con una specie di terrore. 'Ha
paura,' pensò Girolamo 'e mi prende per un pazzo.' Nonostante
fosse molto deluso da questo suo primo bacio d'amore, pure un
certo ardore puntiglioso gli impedì di desistere da un'impresa che
³⁰ gli sembrava ormai quasi fallita; continuò così a disseminare baci
sulla bocca, sul collo, sulla fronte; anzi, ad un certo momento,
afferrò il braccio che la ragazzetta teneva piegato sopra la testa e se
lo girò intorno al collo, come per farle capire che era necessario
contraccambiare in qualche modo queste sue tenerezze. Ma il brac-
³⁵ cio restò come egli l'aveva messo, inerte e docile; e Girolamo

scoraggiato stava già pensando di rinunziare definitivamente ai suoi propositi di seduzione quando, improvvisamente, fu bussato due volte alla porta.

Rosso in volto, più per lo sforzo che per l'eccitazione, più annoiato che pauroso, Girolamo si tirò indietro. Ma il suo aspetto era certo molto più scomposto di quel che immaginava, perchè, ad un tratto, contro ogni previsione, vide la ragazzetta sorgere dal letto, e con un gesto amorevole ed imperioso, passargli prima una mano sopra i capelli in disordine e poi ravviargli le coltri rovesciate. Ciò fatto, soddisfatta, ella si distese di nuovo, e con una placidità quasi ipocrita, gridò allo sconosciuto visitatore di entrare.

Era la posta. Ma quel gesto della ragazzetta era stato così spontaneamente femminile e complice, che Girolamo si sentì ad un tratto invaso da un turbamento straordinario, quale non aveva mai provato. Subitamente la sua piccola amica cessò di sembrargli puerile. 'La sa più lunga di me,' [34] pensò guardandola prendere dalla mano del postino, con la più grande calma, le lettere di quel giorno. L'uscio non si era ancora richiuso del tutto, che egli s'era già ributtato fuori dalle coltri e premeva con le sue labbra quelle immobili della fanciulla.

L'atteggiamento della Polly fu poi sempre lo stesso, ella non si mosse nè parlò neppure una sola volta e conservò quella sua ipocrita immobilità fino all'ultimo momento. Un poco a causa di questa passività, un poco perchè s'era aspettato molto di più, Girolamo non trovava molto sugo [35] in questa sua opera di seduttore; si consolava però pensando che anche lui aveva finalmente fatto questa esperienza indispensabile, e che, in tal modo, non avrebbe più dovuto vergognarsi in presenza del Brambilla. Ma certe rapide chiaroveggenze, non tanto della qualità morale, quanto della goffaggine e della scompostezza dei suoi atteggiamenti (gli avvenne per esempio, ad un certo momento, di sentir freddo alle reni e di accorgersi che a furia di sporgersi era uscito quasi del tutto fuori del

[34] *la sa . . . di me* she knows a lot more than I do
[35] *non trovava molto sugo* was not having much pleasure

proprio letto) gli facevano dubitare persino dei vantaggi che il
suo amor proprio poteva trarre da una tale esperienza, e gli davano
piuttosto il senso di un decadimento nel quale sarebbe stato quasi
voluttuoso lasciarsi affondare del tutto. 'Commetto azioni perverse
5   e assurde,' era press'a poco il suo pensiero, 'ma tanto sono perduto...: a che servirebbe trattenermi?'

La camera era oscura e silenziosa, i due letti gemelli vi facevano
una gran macchia bianca; nell'ombra delle pareti si distinguevano
confusamente varii oggetti, fiori, fotografie, vestiti, e davano a
10   Girolamo un senso di lusso e di intimità. Ogni tanto, egli si tirava
indietro sul letto, guardava intorno, ascoltava con piacere i rumori
dell'esterno, come, per esempio, i sonagli di certe slitte non si
capiva bene se in arrivo o in partenza, e avrebbe voluto non aver
fatto nulla e poter tornare ai passatempi innocenti di una volta; ma
15   il pallore, l'immobilità imbarazzata, l'espressione d'attesa della
Polly gli facevano capire l'assurdità di queste nostalgie; e senza
entusiasmo tornava alla sua impresa di seduttore.

Ma nel corridoio, mentre l'austriaco lo trascinava verso la sua
stanza, gli venne una specie di fierezza per quello che aveva fatto;
20   ché gli tornava in mente il Brambilla, e già immaginava di raccontargli l'accaduto, di ridere insieme con lui dell'innocenza della
sua piccola amica, di sentirsi finalmente uomo a fianco di quel-
l'uomo. Le guance gli ardevano; sicuro di essersi meritata tutta la
stima del suo compagno di stanza, si sentiva quasi felice; avrebbe
25   voluto parlare all'infermiere, oppure interpellare le cameriere che
andavano da una camera all'altra portando i vassoi delle cene. Fu
tratto da questo stato di ebbrezza, nell'ascensore, dalla voce del-
l'infermiere il quale, come il solito, si era seduto in fondo al letto:

'E così, signor Girolamo,' incominciò l'austriaco 'ora le toc-
30   cherà [36] cambiare compagnia.'

'Perchè?'

---

[36] *le toccherà*   you'll have to

'Ah già...., forse non lo sa...,' spiegò l'infermiere. 'Il signor professore ha visitato poco fa il signor Brambilla e l'ha trovato guarito...e così il signor Brambilla ci lascerà tra una settimana.' Con un ronzio monotono l'ascensore saliva. Immobile in fondo al suo letto, il ragazzo guardava il viso rosso e stupido di Joseph e rivolgeva in mente questi due pensieri: 'Il Brambilla è guarito,' 'Il Brambilla se ne va.' Individia non ne provava, ma piuttosto una vergogna acuta di aver fatto invano tutta quella sua opera di seduttore; capiva che ormai sarebbe stato stupido e inutile vantarsi col commesso viaggiatore dei suoi amori quasi infantili; il Brambilla era guarito, partiva, e non l'avrebbe neppure ascoltato; il Brambilla se ne andava ed egli restava in quella sua triste e meschina prigione, tra gli altri malati, le braccia ingombre di questa cattiva azione che ormai non serviva più a nulla. Intuiva inoltre d'essere stato il solo a prendere sul serio [37] il giuoco, a considerare la malattia e il sanatorio come uno stato normale, mentre, con ogni probabilità, il commesso non aveva mai cessato di ritenere la propria infermità, e tutto quello che essa comportava di amicizie, abitudini, stati d'animo e piaceri, come cose transitorie e soltanto per questo tollerabili. Al Brambilla la sua compagnia appassionata aveva fatto comodo, ecco tutto; ora se ne andava, lasciandolo nella sua malattia e nella sua ridicola e abbietta buona fede.

L'urtare che fece il letto contro lo stipite della porta della sua stanza, lo destò da queste amare riflessioni. Alzò gli occhi e vide, là nella cameretta, il posto vuoto che stava per rioccupare il suo letto, la lampada accesa, e il Brambilla che seduto fuor delle coltri lo guardava venire con la faccia di chi ha da annunziare una grande notizia. 'So già tutto,' avrebbe voluto gridargli Girolamo, e poi avrebbe voluto mettere la testa sotto le lenzuola e piangere o dormire, ma soprattutto non udire, non vedere più nulla; invece per uno scrupolo di dignità si rassegnò a far la parte dell'ignorante.

'E così,' disse il Brambilla, appena la porta si fu chiusa, con una

---

[37] *prendere sul serio* to take seriously

faccia che pur nella contentezza serbava tutta la sua brutalità,
'la sa la canzone:

> Saluti, salutissimi,
> lontano me ne andrò,
> e mai più ritornerò.'

'Sarebbe a dire?' domandò Girolamo.
'Questo vorrebbe dire,' rispose il commesso viaggiatore 'che
parto...me ne vado...che il professore mi ha visitato e mi ha trovato
guarito.'
'Ah benissimo,' incominciò Girolamo che credeva di dover
congratularsi; ma fu interrotto dal Brambilla.
'L'avevo sempre detto io,' continuava costui, 'che era una cosa da
nulla la mia...e ora me ne vado, caro il mio signor Girolamo, tra
una settimana sono a Milano...e voglio esser dannato se due giorni
dopo non sono già a cena al Cova con qualche bella donnina.'
'Sì...ma nei primi tempi,' insistette Girolamo con una prudenza
e un altruismo pieni di buona volontà, 'farà bene a stare attento...'
'Perchè attento? ma mi faccia il piacere...attento a che cosa...?
Il professore mi ha detto che posso fare tutto quello che voglio...e
poi starei proprio a seguire i suoi consigli...; pensi a guarire lei
stesso prima di dare consigli agli altri...bella questa...! Uno che è
malato e che vuol consigliare chi ha saputo guarire sul da farsi e
non farsi.'
Il Brambilla parlava. Mortificato Girolamo lo guardava e pensava con amarezza che quell'inferiorità sua di fronte al commesso
si rinnovava una volta di più sotto altre forme; prima erano le
esperienze amorose, ora la malattia; se prima sarebbe forse bastata
la seduzione della piccola inglese a procurargli quella stima tanto
agognata, ora questo scopo egli non avrebbe potuto raggiungerlo
che ridiventando sano. E così evidente era il disprezzo del Brambilla, così profondo il suo senso di umiliazione, che, ad un tratto,
per la prima volta da quando era nel sanatorio, gli parve di
distinguere chiaramente tutta la deformità viziata della propria
persona e delle cose che faceva. Questo stesso fatto di essersi

abituato a considerare la malattia come uno stato normale, come un'atmosfera respirabile gli sembrò una prova di più della propria irreparabile anormalità; non c'era dubbio: il Brambilla era sano e lui era malato; persino quelle 'belle donnine' di cui il commesso aveva parlato, avevano in loro qualche cosa di lecito e di puro, mentre invece tutto nei suoi rapporti con la piccola inglese era illecito, triste, torbido.

Queste considerazioni lo convinsero definitivamente di essere guasto, senza rimedio. Allora, mentre il Brambilla, tutto inebriato da questa sua improvvisa guarigione, parlava di quel che avrebbe fatto e della gente che avrebbe veduto a Milano, per una reazione dell'amor proprio abbastanza simile a quella che lo spingeva ad umiliarsi spontaneamente per non essere umiliato, Girolamo pensò ad un tratto che poichè era malato e viveva in sanatorio, ero meglio non soltanto non vergognarsi di questo suo stato, ma, come per sfida, mostrarsene persino soddisfatto e spingerne fino all'estremo limite le conseguenze pratiche e morali. Quali poi potessero essere queste conseguenze egli non avrebbe saputo dire chiaramente: con ogni probabilità affondare con maggior consapevolezza in questa specie di oscurità in cui gli pareva di vivere, sforzandosi di arrivare alla completa seduzione della sua piccola amica; dare, insomma, a se stesso e agli altri l'impressione di una certa disinvoltura, come di animale immerso nel proprio naturale elemento. Questa decisione calmò tutti i suoi risentimenti, gli parve d'essersi messo al sicuro con un tale pieno riconoscimento della propria debolezza, e nello stesso tempo di aver fornito a se stesso una giustificazione sufficiente di quelle azioni altrimenti condannabili che stava per compiere.

Ma i giorni che seguirono quella sera furono forse i più neri di quel suo inverno nel sanatorio. Il tempo che continuava ad oscillare tra un sole sfarzoso ma labile e subitanei e minacciosi oscuramenti seguiti da raffiche di neve, impediva una cura efficace. Il Brambilla, che cominciava ad alzarsi, scendeva in slitta al villaggio e ne riportava descrizioni di donne, di grandi alberghi, di lussuosità, di divertimenti di ogni genere, piene di una insolente felicità che facevano soffrire il ragazzo più di tutti i sarcasmi di un tempo. E quanto a Girolamo, egli si accorgeva che quell'abbandono, quel riconoscimento della propria miseria non gli davano alcuna forza.

⁵ 'Le sembrerà strano,' provò a dire al Brambilla, 'ma non ho alcun desiderio di alzarmi...qui al sanatorio mi trovo benissimo.'
'Tutti i gusti son gusti,' [38] gli rispose il commesso viaggiatore, 'ma io preferisco camminare e star bene.'
Quasi ogni giorno egli si faceva portare a pianterreno, presso la sua piccola amica. Ci andava con una cupa voglia di scandalo,
¹⁰ che sia per l'infantilità della ragazzetta, sia per le intenzioni che egli ci metteva, gli pareva di una perversità tutta gratuita, neppure giustificata dal bisogno di meritare la stima del Brambilla. Quel che succedeva poi durante queste visite gli lasciava un disgusto stupito. La Polly era sin troppo docile, tanta passività destava
¹⁵ in lui una crudele irritazione. 'La Polly,' pensava, 'se lo volessi tornerebbe con lo stesso zelo e la stessa indifferenza ai giuochi innocenti di prima.' Avrebbe voluto essere meno obbedito, questa autorità gli pesava, gli pareva di usarla male; una volta pensò persino di confidarsi al Brambilla ma poi ci rinunciò; e il proposito
²⁰ di raddrizzare i suoi rapporti con la ragazzetta, sia curiosità, sia debolezza, restò allo stato d'intenzione.
Le visite duravano da due a tre ore. Quando Girolamo tornava in camera, si sentiva insieme spossato e febbricitante; la febbre, che era il risultato più tangibile di questi suoi strapazzi, era abbastanza
²⁵ alta, durava fino a notte, e s'accompagnava con leggeri dolori al ginocchio malato, il quale, dopo di aver dato in un primo tempo segni evidenti di miglioramento, ora pareva essersi di nuovo aggravato. Ma Girolamo considerava tutti questi minacciosi indizi con la più grande indifferenza; non sperava nè desiderava più
³⁰ guarire; pensava che se la sconfitta aveva da esserci, era meglio che fosse completa. L'idea della morte non sfiorò mai la sua mente, è vero, ma gli si presentò spesso sotto l'aspetto quasi allettante di una

---

[38] *tutti i gusti son gusti*   there is no accounting for tastes

catastrofe imprecisata che presto o tardi avrebbe dovuto venire a
troncare una situazione ormai senza scampo nè via d'uscita.
Venne il giorno della partenza del Brambilla. Costui, subito
dopo pranzo, si alzò dal letto e procedette ad una accuratissima
toletta: si fece la barba, s'incipriò, si profumò con l'acqua di
Colonia, con un pettine spartì quei suoi capelli biondi nel mezzo
della testa e con la brillantina li rese lisci e lustri; da un suo bauletto
trasse un vestito turchino, un paio di scarpe di coppale, un soprabito nero con bavero di velluto e un cappello nero duro; poi
incominciò a vestirsi.

Aveva nevicato tutta la mattina; il cielo era di un biancore trasognato e sporco; nella stanza c'era poca luce; attraverso la doppia
finestra senza tendine si vedevano passare e ripassare, là di fuori,
sulla terrazza, contro quel cielo bianchiccio, le figure nere di due
infermieri che, armati di grandi pale, buttavano via la neve accumu-
lata dalla tormenta. Immobile in fondo al letto in disordine, i
capelli tutti arruffati e pendenti sul viso pallido e ardente, Girolamo
guardava ora il Brambilla, che, ritto in mutande rigate davanti allo
specchio, si sforzava, in quella luce incerta, di mettersi un colletto
troppo stretto, ora gli spalatori. Si sentiva già un po' febbricitante,
i tonfi che le palate di neve facevano cadendo sul piazzale disotto,
destavano in lui un formicolío di immagini frettolose. Pensava al
freddo, alla mortale tranquillità, al silenzio che certo erano di fuori.
Immaginava che gli infermieri ogni tanto si soffermassero nel loro
lavoro e con quella nuvoletta del respiro davanti alle bocche
ansanti, appoggiati sulle pale, indugiassero a guardare il paesaggio
nevoso. Gli pareva di vedere questo paesaggio, tutto bianco, con
certi alberi e certe casupole d'una nerezza fradicia e come carboniz-
zata, e il fumo dei comignoli sospeso tra il cielo e i pendii, meno
candido della neve, meno bigio delle nuvole. Ad un tratto, uno
stuolo di corvi si leva dal fondo della valle, compatto, ordinato,
che fa sul cielo bianchiccio un disegno nero ed elegante. Questo
stuolo si avvicina volando basso, ora addensandosi, ora disper-
dendosi, ma sempre conservando quel suo ordine preciso; più si
avvicina, più pare numeroso, ad un certo momento il cielo ne è

pieno, e lo stuolo è così basso che si possono distinguere le ali, le code aguzze dei corvi. Ed ecco, da dietro una collina rotonda, parte un colpo di fucile che esplode come una bomba nel mezzo dello stuolo. Ora i corvi sono tutti stramazzati sopra la neve, morti e stecchiti, ogni cadavere fa su quel candore una macchia nera diversa da tutte le altre, sia che tenga aperte tutte e due le ali, o una sola, ed abbia la coda spalancata a ventaglio o ben chiusa come un tulipano, sia che giaccia sul fianco o sul dorso con le zampe in aria; macchie nere più piccole e persino appena visibili, fanno sulla neve penne e pelurie lanciate in tutti i sensi dall'esplosione... Questa immagine della strage dei corvi tornava insistente nella mente di Girolamo, egli provava una specie di angosciosa delizia a imaginare i funebri uccelli disseminati sul pendío nevoso, sotto il cielo stupito; avrebbe voluto pensare alla sua piccola amica, ma non ci riusciva e pieno di malumore, pur guardando il Brambilla vestirsi, tornava a quei suoi sogni febbrili. In questo momento fu bussato alla porta e Joseph entrò.

'È venuto per portarmi dalla Polly,' pensò Girolamo; e, tiratosi a sedere [39] sul letto, incominciò a cercare sulla tavola accanto lo specchio e il pettine per ravviarsi i capelli scomposti; ma fu fermato in questo suo affaccendamento da un gesto dell'infermiere.

'Niente visita oggi, signor Girolamo,' disse l'austriaco con una grande sobrietà di tono, quasi seccamente; e poi rivolto al commesso viaggiatore: 'La slitta è pronta, signor Brambilla.'

'Perchè?' domandò Girolamo già preso, di fronte a questa freddezza dell'infermiere, da un malessere profondo. 'Forse la signorina Polly sta poco bene?'

'La signorina Polly ha delirato tutta la notte,' rispose l'infermiere sempre con la stessa rigidità 'e ora sta meglio...ma lei signor Girolamo non potrà andarci nè oggi nè i giorni prossimi...mai più.'

'Hanno scoperto ogni cosa,' pensò il ragazzo; il respiro gli mancò, sentì ad un tratto un gran freddo alle tempie e si abbandonò sui cuscini come chi sta per svenire. L'infermiere intanto s'era

[39] *tiratosi a sedere* having raised himself up to sit

chinato e legava il bauletto del Brambilla, là, presso la porta; il commesso già tutto vestito, col cappello in testa e il soprabito addosso, sorvegliava quest'operazione serio e accigliato.
'Perchè mai più?' domandò alfine il ragazzo con una voce esile.

'Ordine del signor professore,' disse l'austriaco, levandosi tutto ⁵ rosso in volto per lo sforzo compiuto; 'il signor professore ha avuto stamane un lungo colloquio con la madre della signorina Polly, la quale è arrivata stanotte; poi mi ha chiamato e mi ha detto:

'Joseph, per nessuna ragione d'ora in poi, nè il signor Girolamo ¹⁰ nè gli altri malati potranno muoversi dalle loro stanze.'
'E non le ha detto perchè?' insistè Girolamo che questa mancanza di cordialità da parte dell'infermiere addirittura atterriva. 'Non ha detto altro?'
L'infermiere aveva una faccia disgustata e severa: ¹⁵
'Lei, signor Girolamo, le ragioni le sa meglio di me...allora perchè far tante domande?'
Il Brambilla che aveva finito di esaminare il suo bauletto, si avvicinò:
'Che è successo?' domandò. 'Il signor Girolamo ne ha fatta ²⁰ ancora una delle sue?' ⁴⁰
'Ma sì,' disse l'austriaco con un viso oscuro; 'e poi, si sa, chi ne risente le conseguenze siamo noi del servizio... Come se si potesse sapere quel che fanno tra di loro i malati nelle loro stanze.'
Immobile il ragazzo guardava con quei suoi occhi brillanti i due ²⁵ uomini, le guance gli ardevano, dalla sofferenza avrebbe voluto gridare; 'ora,' pensava, 'il Brambilla domanderà i particolari e mi canzonerà ⁴¹ come il solito.' Non voleva confessarselo, ma, in verità, quel che soprattutto desiderava in quel momento, era che il commesso gli buttasse in faccia quei suoi soliti sarcasmi grossolani; ³⁰ una tale specie di interesse gli pareva mille volte preferibile a questo freddo riserbo; trepidante, aspettava una frase, come per

---

⁴⁰ *ne ha fatta . . . sue?* has [he] played one of his usual tricks again?
⁴¹ *mi canzonerà* will make fun of me

esempio, 'ah lei seduce le bambine,' che gli avrebbe permesso, modesto satellite, di rientrare, sia pure di soppiatto,[42] in quell'orbita superba.

Fu invece deluso.

'Sempre così,' proferì sprezzante il Brambilla che non pareva voler sapere più di quel che già era stato detto, 'questi figli di papà sono tutti eguali, non pensano che a loro stessi..., che poi gli altri abbiano a soffrire le conseguenze delle loro stupidaggini, che importa loro? son cose che non li riguardano...'

'Ma che c'entra Joseph con quello che io faccio?' incominciò Girolamo a cui la freddezza dei due uomini faceva perdere la testa. 'Io posso fare quello che voglio...'

Il Brambilla che riuniva certi giornali, si voltò: 'Ma stia zitto,' interruppe 'si vergogni...'; poi, rivolgendosi all'infermiere: 'Allora,' disse, 'possiamo anche andare.'

Joseph spalancò la porta, si chinò, e caricò sulle spalle il bauletto. 'Del resto,' disse al ragazzo prima di uscire 'neppure lei, signor Girolamo, la passerà così liscia...; il signor professore è arrabbiatissimo...; sentirà domattina.'

Girolamo affidava ormai le sue ultime speranze agli addi del commesso. Quel riserbo, quella riprovazione dei due uomini l'avevano riempito di un tale acuto senso di colpevolezza, era così convinto della propria indegnità, che, in quel momento, un movimento affettuoso del suo compagno di stanza lo avrebbe certo commosso fino alle lagrime, come il segno di una bontà quasi sovrumana. Guardava perciò il Brambilla con occhi ansiosi: 'quasi nove mesi passati insieme,' pensava, 'non dovremmo forse abbracciarci?'

Ma il Brambilla che aveva finito di radunare la sua roba, era già più vicino alla porta che al suo letto.

'Mi pare di non lasciare nulla,' disse alfine dalla soglia, girando per la stanza già piena della penombra del crepuscolo, uno sguardo

---

[42] *di soppiatto*   secretly

scrutatore. Il ragazzo lo vide esitare, quindi aprir l'uscio. 'Allora arrivederci e auguri,' arrivò improvvisamente a Girolamo dall'ombra che avvolgeva la soglia. Egli avrebbe voluto alzarsi sul letto, dir qualche cosa, ma non ne ebbe il tempo; la porta era già chiusa.

La notte era intanto caduta del tutto, un'ombra nera interrotta soltanto dal biancore confuso delle lenzuola rovesciate sul letto del Brambilla, riempiva la stanza. Per un poco il ragazzo restò immobile ascoltando avidamente i rumori che giungevano dall'esterno; udì così il tintinnío dei sonagli della slitta che portava via il commesso, allontanarsi nella notte gelata e poi morire affatto, udì anche l'uscio della stanza attigua sbattere, e qualcuno parlare; a questo punto un brivido di freddo, probabilmente originato dalla febbre, percorse il suo corpo; macchinalmente egli si rannicchiò come poteva e tirò fin sopra le orecchie le coltri in disordine.

Tutto quello che l'infermiere, con quel suo tono oscuro e disgustato, gli aveva detto a proposito della sua piccola amica, ora gli tornava in mente con l'intensità propria ad ogni stato febbrile. L'idea che la bambina avesse delirato tutta la notte gli ispirò dapprima un rimorso impietosito e amaro; si raffigurò la ragazzetta come l'aveva tante volte veduta, bianca e immobile sotto la luce bassa della lampada; gli parve ad un tratto di intuire un nesso tra il fisso terrore che aveva spesso sorpreso in quegli occhi cilestri e questo delirio seguìto dalla rivelazione, dallo scandalo, e dall'intervento materno. 'Evidentemente,' pensò, 'ella aveva per me, benchè non me lo avesse mai detto, un grandissimo rispetto, una specie di adorazione...ed è per questo che mi ha lasciato agire senza protestare, senza neppure avere il coraggio di respirare..., ma poi ciò che è accaduto l'ha riempita, suo malgrado di vergogna e di paura, ella non ha cessato di pensarci e finalmente, dopo una notte di deliri, appena ha veduto sua madre, non si è più trattenuta e piangendo ha confessato ogni cosa...' Queste immagini gli fecero ad un tratto capire che anche la sua piccola amica s'era messa, e con ragione, da quella parte dove già stavano il Brambilla e

l'infermiere: 'sono solo,' pensò ancora, 'nessuno vuol più saperne
di me.' [43]

L'entrata improvvisa di una infermiera che portava il vassoio
della cena, lo fece balzare seduto sul letto e accendere la luce. La
donna, una bruna piuttosto piccola, di forme sode e non brutta, ma
dotata di una particolarità insolita, e cioè di una peluria vellutata e
scura che le copriva gli avambracci, le guance, il labbro superiore e
persino il collo, e faceva pensare a un corpo furiosamente villoso,
posò dapprima il vassoio sopra la tavola, e poi, sempre senza dire
parola, si diede a disfare il letto del Brambilla. Costei era solita,
ogni volta che entrava in quella stanza, indugiare a chiacchierare col
ragazzo e soprattutto col Brambilla al quale quella particolarità
della peluria ispirava una grande attrazione. Girolamo che l'aveva
veduta anche troppo cordiale e non senza una certa sua scurrilità,
risentì subito questa ostentata freddezza come un rimprovero e una
condanna. 'Anche lei sa tutto,' pensò disperato, 'e mi disprezza
come tutti gli altri.' Ora la sua persona intera si tendeva nel desiderio di ottenere almeno da questa donna un segno di stima o di
misericordia; avrebbe voluto dire una frase, fare un gesto che avessero invincibili virtù di convinzione, ma gli bastava guardare a
quella figura curva sul mucchio delle lenzuola, là, nell'angolo, per
sentirsi incapace persino di aprire bocca.

Ma nel momento in cui l'infermiera stava per andarsene, gli
riuscì alfine di vincere la timidezza. 'Dica,' domandò con sforzo
'come sta la signorina Polly?'

La donna col fagotto delle lenzuola sotto il braccio, era già presso
la porta.

'Proprio lei,' esclamò con violenza, 'proprio lei ha il coraggio di
farmi questa domanda...! bel tipo!' soggiunse con un riso sarcastico,
'prima fa il male, poi come se nulla fosse, in tono indifferente,
s'informa della salute...'; ci fu un istante di silenzio; a Girolamo
ardevano persino le orecchie. 'La signorina Polly sta meglio,'
concluse seccamente l'infermiera, 'desidera altro?'

---

[43] *nessuno . . . di me*   nobody wants to hear any more about me

'E il professore,' domandò ancora Girolamo, 'quando farà la sua visita?'

'Domattina...e sentirà che musica... Desidera altro?'

'Ma come,' insistette Girolamo che s'era ad un tratto fatto pallidissimo 'che vuol dire...? perchè che musica?'

La donna lo guardò di traverso. Non sapeva neppure lei che cosa avesse voluto dire con quella frase, nè quello che avrebbe deciso il professore il giorno dopo, ma, nella sua sincera indignazione, ogni più severa condanna le pareva troppo mite.

'Che cosa vuol dire?' ripetè alfine 'vuol dire che dopo quel che lei ha fatto, il professore può anche mandarla via... Desidera altro?'

'Porti via la cena,' disse il ragazzo con un vago desiderio di impietosire la donna con questo suo digiuno; stasera non mangio.'

Ella ebbe daccapo quel suo riso sarcastico.

'Ora non faccia la vittima,' disse, 'mangi..., tanto, quando non avrà mangiato, la signorina Polly non starà meglio... Desidera altro?'

'Nient'altro.'

La porta si chiuse. Per un istante Girolamo restò come era, seduto sul letto; poi, senza toccare il cibo che conteneva il vassoio, si rannicchiò di nuovo sotto le coltri, il viso rivolto verso la finestra. I suoi pensieri erano confusi, gli pareva di essere perduto; 'mandarmi via,' pensava, 'il professore mi manderà via'; sebbene fosse convinto di meritare questa punizione, pure una tale prospettiva gli ispirava uno sgomento indicibile. Sapeva che la sua famiglia non l'aveva mandato senza sacrifici in quel sanatorio, e con quella intensità che gli dava la febbre gli pareva di vedere, momento per momento, quel che sarebbe successo: la partenza dal sanatorio, l'arrivo a casa, le lagrime di sua madre, i rimproveri di suo padre, tutti quei contrasti, insomma, tra umilianti e dolorosi, che un tale avvenimento avrebbe prodotto in una famiglia già stretta da angustie di ogni genere com'era la sua, e verso la quale, per certi suoi scrupoli puerili che non avevano alcuna rispondenza nella realtà, era convinto di avere un debito di gratitudine pressochè inestinguibile.

Queste immaginazioni gli diedero una specie di agitazione, come se il professore fosse già lì a imporgli di andarsene; incominciò a muoversi sotto le coltri, a scuotere la testa: 'no, questo no,' pensava tra questi movimenti, 'tutto fuorchè questo.' Non se lo confessava,

5 ma quel che lo faceva soprattutto soffrire in questa amara prospettiva dell'essere scacciato, era perdere la stima e l'affetto dei genitori; non avendo mai fatto alcuna differenza tra loro e la gente del sanatorio, Girolamo era sicuro che appena avessero saputo la verità, l'avrebbero disprezzato anch'essi come tutti gli altri; e con spavento

10 immaginava la vita a casa, malato e disprezzato, ragione di dispiacere e di noie senza fine, con poca speranza di guarigione e nessuna di felicità. 'No, tutto fuorchè questo,' si ripetè atterrito, 'tutto fuorchè questo.'

Era stanchissimo, ad un tratto gli venne una gran voglia di

15 dormire, di dimenticare ogni cosa, lasciandosi cadere nel nero abisso del sonno; spense la luce, e non erano infatti ancora passati cinque minuti che già dormiva profondamente. Ma subito incominciò a fare sogni imbrogliatissimi; gli pareva di stare, disteso sul suo letto di ferro, in una grande stanza vuota, dalle pareti grige e disadorne;

20 nel mezzo c'era una tavola di legno scolpito alla quale si appoggiava con negligenza un uomo ancora giovane: suo padre. Parlano con calma e suo padre gli dice che non ha più abbastanza soldi per mantenerlo al sanatorio; non pare disgustato o irritato suo padre, sorride con rassegnazione; egli è d'accordo con suo padre, è evi-

25 dente che se non ci sono più quattrini non è più possibile continuare la cura, ma pensa, riflette con ostinazione cercando un rimedio, gli pare improvvisamente di averlo trovato: 'sposerò la Polly,' esclama. Questa proposta incontra la piena approvazione di suo padre; ma bisogna portare la notizia alla piccola inglese. Il padre di

30 Girolamo si leva dalla tavola e comincia a tirar fuori dalla stanza il letto del figlio. Sono ora nel corridoio oscuro del sanatorio, il padre guida con difficoltà il letto del ragazzo, non ha l'abilità di Joseph, d'altra parte il corridoio nero è pieno di letti bianchi guidati in tutti i sensi da infermiere e infermieri. Altro fatto che rallenta

35 il passaggio sono le fermate davanti le numerose botteghe che, non

si sa come, aprono le loro vetrine sfarzose da ambo i lati del corridoio. Queste botteghe sono davvero luminosissime; dentro le vetrine profonde come caverne, in mezzo ad un grande sfarzo di luce, si vedono esposti oggetti rari d'oro e d'altri metalli preziosi, chincaglierie, vestiti, bronzi, armi. Tutte queste belle cose attirano gli sguardi di Girolamo; egli pensa ad un tratto di fare una improvvisata alla sua futura moglie, portandole addirittura un corredo completo. Detto e fatto: [44] il padre entra in una di quelle botteghe e poco dopo ne riesce con uno splendido vestito di sposa, tutto bianco, luccicante, ornato di un grande strascico di veli vaporosi; da un'altra bottega riporta una corona di fiori d'arancio; da un'altra ancora altri indumenti; ogni cosa viene deposta sul letto di Girolamo; il vestito di sposa, con tutti i suoi veli, fa una grande e abbagliante macchia bianca in quella oscurità nera; essi riprendono il viaggio nel corridoio. Arrivano alfine all'ascensore, che li porterà a pianterreno; sono già dentro, l'ascensore comincia a discendere. Ed ecco, la discesa pare più lunga del solito, e quel ronzio elettrico che l'accompagna più forte e insistente; Girolamo guarda il vestito di sposa, là in fondo al letto, un'angoscia assurda l'opprime, 'bisogna fermarsi,' si ripete, 'bisogna fermarsi.' Ma la discesa continua, e il ronzio cresce, si trasforma crescendo, diventa una specie di ululato... A questo punto le immagini si spezzarono e il ragazzo si destò.

La nota oscurità della sua stanza empiva i suoi occhi sbarrati, ma quell'ululato del sogno era restato e pareva anzi crescere d'intensità di momento in momento, e riempire, per così dire, di sè, ogni più piccolo ripostiglio di silenzio. Dapprima, ancor tutto insonnolito, non capì che cosa fosse, poi un rumore di passi precipitosi giù per la scala di legno del sanatorio, che non era lontana dalla sua stanza, come di gente in fuga, gli fece ad un tratto capire la verità: 'È la sirena del campanile, per gli incendi,' pensò, 'il fuoco è nel sanatorio...e questo rumore è quello degli infermieri che scappano.'

---

[44] *detto e fatto*   no sooner said than done

Accese in fretta la luce, la tranquillità della propria stanza, in quel momento, con quell'ululato della sirena per l'aria, con quello scalpicciare, giù per la scala, là di fuori, gli parve tremenda. 'Il sanatorio è quasi tutto di legno,' pensò, 'e brucerà in un istante...e c'è un solo ascensore che può portare un solo letto per volta... e ci sono più di ottanta letti...' Tra questi colcoli guardava la porta, l'ululato della sirena cresceva sempre più, giù per la scala continuava il rumore affrettato dei passi. Ad un tratto, benchè sapesse benissimo che, attaccato com'era per un piede alla carrucola del suo apparecchio di trazione, da solo non avrebbe mai potuto liberarsi, incominciò a dibattersi dentro il letto. La carrucola cigolava, il letto gemeva, dopo un poco Girolamo cambiò sistema e diresse tutti i suoi sforzi a smuovere il letto nella direzione della porta, ma il letto non si mosse. 'Dovrò restar qui,' pensò alfine, abbandonandosi sui cuscini, con più ira che spavento, 'attaccato per un piede...restare qui in questa trappola ad aspettare la morte...' Gli pareva che questa morte sarebbe stata l'ultima ingiustizia dopo una lunga serie di sfortune immeritate. Improvvisamente lo prese una rabbia terribile contro questa specie di fatalità che colpiva lui e risparmiava gli altri. 'Maledizione,' incominciò a ripetere, guardandosi intorno, bianco in volto, fremendo e digrignando i denti, con un preciso desiderio di mordere, di far del male, di vendicarsi di tutti i suoi patimenti in questo suo estremo momento; 'maledizione..., maledetto il sanatorio, maledetta la Polly, maledetti i medici...' Gli occhi gli si posarono sul vassoio della cena, carico di piatti e di pietanze fredde; si protese e lo spinse fuori della tavola: ci fu un gran fracasso di porcellane rotte; poi fu la volta del calamaio e degli altri oggetti; non si fermò se non quando si sentì estenuato, e non ci fu più nulla da distruggere.

Allora si accorse con stupore che quell'ululato della sirena, e quello scalpiccio giù per la scala erano cessati, e che, d'altra parte, nè il crepitio, nè le fiamme, nè il fumo, nè alcun altro insomma dei funesti segni dell'incendio erano venuti a turbare la tranquillità della stanza. E ad un tratto capì la verità: con ogni probabilità s'era appiccato il fuoco a qualche fienile, e quella gente che scendeva la scala non correva per salvarsi, bensì invece per andare ad ammirare lo spettacolo insolito di un incendio su quella neve, nel cuor della notte invernale.

Dal sollievo gli occhi gli si riempirono di lagrime, poi vide i rottami dei piatti, là, sul pavimento, si ricordò di quei suoi contorcimenti, di quelle sue maledizioni di poc'anzi, e un'improvvisa, intollerabile vergogna l'invase. L'essere giunto, in quell'istante di smarrimento, a maledire la bambina che sapeva di aver offeso, gli pareva il segno più chiaro di un'oscurità nella quale, senza accorgersene, s'era da tempo lasciato cadere. 'Avrei davvero meritato di morire,' pensò con convinzione. Si sentiva pieno di pentimento e di buoni propositi, avrebbe voluto poter camminare per andare dalla sua piccola amica e domandarle perdono; pensò anche per un istante di promettere solennemente di sposare la bambina appena si fosse fatta donna, ma abbandonò subito questo progetto per la sua evidente assurdità. Gli pareva di essere l'ultimo degli uomini e il più malvagio, l'idea che il professore il giorno dopo l'avrebbe scacciato dal sanatorio, non lo spaventava più, gli recava anzi una specie di sollievo; 'come lo merito,' pensò. Ora quell'umiliazione, quel disprezzo, quell'inferiorità ai quali andava incontro, gli parevano desiderabili; gli piaceva di immaginarsi punito con giustizia; pensava che in tal modo, attraverso questi nuovi patimenti, si sarebbe alfine liberato di quella specie di oscura rabbia che gli pesava addosso dalla sera in cui, per la prima volta, aveva baciato la ragazzetta, e avrebbe potuto con animo placato rivolgere il pensiero alla guarigione. Questa idea che il giorno dopo qualcuno l'avrebbe punito con giusta severità e con pieno diritto, gli ispirava una fiducia, una tranquillità illimitate; chiusi gli occhi, con uno stato d'animo molto simile a quello di un bambino che, dopo uno spavento o qualche capriccio, si addormenta tra le braccia di sua madre, passò alfine dallo stato di veglia al sonno.

Fu destato a mattino inoltrato da un raggio di sole non caldo ma straordinariamente limpido e rutilante che, passando sotto l'angolo della finestra, veniva a battere su tutta quella parte della stanza dove era situato il letto. Aprì gli occhi e il primo pensiero

fu di gioia per la bella giornata; 'che splendido cielo azzurro,'
pensò guardando alla finestra; 'oggi potrò finalmente fare la cura
del sole.' E già si meravigliava che non fossero venuti a destarlo
per tirarlo sulla terrazza, quando gli giunse dalla stanza attigua
un rumore di voci virili, delle quali una più sicura e imperiosa
sembrava domandare e comandare, e le altre rispondere in tono
di deferenza e di sottomissione; 'è il professore,' capì ad un tratto,
invaso a questo pensiero da un malessere intollerabile, 'ed è già
arrivato dai miei vicini...e tra poco sarà qui...'
    Gli tornarono in mente tutti gli aspetti della realtà che l'oppri-
meva: la bambina, lo scandalo, la cacciata dal sanatorio, e, per un
istante, un'angoscia, un orgasmo straordinari lo invasero. 'Tra
poco sarà qui,' pensò, 'e io non sono lavato nè pettinato...e tutta
la stanza è in disordine...e c'è ancora per l'aria il puzzo della
notte...'; si muoveva, non sapeva da che parte incominciare per
mettere un po' d'ordine intorno a sè. Ad un tratto quei suoi occhi
smarriti si posarono sul pavimento, e vide, là in terra, tra i due
letti, il vassoio, i piatti spezzati, e, tra le scheggie di porcellana, i
cibi raggrumati nella cera scura degli intingoli. 'E io che me ne ero
dimenticato,' pensò in furia. Esitò, poi si protese con la testa in giù,
con l'intenzione di spingere quei rottami sotto il letto. In questo
momento le voci virili accompagnate da un rumore di piedi, si
fecero oltremodo distinte e vicine, poi la porta si aprí e, seguito da
Joseph e dal medico assistente, il professore entrò.
    Questo professore, terrore di Girolamo, e, per tutt'altre ragioni,
di tutto il corpo sanitario, dall'assistente fino al più umile degli
infermieri, incarnava abbastanza bene certo tipo di medico moderno,
non tanto scienziato quanto abile e interessato amministratore al
tempo stesso del proprio ingegno e dell'immensa credulità dei
malati. Privo di qualsiasi originalità creativa, ma buon chirurgo,
dotato soprattutto di intuito psicologico e, come dire?, politico,
lo spettacolo della viltà di fronte al dolore, e l'altro non meno
istruttivo dell'ignoranza e dell'insufficienza dei medici, gli avevano
ispirato fin da giovane il più grande disprezzo per gli uomini, e la

convinzione che per farsi strada, in questo come in tutti gli altri campi, servissero soprattutto il cipiglio, la sicurezza del linguaggio, il tono duro e convinto, tutti insomma quei segni esteriori di autorità dietro i quali la folla immagina si nascondano lumi equivalenti e infallibili di sapienza e di genio. Di persona questo professore era alto e poderoso, aveva mani pallide e corte sparse di peli lunghi, neri e rari, capelli tagliati a spazzola, occhi folgoranti e freddissimi, naso adunco, baffi e barba in punta: era la testa di un moschettiere o di un inquisitore. Se a tutto questo si aggiunge un modo di muoversi, di parlare, di guardare, brusco e imperioso, e certe risate, certe bonomie rare ma sempre adoperate a tempo, che facevano dire ai suoi ammiratori: 'è brusco, si sa..., ma quanta bontà c'è nel suo riso,' si avrà un'idea press'a poco esatta del personaggio.

Al rumore che fece la porta aprendosi, Girolamo, che, intento a cacciare i rottami della cena sotto il letto, stava proteso fuor delle coltri con tutto il busto, e coi capelli pendenti quasi toccava il pavimento, si rizzò con vivacità, e pur guardando fissamente il professore che seguito da Joseph e dall'assistente si avvicinava con lentezza e, si sarebbe detto, quasi con circospezione, rimise a posto le coltri, e, come poteva, si ravviò i capelli. Il cuore gli batteva, dall'ansietà il respiro gli mancava. Poi si ricordò della ragione di questo suo sgomento e come per incanto si calmò; 'ora dirà che mi rimanda a casa,' pensò stringendo i denti [45] per superare il malessere che l'opprimeva; 'che ho fatto una cosa orribile...; sono pronto a obbedire, a subire qualsiasi punizione, purchè faccia presto.' Avrebbe voluto gridarlo al professore: 'presto..., faccia presto'; invece seppe trattenersi, e, rosso in volto, guardò venire il chirurgo e i suoi due compagni.

Come se avesse voluto contraddire apposta quel desiderio di Girolamo, il professore non pareva invece avere alcuna fretta. Si avvicinò, a due passi dal letto si fermò e scosse la testa in modo

---

[45] *stringendo i denti* clenching his teeth

ironico, vedendo sul pavimento i piatti rotti e il vassoio; poi
guardando il ragazzo:

'Ne ho sentito delle belle [46] sul conto suo.'

Girolamo impallidì; 'ci siamo,' pensò; dalla sofferenza avrebbe
voluto gridare.

'Ma se debbo andarmene,' gli riuscì alfine di proferire con voce
tremante, 'la prego, signor professore, di farmi partire il più presto
possibile...'

Il medico lo guardò:

'Andarsene...? Chi le ha detto che deve andarsene?'

Una specie di densa nebbia avvolgeva ormai gli occhi di Girolamo.

'Ma a causa di quello che ho fatto,' balbettò ancora, 'la Polly...il
primo piano...'

Il professore capì finalmente.

'Ah...è per questo!' esclamò con freddezza, avvicinandosi al letto
e facendo segno agli altri due di seguirlo: 'ma in tal caso, ragazzo
mio, lei si sbaglia... La condotta dei malati non ci riguarda...non è
una casa di correzione, questa, ma una clinica... Noi ci occupiamo
del suo corpo, non della sua anima, soltanto del suo corpo, anzi
di una parte del suo corpo... Ho già dato ordine che non la si faccia
più scendere a pianterreno, ecco tutto...e in quanto all'andarsene,
lei se ne andrà quando noi giudicheremo che sarà necessario...' Si
voltò verso l'infermiere e con un gesto: 'Tiratemi via queste
coperte,' ordinò.

L'austriaco obbedì. Nudo, Girolamo rabbrividì; troppa confusione era nella sua mente, perchè gli fosse possibile pensare; gli
pareva di essere annientato e al di là di questa amara sensazione di
nullità non sapeva andare. Intanto il professore si era chinato,
riflessivamente e palpava con quelle sue mani pallide e tozze il
ginocchio malato. Girolamo lo guardava, e gli pareva di non essere
più che un corpo senza volontà e senza intelligenza. Poi il professore si alzò:

---

[46] *Ne ho sentito delle belle* I have heard some fine things

'Mi faccia vedere le radiografie,' disse all'assistente.

Costui aveva un fascio di buste metalliche sotto il braccio. Ne trasse le tre fotografie del ginocchio di Girolamo e le porse al chirurgo; che, mettendole contro luce, le scrutò a lungo confrontandole. La prima di queste fotografie mostrava, sopra un 5 fondo nero, il nucleo biancastro, formato dalla rotula e dalla congiunzione del femore con la tibia, tutto annebbiato e deformato; nella seconda negativa questo annebbiamento, questa deformazione erano già rimpicciolite e circoscritte da un orlo oscuro; ma neila terza radiografia la nebulosità e la deformazione erano le stesse 10 della prima, anzi, semmai, parevano leggermente aumentate. Il professore rese le fotografie all'assistente e si volse verso il ragazzo.

'Lei,' pronunziò, 'è tornato alle stesse condizioni nelle quali si trovava quando arrivò qui al sanatorio...è contento?'

'Come, quali condizioni?' incominciò il ragazzo; ma l'altro lo 15 interruppe: 'Pensi,' disse, 'a guarire... Io, se fossi al suo posto, non prenderei così sottogamba la malattia...; e ora vada a fare la cura... Joseph, mettetelo fuori sulla terrazza'; e senza aspettare la risposta di Girolamo, seguito dall'assistente, il medico uscì.

Joseph spalancò la finestra, diede al ragazzo gli occhiali affumi- 20 cati e il pannolino per il ventre, tolse via del tutto le coperte, poi, con pochi strattoni delle braccia robuste, tirò il letto sulla terrazza. In un atteggiamento vergognoso, nudo, rannicchiato sopra il materasso, il ragazzo si trovò ad un tratto all'aria aperta. Faceva freddo, era molto se il sole gioioso e limpido che inondava di luce 25 la terrazza, impediva di gelare. Altri letti, coi loro bruni corpi distesi sulle lenzuola accecanti, stavano già esposti al sole, persino le piaghe, le fistole, gli ascessi che qua e là deformavano quelle membra inerti, parevano meno ripugnanti nella bella luce del mattino invernale. Alcuni di questi malati leggevano, altri giace- 30 vano supini senza far nulla, immobili come morti, altri ancora, laggiù, in fondo alla terrazza, avevano messo in movimento un loro grammofono, se ne udivano a intervalli, portati dal vento, i suoni facili e discordi La giornata non avrebbe potuto essere più splendida: fin dove l'occhio poteva arrivare, si vedevano con net- 35 tezza, contro quel cielo duro e limpido, i picchi accidentati e nevosi delle montagne che facevano corona [47] intorno la valle; le foreste di abeti erano tutte impolverate dalle recenti tormente; si distinguevano sui pendii luccicanti le figurette nere degli sciatori che scivolavano in tutte le direzioni, cadevano, si rialzavano, disparivano dietro le bianche colline, riapparivano. Ma Girolamo guardava questo festoso paesaggio con occhi pieni di lagrime: nulla era successo, non avrebbe più rivisto nè il Brambilla, ne la piccola inglese; era solo; e la guarigione sembrava ormai oltremodo lontana.

---

[47] *facevano corona*   surrounded

Ritorno al mare

La campagna era bassa, con grandi prati sui quali le margherite spandevano largamente il loro soffice biancore. All'orizzonte la pineta sbarrava i prati con una lunga, ininterrotta muraglia di verdura gonfia e immobile. La macchina avanzava piano e come malvolentieri, sobbalzando sulle buche della strada disselciata; attraverso il vetro del parabrise, Lorenzo poteva vedere la massa della pineta venirgli incontro, come se si muovesse, malinconica, misteriosa e ostile. Lorenzo aveva inventato la gita come un mezzo per addolcire i rapporti con sua moglie. Ma ora, di fronte al mutismo di lei, si sentiva ripreso dalla timidezza. Tuttavia, come giunsero a non grande distanza dai pini, disse: 'Ecco la pineta.'

La moglie non rispose nulla. Egli levò la mano e aggiustò lo specchietto sopra il parabrise. Al momento di partire l'aveva girato verso di lei e per tutto il tempo della gita non aveva fatto altro

che guardarla. Ella stava ferma ed eretta, la mano guantata sullo sportello, la giubba ripiegata sulle ginocchia, in una camicetta di lino bianco aperta sul petto. Il collo sottile, venendo su dalla camicetta, era grazioso come uno stelo; sul viso riarso e sulla bocca
5 rossa le lentiggini e la peluria del labbro mettevano come un velo di ombrosa sensualità. Ma gli occhi piccoli e neri guardavano in avanti con ostinazione; e il ciuffo di capelli che continuava la fronte, dava a tutto il viso un'aria aggressiva e dura. Ella aveva un po' della scimmia,[1] pensò Lorenzo; non tanto nei tratti quanto
10 nell'espressione triste, decrepita e innocente, come è appunto quella di certe piccole bertucce. E come una scimmia, infatti, simulava un atteggiamento di dignità offesa di cui egli la sapeva del tutto incapace.

La pineta ormai era vicina e appariva meno fitta che da lontano,
15 con i tronchi rossi che s'inclinavano d'ogni parte come se stessero per cadere gli uni contro gli altri. La macchina lasciò la strada, imboccò un tracciato di terreno brullo e soffice sul quale le ruote rimbalzavano mollemente. La pineta era deserta; a distanza s'intravedeva nell'ombra qualche chalet disabitato, con tutte le persiane
20 chiuse. Poi la pineta si schiarì,[2] apparve in fondo un'aria bianca e mossa: il mare.

Lorenzo avrebbe voluto annunziare il mare come aveva già annunziato la pineta. Ma questa volta il silenzio della moglie gli sembrò ancor più sicuro; giacchè l'apparizione del mare destava in
25 lui una gioia così sincera che ella non avrebbe resistito alla tentazione di mortificarlo. Tacque e spinse la macchina sullo spiazzo. La macchina si fermò e per un momento stettero fermi, nell'ombra del mantice abbassato. Il mare non lo vedevano ancora ma lo udivano, ora che il motore si era spento, con il suo rumore diffuso e
30 vario in cui pareva già di riconoscere la diversità di voce di ciascuna onda. 'Vogliamo scendere?' egli propose infine.

La moglie aprì lo sportello mettendo fuori le gambe impacciate

---

[1] *ella . . . . scimmia*   she looked slightly like a monkey
[2] *si schiarì*   thinned out

dalla strettezza della gonna. Lorenzo discese a sua volta a chiuse lo
sportello. Subito furono investiti dal vento marino, forte e tiepido,
che soffiava impetuosamente sollevando nuvole di sabbia dallo
spiazzo. 'Vogliamo andare verso il mare?'   5
'Andiamo pure.'
Si avviarono per lo spiazzo. I bombardamenti avevano rovesciato
gran parte della balaustrata, larghi squarci si aprivano in due o tre
punti nel lastrico di cemento. Alcune colonnine stavano ancora
ritte, le altre, a terra, le ricopriva la sabbia che il vento spingeva in   10
lunghe lingue fin nel mezzo dello spiazzo. Come si affacciarono
alla spiaggia, scoprirono che era percorsa in tutti i sensi [3] da reticolati. Il vento soffiava sotto i reticolati levigando la sabbia; in
lontananza, i fili di ferro spinati scomparivano avvolti in un
bianco e furioso polverio.   15
Trovarono un passaggio tra i reticolati, delimitato da paletti, che
portava al mare. Lorenzo lasciò che la moglie lo precedesse e la
seguì a qualche distanza. Lo faceva per guardarla a suo agio; come
già prima nello specchietto della macchina. Si rendeva conto,
mentre si lasciava andare a queste manovre, che forse l'aspetto più   20
disgraziato di tutta la sua disgrazia era questo suo improvviso e
tardivo innamoramento di sua moglie. Non l'aveva mai amata,
l'aveva sposata in fretta, al fine di mettersi in regola per la car-
riera politica. E ora che la fortuna rumorosa e vuota che l'aveva
stordito per tanti anni, l'aveva abbandonato, si era innamorato   25
di lei che non voleva più saperne.[4] O meglio, gli si era accesa nel
sangue una specie di acre libidine, timida e maldestra come un
amore giovanile. Seguendola, l'osservò con una avidità triste e
sorniona che meravigliò lui stesso. Era grande, magra, elegante,
simile in tutto ad un ragazzo; e le gambe robuste e persino pesanti   30
rispetto alla snellezza del busto, muovendosi goffamente sulla sabbia
ineguale, ricordavano quelle dei puledri ancora inabili a camminare.

---

[3] *che era . . . . i sensi* that it was crossed in every direction
[4] *non voleva più saperne* didn't want anything to do with it

Lorenzo guardava soprattutto a queste gambe sulle quali, nella transparenza delle calze, si vedevano moltissimi peli neri e lunghi come uccisi e senza vita, appiccicati alla pelle. Ella non si depilava come fanno tante donne: in un gesto che fece portando la mano alla testa per trattenere i capelli sconvolti dal vento, gli parve di indovinare attraverso il lino della camicetta la nerezza dell'ascella e si sentì ad un tratto tutto turbato.

Giunsero al mare. A poca distanza dalla sponda il vento riusciva a spingere e ad accavallare l'una sull'altra le lunghe e sonore ondate primaverili; ma più lontano il mare era quasi calmo, con strisce alternate di un torbido verde e di un violetto scuro. Per un poco, ritto accanto alla moglie, Lorenzo guardò le onde. Ne sceglieva con gli occhi una, più lontano che poteva, proprio al suo nascere e poi la seguiva mentre si alzava, si rovesciava sulle reni di quella che la precedeva, la raggiungeva, la sorpassava. Come l'onda ritardata e sviata dal risucchio, veniva a morire ai suoi piedi, il suo sguardo saltava di nuovo sul mare a cercarne un'altra. Desiderava, non sapeva per qual motivo, che almeno una di quelle ondate, tra le innumerevoli che si infrangevano sul litorale, riuscisse ad evitare gli intoppi delle onde rivali, il rallentamento del risucchio e con tutta la sua forza si scagliasse sulla riva oltrepassando loro due e risalendo la spiaggia, fino ad investire con le spume estreme i reticolati e lo spiazzo. Ma era un vano desiderio; e ad un tratto comprese perchè lo desiderasse tanto: bambino, nei giorni di tempesta, amava osservare la diversa impetuosità delle ondate e talvolta, vedendone una più forte e più grossa propagarsi con velocità su su per la spiaggia fino ai capanni, pensava con ambizione: 'Io sarò come quell'onda.' Scosse con forza la testa per scacciare questo ricordo e, volgendosi verso la moglie, le domandò: 'Ti piace?'

'Il mare,' ella disse con indifferenza, 'non è la prima volta che vedo il mare.'

Lorenzo avrebbe voluto spiegarle il sentimento che provava; magari raccontarle quella sua illusione infantile; ma non sapeva che disperata timidezza gli impedì di parlare. Gli venne un impulso forte di liberarsi di questa ansietà, di apparire disinvolto. Si chinò, raccolse una pietra con l'intenzione di lanciarla più lontano che poteva. Contava sulla violenza dell'atto per scagliare via insieme con la pietra anche l'angoscia che l'opprimeva. Ma la pietra era ingannevole. Grossa come un pugno, era invece leggera, una ⁵ pietra pomice tutta sforacchiata. E ricadde non lontano dalla riva, quindi, galleggiando sulla cresta di un'ondata, venne ad arenarsi ai suoi piedi. Ne provò un senso acerbo, come di una muta risposta della realtà alle sue aspirazioni. Anche la sua pena, come quella pomice, non valeva lanciarla lontano; gli sarebbe sempre tornata ¹⁰ indietro insieme con i detriti e la nera minutaglia che il mare agitato vomitava sulla sponda.

Si accostò alla moglie, la prese sottobraccio. Voleva camminare con lei lungo il mare, nel vento salutare che soffiava loro incontro, in quella solitudine clamorosa delle onde che si gettavano sul lito- ¹⁵ rale. Ma ella lo respinse con uno stupore caparbio. 'Che ti prende ora?'

'Non vogliamo passeggiare?'

'C'è troppo vento.'

'A me piace il vento,' egli disse. E tutto solo mosse qualche ²⁰ passo ⁵ lungo la sponda. Gli pareva di agire come un pazzo, fuori da ogni calcolo ragionevole, disperatamente. E questo senso di pazzia gli era accresciuto dal fracasso delle onde e dai capelli che il vento gli faceva volare negli occhi. 'Ho perso completamente la testa,' pensò con freddezza. Intanto si avviava verso un monticello ²⁵ di sabbia che non lontano si era formato intorno non si capiva che carcassa rugginosa.

'Ma che fai?' udì la voce corrucciata della moglie. 'Dove vai...? e poi ci sono le mine.'

'Che m'importa delle mine,' egli rispose con una spallucciata. ³⁰ Avrebbe voluto soggiungere: 'Magari saltassi in aria,' ⁶ ma per pudore tacque. Si voltò per vedere che cosa facesse la moglie.

---

⁵ *mosse qualche passo*   took a few steps
⁶ *magari saltassi in aria*   I wish I were blown up (by a mine)

Ella era rimasta in piedi di fronte al mare, con aria irritata e irresoluta. Poi disse: 'Non fare l'eroe... Anche a te preme vivere.'[7] Con un disprezzo che lo ferì e gli parve ingiusto. Tornò indietro con un salto e la prese per un braccio. 'Tu mi devi credere se ti dico che in questo momento non soltanto non m'importa niente di morire, ma anche sarei contento.' Stringeva forte quel braccio tondo e solido e si accorgeva con dolore che a quel contatto la sua disperazione si cambiava facilmente in desiderio e gli diventava suo malgrado insincera. Ella lo guardò e disse con intonazione incredula e ingiuriosa: 'Ma lasciami...sono le tue solite storie...e poi,' soggiunse dopo un momento, 'fa quello che vuoi...ma io non ti seguirò...non voglio mica morire io.'

Lorenzo la lasciò e si diresse con decisione verso il rottame. I suoi piedi affondavano, le sue scarpe si gonfiavano di sabbia. Il rottame non distava più di una cinquantina di metri. Lo raggiunse e scoprì che era un vecchio bidone di benzina. Il mare l'aveva corroso e arrugginito, il vento l'aveva riempito per tre quarti di sabbia. Dopo il rottame, la spiaggia continuava a perdita d'occhio,[8] spazzata dal vento radente, percorsa da fini reticolati neri che parevano cicatrici rimarginate sulla bianchezza soffice della rena. Egli si fermò un momento, indeciso, abbagliato dal riflesso del cielo nubiloso, quindi tornò indietro.

La moglie non c'era più. Lorenzo si avviò per lo stretto passaggio tra i reticolati verso lo spiazzo. La moglie stava ritta presso la macchina, una mano sullo sportello, l'altra sulla fronte a trattenere i capelli. 'Allora cosa vogliamo fare?' domandò.

'Vogliamo mangiare?' egli rispose in tono allegro. Ma in realtà si sentiva incapace di parlare nonchè di apparire lieto.

'Dove?'

'Possiamo andare nella pineta.' Senza aspettare risposta, egli prese dal sedile posteriore della macchina la borsa delle provviste e si avviò verso i pini. La moglie lo seguì.

---

[7] *anche a te preme vivere*   you also hold your life dear
[8] *a perdita d'occhio*   as far as the eye could see

Attraversarono lo spiazzo dirigendosi verso le rovine di quello che era stato un tempo il ristorante del luogo. Nella luce bianca e piena di polvere, le rovine, ridotte ai seminterrati, venivano su dal terreno sconvolto, con mozziconi ritti, pallidi di fuori e colorati di dentro, simili a denti cariati. La scala di cemento che portava alla grande sala dove si mangiava in vista del mare saliva con qualche gradino e poi cessava bruscamente sopra uno sprofondato caos di pezzi di soffitto, di ferri contorti e rugginosi, di blocchi di calcinacci e di mattoni. Le altre stanze, tra le pareti sgretolate, erano riconoscibili per altre macerie simili, agglomerate in una sola polverosa poltiglia. Girarono intorno le rovine e Lorenzo disse: 'Ti ricordi quando siamo venuti qui l'ultima volta?'

'No.'

'Due anni fa... Già le cose andavano male, ma io non volevo accorgermene...avevi una fascia intorno il petto e un'altra intorno ai fianchi che ti passava tra le gambe...eri bruna, bruna...avevi un piccolo turbante intorno la testa...ora,' egli continuò con voce improvvisamente strangolata, 'mi accorgo che sei molto bella...ma allora era come se non ti vedessi...non pensavo che alla politica...e lasciavo che ti facessero la corte tutti quegl'imbecilli che ci tiravamo dietro [9]...'

'E allora?' ella disse seccamente.

.'Nulla.'

Dietro il ristorante c'era un prato in cui l'erba dura e sporca appariva tutta mescolata di sabbia. Fitti cespugli, alberi storti dai rami protesi come braccia crescevano ai margini di questo prato. Nel mezzo del prato il bombardamento aveva fatto volare un pezzo del pianoforte del caffè: la tastiera con pochi tasti bianchi e un gran pezzo di legno scheggiato in tutto simile ad una mascella di animale con pochi denti e una parte putrefatta. Tutta l'erba intorno era piena dei martelletti di feltro del pianoforte. Un'altra parte dello strumento, l'arpa, era stata scagliata nell'inforcatura di un

---

[9] *ci tiravamo dietro*   we dragged along

albero. Ne pendevano, brevi e lunghe, le corde metalliche tutte arricciate come propaggini pendule di un insolito rampicante. Lorenzo cercava un luogo appartato con una premeditazione accecata e assorta, come se non d'amore si fosse trattato ma di un delitto. La moglie lo seguiva a distanza con un atteggiamento che egli sentiva sempre più malcontento e restio. La pineta era piena di piccole radure erbose delimitate irregolarmente dai cespugli del sottobosco. Finalmente gli parve di aver trovato quel che cercava. 'Sediamoci qui,' disse lasciandosi cadere in terra.

Ella rimase un momento in piedi, guardandosi intorno. Poi, piano piano, con una contegnosità sdegnosa, si lasciò cadere sulle proprie gambe e sedette tirandosi duramente la veste sulle ginocchia. Lorenzo finse di non guardarla e cominciò a trarre fuori dalla borsa le provviste. C'erano molti pacchi e pacchetti tutti avvolti con cura in carta velina bianca, di quella che serve alle modiste. E c'era anche una bottiglia di vino. 'Sei tu che hai preparato questa borsa?'

'No, l'ho fatta fare alla cameriera.'

Egli spiegò sull'erba un tovagliolo e vi depose sopra con cura le uova, la carne, il formaggio, la frutta. Quindi stappò la bottiglia e la richiuse con il suo tappo. "Vuoi delle uova?'

'No.'

'Della carne?'

'Dammi un panino con una fetta di carne.'

Lorenzo prese uno dei panini già tagliati per metà e imburrati, vi mise dentro due fette di carne e glielo porse. Ella lo prese schifiltosamente, senza ringraziare, a fronte bassa. Lorenzo prese un uovo sodo e vi morse dentro con avidità, riempiendosi poi subito dopo la bocca di pane imburrato. Provava una fame triste che gli pareva della stessa natura del suo desiderio per sua moglie. Fame e libidine crescevano prosperose sulla sua disperazione, egli pensò, anzi si nutrivano di essa. Come se lui non fosse stato più che un corpo esanime e senza volontà e le voglie gli fossero cresciute addosso allo stesso modo che crescono addosso ai morti i peli della barba. Mangiò un primo uovo, poi un secondo, poi un terzo, esitò e mangiò anche il quarto uovo. Gli piaceva mordere nel bianco quasi elastico e sentire sotto i denti lo sbriciolío soffice del tuorlo. Masticava con enfasi e ogni tanto portava alla bocca la bottiglia e tirava lunghi sorsi. Dopo le uova fu la volta della carne di cui c'erano due qualità: rosbiff in larghe fette rosse e cotolette panate e fritte. Non guardava la moglie, mangiava e sentiva via via che mangiava una turgida vitalità gonfiargli le vene pur restando il suo animo triste e vuoto. Questa vitalità congiunta a tanta disperazione lo desolava come una ricchezza inutile e ironica. Finalmente levò gli occhi e le offrì mutamente la bottiglia. Ella aveva ancora il suo panino di cui non aveva mangiato che la metà. Rifiutò con un cenno del capo.

'Non mangi?'

'Non ho fame.'

Lorenzo finì di mangiare, quindi raccolse tutte le bucce e i rifiuti, li avvolse in una carta e li gettò lontano. Nella borsa rimise la bottiglia semivuota. Faceva tutti questi atti con una volontà ostinata, come se si fosse trattato di riordinare la propria mente sconvolta e non le provviste. La moglie che aveva finito allora il suo panino, prese a ritoccarsi il viso con lo specchio e il rossetto. 'Allora,' disse, 'vogliamo andare?'

'Dove?'

'A casa.'

'Ma è presto.'

'Hai visto il mare,' ella disse con cattiveria, 'hai fatto colazione... non vorrai mica dormire qui.'

Lorenzo la guardò, incerto se dovesse sentirsi più infuriato o più avvilito per questa tenace ostilità. Poi pronunziò a bassa voce: 'Senti, debbo parlarti.'

'Parlare a me...? ma abbiamo già tanto parlato.'

Egli strisciò con fatica sull'erba e venne a mettersi accanto a lei.

'Io vorrei sapere che cos'hai contro di me.'

'Non ho niente: soltanto non vedo perchè dobbiamo continuare a vivere insieme...ecco tutto.'

'Tu non senti più nulla per me.'

'Non ho mai sentito nulla...e oggi meno che mai.'

'Ma un tempo,' insistette Lorenzo, 'quando ti portavo qualche regalo o ti davo una busta piena di denaro...mi saltavi al collo, mi abbracciavi, mi baciavi, dicevi che mi amavi.'

⁵ 'Mi faceva piacere ricevere dei regali,' ella disse con evidente disappunto per questa rievocazione delle sue puerili avidità, 'ma non ti amavo.'

'Fingevi, però.'

'No, non fingevo.' Lorenzo capì che era sincera. In una donna
¹⁰ come lei la gratitudine per i doni rassomigliava assai all'amore; anzi forse era il solo amore di cui fosse capace.

'E io invece,' disse a testa bassa, 'sento per te...da quando le cose mi vanno male... per la prima volta in vita mia...ecco...non so neppure come dirlo.'

¹⁵ 'Per carità, non dirlo,' ella esclamò con facile disprezzo.

'Ma, insomma, si può sapere che cos'hai contro di me?'

'Ho,' ella rispose stizzita, 'che non voglio più essere la moglie di un galeotto.'

'Sono stato in prigione soltanto pochi giorni,' egli osservò, 'e poi
²⁰ si trattava di motivi politici.'

'Lo dici tu,' ella ribatté; 'invece la gente dice che c'è dell'altro e...che potresti andare dentro di nuovo anche domani.'

Lorenzo fu colpito dall'accento incerto di queste parole, come di cose sentite dire piuttosto che pensate. 'Tu parli di cose che non
²⁵ sai..., scommetto che ignori persino chi io fossi e che cosa io abbia fatto per tutti gli anni che siamo stati insieme.'

'Come no,' ¹⁰ ella disse sdegnosamente.

'E allora dillo.'

'Eri,' ella esitò, 'eri insomma uno di quelli che comandavano.'
³⁰ 'Ma non basta,' egli disse, 'che carica avevo?'

'Che ne so io della carica,' ella disse con dispetto; 'so soltanto che tutti parlavano di te come di un'autorità...e poi tu cambiavi

---

¹⁰ *come no* I certainly do

sempre, ora eri una cosa, e ora un'altra...avevo altro da pensare io
che alle tue cariche."

'Sì,' disse Lorenzo dolcemente, 'avevi da pensare a Rodolfo, a
Mario, a Gianni.'

Ella finse di non avere udito i nomi di questi suoi amanti, tutti ⁵
giovani e sciocchi come lei. Lorenzo riprese: 'E almeno sai che
cosa è successo dal tempo che io avevo le cariche? lo sai?'
La vide alzare le spalle con stizza. 'Ecco, ora mi prendi per una
stupida e invece sono molto più intelligente di quanto non credi.'
'Non ne dubito affatto...ma dimmi che cosa è successo.' ¹⁰
'È venuta la guerra...e poi è andato via il fascismo...ecco cos'è
successo...sei contento ora?'
'Brava...e secondo te perchè io ho perso la carica?'
'Perchè,' ella disse incerta, 'ora sono andati al governo i nemici
del fascismo.' ¹⁵
'E chi sono i nemici del fascismo?'
Questa volta ella levò gli occhi al cielo, strinse le labbra e non
disse nulla. Una specie di rabbia si impossessò di Lorenzo. Questa
ignoranza, egli pensò, era molto peggio di qualsiasi condanna. Così
anche i suoi errori, nonchè i suoi pochi meriti, cadevano nel vuoto; e ²⁰
della sua vita non restava più traccia che dei suoi passi di pòco
avanti sulla sabbia lungo il mare. 'E che cos'era il fascismo?' inter-
rogò ancora.

Medesimo silenzio. Lorenzo l'afferrò ad un tratto per un braccio
e la scosse. 'Rispondi, bestia...perchè non rispondi?' ²⁵
'Lasciami,' ella disse in tono caparbio, 'io non ti rispondo perchè
so che tu vuoi confondermi e farmi cambiar idea...e io invece ti
dico che con te non voglio più rimanerci...ecco tutto.'

Lorenzo non l'ascoltava più. Al contatto di quel braccio gli si
era ridestato il desiderio. Guardava alla veste stretta che le cosce, ³⁰
stando ella così seduta sulle gambe, tendevano fortemente comunicando alla stoffa quasi la morbidezza, il calore e il peso della
carne e a questa vista sentiva la sua mente svuotarsi e il respiro
mancargli. Disse tuttavia, lentamente: 'Non ti rendi conto che mi
lasci proprio nel momento in cui un'altra donna mi resterebbe ³⁵

fedele...e per motivi che non ti sono chiari, per qualche chiacchiera o qualche capriccio?' 'Io mi rendo conto che molte signore non mi invitano più, non mi salutano più. Io ho avvisato la mamma che voglio tornare da
⁵ lei... Basta, con te non voglio più starci.' Così dicendo, si levò in piedi. Lorenzo la guardò di sotto in su. Ella stava ritta e sprezzante ma con le gambe in goffo atteggiamento per via della gonna troppo stretta e della scarpe troppo alte. Egli capiva che sarebbe stato
¹⁰ facile abbatterla sull'erba come sarebbe stato facile disarmare il suo disprezzo. ·Quelle gambe impacciate dall'angustia della veste ¹¹ troppo rassomigliavano al suo carattere che la sciocchezza rendeva vacillante e fiacco. Gli venne un desiderio violento di annientare quell'atteggiamento. Con una sola spinta di tutto il corpo si gettò
¹⁵ sulle gambe di lei e la rovesciò sul prato. Ella cadde riversa, con un viso sorpreso, e disse subito, stizzita: 'Lasciami... che ti prende¹² ora?'

Lorenzo non rispose nulla ma si gettò su di lei, schiacciandola sotto il suo corpo. 'Io sono quello che sono,' proferì poi, tenendole
²⁰ le labbra sulle labbra, come se avesse voluto mandarle ogni parola dentro la bocca. , 'Ma tu non sei davvero meglio di me...sei una stupida, vuota, corrotta ragazza...finchè ti faceva comodo,¹³ sei rimasta con me...ebbene, ora che non ti fa più comodo ci resterai egualmente.'

²⁵ La vide fare un viso impaurito; e poi dire di nuovo, quasi supplichevolmente: 'Lasciami.'

'Non ti lascerò,' disse Lorenzo a denti stretti. Sapeva, per averlo già sperimentato in passato, che la moglie con tutto il suo rancore non avrebbe resistito alla fine alla sua violenza. Pareva che in lei,
³⁰ ad un certo momento, sopravvenisse una specie di languore o di complicità con la forza che subiva e allora ella cedeva e si faceva

---

¹¹ *dall'angustia della veste*   by her tight dress
¹² *che ti prende*   what's the matter with you
¹³ *finchè ti faceva comodo*   as long as it was convenient to you

passivamente amorosa come se tutte le ripulse anteriori non fossero state che premeditate civetterie. Era questo un tratto di più della sua sciocchezza: non saper portare fino in fondo nessun sentimento nè ostile nè amichevole. E infatti, come presero a lottare, lei dibattendosi e lui cercando di vincere la sua resistenza, Lorenzo vide ad un tratto negli occhi piccoli e innocenti di lei affacciarsi uno sguardo che ben conosceva, tentato, passivo, languido. Gli parve pure che si dibattesse con meno forza. Poi ella proferì a bassa voce: 'Lasciami, ti dico...potrebbero vederci.' E questo era già un invito a continuare. Gli venne un disgusto improvviso di questa sua vittoria. Pensò che anche se ella avesse ceduto, poi niente sarebbe cambiato. Lui si sarebbe levato senza amore da quel corpo posseduto; lei, indispettita e arruffata, avrebbe tirato giù la veste gualcita; e alla prima parola il loro contrasto sarebbe ricominciato. Con in più il disgusto di quell'accoppiamento meccanico che non significava niente. Ora non era questo che egli aveva voluto ottenere portandola quel giorno in gita. Tutto ad un tratto la lasciò e si tirò da parte sull'erba. Ella si levò a sedere con aria strapazzata e delusa. 'Non sai che la violenza non serve a nulla,' disse imbronciata.

Lorenzo avrebbe voluto mettersi a ridere e rispondere che la violenza era con lei forse la sola cosa che servisse. Ma al tempo stesso non poteva fare a meno di riconoscere che era vero: per quello di cui aveva bisogno la violenza non serviva proprio a nulla.

Disse tuttavia con crudeltà: 'Questo non toglie che se ti stavo addosso un altro poco, tu le gambe le aprivi.'

'Come sei volgare,' ella rispose con sincero disgusto. Si levò in piedi, e, scavalcando i cespugli, si avviò decisamente verso lo spiazzo.

Lorenzo rimase seduto in terra, gli occhi rivolti all'erba. Ora, ripensando alle risposte incerte che gli aveva dato la moglie, gli pareva anche lui di non sapere più che cosa avesse fatto, che cosa fosse stato per tutti quegli anni. 'Ha ragione lei,' pensava· 'è stato tutto un vaneggiamento, un delirio...e ora mi sono destato.'

Riandando con la memoria a quel tempo della sua vita, si accorgeva di non ricordarsi d'altro se non d'essere stato sempre e inalterabilmente cordiale con i propri inferiori, con i propri superiori, con gli amici, con i nemici, con gli estranei, con sua moglie. Questa cordialità, riflettè, doveva aver sortito alla fine un brutto effetto: infatti dopo aver tanto parlato e sorriso a vanvera [14] ora si sentiva incapace di discorrere e di essere allegro come se la lingua gli si fosse disseccata e gli angoli della bocca piagati. In queste condizioni perfino una sciocca come sua moglie aveva buon gioco.

Trasalì ad un lontano rombo di automobile, stette un momento fermo tendendo l'orecchio, poi gli venne un sospetto e, levatosi in piedi, prese a correre attraverso i pini, saltando i cespugli e le ineguaglianze del terreno, verso lo spiazzo. Vi giunse ansimante e lo trovò vuoto. Per l'aria era ancora la polvere sollevata dalla macchina con la quale la moglie era fuggita.

Gli parve una degna conclusione della giornata e non si sentì neppure irritato. Pensò che sarebbe ritornato con un camion militare. Alla peggio avrebbe fatto a piedi [15] qualche chilometro fino alla strada maestra. Lì gli autocarri erano frequenti e facilmente avrebbe ottenuto un passaggio.

Ma come si avviava verso il tracciato della pineta, sentì l'appello del mare. Come un desiderio di riaffacciarsi a quell'eterno movimento, a quell'eterno clamore prima di tornare in città. E poi voleva fare una cosa che in presenza della moglie non aveva avuto il coraggio di fare: togliersi le scarpe, rimboccare i pantaloni e camminare lungo il mare, nell'acqua bassa e fluida del flusso e riflusso delle onde.

Si rendeva conto che faceva questa passeggiata lungo il mare anche per dimostrare a se stesso che era indifferente alla fuga della moglie. Ma sapeva che non era vero; e come sedette sulla sabbia per levarsi le scarpe, si accorse che le mani gli tremavano.

Si tolse le scarpe e le calze, rimboccò i pantaloni fin sotto il

---

[14] *a vanvera* indiscriminately
[15] *alla peggio* . . . *piedi* at the worst he would have walked

ginocchio e si avviò tra i reticolati, verso la riva. Prese a camminare
nell'acqua che andava e veniva, le scarpe in mano, la testa bassa, gli
occhi rivolti a terra. Era un atteggiamento pensoso, ma in realtà non pensava nulla.
Gli piaceva di vedere l'onda sorpassare i suoi piedi, salendo lungo   5
le gambe e formando una groppa d'acqua intorno i malleoli e poi
rifluire rapinosamente portandogli via la sabbia sotto le piante, con
un solletico vivo, come di cosa animata. Gli piaceva anche guardare
in basso e non vedere che acqua a destra e acqua a sinistra, torbida,
vorticosa, sparsa di bianchi anelli di spuma. Il mare presso la   10
sponda era pieno di una nera minutaglia che ogni onda gettava
sulla spiaggia e poi nel riflusso riportava indietro. Erano rametti
come di ebano, scaglie ovali e lisce, frantumi minimi di legno,
miriadi di corpuscoli neri che il movimento dell'acqua torbida e
piena di sabbia manteneva in continuo rimescolío. Diafani granchi   15
morti, alghe verdi, gialle radici mettevano qualche macchia di
colore in questo carbonizzato tritume. Se l'onda si ritirava, la
minutaglia restava invescata sui suoi piedi rabescandone di nero la
lucida bianchezza. Qualche detrito più grosso galleggiava nelle
pause tra un'onda e l'altra, nel ribollire di vetro pestato dell'acqua   20
schiumosa. Ne vide uno a non grande distanza, di colore e forma
incerta, che faceva pensare ad un animale; ma come si avvicinò,
vincendo la resistenza dell'acqua, scoprì che era lo zoccolo di legno
di una scarpa ortopedica di donna. Conchigliette di un pallido
colore ametista avevano proliferato fittamente sulla punta formando   25
come una grossa nappa, il tacco era ancora ricoperto di stoffa rossa.
Mentre osservava il relitto, un'onda alta e senza spuma trascorse via
rapidamente bagnandolo fino all'inguine. Gettò via la scarpa e
tornò più vicino alla riva.
Non seppe neppur lui quanto tempo camminasse lungo la   30
sponda, nell'acqua riottosa, sulla molle sabbia sfuggente. Ma a
forza di guardare in basso, alle onde che senza posa [16] si gettavano
sulle sue gambe e le oltrepassavano nella corsa verso l'invisibile

---

[16] *senza posa*   unceasingly

spiaggia gli venne una specie di capogiro. Levò gli occhi verso il mare, e per un momento gli parve di vederlo alto e ritto, simile ad una liquida parete. Non più che una striscia vaporosa era il cielo all'orizzonte, qualche uccello marino vi sfiorava il pelo dell'acqua in un volo remoto e rischioso che faceva pensare all'ebbrezza e alla violenza del vento. Abbagliato, vacillò sotto l'urto di un'onda più forte. Anche il clamore marino gli parve ad un tratto farsi più alto e più accanito, come raddoppiato dalla speranza di un suo crollo. Quasi con paura si voltò verso la spiaggia pensando di uscire dall'acqua e sedersi per un momento sulla sabbia asciutta. Aveva camminato molto; lontano era lo spiazzo con le rovine; in quel punto la spiaggia era in salita, tutta percorsa da reticolati legati a paletti che davano l'idea di persone che si tenessero per mano a braccia tese per impedire il passaggio. Attrasse la sua attenzione un grosso banco di alghe nere e lustre sotto le quali le onde avevano profondamente scavato la sabbia. Salì fino al banco e, ponendo una mano in terra, vi saltò sopra.

Il torrente di alghe e di sabbia che si levava in aria con eco tonante, oscurò per un momento ai suoi occhi il cielo mentre piombava indietro nel risucchio dell'esplosione. Credette un momento di cadere riverso per sempre in un perpetuo fracasso di cateratta. Seguirono invece il silenzio e l'immobilità. Egli stava supino sull'acqua, il rumore e il movimento del mare erano singolarmente dolci e remoti sotto il cielo tornato sgombro. L'acqua lo tirava di sotto per i capelli; in un movimento che fece il suo corpo, testa in giù e piedi in alto, per il passaggio di un'onda, vide già lontano una larga chiazza rossa trascorrere verso la riva insieme con gli anelli di spume e i neri detriti. Poi un'altr'onda sopravvenne e lo sommerse mentre chiudeva gli occhi.

EXERCISES

Non è il momento

A. *Rispondere alle domande che seguono:*

1. Perchè il narratore, qualche volta, aveva nostalgia dell'amico Paolino?
2. Per quale motivo non lo vedeva più tanto spesso?
3. Descrivere brevemente la fisionomia di Paolino.
4. Quali aspetti della vita attiravano immancabilmente l'attenzione del giovane?
5. Per quale ragione Gigi aveva deciso di andare a piazza Navona la sera della Befana?
6. Quando e come si celebra la festa della Befana?
7. È vero che Paolino si rendeva conto dello stato d'animo di Gigi? Perchè?
8. Cosa stava facendo l'amico americano di Iole?
9. Cosa rispose la ragazza all'invito di Gigi?
10. Descrivere lo scherzo chiassoso del gruppetto di giovani a piazza Navona.
11. Perchè i tranvieri si erano riuniti nella saletta del secondo piano?
12. Come si è comportato Gigi al ristorante? Lei prova compassione per lui? Perchè?

172   *Exercises*

13. Verso la fine del pranzo sociale cosa propose di fare uno dei tranvieri?
14. Dopo qualche minuto com'era la saletta del ristorante? Perchè?
15. Cosa fecero Iole e l'americano dopo di essere usciti dal ristorante?
16. Ricorda l'ammonizione di una delle guardie?
17. Qual è, secondo lei, l'aspetto più buffo di questo racconto?
18. Su chi cade la bonaria ironia dello scrittore?
19. Le sembra che l'accaduto sia un inevitabile scherzo del caso?
20. Esamini le azioni di Gigi. Che tipo di uomo è? Come si regola con le donne? Come reagisce nei momenti critici?
21. Immagini di essere il tranviere "poeta" del racconto e componga una breve poesia, un po' scherzosa, che celebri la solidarietà tra compagni di lavoro.
22. Che cosa rappresenta per Iole il giovane americano? Che funzione ha nel racconto?
23. Che sentimento suscita Paolino nell'animo del lettore?
24. Che genere di persone presenta lo scrittore nel racconto?
25. In quale periodo potrebbero essere accaduti i fatti del racconto? Perchè?

B. *Completare considerando lo stile del testo:*

1. Questo ragazzo ha una bocca grandissima che va _____.
2. Non so che cosa Mario (*has*) _____ nella testa.
3. '_____ trovai _____ lui' dice Gigi.
4. Era tardi, faceva freddo ed allora noi (*started out*) _____ verso la piazza.
5. 'Ma perchè tanta voglia (*to clown*) _____?'
6. (*As soon as I entered*) _____ compresi il mio errore.
7. (*He wore*) _____ giacca a vento a scacchi verdi e neri.
8. 'Due parole sole. Poi ti lascio e non mi vedi _____.'
9. (*At last*) _____ quei giovanotti si allontanarono (*shouting*) _____ 'Gigi, non è il momento.'
10. Nella saletta c'era una tavola (*shaped like a horseshoe*) _____.
11. Pietro uscì (*splitting his sides with laughter*) _____.
12. Benchè loro (*were making fun of me*) _____ io non dissi niente.
13. Sembrava proprio che quella gente (*were drunk*) _____.
14. Loro aggredirono l'americano e me (*who had nothing to do with the matter*) _____.
15. Aveva comperato (*a big, long car*) _____.

C. *Formare delle frasi usando i verbi indicati:*

1. farsi delle risate
2. far cagnara
3. voler bene
4. avvicinarsi

5. stringersi
6. squadrare
7. canzonare
8. filare

D. *Da quali parole derivano le seguenti forme alterate?*

1. ragazzotto
2. piccoletto
3. fischietto
4. cappottino

5. difettuccio
6. bonaccione
7. omaccione
8. macchinone

Primo rapporto sulla terra dell''inviato speciale' della luna

A. *Rispondere alle domande che seguono:*

1. Quando l''inviato speciale' arriva sulla terra ha un'idea precisa di quel che vuol dire 'uomini ricchi' e 'uomini poveri'?
2. Da dove erano venuti i poveri?
3. Quali erano, a prima vista, le loro caratteristiche più evidenti?
4. Erano colti i poveri? Amavano la pittura, la musica o la poesia? Perchè?
5. Era vero che gli uomini ricchi e quelli poveri godevano le bellezze della natura?
6. Invece di lavorare nelle fabbriche, nelle campagne o nelle miniere, cosa avrebbero dovuto fare i poveri, secondo i ricchi?
7. Che concetto si forma l''inviato speciale' di ciò che si definisce 'lavoro'?
8. Come si manifesta il pessimo gusto dei poveri nella scelta dei cibi e delle bevande?
9. A quali conclusioni sono arrivati gli studiosi?
10. Perchè le misure di polizia sembrano più efficaci della persuasione?
11. C'è comprensione fra i due tipi di uomini? Perchè?
12. Secondo i poveri, qual è l'elemento che determina le differenze sociali?
13. È vero che l''inviato speciale' presta fede ai poveri? Perchè?

14. Perchè la maggior parte delle informazioni viene dai ricchi? Come mai i poveri sono così restii a parlare?
15. Secondo lei, come si protrebbe definire l'atteggiamento dei ricchi di questo racconto?
16. Lei crede che la necessità di lavorare ostacoli sensibilmente il godimento del bello?
17. Quale sarebbe, secondo i poveri, la vita ideale? Se riuscissero ad ottenerla, potrebbero essere felici?
18. Perchè l'"inviato speciale' trova strano che la differenza tra gli uomini sia contituita da una certa carta colorata e da pezzetti di metallo di forma tonda?
19. Cosa sembra voler concludere l'autore?
20. Le sembra giusto che gli uomini siano divisi in ricchi e poveri?
21. Per quale motivo i poveri non riescono a guadagnarsi la fiducia dell'"inviato speciale'?

B. Mettere al plurale:

1. Il suo vestito è sudicio e rattoppato, la sua casa squallida, la sua vita triste ed inutile.
2. Il divertimento del povero, spiega il ricco, è quanto di più rozzo si possa immaginare.
3. Tu preferisci al mare la piscina municipale, e alla campagna un rognoso prato della periferia.
4. Quando vuole lavorare si inabissa in una galleria profondissima e lì, al buio, si diletta ad estrarre pietre.
5. Non cerchi uno svago, non ti piace nessun gioco, non vuoi neanche vedere qualche amico.
6. Per me non esiste nessun delizioso manicaretto, il vino vecchio o un dolce squisito.
7. Non consultava il medico, restava chiusa in casa e non si faceva vedere dalla sua amica.
8. Non si finirebbe mai di parlare di quel povero del suo attaccamento per quella cosa nociva, rozza e stravagante.
9. La ragazza era sempre simpatica e comprensiva ma suo fratello, scettico e diffidente, non tollerava la presenza di nessuno.
10. Distese una tovaglia bianca sulla travola.

C. Usare i verbi indicati in altrettante proposizioni:

1. fare difetto   3. premere (importare)
2. sentire l'altra campana   4. esporsi

5. deplorare
6. figurarsi
7. dilettarsi

8. venire in mente
9. disdegnare
10. inabissarsi

D. *Trovare gli aggettivi che corrispondono ai nomi seguenti e usarli in brevi proposizioni:*

1. perfezione
2. squallore
3. popolo
4. lusso
5. municipio
6. fumo
7. violenza

8. mistero
9. profondità
10. negligenza
11. studio
12. scetticismo
13. difetto
14. calore

Lo scimpanzè

A. *Rispondere alle domande che seguono:*

1. Qual era lo stato d'animo del protagonista mentre camminava per il viale di Villa Borghese?
2. Cosa avrebbe voluto fare? La pioggia lo deprimeva?
3. Che aspetto presentava il parco in quel momento? Com'era il cielo? Perchè si sarebbe pensato che fosse marzo?
4. Cosa cerca di mettere in evidenza lo scrittore all'inizio del racconto?
5. Cosa pensava della sua vita il giovanotto?
6. Qual era la causa della sua felicità? Era quello il loro primo appuntamento?
7. È proprio esatto dire che il giovane non aveva nessuna preoccupazione? Dove lavorava? Cosa faceva?
8. Perchè il giovane contava sul sentimento? Per quale ragione anche Gloria avrebbe dovuto avere i suoi stessi gusti?
9. Che effetto fa la ragazza appena la si vede spuntare da uno dei viali?
10. Come ce la descrive Moravia? Ne analizzi le maniere e cerchi d'indovinare alcune delle sue caratteristiche morali.
11. Cosa propone di fare Gloria?
12. Come accetta la proposta del giovane?

13. Che mezzo usa Moravia per farci capire che, in fondo, la ragazza è molto esigente solo in apparenza?
14. Al giovanotto, c'è bisogno di dirlo? — piacevano gli animali. Secondo Lei la sua ammirazione per essi era eccessiva o normale?
15. Racconti la scenetta che si svolge davanti al recinto degli elefanti. Cosa finisce per fare Gloria? Che osservazione fa a proposito dell'ippopotamo?
16. Cosa pensava il giovanotto della sgarbatezza di Gloria? A lei sembra che egli sia veramente imparziale?
17. Si ricorda cosa è accaduto mentre i due protagonisti si stavano dirigendo verso le gabbie dei leoni?
18. Cosa sembrava che facessero le foche? Di quale foca si sarebbe interessata Gloria?
19. Su quali animali si concentra poi l'attenzione della ragazza? Lo fa sinceramente o per una ragione particolare?
20. Quale aspetto ironico introduce lo scrittore in questo episodio?
21. Il giovane si lascia convincere dall'improvviso interesse di Gloria per le scimmie?
22. Cosa facevano gli scimpanzè? Descriva ciò che ha fatto quello che stava sull'altalena.
23. Come si sarebbe comportato Lei se si fosse trovato al posto di Gloria?
24. Il giovane accompagna la ragazza fuori dello zoo?
25. Che genere di persona ha tratteggiato Moravia nel descrivere il protagonista di questo racconto?
26. Le sembra che lo scrittore provi più simpatia per Gloria o per il giovanotto? Lei per chi ne sente di piú?

B. *Trovare nel dizionario i verbi che si usano per indicare la voce dei seguenti animali:*

1. l'orso	5. il cane	9. la pecora
2. il leone	6. l'anitra	10. la scimmia
3. il gatto	7. l'elefante	11. il cavallo
4. la gallina	8. la mucca	12. l'asino

C. *Mettere all'imperfetto dell'indicativo i verbi in parentesi:*

1. Il giovanotto (scendere) _____ giù per il viale di Villa Borghese.
2. Mentre i fidanzati (passeggiare) _____ (piovere) _____ a dirotto.

3. Io (sentirsi) _____ felice e (volere) _____ restare ancora nel parco.

4. (Tirare) _____ vento ma il sole (risplendere); i bambini ritornati nel viale (correre) _____ e (gridare) _____ allegramente.

5. Gloria (andare) _____ allo zoo malvolentieri perchè non (interessarsi) _____ affatto degli animali.

6. Quel bravo giovane (illudersi) _____ che la ragazza lo comprendesse.

7. Ogni volta che voi (visitare) _____ i nonni, (restare) _____ da loro per qualche giorno.

8. Tu (essere) _____ tutta infronzolata: (avere) _____ un cappotto nuovo, (portare) _____ un cappellino eccentrico però non (sembrare) _____ più la ragazza che mi (piacere) _____ tanto.

9. Gli elefanti simpatici li (guardare) _____ fisso con i loro occhietti intelligenti.

10. Mi (parere) _____ che il cielo fosse diventato grigio; la pioggia, infatti, mi (infastidire) _____ ed io (essere) _____ un'altra volta di cattivo umore.

D. Coniugare all'imperfetto le frasi che seguono:

1. prendere l'erba e darla all'elefante
2. leggere il giornale e mangiare un panino
3. andare a casa presto e fare colazione
4. aprire il libro e copiarne una pagina
5. dondolare la testa e suscitare l'ilarità generale
6. trovare le parole nuove e impararle a memoria
7. nuotare e saltare nell'acqua
8. scendere dal letto e affacciarsi alla finestra
9. rallentare il passo e guardare le vetrine dei negozi
10. sapere sempre la lezione e venire ricompensato

E. Usare le seguenti espressioni in altrettante frasi:

1. fare buio
2. in santa pace
3. mettere un piede in fallo
4. tirar via
5. avere la passione di

6. farsi coraggio
7. piovere a dirotto
8. un fuggi fuggi
9. aversene a male
10. avercela con qualcuno

La vita è una giungla

A. Rispondere alle domande seguenti:

1. Qual è il contrasto che il giovane nota quando sente al telefono la voce della signorina?
2. Cosa avevano deciso di fare Girolamo e la signorina?
3. Quando la ragazza si allontanò dal telefono cosa potè sentire Girolamo?
4. La signorina sarebbe andata sola all'appuntamento? Con chi sarebbe andata?
5. Girolamo come passò l'ora di attesa? Che cos'è la periferia di una città?
6. Che stagione era? Com'erano gli alberi? Di quale tipo di alberi si parla?
7. Il fabbricato in cui abitavano le signorine era lussuoso e moderno, ma dove si trovava il loro appartamento?
8. Cosa gli disse di fare la voce sgarbata dall'interno della stanza?
9. Dove andò Girolamo? Com'era il tempo?
10. Erano molto simili le due donne?
11. Quali caratteristiche avevano in comune?
12. Faccia una descrizione del loro abbigliamento.
13. Con che cosa contrastava il biondo artificiale dei capelli?
14. Perchè nella trattoria c'era una quantità di tavole vuote?
15. Cosa domanda Cloti a proposito del denaro del giovanotto?
16. Il cameriere diede qualche segno di sorpresa alle parole della ragazza?
17. Qual è l'atteggiamento di Girolamo nella prima parte del racconto?
18. Cosa cerca di fare Maia per rassicurare Girolamo?
19. Che osservazione fa Cloti a proposito del nome del giovane?
20. Cosa denota il tipo di diminutivi che usano Clotilde e Marianna?
21. Cloti dimostra il benchè minimo interesse per il giovanotto? Perchè?
22. Malgrado il modo di agire della ragazza, cosa pensava Girolamo di Cloti?
23. Osservando bene i lineamenti di Cloti che cosa si noterebbe?
24. Quale fu, infine, l'osservazione che fece Girolamo?

25. Dal modo di agire delle due donne, cosa si potrebbe dedurre a questo punto?
26. Perchè Girolamo non era partito per le vacanze?
27. Le sembra sincera la spiegazione di Cloti? Quale altro motivo poteva esserci per spiegare la loro mancata partenza?
28. Come avrebbe dovuto agire la signorina Clotilde secondo Girolamo?
29. Perchè Cloti era così scortese?
30. Un simile modo di pensare sembra naturale o almeno giustificabile?
31. Quale conseguenza provoca spesso questo tipo di difesa?
32. Nel caso lei avesse dei dubbi sulla natura "difensiva" di questo atteggiamento, li esponga ed offra un'altra spiegazione.
33. Chi è la vittima di questo racconto?

B. Nelle frasi che seguono usare il passato remoto dei verbi in parentesi:

1. Giuliano non (ricordarsi) _____ di comperare i fiori.
2. Io (venire) _____ perchè il tempo era buono.
3. Girolamo (udire) _____ i tacchi della ragazza allontanarsi sul pavimento e dopo qualche minuto (uscire) _____.
4. Era malcontento e (pensare) _____ che non valeva la pena di aspettare più a lungo.
5. I giovanotti (entrare) _____ nell'ingresso e (scoprire) _____ che l'appartamento stava nel seminterrato.
6. Noi (dire) _____ ridendo che avevamo contato bene i nostri soldi.
7. La mamma (leggere) _____ il telegramma e dopo qualche ora (scrivere) _____ una lettera di risposta.
8. La più giovane delle ragazze (prendere) _____ del vino bianco.
9. Tu (accorgersi) _____ che non era ancora tempo di partire.
10. Tutti gli ospiti (rimanere) _____ sorpresi quando (sapere) _____ che il padrone di casa celebrava l'ottantesimo compleanno.
11. Io (promettere) _____ che non avrei invitato mai più quell'ubriacone.
12. I miei colleghi non ricordavano la parola e la (cercare) _____ nel vocabolario.
13. La ragazza (stare) _____ zitta per un momento e poi (riprendere) _____ a parlare.

C. *Riscrivere le frasi seguenti sostituendo le parole in corsivo con i corrispondenti pronomi atoni:*

1. Mario, tu devi invitare *la mamma.*
2. Chiudete *il portone,* per favore.
3. Pensavo di dare *la macchina da scrivere a voi.*
4. Mirella si è fatta male tagliandosi *le unghie.*
5. Portate *queste rose alle zie.*
6. Ripeta *questi verbi* almeno due volte!
7. Bisogna restituire tutto *il denaro a Giovanni.*
8. È venuto per fare gli auguri *a me* ed *a te.*
9. Con grande ansietà leggemmo *la lettera* più volte.
10. Carlo si alza e rimette *le sedie* a posto.

D. *Coniugare all'imperativo i verbi seguenti:*

1. fare colazione
2. dire la verità
3. andare a riposare
4. accomodarsi nel salotto
5. non sgridare il bambino

6. venire più presto
7. rispondere con cortesia
8. voltarsi verso il professore
9. non chiedere troppe cose
10. non aprire tutte le finestre

E. *Mettere al plurale i nomi e gli aggettivi che seguono ed usarli in alcune frasi:*

1. fuoco
2. monaca
3. violinista
4. roccia
5. greco

6. medico
7. specie
8. uovo
9. moglie
10. dio

11. miglio
12. braccio
13. frutto
14. catalogo
15. bacio
16. banca

La contrafigura

A. *Rispondere alle domande seguenti:*

1. Quale similitudine usa Moravia per descrivere il cambiamento di Agata?
2. Fu un cambiamento improvviso o graduale? Quali scuse trovava Agata per diradare le sue visite?

3. Andava in orario agli appuntamento? Ci restava a lungo?
4. Oltre a mostrare una certa aria di sufficienza, come accettava Agata l'affetto di Gino?
5. Diminuisce l'amore di Gino? Il giovane si adatta alla nuova situazione?
6. Quando Gino, a piazzale Flaminio, tenta d'impressionare Agata, che risposta riceve?
7. A quale scopo Gino analizza i difetti della ragazza? Cosa sperava di ottenere da ciò?
8. Lei ricorda alcuni dei difetti della ragazza?
9. Come ci fa capire Moravia, a questo punto, che Gino ama ancora Agata? Perchè gli piace?
10. Che effetto avevano su di lui la vanità e la civetteria della ragazza? Quali espressioni usa il giovane per descrivere la sua condizione?
11. Illudendosi di riconquistare l'affetto perduto, cosa si propone di fare Gino?
12. Segue poi fedelmente i suoi piani?
13. In qual modo lo scrittore fa vedere la tenace, ingenua speranza di Gino nell'episodio dell'appuntamento alla fermata del tram?
14. Si ricorda il mazzo di violette che Gino aveva comperato? Che fine fecero quei fiori?
15. Secondo Lei l'indulgenza del giovanotto deriva unicamente dal suo amore per Agata?
16. Quale riflessione Moravia fa fare al giovane subito dopo l'episodio suddetto?
17. Con quale scusa Agata spiega il suo mancato arrivo all'appuntamento?
18. Quale altra specie d'amore sperava che esistesse il giovane?
19. Come si rivelano in questa fase del racconto gli impulsi e l'ostinazione di Gino?
20. Perchè Gino, che dice di essere nato per fare l'attore, fa solo la comparsa?
21. In che cosa consiste il lavoro di una comparsa? E di una controfigura?
22. La parte di controfigura permetteva a Gino di rappresentare un po' se stesso?
23. Perchè il pensiero del giovane si sofferma con una certa insistenza sui termini 'uomo di paglia,' 'pupazzo,' 'sosia di occasione'?
24. Che cosa promise di fare l'aiuto-regista per aiutare l'amico?
25. Quale altro aspetto del carattere di Agata veniamo a conoscere a questo punto?

182   *Exercises*

26. Che sentimento suscita in Gino e nel lettore l'atteggiamento della ragazza? Descriva com'era Agata in quella particolare occasione.
27. Perchè Agata fece pena al giovanotto appena egli la rivide?
28. Come accetta Agata la proposta di matrimonio fattale da Gino?
29. È per pura cattiveria che Gino rivela ad Agata il trucco dell'intervista? Perchè lo fa?
30. Perchè soltanto in quel momento e non prima Gino comprese di aver perduto Agata per sempre?
31. L'episodio finale si presterebbe, secondo lei, ad essere filmato? Perchè? (In caso affermativo descriva accuratamente gli atti dei personaggi e l'ambiente, aggiungendo magari altri elementi che Lei considera necessari.)

B. *Mettere al trapassato prossimo i verbi in parentesi:*

1. Quella sera tutti (divertirsi) _____ ed (rimanere) _____ da noi più del previsto.
2. Gino (adattarsi) _____ a fare la controfigura.
3. Attraversai il corridoio lungo e nudo per dove Anna (passare) _____ qualche minuto prima.
4. Gli (sembrare) _____ di non poter più vivere senza di lei.
5. Giovanna (pronunciare) _____ quelle parole a labbra strette, senza guardare l'amico negli occhi.
6. Ho detto che io (tentare) _____ di telefonarle ma che non (riuscire) _____ a trovarla in casa.
7. 'Forse io non (spiegarsi) _____ bene,' ha detto il giovane.
8. Lei rispose subito: 'Ti (spiegarsi) _____ benissimo.'
9. Più tardi venimmo a sapere che essi (decidere) _____ di partire più presto, che (preparare) _____ i bagagli ma che (dimenticare) _____ di cambiare i biglietti.
10. Mia zia mi assicurò che non (andare) _____ mai in quel locale ma che ne (sentire) _____ parlare molto dal babbo.
11. Al momento di entrare nella cabina telefonica gli (venire) _____ quasi la nausea però (formare) _____ lo stesso quel maledetto numero.
12. L'amore non ci (fare) _____ vedere la realtà; (continuare) _____ a sognare cose impossibili.
13. Non ci (vivere) _____ che poche settimane all'anno.
14. Marta (sedersi) _____ un po' in disparte ed (fingere) _____ di non vedermi.

C. *Completare le frasi che seguono usando le forme toniche dei pronomi:*

1. Io spiego questo verbo (*for her*) _____.
2. Spedì la lettera (*to me and to him*) _____.
3. Verremo a passare un'oretta (*with you; polite plur.*) _____.
4. Lo sanno tutti che faccio questa cosa solo (*for you; fam. sing.*) _____.
5. Pensa sempre (*of himself*) _____ e mai agli altri.
6. Ha detto che si sarebbe rivolta (*to me*) _____.
7. Questa notizia non è partita (*from us*) _____.
8. Mi hanno parlato spesso (*of you; fam. plur.*) _____.

C. *Trovare le forme femminili dei nomi che seguono ed usarle in brevi frasi:*

1. poeta
2. direttore
3. professore
4. dio
5. fratello
6. uomo
7. eroe
8. leone
9. montone
10. cavallo
11. padre
12. genero
13. re
14. imperatore
15. frate
16. studente

D. *I nomi che seguono hanno una forma plurale maschile ed un'altra femminile. Indicarne il diverso significato in brevi frasi:*

1. labbro
2. osso
3. fuso
4. dito
5. braccio
6. filo
7. membro
8. ciglio
9. muro
10. fondamento

L'equivoco

A. *Rispondere alle domande che seguono:*

1. Che cosa invogliò l'Urati, giovane incensurato, a meditare un furto?
2. Osservando l'Urati, cosa si sarebbe pensato?
3. Cosa disse l'Urati al Lopresto per convincerlo a tentare il furto?

184 *Exercises*

4. Chi abitava nella villa quando l'Urati vi lavorava come cameriere?
5. Di che male soffriva il Sangiorgio?
6. Cosa piaceva al Sangiorgio? Era contento di vivere da solo?
7. Quale errore commise il Sangiorgio scegliendo Gilda per moglie?
8. Come concepiva quel matrimonio Gilda?
9. Cosa fece il Sangiorgio per vedere se i suoi sospetti erano fondati?
10. Come passò la sera e le prime ore della notte il Sangiorgio?
11. Qual era il suo stato d'animo mentre ritornava a casa sua?
12. Che effetto ebbe su di lui la presunta prova dell'infedeltà della moglie?
13. Per quale ragione 'un sospetto che si faccia ad un tratto realtà pare cosa tutta nuova'?
14. Quale sorpresa attendeva l'Urati nel salotto e nelle altre stanze del pianterreno?
15. Perchè il nuovo proprietario non aveva completato l'arredamento di quelle stanze?
16. Che impressione davano i mobili di stile Luigi quindici in quel salotto?
17. Cosa fece il Lopresto quando l'Urati decise di salire al piano superiore?
18. Cosa trovò l'Urati nella prima stanza del piano superiore?
19. Chi dormiva di solito in quel luogo? Perchè?
20. Quale elemento insospettato distrasse l'Urati dalla ricerca di oggetti da rubare?
21. Veniamo a sapere il motivo principale che lo spingeva a commettere queste azioni? Qual era?
22. Qual è, dunque, una delle idee fondamentali del racconto? Perchè?
23. Com'era l'aspetto di Gilda?
24. Quale 'rito' si ripeteva ogni sera davanti alla psiche? Spieghi 'lo stupore senza fondo' di quella donna.
25. Che errore commise l'Urati quando vide entrare il Sangiorgio?
26. Come usa il Moravia il motivo dell'onore?
27. Che espediente ideò l'Urati per fronteggiare l'ira del Sangiorgio?
28. Riesce bene l'espediente dell'Urati? In che modo?
29. Quali effetti provoca in questo racconto l'innocenza di Gilda? A qual fine lo scrittore usa questo elemento?
30. Cosa pensava la donna dell'inaspettato ritorno di suo marito?
31. Oltre alle parole irritanti, che altro contribuisce ad esasperare il marito?
32. Quali pensieri occupavano la mente del Sangiorgio dopo la morte della moglie?

33. Cosa era accaduto, intanto, all'Urati ed al Lopresto?
34. Era sincero il Sangiorgio quando gridò che l'Urati era l'assassino della moglie?
35. Perchè alla guardia conveniva che l'ucciso non fosse solo ladro ma anche assassino?
36. Quanti equivoci vi sono in questo racconto?

B. *Completare usando i pronomi relativi:*

1. L'Urati, (*who*) _____ aveva preparato il piano per il furto, cercò di trovare un complice (*with whom*) _____ poter penetrare nella villa.
2. I giornali (*that*) _____ leggerete sono stampati in Italia.
3. (*To whom*) _____ pensi di lasciare questa grande fortuna?
4. (*He who*) _____ crede senza riflettere, potrebbe pentirsi.
5. La persona (*whom*) _____ l'Urati non prevedeva di trovare, stava entrando proprio allora.
6. La chiave (*with which*) _____ aveva aperto la porta non era la mia.
7. (*By whom*) _____ potremmo essere riconosciuti in questo paesello?
8. La casa (*in which*) _____ abito, non è poi così costosa.
9. Il poeta (*whose*) _____ opere tu ammiri tanto profondamente, parlerà alla nostra scuola.
10. (*For whom*) _____ lavoriamo se non per voi?
11. (*Whose*) _____ sono queste cravatte nuove?
12. Era andato a Bologna dove lo aspettava un certo affare (*which*) _____ per via delle nozze aveva rimandato.
13. (*What*) _____ aveva preparato il Sangiorgio?
14. (*What*) _____ mi fa disperare è proprio la tua indifferenza!

C. *Mettere prima al condizionale presente e poi al passato i verbi in parentesi:*

1. (Venire) _____ anche tre volte alla settimana.
2. (Potere) _____ consigliarlo sul da farsi.
3. (Consultare) _____ un buon avvocato e (togliersi) _____ dall'imbarazzo.
4. (Essere) _____ un viaggio relativamente breve e (divertirsi) _____ ugualmente.
5. Che (pensare) _____ di ciò i tuoi genitori?

6. Secondo quest'informazione l'aereo (atterrare) _____ in quest'aeroporto e (ripartire) _____ dopo qualche minuto.
7. Quanti studenti (mettere) _____ tu in questa classe?
8. Il Sangiorgio (scoprire) _____ l'innocenza della moglie e non (commettere) _____ un omicidio.
9. Luigina (andarsene) _____ troppo presto e non (avere) _____ modo di conoscerla.
10. Voi (convincersi) _____ dell'inutilità di quel metodo e lo (fare) _____ cambiare.

D. *Completare le frasi che seguono con le preposizioni quando ciò sia necessario:*

1. Era andato _____ aprire la finestra dello studio.
2. 'Sono felice _____ rivedervi,' disse Maria Luisa.
3. Desidero _____ restare per un'oretta sulla spiaggia.
4. Erano stanchi _____ fare la stessa cosa.
5. Corse _____ vedere se il treno era arrivato.
6. Si scostò _____ evitare di venire investito dall'autobus.
7. Vuole _____ considerare con calma tutte le possibilità.
8. Mi dispiace _____ non esser potuto venire alle vostre nozze.
9. Sanno _____ suonare il piano con grande maestria.
10. Potevano _____ vederle entrare nel porto dal molo.

Il tacchino di Natale

A. *Rispondere alle domande seguenti:*

1. Cosa vuol dire l'espressione 'c'era il tacchino'?
2. Cosa vuol dire 'avere la passione della gola'?
3. Dove sperava di trovare il tacchino il commerciante Policarpi-Curcio?
4. Quale gioco di parole usa Moravia appena presenta la moglie del commerciante? Cosa significa?
5. Quale scopo aveva la visita del tacchino secondo la signora?
6. Perchè quella donna dimostrava un così grande entusiasmo?
7. Quale dei modi dell'ospite irritava soprattutto il Curcio? Perchè?
8. Aveva forse un complesso d'inferiorità il Curcio? Perchè?

9. Che linguaggio usava il tacchino quando si rivolgeva alla signora Curcio?
10. Di quali argomenti parlò l'ospite per fare impressione su Rosetta e sua madre?
11. Descriva l'abbigliamento del tacchino.
12. Rosetta accettò subito l'ammirazione del tacchino?
13. Cosa temeva in cuor suo il Curcio?
14. Cosa avrebbe dovuto fare il tacchino per regolarizzare la sua posizione?
15. Aveva intenzione di farsi una famiglia il tacchino?
16. Che proposta fece alla ragazza?
17. Chi fuggì durante la notte di luna?
18. Cosa fecero le persone addette alla polizia quando il Curcio espose il suo caso?
19. Perchè la legge non poteva intervenire?
20. Cosa fu costretto a fare il commerciante per riavere in casa la figlia?
21. Consideri l'operato della signora Curcio. Come la giudicherebbe lei?
22. Racconti brevemente l'accaduto, ma dal punto di vista di Rosetta.
23. Che tipo di persona rappresenta il tacchino? Per quale ragione il Moravia gli ha dato questa parte?
24. Secondo lei, di che cosa si preoccupava maggiormente il Curcio?

B. *Mettere al congiuntivo presente i verbi in parentesi:*

1. È giusto che tu (dire) _____ quel che pensi.
2. Rosetta è ansiosa che il tacchino (regolarizzare) _____ la sua posizione.
3. Mi sembra che il posto del tacchino (essere) _____ nella pentola.
4. Desidera che voi (fare) _____in modo da risolvere il problema.
5. Crede che le sue magagne non (venire) _____ all'orecchio del Curcio.
6. Ci dispiace che la storia di Rosetta non (concludersi) _____ felicemente.
7. Preferiscono che lei (sapere) _____ anche la letteratura contemporanea.
8. Dubito che il Curcio (riuscire) _____ a trovare un buon partito per sua figlia.
9. Lei crede che la madre di Rosetta (piangere) _____ ancora e (invocare) _____ la figlia?
10. Mi meraviglio che il tacchino (avere) _____ così tanta fortuna.

C. Mettere al congiuntivo passato i verbi in parentesi:

1. Ci dispiace che l'agente non (arrivare) _____ in tempo.
2. Penso che (comprare) _____ il giornale e (mettersi) _____ a leggerlo.
3. Sperano che tu e Luisa (trovare) _____ una soluzione accettabile.
4. È bene che (finire) _____ già i compiti per domani.
5. È un vero peccato che i tuoi cugini non (fare) _____ questa gita con noi.
6. A chi credete che Rosetta (prestare) _____ fede: al tacchino o a suo padre?
7. Non mi sembra che il Curcio (intuire) _____ le idee della figlia.
8. Non so se il pacco (arrivare) _____ a destinazione o se sia ancora in viaggio.
9. Siete davvero contenti che questa vostra parente (essere) _____ così esplicita in quell'occasione?
10. Penseranno che tu (scordarsi) _____ di loro.

D. Completare usando il comparativo di maggioranza e di minoranza:

1. Crede _____ a Gina _____ a voi.
2. La tavola è _____ lunga _____ larga.
3. Erano _____ felici di vivere a Genova _____ qui.
4. I suoi articoli saranno _____ convincenti _____ tuoi.
5. Preferiscono _____ leggere _____ lavorare.
6. È vero che hanno studiato _____ per me _____ per lei.
7. Questo libro è _____ lungo _____ divertente.
8. Sei una persona che vale _____ pensino gli altri.

E. Completare con le varie forme del comparativo di uguaglianza:

1. Si sentiva _____ a suo agio con Rosetta _____ con la madre.
2. Ha dipinto un ritratto che è vivo _____ il soggetto stesso.
3. È _____ cortese _____ intelligente.
4. Amava _____ le arti _____ gli sport.
5. Le piaceva _____ discutere _____ meditare.
6. Nel bicchiere c'era _____ acqua _____ vino.
7. Non sei _____ studioso _____ tuo padre.

Romolo e Remo

A. Rispondere alle domande che seguono:

1. Tra quali bisogni fa un paragone lo scrittore? Come conclude?
2. Da che cosa è tormentato Remo all'inizio del racconto?
3. Come apparve agli occhi di Remo il traffico del Corso? Perchè?
4. A quale inganno di prospettiva accenna lo scrittore parlando delle cose?
5. Cosa pensò di fare Remo in un primo momento?
6. Come e dove viveva Remo in quei giorni?
7. Cosa accadde quando dette un urtone alla guardia?
8. Cos'è il Pantheon? Ne descriva la struttura. Quali uomini celebri vi sono sepolti?
9. Cosa comprese Remo quando vide la vetrina della trattoria di Romolo?
10. Che aspetto aveva Romolo? Come si erano conosciuti i due amici?
11. Perchè nel racconto si menziona la lupa? Cosa ricorda Lei a proposito della lupa e dei gemelli Romolo e Remo?
12. Che cosa accomuna i due personaggi del racconto?
13. Provò qualche scrupolo Remo mentre ordinava il pranzo?
14. Perchè i due bambini di Romolo uscirono subito dopo?
15. Cosa voleva dire quel fatto?
16. Fino a quando i due amici continuarono a dirsi pietose menzogne?
17. Di quali argomenti prese a parlare Romolo?
18. Perchè i due amici diventarono sempre più loquaci?
19. Perchè Romolo, l'oste, accettò gli spaghetti che gli dava il suo cliente?
20. In che modo la vita si prende gioco dei due amici?
21. Quali constatazioni faceva Remo mentre soddisfaceva il suo appetito?
22. Come si considera l'amicizia in questo racconto?
23. Cosa rivelava il viso della moglie di Romolo?
24. Di quale elemento irrazionale parlano il marito e la moglie?
25. Remo cercò di mettere pace fra i litiganti?
26. Come reagiscono Romolo e la moglie sotto i colpi della sfortuna? È una situazione frequente?

B. Mettere all'imperfetto del congiuntivo i verbi in parentesi:

1. Bisognava che Remo (trovare) _____ il modo di calmare il suo appetito.
2. A causa della fame gli sembrò che le cose (essere) _____ vacillanti e deboli.
3. Pensava che Romolo, proprietario di una trattoria, (trovarsi) _____ in buone condizioni finanziarie.
4. Generalmente i clienti volevano che l'oste (servire) _____ loro solamente il vino.
5. Il povero Remo non poteva supporre che la vetrina della trattoria (contenere) _____ in tutto e per tutto una mela.
6. Era praticamente impossibile che, giunto a quel punto, (rivolgersi) _____ a qualche altra persona.
7. Pareva che anche nella famiglia di Romolo (regnare) _____ la miseria più nera.
8. Mancò poco che la moglie non (ammazzare) _____ Romolo con un coltellaccio lungo e affilato.
9. Il marito, a sua volta, credeva che la moglie gli (portare) _____ iettatura.
10. A Remo sembrò che quello (essere) _____ il momento giusto di tagliar la corda.

C. Mettere al trapassato del congiuntivo i verbi in parentesi:

1. Temevano che gli amici non (ricevere) _____ la lettera d'invito.
2. Remo sperava che almeno l'amico (fare) _____ fortuna.
3. Era contento che Mario (potere) _____ trovarsi un buon impiego.
4. Bisognava che (completare) _____ almeno due anni d'università.
5. Credevano che tu (vivere) _____ in Inghilterra e che (imparare) _____ l'inglese per pratica.
6. Sarebbe stato meglio se Remo (chiedere) _____ un pasto gratis.
7. Come potevate pensare che Romolo (intuire) _____ fin dal primo momento le intenzioni dell'amico?
8. Avevi segretamente sperato che Marta (ritornare) _____ solo per te.
9. Fui contento che essi (avviarsi) _____ verso casa un po' prima di me.
10. Si era illusa che tutti voi (accorgersi) _____ del dolore che l'angosciava.

D. *Completare le proposizioni seguenti con il superlativo relativo di maggioranza o di minoranza.*

1. Era (lunga) _____ conferenza della serie.
2. Voi sapete (grande) _____ segreto della sua vita.
3. Non ricordavano di aver conosciuto _____ donna (nobile) _____ e (fiera) _____ di quella famiglia.
4. Perfino _____ persona (ingenua) _____ avrebbe compreso una domanda simile.
5. Doveva scegliere proprio _____ libro (noioso) _____ della collana.
6. In ogni occasione Fabrizio era (buono) _____ di tutti.
7. Aveva solamente un difetto: credeva di essere _____ uomo (colto) dell'università.
8. La fame gli fece passare (brutti) _____ momenti della sua vita.
9. _____ decisione (sensata) _____ che potesse prendere fu appunto quella di andarsene alla svelta.

Passare il tempo

A. *Rispondere alle domande che seguono:*

1. Perchè Ernesto, invece di rispondere al telefono, corse ad aprire la porta?
2. Chi poteva essere alla porta, secondo Ernesto?
3. Che sorpresa lo attendeva all'ingresso dell'appartamento?
4. In quale stato d'animo venne a trovarsi Ernesto dopo la telefonata di Alina?
5. A che cosa attribuisce Lei questo modo di agire?
6. Cosa fece nello studio?
7. Che effetto gli facevano la lettura del romanzo e la musica del violino?
8. Perchè, in quel momento, si sentiva incapace d'impegnarsi nel suo lavoro?
9. Che sensazione ebbe quando si chinò sul tavolo da disegno?
10. In che consiste la differenza fra il tempo dell'orologio e i tempi della lettura, della musica o del lavoro?
11. Quale vantaggio avrebbe offerto un'occupazione del tutto meccanica?

12. Perchè il tempo psicologico, sentimentale, non sarebbe servito ad Ernesto durante l'attesa?
13. Cosa si mise a fare, allora, Ernesto?
14. Benchè questa fosse un'azione meccanica, come mai, ad un certo punto, fu preso dalla svogliatezza?
15. Perchè, secondo lo scrittore, un'azione completamente meccanica ed assurda è difficile a trovarsi?
16. Quali azioni riescono più spontanee alla natura dell'uomo?
17. È vero che la combinazione della meccanicità con l'assurdità poteva servire a far passare il tempo?
18. Quanto durò la conta dei chicchi di caffè?
19. A quale conclusione giunse Ernesto dopo quest'esperimento?
20. Ad un certo momento Ernesto ebbe il sospetto che il tempo non sarebbe mai passato. Come giunse a questa conclusione?
21. Quale condizione sarebbe venuta a crearsi in questo modo? Quale immagine viene evocata?
22. Perchè Alina era in ritardo?
23. Qual era stato il pensiero di Alina durante l'attesa?
24. Qual è la differenza tra Alina ed Ernesto a proposito di quell' 'eternità' di tempo che dovevano far passare?
25. Cosa potrebbe denotare, in un individuo, la difficoltà di far passare un certo periodo di tempo?
26. Lei accetta il principio esposto nel racconto secondo il quale non poter fare assolutamente niente significa 'sospendere il tempo'?
27. Secondo lo scrittore, con che cosa si identifica il tempo, in questo caso?

   B. Completare le seguenti frasi con le forme corrette del congiuntivo:

   1. Pensò che il suono del campanello _____.
   2. È necessario che Stefania _____.
   3. Si rammaricavano che tu _____.
   4. Vuole che anch'essi _____.
   5. Crederà che Alina _____.
   6. Desideravano che i libri _____.
   7. Gli parve che il tempo _____.
   8. Anche Alina temeva che l'attesa _____.
   9. Non le importa che il telefono _____.
   10. Spera che la musica _____.
   11. Le sembra che questo racconto _____.
   12. Peccato che Ernesto non _____.
   13. Dubito che contare i chicchi di caffè _____.

C. *Trovare il superlativo assoluto e usarlo in brevi frasi:*

1. ricco
2. lungo
3. ampio
4. integro
5. benevolo

6. misero
7. savio
8. pratico
9. salubre
10. profondo

11. celebre
12. simpatico
13. contrario
14. povero

D. *Usare i superlativi che seguono in brevi frasi dopo di averne trovato il significato:*

1. pessimo
2. minimo
3. ottimo

4. massimo
5. infimo

6. estremo
7. supremo

E. *Usare l'avverbio molto in cinque esempi.*

F. *Usare l'aggettivo molto (a — i — e) in cinque esempi.*

Ci vorrebbe Ugo

A. *Rispondere alle domande seguenti:*

1. Che concetto si era formato Ugo delle donne di Roma?
2. A che cosa era dovuto il suo risentimento?
3. Come pensava di risolvere questo suo problema?
4. Dove si svolgono i fatti narrati nel racconto?
5. Quale espediente usano i due giovani per attaccare discorso con le ragazze?
6. Che impressione fecero su Attilio le due ragazze?
7. Perchè la bruna, Luciana, accetta l'invito dei due giovani?
8. Chi aspettavano quella sera Fedora e Luciana?
9. Perchè il loro amico Ugo non le aveva aspettate?
10. Che sentimento rivela Fedora per l'amico Ugo?
11. Che osservazione fa Fedora a proposito dei soldi? Di quale altro racconto si ricorda Lei?
12. Le osservazioni di Fedora confermano i dubbi di Ugo?
13. Come apparve ai giovani il Luna Park a quell'ora?
14. Fedora decise di passare molto tempo con i due amici?

15. Cosa dice Fedora ad Attilio quando Luciana e Ugo si allontanano?
16. Per quale motivo Fedora ammirava Ugo così profondamente?
17. Come camminavano Ugo e Luciana?
18. Cosa pensava Luciana di Ugo che era assente?
19. Che tipo di uomo emerge dalla descrizione delle due ragazze?
20. Luciana decise di andare con la sorella? Cosa fece Ugo?
21. Chi arriva improvvisamente?
22. Vediamo mai il famoso Ugo del racconto?
23. Quale aspetto dà lo scrittore al misterioso personaggio?
24. Che rapporto esiste tra l'attegiamento di Fedora ed il carattere del tanto ammirato Ugo?
25. Che cosa rappresenta 'l'infornarsi' delle ragazze nel tubetto gigantesco?
26. Con quale affermazione si conclude il racconto? Quali sembrano essere le caratteristiche rilevanti di queste due ragazze? Ugo finisce per cambiare parere a proposito delle donne della sua città?

B. *Completare convenientemente le frasi seguenti con la costruzione ipotetica riferita al presente:*

1. Ugo (essere) _____ felice se Luciana (accettare) _____ il suo invito.
2. Fedora (comportarsi) _____ più gentilmente se (sapere) _____ che i due giovani sono ricchi.
3. Queste cose non (succedere) _____, se certe persone (avere) _____ più dignità.
4. Se tu (trovarsi) _____ al mio posto cosa (fare) _____?
5. Se lei (stare camminando) _____ per la strada e (vedere) _____ una ragazza che le piace, la (fermare) _____?
6. Come (passare) _____ lei il tempo se (potere) _____ trascorrere qualche ora al Luna Park?
7. Se Ugo (puntare) _____ bene la pistola, (colpire) _____ i palloncini.
8. Se noi (cadere) _____ da questo muro, (farsi) _____ male alle gambe.
9. Se voi (volere) _____ conoscere Fedora, (dovere) _____ andare all'E.U.R. verso sera.
10. Se io (sentire) _____ fare la pubblicità di un dentifricio, (pensare) _____ ad Ugo ed alla sua macchina-tubetto.

C. Usare le varie forme del partitivo nelle frasi che seguono:

1. Giovanni ha preso solamente _____ fetta di pane.
2. Se apro il frigorifero, trovo _____ minestra in una scodella.
3. C'erano _____ giovanotti e _____ ragazza che si divertivano al tiro a segno.
4. Ho comperato un chilo di mele ma ne darò _____ a Maurizio.
5. No, grazie. Non prendo zucchero nel caffè. Però vorrei metterci _____ latte.
6. È andato al Luna Park e c'è rimasto _____ ora, poi ha trovato _____ amici e si sono incamminati verso il Corso.

D. Volgere al passivo le seguenti frasi:

1. Gli studenti ricevono il professore.
2. Carletto vedrà le zie di Ascoli Piceno.
3. L'impresario ha firmato il contratto.
4. Il primo cliente comperò l'orologio d'oro.
5. I bravi ragazzi non avevano calunniato la signora Malatesta.
6. Di solito Giustino precedeva i visitatori.
7. La commissione accetterebbe l'offerta senza troppe difficoltà.
8. È bene che tutti gli studenti scrivano le frasi modello.

Hai dormito

A. Rispondere alle domande che seguono:

1. Quale abitudine della madre veniamo a conoscere al principio del racconto?
2. Cosa cercava Girolamo?
3. Con chi andò Girolamo verso le celle?
4. Dove si diresse il padre del ragazzo?
5. Che impressione ebbe il ragazzo quando sentì che i cani ululavano?
6. Perchè Girolamo aveva deciso di prendere il grifone nero?
7. Si mostravano preoccupati i genitori sapendo che il grifone nero non era più nella sua cella?
8. Che osservazione fa il padre a proposito di certe persone?
9. Perchè, secondo il padre, i cani bastardi soffrono di più?
10. Cosa pensa la madre a questo proposito?

11. Che cosa tenta di fare il cagnolino bianco e giallo?
12. Perchè Girolamo sente più compassione per il cane lupo?
13. In quel momento il ragazzo sapeva cosa sarebbe accaduto ai cani dopo un certo tempo?
14. La madre partecipa all'angoscia del figlio quando gli parla del cane da caccia?
15. Cosa spiega l'inserviente al padre di Girolamo?
16. Perchè il grifone nero non era più nella sua cella?
17. Cosa nota in cuor suo il ragazzo appena esce dal canile?
18. Quale pensiero lo fa soffrire maggiormente: la morte del grifone? Un'altra cosa?
19. Cosa rappresenta l'angoscia di Girolamo? È veramente malato il ragazzo?
20. Qual è il tema del racconto?
21. In quali elementi troviamo una profonda differenza tra gli adulti e Girolamo?
22. Che reazione provoca nel ragazzo il modo di fare dei grandi? Come gli sembrano?
23. Considerando l'attitudine dei genitori e del ragazzo, verso quale conclusione ci porta il racconto?

B. *Completare convenientemente le frasi seguenti con la costruzione ipotetica riferita al passato:*

1. Se la madre di Girolamo (essere) _____ meno indifferente, il grifone nero non (morire) _____.
2. L'inserviente (accettare) _____ la sigaretta se tu gliela (offrire) _____.
3. Se (potere) _____ farlo, Girolamo (rimproverare) _____ i genitori.
4. Se la gente non (avvicinarsi) _____ troppo alla gabbia, il cane lupo non (muoversi) _____.
5. Se (andare) _____ a lavorare nei campi, (trascorrere) _____ il tempo più piacevolmente.
6. 'Anche tu (avere) _____ paura se (perdersi) _____' disse la madre a Girolamo.
7. Se non (esserci) _____ troppi cani randagi, non (essere) _____ necessario eliminarli.
8. Fabrizio (conoscere) _____ anche mio fratello se (rimanere) _____ a casa mia altri dieci minuti.

9. Se tu gli (parlare) _____, Giuliano (decidersi) _____ a partire.
10. Quel film (riuscire) _____ più convincente se il regista (seguire) _____ i consigli dell'attore.

C. *Volgere alla forma impersonale le seguenti proposizioni passive:*

1. I ragazzi sono rimproverati quando agiscono svogliatamente.
2. La cometa fu veduta a notte tarda.
3. La spedizione sarà preparata in tutta fretta.
4. Nessuno potrà dire che non siano state considerate tutte le soluzioni possibili.
5. Il vino è imbottigliato in questo locale.
6. Queste cose non sono dette in pubblico.
7. Un libro come quello è letto con molta attenzione.

D. *Usare gli aggettivi indicati nelle frasi seguenti:* ciascuno, nessuno, qualche, qualsiasi, nessuna, qualunque

1. Era sempre disposto a fare _____ cosa.
2. Per quanto tenti, non riesce mai a convincere _____ candidato.
3. È un problema così facile che _____ studente lo svolgerebbe in pochi minuti.
4. Restituì il quaderno a _____ studente.
5. _____ volta bisogna ascoltare con molta pazienza le persone noiose.
6. Sarà bene che tu faccia questo lavoro, anche se non riceverai _____ ricompensa.

Il camionista

A. *Rispondere alle domande che seguono:*

1. Che costituzione fisica deve avere un camionista secondo il narratore? Perchè?
2. Come dev'essere spiritualmente? Perchè?
3. Che tipo d'uomo era Palombi? Era adatto per il suo lavoro?
4. Quando si schiariva l'intelligenza del Palombi? Racconti il fatto accaduto all'osteria di Itri.

5. Come doveva essere, in simile compagnia, lo stato d'animo di chi racconta?
6. Quale novità ruppe, ad un certo momento, la monotonia dei viaggi sulla Roma–Napoli?
7. Perchè Italia non avrebbe dovuto viaggiare nel camion?
8. Di che cosa si avvaleva la ragazza per farsi dare un passaggio dai camionisti?
9. Cosa desta nel narratore una così forte attrazione per Italia? Cosa gli parve di aver trovato?
10. Come si comportava la ragazza?
11. Quale trasformazione notiamo nel narratore col passare del tempo?
12. Perchè, a volte, gli pareva di essere perfino troppo debole?
13. Cosa avrebbe voluto dire con i fari del camion?
14. Palombi conversava a lungo con la ragazza?
15. Quando si accorse del doppio senso della scritta 'Viva l'Italia'? Cosa disse?
16. Perchè fino ad Itri il camionista non fu preso dal sonno?
17. Il pensiero d'Italia lo tenne sveglio fino a Terracina?
18. Quale fu la prima preoccupazione di Palombi?
19. Cosa trovarono un po' più tardi?
20. Com'era l'uomo dell'osteria?
21. A quale strana scena assistono i due camionisti?
22. Quale trasformazione avviene in Palombi alla fine dell'episodio?
23. Perchè l'altro camionista non vuol più sentire le sue lamentele?
24. L'inganno della donna cambia in qualche modo i rapporti tra i due uomini?
25. Cosa spinse il narratore a cambiare lavoro?
26. Sarebbe possibile trovare il Palombi ne' 'Il ritrovo dei camionisti'?

B. *Usare le forme che seguono in altrettante frasi:*

1. avere grilli per la testa
2. di straforo
3. tanto vale che
4. fatto sta che
5. ci voleva
6. con tutto che
7. essere di peso a
8. a fior di labbra

C. *Completare opportunamente le frasi che seguono:*

1. un gregge _____
2. all'altezza di _____
3. mi innamorai _____
4. l'avete fatta _____
5. _____ il passo
6. _____ alla robespierre
7. vedere il gobbo e l'Italia insieme mi faceva _____
8. era ingrata e senza_____

D. *Usare i verbi in parentesi nella forma corretta:*

1. Ho ripetuto la frase affinchè tutti la (capire) _____.
2. Benchè tu (arrivare) _____ tardi, non hai perduto l'autobus.
3. Ci siamo divertiti moltissimo quantunque (fare) _____ freddo.
4. Lo aiuteremo nonostante (agire) _____ male verso di noi.
5. Malgrado (tentare) _____ di finire la lezione presto, non ci è riuscito.
6. Ancorchè tu lo (conoscere) _____ poco prima, non te ne ricordavi più il nome.
7. Regalò molto del suo agli indigenti benchè non (disporre) _____ di grandi ricchezze.
8. Parlano italiano meglio che non lo (scrivere) _____.
9. La tua macchina funzionò peggio di quel che tu non (aspettarsi) _____.
10. Finì la sua porzione di minestra in men che non si (dire) _____.
11. Lavorano più di quel che tu non (immaginare) _____.

Una strana malattia

A. *Rispondere alle domande che seguono:*

1. Qual era lo scopo del viaggio dei due scienziati?
2. Che nome era stato dato alla malattia? Perchè?
3. Il malato quando entrava nella prima fase del morbo?
4. Quanto tempo durava quella fase?
5. Come si comportava il malato in seguito? Come si chiamava quest'altra fase? Quali ne erano i sintomi?
6. Cosa accadeva al malato prima di morire?
7. Perchè quella malattia veniva chiamata anche 'alcoolismo secco'?
8. A che cosa somigliavano le mostruose allucinazioni descritte dai due scienziati?
9. C'è dell'ironia nella frase 'nostra bella civiltà occidentale'?
10. Qual era la tesi di uno dei più giovani dottori?
11. Cosa propose di domandare il vecchio scienziato?
12. Fu soddisfacente la risposta dello straniero?
13. Secondo lo scienziato esisteva una realtà nel paese straniero?
14. Come considerava la natura lo straniero?

15. Si giunse a qualche soluzione? Perchè?
16. Secondo lo scrittore, chi è malato: lo scienziato straniero o coloro che lui considera malati? Qualcun altro?
17. Perchè era impossibile spiegare la realtà ai malati?

B. *Usare i verbi in parentesi nella forma corretta:*

1. Avrete il mio aiuto, purchè si (agire) _____.
2. Resteremo qui fino a domani, a meno che Giovanna non (decidere) _____ di ritornare più presto.
3. Scrivetegli qualora ve ne (dare) _____ motivo.
4. Non li chiameremo, eccetto che non lo (richiedere) _____ essi prima.
5. Leggerò quel brano, a condizione che voi l' (ascoltare) _____ con la massima attenzione.
6. Qualora questa rivista non (essere) _____ quella richiesta, ditemelo e la farò cambiare.
7. Nel caso Mario (sentirsi) _____ solo, fategli un po' di compagnia.
8. Se la ragazza (dovere) _____ usare il mio studio, lasciate pure che lo faccia.
9. Parlava come se ciò gli (costare) _____ gran fatica.
10. Caso mai (piovere) _____, chiudete le finestre.
11. Posto che tu (volere) _____ andare all'università, noi ti ci manderemo di buon grado.
12. Urlavano quasi (essere) _____ pazzi.

C. *Usare i vocaboli seguenti in altrettante frasi:*

1. rimedio	5. coscia	8. stuolo
2. febbre	6. palliativo	9. allucinazione
3. malessere	7. morbo	10. ciarlatano
4. sintomo		

D. *Completare le proposizioni usando le forme indicate: gruppetto, riunione, gregge, banda, branco, pattuglia*

1. Un _____ di pecore si era sparso per i campi.
2. I predoni avevano attaccato i passeggeri come un _____ di lupi.
3. Un _____ di studenti si era riunito nella piazza del paese.
4. Una _____ di soldati arrivò alla fortezza.
5. Fu necessario arrestare tutta la _____ di malfattori.
6. Si fece una _____ dei membri.

E. *Trovare gli avverbi corrispondenti:*

1. umile
2. raro
3. reale
4. serio
5. franco
6. necessario
7. semplice
8. utile
9. feroce
10. tenace

Inverno di malato

A. *Rispondere alle domande che seguono:*

1. Quale problema sociale emerge all'inizio del racconto? Come lo prospetta il Brambilla? Come risponde Girolamo?
2. Quali conseguenze psicologiche descrive lo scrittore quando accenna al senso di colpevolezza di Girolamo?
3. Che genere di 'realtà' finì per crearsi il ragazzo restando così a lungo nel sanatorio? Cosa lo faceva soffrire, a volte?
4. Giacomo disprezzava il Brambilla? Prendeva sul serio la vanagloria del commesso viaggiatore? Qual era il tipo ideale di uomo da imitare?
5. Com'era stato l'atteggiamento di Girolamo verso la Polly prima dell'arrivo del Brambilla? E poi, perchè era cambiato?
6. Come si comportava il ragazzo quando gli amici ed i parenti andavano a visitarlo? Perchè?
7. Cosa desiderava meritare Girolamo? Quali erano gli aspetti contrastanti dell' 'amara commedia.'
8. Quali conseguenze morali provocò nella mente di Girolamo il proposito di sedurre la ragazzina inglese?
9. Perchè il ragazzo voleva essere considerato cattivo? Attraverso quali passaggi psicologici arriva a quest'idea?
10. Quale sentimento prevalse in Girolamo durante la visita alla Polly?
11. In che modo lo incoraggiò la ragazzina?
12. Quali pensieri passarono per la mente di Girolamo quando seppe che il suo compagno di stanza sarebbe partito?
13. Perchè la partenza del Brambilla rappresenta un'altra umiliazione per Girolamo?
14. Riconobbe, in quel momento, la sua debolezza fondamentale?

15. Dopo quella constatazione, cambiarono, in qualche modo, i suoi sentimenti per la Polly? Perchè?
16. Quale immagine tornava spesso alla mente di Girolamo? Che significato aveva?
17. Come fu, per il ragazzo, la separazione definitiva dal Brambilla?
18. Quando cominciò Girolamo a rendersi conto della gravità della sua situazione?
19. Che cosa provocava, in realtà, il risentimento degli inservienti dell'ospedale verso il ragazzo?
20. Cosa ci rivela il sogno tormentoso del ragazzo?
21. Con quale speranza si addormentò quella notte?
22. Perchè il professore del sanatorio era un uomo di successo?
23. Il professore si preoccupava dello stato d'animo di Girolamo e dei suoi pazienti?
24. Cosa sgomentò il ragazzo anche in quest'occasione?
25. Il problema dell'isolamento di un adolescente. Come lo presenta il Moravia in questo racconto?
26. Perchè lo scherno e l'indifferenza degli adulti per l'adolescente hanno un'importanza notevole nel racconto?

B. *Completare le frasi seguenti:*

1. Cercava dei libri che (istruire) _____ divertendo.
2. Avrebbe desiderato trovare qualcuno che gli (dimostrare) _____ un po' di simpatia.
3. Chi volete che (venire) _____ a quest'ora?
4. Chi credete che (fare) _____ una tale azione?
5. Non c'è cosa che (piacere) _____ a quei ragazzi.
6. Era il solo aereo che (fermarsi) _____ in quella città.
7. Non fece mai cosa che non (essere) _____ generosa ed onesta.
8. È la prima cura che (ricevere) _____ al sanatorio.

C. *Usare le forme che seguono in altrettante proposizioni:*

1. abboccare all'amo
2. prendersi beffa di
3. trattarsi di
4. prendere gusto
5. far ridere i polli
6. condurre a compimento
7. saperla lunga
8. trovarci sugo
9. prendere sul serio
10. di soppiatto
11. detto e fatto
12. fare corona

Ritorno al mare

A. *Rispondere alle domande che seguono:*

1. Come ci viene presentato il paesaggio all'inizio del racconto?
2. Per Lorenzo quella era una semplice gita di piacere?
3. Ispirava simpatia, in quel momento, la moglie? Perchè faceva pensare a una scimmia?
4. Cosa creava in Lorenzo la vista del mare? Perchè non disse nulla?
5. Che aspetto offriva lo spiazzo dove s'era fermata la macchina?
6. Perchè i rapporti fra Lorenzo e la moglie non erano buoni? Cosa stava accadendo in lui per la prima volta?
7. Di che natura era l'attrazione che l'uomo sentiva per la donna?
8. Perchè, guardando il mare, Lorenzo aveva pensato alla sua fanciullezza?
9. Come si rivela, in quest'episodio, il distacco sentimentale della moglie?
10. Lorenzo potè scagliare lontano la pena che l'opprimeva? Tentò di farlo?
11. Quali ricordi suscitarono in Lorenzo le rovine del ristorante?
12. Cosa sta a significare la fame triste di Lorenzo?
13. Di quali fatti ci rendiamo conto seguendo il diverbio dei protagonisti?
14. Perchè Lorenzo comprese che una facile vittoria sulla moglie non avrebbe risolto il suo problema sentimentale?
15. Lei crede che quella donna avrebbe potuto mai intuire il bisogno spirituale di Lorenzo? Perchè?
16. Dopo la fuga della moglie a quale impulso si lasciò andare Lorenzo?
17. Le sembra, in un certo senso, che il mare sia pietoso con lui?
18. Parli del procedimento seguito dallo scrittore nell'esporre i motivi che rendono i due protagonisti estranei ed ostili.
19. Quali fattori storici e politici intervengono nel racconto?
20. Che significato hanno le immagini frequenti della spiaggia e della pineta in rapporto alle vicende dei protagonisti?

B. *Completare le proposizioni che seguono:*

1. Non si diventa colti (*all of a sudden*) _____.
2. Il carattere di quest'uomo è (*rather*) _____ superficiale.
3. Ci raccontò delle cose (*somewhat*) _____ inverosimili.
4. Sì, porteremo i documenti richiesti (*at once*) _____.
5. Ci recavamo in città (*from time to time*) _____.
6. (*Rather than*) _____ restare chiuso in casa, preferisco uscire anche se piove.
7. Inviterà (*all of you*) _____.
8. Cadde nell'acqua e si bagnò (*all over*) _____.

C. *Usare in altrettante proposizioni:*

1. in avvenire
2. in lode
3. in mare
4. a volo
5. a paragone di
6. a poco a poco
7. a bocca aperta
8. d'inverno
9. di giorno
10. in luogo
11. con suo comodo
12. per paura di
13. per ora (adesso)
14. con lo scopo di

D. *Completare con le preposizioni o con gli articoli:*

1. Il treno si fermò prima _____ scambi.
2. La cagnetta passa dietro _____ te.
3. Entrerò dopo _____ voi.
4. La macchina è fuori _____ rimessa.
5. Il capo teneva tutti sotto _____ sè.
6. Improvvisamente è comparso davanti _____ noi.
7. Lorenzo si era seduto accanto _____ moglie.
8. Più tardi si diresse verso _____ alghe.

VOCABULARY

The vocabulary comprises those words with which the second-year student is generally unfamiliar. Verbs are given in their infinitive form. Nouns ending in -o are masculine and in -a are feminine; the gender of other nouns is indicated with *m.* (*maschile*) and *f.* (*femminile*).
Definite and indefinite articles, direct and indirect pronouns, relative pronouns and past participles used as such in the context have not been included.

abbacchio   lamb
abbagliare   to blind, to dazzle
abbaglio   mistake
abbietto   abject, base
abbordabile   accessible, approachable
abbottonare   to button
abete *m.*   fir tree
abisso   abyss, gulf
abitudinario   customary
accanimento   obstinacy
accanto   near, by
accatastare   to pile up
accavallare   to cross, to overlap
accecante   blinding ·
accendere (il motore)   to start

acchiappare   to catch, to seize
acciambellato   curled up
accidentato   uneven
accigliato   frowning
accingersi   to set up
accoglienza   reception, welcome
acconciato   attired, arranged
acconciatura (dei capelli) *f.*
   head-dressing, hairdo
accoppiamento   coupling
accordo   accord, agreement;
   restare d'—   to agree
accorgersi   to perceive, to be
   aware
accorrere   to run

accostarsi to draw near, to approach

accosto near, at hand

accrescere to increase, to accentuate

accucciato crouched

acerbo bitter

acre acrid, sharp, bitter

addietro ago, before, behind

addirittura really, quite

addolcire to soften, to allay

addossare to lay (the blame), to throw (the blame)

addosso on, upon

adescamento enticement, allurement

adescare to entice, to allure

adesso now

adoperare to use

adunco hooked

affannarsi to do one's best, to busy oneself

affaticato tired

afferrare (a volo) to catch (in the air), to grab

affezionato fond of

affilato sharp

affittare to rent, to let

affumicati: occhiali — *m. pl.* sunglasses

aggiungere to add

aggiustare to repair, to fix

aggrapparsi to grasp, to cling to

aggravarsi to grow worse

aglio garlic

agro sour

aguzzo pointed, sharp; stringy

aiuto-regista *m.* assistant director

alba dawn

alfiere *m.* bishop (chess)

allargarsi to surge

allineare to range, to set in a row

alloggiato lodged

allungare della bocca to pucker

alpestre alpine, mountainous

altalena swing

altolocato in a high position

altoparlante *m.* loud-speaker

altrove elsewhere

amante *m.* lover, suitor

ambagi: senza — plainly

ammazzare to kill

ammiccare to wink

ammonticchiato heaped up

ammutolire to become dumb, to become confused

amor proprio *m.* self-respect

amorevole loving

anca hip

andare to go, to walk; — a spasso to take a walk; andarsene to go away

angolo corner

angustia misery, distress

angusto narrow

anima soul

annebbiato dim, foggy

annientare to annihilate

anteporre to place before; to prefer

anticamera waiting room

apparecchio cast

apparire to appear

appiccarsi to spread (fire)

appiccicato stuck

appoggiare to lean

apposta on purpose

appostare to waylay

appostarsi to lie in wait

appresso near, after, close by

appurare   to verify, to ascertain
aragosta   lobster
arcobaleno   rainbow
ardere   to burn
ardito   bold, daring
arenarsi   to stop
argento   silver
armamentario   equipment, paraphernalia
arredamento   interior decoration; fitting
arrendersi   to surrender, to give oneself up
arricciato   curled
arrossire   to blush
arrotolare   to roll
arroventare   to make hot
arruffato   ruffled up
ascella   armpit
ascendente m.   influence
ascensore m.   elevator, lift
ascesso   abscess
asciugare   to dry
asciutto   dry
asilo   kindergarten
aspirare   to aim, to aspire
assumere   to assume (an air)
atrio   entrance hall
attaccamento   attachment
atterrire   to frighten, to terrify
attiguo   adjacent, adjoining
attillato   tight
attonito   dumbfounded, amazed
attorcigliarsi   to twist, to wind
attore m.   actor
attrice f.   actress
augurare   to wish
austriaco   Austrian
avambraccio   forearm
avvelenato   poisoned, embittered

avvenente   good-looking, handsome, pretty
avvenire   to happen, to occur
avventore m.   client, patron
avverarsi   to prove, to be accomplished
avvertire   to warn
avviarsi   to start, to set out
avviato: ben —   thriving
avvicinarsi   to get close
avvolgersi   to wind
azzeccare   to hit, to guess right
azzimarsi   to dress up

bacio   kiss
badare   to watch, to pay attention, to mind
badiale   large, huge
baffo   mustache
bagnato   wet
baiocco m.   coin, money
balaustrata   balustrade
balbettare   to stammer
balia   wet nurse
balla   bale
ballo   dance
bambola   doll
banco   bank
baracca   booth
barattolo   jar
bargiglio   wattle
basso   low
baule m.   trunk
bavero   lapel
becco   beak
Befana   Epiphany (January 6)
beffare   to make fun of, to ridicule
belletto   make-up

benchè   although
benestante   rich, well-to-do
bensì   but
bersaglio   target
bertuccia   monkey
biancore *m.*   whiteness
bidone *m.*   barrel, drum
bilioso   peevish, bilious
biscotto   cookie
bisognare   to be necessary
bistrattare   to treat badly, to ill-use
bitorzoluto   knotty
bobina   roll
bocca   mouth
boccolo   lock, curl
bombardamento   bombardment, bombing
bonaccione *m.*   good fellow
bonomia   kindness, good nature
borghese *m.*   civilian
borseggiare   to rob, to pick (a pocket)
bosco   woods
botta   blow
bottega   shop, store
bottino   prize, loot
braccio   arm
bracco   hound
brandire   to brandish
bricco   kettle
briciola   crumb
brillantina   brilliantine
brivido   shiver, shudder
brontolare   to grumble
bronzo   bronze, bronze object
brullo   barren
bruscamente   suddenly
brusco   sharp, harsh; sudden
brutto: farsi —   to become angry
buca   hole

bucare   to make a hole
buccia   peal, shell
bue *m.*   ox
bugia   lie
bugiardo   lier
burlarsi   to make fun of
bussare   to knock
buttare   to throw

cabina   booth
caccia: cane da — *m.*   hunting dog
cacciarsi   to intrude
cacciata   expulsion
cacciato   driven out
cadere   to fall
cagnara   fuss, bustle
calamaio   inkstand
calare   to lower
calcinacci *m.pl.*   rubbish (of plaster)
calcio   gunstock, kick
calloso   hardened, having horns
calotta *m.*   cap
calvo   bald .
calzare   to put on (footwear)
camice m.   gown, coverall
camion *m.*   truck
camoscio   suede, chamois
campanello   bell
campanile *m.*   belltower
camuso   flat, snub
canarino   canary
cancello   gate
cane da caccia *m.*   hunting dog
canile *m.*   kennel
canterellare   to hum
cantiere *m.*   yard, building yard
cantuccio   corner

canzonare to make fun
canzonatura joke, irony
caparbio stubborn, obstinate
capelli: acconciatura dei —
 head-dressing, hairdo
capezzale *m.* headboard
capitare to meet with
capitello capital (*architectural*)
capitombolare to tumble down
capogiro dizziness
capomastro master builder
capovolgersi to overturn
cappotto topcoat
capra goat
capriola somersault
carbone *m.* coal
carbonella charcoal
carciofo artichoke
cariato decayed
carica office, appointment
caricare to load
carico dark (in color); *m.* load
carnagione *f.* complexion
carretto cart
carrozzeria body (of an automobile)
carrucola pulley
carta gommata scotch-tape
cartello sign
cartoccio paper bag, wrapping
casalingo homely; home-made,
 home style
cascante falling, baggy
cassa cash register
cassiere *m.* cashier
castano brown
casupola hovel, hut
cattiveria nastiness
cavallo: ferro di horseshoe
cavarsela to get off

caverna cave
cena supper
cenere *f.* ashes
cenno sign
cera wax
cervello brain
cespuglio bush
cessare to cease, to end
chiaroveggenza clearsightedness
chiasso noise
chiazza spot, stain
chicco bean, seed
chiedere to ask
china slope
chinarsi to stoop
chincaglieria small fancy
 articles
chiodo nail
chirurgo surgeon
ciarlataneria quackery
ciarliero talkative
cicatrice *f.* scar
cicoria chicory
cigolare to creak, to squeak
cilestro sky-blue
cima top
ciocca lock (of hair)
cioccolatino *m.* little chocolate
cipiglio frown, scowl
cipolla onion
cipria powder
ciuffo forelock
civetta flirt, owl
clamore *m.* clamor, noise
coda tail; (*colloq.*) — alla
 vaccinara steer tail (Roman
 style)
coetaneo of the same age
collera anger, rage
colletto collar
collina hill

collo neck
colmo full
colonna column, pillar
colonnato colonnade
colpa fault
colpevolezza guilt
colpire to hit
colpo shot
coltellata cut, stab
colto p.p. of cogliere caught
coltre f. sheet, blanket
commesso: — viaggiatore traveling salesman
commettere to commit
commissariato police office
compagnia: dama di — lady companion
comparsa walk-on, supernumerary
compiacimento pleasure, satisfaction
complesso: nel — on the whole
comporre to compose
comportarsi to behave
compunto afflicted, sorry
conchiglia shell
concitato excited, agitated
condotta behavior
congedarsi to take one's leave
conoscere to know
consumare to consume, to take some food or drink
contabile m. accountant, bookkeeper
contegno behavior
contegnosità f. gravity
contegnoso grave, solemn
contenersi to restrain oneself
conto bill; rendersi — to realize

contorcimento contortion, twisting
contraccambiare to reciprocate, to return
contrariato upset, vexed
controfigura stand-in
controluce against the light
controveleno antidote
convivenza cohabitation, coexistence
coperta blanket
copia abundance, quantity
coppale m. copal varnish
corallo coral
corazza armor
corda string
coricarsi to go to bed
cornice f. frame
cornicione m. entablature
corona crown
corpulento burly, fat
corpuscolo particle
corredo trousseau
corrodere to corrode
corrucciato worried, angry
corsa: di — running
corteggiare to court
corvo raven
coscia thigh
cosiddetto so-called
costernato dismayed, consternated
costola rib
cotica pig skin
covare to brood, to smoulder
credulità f. credulity
cremoso of the color of cream
crepitio crackling
crepuscolo twilight
crespo crisp, curly
cretino foolish, stupid

cucciolo puppy
cucina cooking; kitchen
cumulo heap
cupo sullen, dark
curvo bent
cuscino pillow

dama di compagnia lady
    companion
dannare to damn
dattilografia typing
debole feeble
decadere to fall
decantare to praise
degente *m. or f.* patient
delimitare to delimit
delirare to be delirious, to rave
delizia delight
deluso disappointed, deluded
denaro money
dentifricio toothpaste
denutrito undernourished, ill-
    fed
depilare to depilate
depilarsi to depilate
destarsi to wake up, to awake
detriti *m.pl.* rubbish
diamine: che —! what the
    devil!
didascalico didactic
diffidente diffident, distrustful
digiuno: essere — to have an
    empty stomach
digrignare to gnash, to grind
dileguarsi to vanish, to fade
    away
dilettarsi to find pleasure in
diminutivo nickname, diminu-
    tive

dinoccolato awkward, clumsy
diradare to make less frequent
dire to say, to tell
dirittura honesty, moral recti-
    tude
disadorno plain, bare, un-
    adorned
discinto untidy, unbraced
discorde discordant
discorrere to talk
disfare to undo
disinvolto extrovert, uncon-
    strained
disistima disesteem, disrepute
disoccupazione *f.* unemploy-
    ment
disparire to disappear
dispettoso spiteful
disprezzare to despise, to scorn
disseccare to dry, to wither
disselciato unpaved
disseminare to scatter, to strew
disserrare to unlock, to open
distinguere to distinguish
disumano inhuman
ditata a finger stroke
ditta firm; business
divampare to flare up, to rage
diversità *f.* difference, diversity
divincolare to twist; to agitate
divincolarsi to struggle
dondolare to swing
drogheria drugstore; grocery
    (store)

ebano ebony
ebbro drunk
efferatezza brutality, cruelty
epidemia epidemic

equivoco   misunderstanding,
  mistake
esanime   lifeless
estero   foreign countries
estraneo   stranger
etnologico   ethnologic

fabbrica   factory
facchino   porter
facciata   façade, front
fagiolo   bean
fagotto   bundle
fallo: senza —   without fail
fanatico   person prone to exag-
  geration
fannullone m.   lazy man
fantoccio   puppet
fare   to make, do; — centro   to
  hit; — il pagliaccio   to clown;
  farsi brutto   to become angry
farinoso   mealy, powdery
faro m.   headlight
fasce f.pl.   swaddling clothes
fastidio   annoyance
febbricitante   feverish
feltro   felt
femore m.   femur, thigh-bone
fenditura   slit
feria f.   vacation, holiday
ferino   wild, feral
ferito   wounded, hurt
ferraglia f.   hardware
ferro   iron; — di cavallo
  horseshoe; — da stiro
  (clothes) iron; rottame di —
  iron scrap
fessura f.   opening, crack
festoso   joyful, merry
fettuccia   strip
fiamma   flame

fianco   side
fiato   breath
ficcare   to put, to thrust
fidarsi   to trust, to rely
fiducia   confidence, trust
fienile m.   hayloft
fieno   hay
fierezza   pride
figura   figure; brutta —   bad
  figure
filare   to go, to run
filippica f.   bitter invective
filo di ferro spinato m.   barbed
  wire
fingere   to pretend
finzione f.   falsehood, imposture
fior: a — di pelle   superficial
fioraio   florist
fischiare   to whistle
fischietto   whistle
fischio   whistle, hiss
fistola   fistula
fittezza   thickness
fitto   thick
fiume m.   river
fiuto   sense of smell
foca   seal
foderato   lined
fogliame m.   foliage
foglietto   bill
folgorante   shining
folla   crowd
fondatezza   ground, truth
fondo: in —   at bottom, in one's
  heart
formicolante   swarming
formoso   shapely
fornello   burner
forza: per —   necessarily, by
  force
fosso   ditch

fradicio wet
fragoroso noisy, loud
frantumi *m.pl.* fragments
freddezza coolness
fregare to strike (a match)
fremere to shudder
frenare to brake (to apply the brakes)
fritto fried food
frivolezza frivolousness, frivolity
fronte *f.* forehead
fucile *m.* rifle
fuga flight, escape
fuggiasco fugitive
fulgido resplendent, bright
funesto fatal, ruinous
fungo mushroom
fuoco fire
furbo shrewd, cunning, sly
furore *m.* fury

gabbia cage
galeotto convict, prisoner
galleggiare to float
gallinaccio turkey
gamba leg
garbo politeness, grace
garzone *m.* errand boy
gazzella gazelle
gelo frost
gemito groan
genero son-in-law
gesso chalk
gesto move, gesture
gettare to throw
ghiaccio ice
gilè *m.* waistcoat, vest
ginocchio knee
giradischi *m.* turntable, phonograph

girare to turn, to spin
girarrosto (roasting) spit
girotondo ring (of people), children's game
giubba jacket
giungere to arrive
giungla jungle
giunta: per — in addition to that
giurare to swear
gnocco dumpling
gobba hunch, hump
gobbo hunchback
goccia drop
godimento pleasure, enjoyment
gomito elbow
gonfio puffy
gonna skirt
gradino step
granchio crab
gregge *m.* herd
grembiale *m.* apron
gremire to fill, to crowd
greve heavy
grifone *m.* griffon
griglia wire fence
grillo cricket
groppa back, hump
grosso big, coarse
grossolano coarse, rude
gru *f.* crane
grugnito grunt
guaito yelp, whine
gualcito rumpled, crumpled
guancia cheek
guanto glove
guardaroba *m.* wardrobe
guardia policeman
guarire to recover, to heal
guizzo start

idraulico   plumber
imbestialire   to become furious
imbestialito   furious, enraged
imbiancato   whitewashed
imbianchino   house-painter, white-washer
imboccare   to enter
imbronciato   pouting
imburrato   buttered
immeritato   undeserved
impacciato   ill-at-ease, awkward
impadronirsi   to get hold of, to take possession
impantanarsi   to sink (in mud)
impazzata: all' — madly
impegnare   to engage
impegno   engagement
impellicciato   wearing a fur
imperioso   peremptory, authoritative
impermalirsi   to take offence
impermeabile m.   raincoat
impiccio   predicament, trouble
impiegato   employee, clerk
impietosito   moved to pity
imporporato   reddened
impotente   unable
impoverire   to grow poor
inabissarsi   to sink, to engulf
inavvertito   unnoticed, unobserved
incarnare   to incarnate, to personify
incastrare   to fit
incauto   imprudent, rash
incendio   fire
incensurato   without a criminal record
inceppato   stuck
inciampare   to stumble
incinta   pregnant

incipriarsi   to powder oneself
inclinato   bent
incollare   to glue
inconsapevole   unconscious
inconsueto   unusual
increspare   to curl up
incrociato   folded (arms)
incubo   nightmare
indolenzirsi   to become painful, to ache
indovinare   to guess
indugiare   to linger, to delay
inebriato   inebriated, excited
ineguaglianza   asperity, unevenness
inerte   motionless, inert
inetto   inept, unfit
infastidire   to annoy, to trouble
infilare   to go through
infischiarsi   not to care
infondato   groundless, unfounded
infronzolato   trimmed up
inforcatura   fork, bifurcation
infrangersi   to break
inganno   deceit, deception
ingarbugliato   confused, entangled
ingegnoso   ingenious
inghiottire   to swallow
ingiurioso   insulting, outrageous
ingombro   cluttered, crowded
ingrato   ungrateful
ingresso   entrance
inguine m.   groin
iniettato   injected
innato   inborn, innate
inoltrato   late
inquieto   apprehensive, uneasy
insediarsi   to install oneself
inseguire   to pursue, to chase

inseguito chased
inserviente m. attendant
insonnolito sleepy
insospettirsi to become suspicious
intascare to pocket
intemperie f.pl. inclemency (of the weather)
interpellare to ask
interrompere to stop, to discontinue
interruttore m. switch
intesa: d'— in an understanding way
intingolo sauce, gravy
intonso uncut
intontito stunned, astonished
intoppo obstacle
intraprendere to undertake
intravvedere to catch a glimpse of
inutile useless
invescato caught
inviato (speciale) m. reporter
inviperito angry, enraged
involto bundle, parcel
irritato infuriated, irritated
irsuto shaggy

juta jute

labbro lip
labile feeble, weak
laccato lacquered
lagrima tear
lama blade
lambire to lap
lamiera metal sheet

lastrico pavement
lastrone slab
laterizio made of brick
latrato bark (of a dog)
latta tin
lavorante m. worker
lealtà f. loyalty
leccio holm oak
ledere to offend, to injure
legare to tie
leggiadro pretty, lovely
legnoso stringy
lembo edge
lentiggine f. freckle
lento slow
lenzuolo bed-sheet
lesto fast, quick
letto bed
levarsi to stand up
levigare to smooth
levigato smooth, refined
leziosaggine f. affectedness
libertinaggio licence, libertinage
libidine f. lust
lino linen
liscio straight, smooth
lista menu
litorale m. beach
locale m. night club, dancing
logoro worn-out
lombata m. loin
losco squint-eyed; dubious
lottare to fight, to struggle
luccicare to shine, to glitter, to sparkle
lume m. light
lupa she-wolf
lupo wolf, German shepherd
lusingare to allure, to entice
lusso luxury

macchiare   to stain
macerie *f.pl.*   ruins, debris
magagna *f.*   fault, defect
maggiorenne   major; of age
mai   never, ever
malcapitato   unlucky, unfortu-
   nate
malconcio   beaten up
maledetto   cursed
malessere *m.*   indisposition, dis-
   comfort
malgarbo   bad manners
malleolo   malleolus
malvagio   wicked
malvolentieri   reluctantly
manata   pat, tap
mancare   to fail
manco   not even
manicaretto   dainty food
manichino   mannequin
manico   handle
manicomio   lunatic asylum
mantice *m.*   top
manto   mantle
marciapiede *m.*   sidewalk
mareggiata   rough sea
margherita   daisy
marmo   marble
martelletto   hammer (in a
   piano)
martello   hammer (tool)
mascella   jaw
maschera   mask, usher
maschio   male
masserizie *f.pl.*   household goods
masso   rock
masticare   to chew
matrimonio   marriage
mattarello   rolling-pin
matto   crazy, insane

mattone *m.*   brick
mazzo   bunch
megafono   megaphone
mela   apple
melanzana   eggplant
mensola   shelf
mentire   to lie
menzogna   lie
mero   mere, pure
meschino   poor, miserable
meticcio   hybrid
miglio   mile
militare   military, soldier
mina   mine
minestra   soup
miniera   mine
minutaglia   shreds
mira   sight
mirino   sight (of a rifle)
misericordia   mercy
misfatto   crime, misdeed
mite   mild
mobile *m.*   piece of furniture
modesto   humble, simple
modista   milliner
mollemente   softly
mollezza   softness, weakness
montagna   mountain; montagne
   russe *f.p.*   roller coaster
morbo   disease
morso   bite
moschettiere *m.*   musketeer
mozzicone *m.*   stump
mucosa   mucus
mugolio   yelping, moan
muraglia   wall
muratore *m.*   mason
musone   sulky, sullen person
mutande *f.pl.*   drawers, under-
   pants
mutismo   obstinate silence

nappa tassel
narice f. nostril
nascondere to hide, to conceal
neanche not even
negare to deny
negato unfit
neghittoso slothful, idle
nerboruto strong, sinewy
nerezza blackness
nero dark black
nervoso nervousness
nesso link, connection
nettezza neatness
ninnolo knick-knack
nocciolina nut
nocivo harmful
nodo knot
noia boredom, trouble
noialtri we
noncuranza carelessness
nonnulla m. trifle, nothing
novero number
nozze f.pl. marriage, wedding
nuca nape
nudo naked
nullità f. nothingness
nuotare to swim

occhiali m.pl. glasses; — affumicati m.pl. sunglasses
occhio m. eye
odio m. hatred
odioso hateful
officina workshop
oleografia oleograph
oleoso oily
oliera oil cruet
oltraggio offense, insult
oltremodo exceedingly, excessively

oltrepassare to pass, to go
  further
ombrello: stecca d'— f. rib
omero shoulder, humerus
opinare to think, to opine
oppure or, or else
orecchia ear
orifizio opening
orizzonte m. horizon
orlo edge
orso bear
osare to dare
ospite m. host; guest
ossigenato peroxide
osso bone
ostentare to show, to manifest
ostinarsi to persist, to insult
ovatta cotton, wadding
ozio leisure, idleness, laziness

pacca blow
padrona boss
padronale with an owner
paesaggio landscape
paese m. country
paffuto chubby, plump
pagliaccio: fare il — to clown
pagliata (colloq.) tripe
paglierino light yellow
pala shovel
paletto stake
palliativo palliative
palloncino air balloon
pallore m. paleness
palpare to feel, to touch
panato breaded
panchina bench
pancia belly
panni m.pl. clothes

218   Vocabulary

pannolino   little towel
pappagallo   parakeet
parabrise m.   windshield
paragonare   to compare
paragone m.   comparison
parete f.   wall, partition
parlantina   talkativeness,
   loquacity
paro: essere a —   to catch up
parrucchiere m.   hair-dresser
pasciuto   (well) fed
passeggiare   to walk
passero   sparrow
pasta   paste
pasticcio   mess
pasto   meal
patimento   suffering
patto   pact, agreement
pattumiera   garbage bin
pavimento   floor
pavoneggiarsi   to strut about, to
   stalk proudly
pazzia   insanity
peccato   sin
pedana   platform
pelle f.   skin; a fior di —
   superficial
pelliccia   fur
pelo   hair
peloso   hairy
peluria   down, soft hair
pena   pity
pendente   hanging
pendere   to hang
pendio   slope
pendulo   hanging
pennello   brush
penombra   shade, faint light
pentirsi   to repent
pentola   pan, pot

pera   pear
percorrere   to travel over, to go
   over
periferia   outskirts
perizia   skill
perlustrazione f.   reconnaissance
permettere   to permit, to allow
pernottare   to spend the night
persiana   Venetian blind
pescatore m.   fisherman
pesce m.   fish
pestato   crumbled, crushed
petto   chest
pezzato   dappled
piaga   sore, wound
piagnucolare   to whine
piangere   to cry
pianta   foot
piantarla   to stop (it)
pianterreno   ground floor, first
   floor
picchiare   to knock, to strike
picco   summit, peak
piè m.   foot
pineta   pine forest
pinguedine f.   fatness
pinzochera   pietist, overzealous
   churchgoer
pioggia   rain
pioli: scala a — f.   ladder
piombare   to fall
pisello   pea
pizzico   pinch
placarsi   to be appeased
placidità f.   placidness
plastron m.   ascot, tie.
platano   plane tree
plenilunio   full moon
poderoso   powerful, mighty
poggio   hill

poltiglia pulp

poltrona armchair, seat

polverío dust

polveroso dusty

pomice *f.* pumice

porcellana porcelain

porchetta roast pig

porgere to give, to hand

porre to put

portabagagli *m.* trunk (of a car)

portasigarette *m.* cigarette case

portiere *m.* doorman

portone *m.* main door

posa: senza — without rest, without cease

posare to place, to set

posata cover

possedere to own, to possess

poveruomo poor fellow

preavviso forewarning

predica preaching, sermon; warning

pregare to pray

preghiera prayer, earnest entreaty

premere to matter, to be important

prendere sottogamba to take lightly

prepotente overbearing, oppressing

presa plug

prestarsi to lend oneself

prevedibilità *f.* prevision

prigione *f.* prison

primario head physician

primizia early fruit, early vegetable

probante probatory, probative

proboscide f. trunk

prodezza bravery, gallantry

prodigarsi to do one's best

produttore *m.* producer

proferire to utter

profilarsi to appear

profumería perfumer's shop

prole *f.* progeny, children

propaggine *f.* vine

proprio just; amor — self-respect

protendersi to lean; to stretch oneself

provare to try

provviste *f.pl.* food

prurito itch

psiche *f.* mirror

pudore *m.* modesty

pugno fist, handful

puledro colt

pulizia cleanliness

pungente piercing (cold)

puntiglioso stubborn, spiteful

pupattola little doll

puzzare to stink

puzzo bad smell

qualche volta sometimes

quartiere *m.* district

qualsiasi any, whatever

querulo complaining, querulous

questura police office

rabbia rage, anger, rabies

rabescare to adorn (with arabesques)

raccattare to pick up

raccogliere to collect

raddoppiare to double

220   Vocabulary

raddrizzare to straighten
rado: di — infrequently, rarely
radura glade; opening
raffica squall, gust
raffreddamento cooling
raffreddore *m.* cold
ragazzo boy
raggrumato clotted
ragione: senza — for no reason
rallentare to slow down
ramo branch
rampicante *m.* creeper
rancore *m.* grudge
randagio stray
rannicchiato crouched
rapa *f.* turnip
rapare to crop one's hair
rapimento kidnapping, abduction
rapinosamente vehemently; quickly
rasoio razor
rassegnazione *f.* resignation
rassomigliare to resemble
rattoppato patched up, mended
rattristato saddened
ravviarsi to comb one's hair
ravvisare to perceive, to see
ravvolgere to roll up
razza race
razzo rocket
re *m.* king
recinto enclosure
recluso convict, prisoner
regalo present, gift
reggere to hold
reggia royal palace
reggipetto brassiere
regista *m.* director
regolarizzare to settle, to regularize

relazione *f.* report
remissione *f.* remission
rendere to make, to render; rendersi conto to realize
reni *f.pl.* loins
restare d'accordo to agree
restio reluctant
reticolato barbed wire line
retta: dare — to listen to, to mind
riaccendere to start again
rialzarsi to get up
riaversi to recover one's senses
ricamare to embroider, to decorate
ricatto blackmail
riccio curl
ricciolo lock, curl
ricevitore *m.* receiver
ricordare to remember
ricredere to change one's mind
ricucire to sew up
ridacchiare to giggle
ridere to laugh
ridiventare to become again
rifiatare to breathe, to gather breath
rifiuti *m.pl.* trash
riflettore *m.* floodlight
rifugiarsi to take (seek) shelter
rigare to furrow
riguardare to concern
riguardo respect, consideration
rimandare to postpone
rimarginare to heal
rimbalzare to bounce
rimboccare to tuck up
rimbombare to echo, to roar
rimescolio mingling, confusion
rimminchionito grown stupid
rimorchio trailer

rimpianto   regret
rimpicciolire   to lessen, to grow smaller
rimprovero   reproach, rebuke
rimuginare   to keep on turning over in one's mind
rincalzo   support
rincasare   to return home
rincorsa   run
rincrescere   to be sorry, to regret
ringhiera   railing
ringhio   snarl, growl
ringhioso   snarling, growling
rinvenimento   discovery, finding
riottoso   agitated, angry
ripararsi   to protect oneself; to take shelter
riparo   shelter
ripescare   to fish out
ripiombare   to plunge again
ripostiglio   recess
risata   laugh; sganasciarsi dalle risate   to split one's sides laughing
riscatto   claim
rischioso   risky, dangerous
riserbare   to keep, to reserve
riserbo   discretion, restraint
risolutamente   resolutely
risputare   to spit again
risucchio   swirl, whirlpool
risvolto   lapel, cuff
ritardo   delay
ritardato   delayed
ritemprare   to strengthen
rito   rite, usage
ritornello   refrain
ritto   upright, erect
riuscire   to succeed
rivalsa   revenge

riverso   on one's own back
rivolgersi   to turn
rivolto   turned
rizzare   to raise, to straighten, to spring up
roba   stuff
robaccia   bad stuff
rodersi (*fig.*)   to gnaw
rognoso   mangy; ugly
romanzo   novel
rombare   to roar
rompere   to break
ronzante   buzzing, humming
rosario   rosary
rotella   wheel
rotolare   to roll
rottame di ferro *m.*   iron scrap, wreck, fragment
rotula   knee-cap
rovescia: alla —   inversely
rovesciare   to overturn, to overthrow
rovinare   to ruin, to spoil
rozzo   unrefined, clumsy
rubare   to steal
rugginoso   rusty
ruggito   roar
rugoso   wrinkled
ruota   wheel
russare   to snore
rutilante   shining, rutilant

salotto   drawing room, reception room
saltaleone *m.*   spring (toy)
saltare   to jump
salute *f.*   health
salvadanaio   money-box
sangue *m.*   blood

santarella   person who pretends to be a prude

Santissimo *m.* the Holy Sacrament

sapere to know

sapido savory

saracinesca rolling shutter

sarta seamstress

sbafare to scrounge, to sponge

sbalordimento amazement, astonishment

sbarrare to bar, to block; — gli occhi to open one's eyes wide

sbarrato wide open (eyes)

sbattere to bump

sborsare to pay

sbriciolio crushing

sbronzo drunk

sbucare to come out, to come in

scacchi *m.pl.* chess

scacchiera chessboard

scacciare to expel, to drive away

scacco square

scaffale *m.* shelf

scaglia *f.* scale

scagliare to throw, to hurl

scala a pioli *f.* ladder

scaloppina scallop

scaldare to warm

scalmanato agitated

scalpicciare to scrape one's feet

scandalizzare to scandalize, to shock

scantonare to round a corner

scappare to run away, to flee

scartafaccio paper

scatenato unrestrained

scatola box

scavalcare to climb over

scegliere to choose

scemo foolish, stupid

scendere to go down, to descend

scendiletto bedside carpet

scettico sceptical

scheggia splinter

scheggiato splintered

schermo screen

scherzare to joke, to jest

scherzo joke

scherzoso playful

schiacciato snub, flat

schiaffo slap

schifiltoso fastidious, hard to please

schifo disgust

schifoso filthy, disgusting

schizzato spattered, splashed

sciatore *m.* skier

scienziato scientist

scimmia monkey

sciocchezza foolishness

sciolto untied, loose (hair); by the glass (of a drink)

sciupato run down, drawn, haggard

scollato with an open collar

scolparsi to justify oneself

scolpito carved

scommettere to bet

scomparire to disappear

scomposto uncomely

sconvolto *p.p.* upset

scopa *f.* broom

scopare to sweep

scoppiare to break out

scoprire to discover, to find out

scorciatoia short cut

scorgere to notice, to perceive

scrutare to investigate, to observe intently

scrutatore investigating, inquisitive

scucchia (*colloq.*) chin

scuotere to shake

scurrilità *f.* scurrility

sdraiarsi to stretch oneself out

seccare to bother

seccato tired, annoyed

seccatore *m.* bore

sedere *m.* bottom

sedurre to seduce

seduttore *m.* seducer

seggiola chair

seggiolone *m.* armchair

segnaletico descriptive

sella saddle

semiaperto half-open, parted

seminterrato basement

senso sense, direction

senza ragione for no reason

serietà *f.* seriousness, gravity

serrato closed, locked; earnest, intent

serva maid, servant

servizio service; serving set

sfarzo magnificence, splendor

sfarzoso gorgeous

sferragliare to make a loud noise

sfida challenge, defiance

sfilacciato frayed

sfilatino long loaf of bread

sfinimento exhaustion

sfiorare to touch lightly

sforacchiare to riddle

sformare to be out of place; to cut a bad figure

sformato deformed

sforzo effort

sfrenato wild, unrestrained

sfrittellato stained

sfuggire to escape (one's attention)

sgabello stool

sganasciarsi dalle risate to split one's sides laughing

sgarbato rude, unmannerly

sgobbare to work hard

sgombro clear, empty

sgomento dismay, discouragement

sgradevole unpleasant

sgradito unpleasant

sgranocchiare to munch

sgretolare to crumble, to smash

sgrinfia *colloq.* claw; a nasty woman

sguaiato vulgar, crude

sibilare to sibilate

singhiozzare to sob

singhiozzo sob

sinistro left, ominous, sinister

sirena siren

slitta sleigh

smanioso eager

smarrimento bewilderment

smentita denial, disproof

smorfia grimace

smorto pale, wan

snellezza agility, slimness

snodarsi to wind

socchiuso half-open, ajar

soccorso rescue

sodo firm, solid

soffitto ceiling

sogghignare to sneer, to jeer

soggiungere to add

soglia threshold

sogno dream

solco fold, furrow

soldi *m.pl.* money

solere   to use, to be accustomed
solleone *m.*   dog days
solleticare   to tickle
solletico   tickle
sollevare   to raise, to lift
sollievo   relief
sommergere   to submerge
sommesso   soft, subdued
sonaglio   bell
soppiatto: di --   secretly, stealthily
soprabito m.   overcoat
sopracciglio *m.*   eyebrow
soprattutto   especially
sopravvenire   to come up
sorgere   to stand, to rise
sornione   sly, sneaking
sorreggere   to hold, to support
sorridere   to smile
sorso   drop, draught
sortire   to obtain
sosia *m.*   counterpart
sospiro   sigh
sotterraneo   underground
sottigliezza   subtlety
sottile   thin, skinny
sottobosco   underbrush
sottogamba: prendere —   to take lightly
sottomissione *f.*   submission
sottoscala *m.*   space under the staircase
sovrumano   superhuman
spalancare   to open wide
spalancato   wide open
spalatore *m.*   shoveling man
spalla   shoulder; stringersi nelle spalle   to shrug one's shoulders
spalmare   to apply
sparare   to shoot

spartire   to part, to separate
spasimo   pang
spasso: andare a —   to take a walk
spazioso   roomy, spacious
spazzare   to sweep
spazzola   brush
specie *f.*   kind, sort
spegnersi   to die out, to go out
spiacevole   unpleasant, disagreeable
spiantato   moneyless, jobless, unsettled
spicchio   section, strip
spiegato   unfurled
spillo   pin
spinato   twilled (cloth)
spintone *m.*   push
spiritoso   humorous
splendere   to shine
spolverare   to dust
sponda   edge, side
sporcarsi   to get dirty
sporco   dirty
sporgente   protruding
sportello   door (of a car)
spossato   weary, fatigued
spostarsi   to move
sprecare   to waste
sprezzante   disdainful, contemptuous
sprofondare   to sink
spulciare   to get rid of fleas
spuntare   to appear, to come out
squadrare   to look over from head to foot
squarciare   to tear asunder, to cut
squarcio   gash
squattrinato   penniless
squillare   to ring

squisito delicious
stabilirsi to settle
staccare to detach
stanchezza tiredness
stappare to uncork
statura size
stecca d'ombrello *f.* rib
stecchino toothpick
stecchito stone dead
stelo stalk, stem
stendere to spread
stia pen, sty
stipite m. doorstep
stiracchiare to pull
stiro: ferro da — (clothes) iron
stivaletto boot
stizzito angry, irritated
stoffa cloth, material
stopposo flaxy, towy
storcere to twist
stordire to stun
storto crooked
stoviglie *f.pl.* earthenware, pottery
straccio rag
stramazzare to fall
strangolare to choke, to strangle
stranito astounded, dumbfounded
strapazzo fatigue, excess
strappare to get, to obtain
strascicare to drag; (*fig.*) to drawl
strascico train (of a dress)
strattone *m.* jerk, pull
straziante heart-rending
strega witch
stridulo shrill
stringere to press, to clench

stringersi to hug; — nelle spalle to shrug one's shoulders
striscia strip
strisciare to drag
strofinare to rub
strombettare to play loudly (trumpet)
stropicciare to rub
stufato bored
stufo tired, sick, annoyed
stuolo multitude, group
stupire to amaze
stupirsi to be surprised, to be amazed
stuzzicare to tease
subitaneo sudden
succedere to help
sudicio dirty
sudiciume *m.* filth, dirt
superbia pride, haughtiness
supino supine, on one's back
suppellettile *f.* furniture, furnishings
supplicare to implore
supplichevole imploring
supplizio torture
sussiego exaggerated gravity, dignity
sussurrare to whisper, to murmur
svago amusement
svaligiare to ransack, to plunder
svelto quick
svenire to faint
sviato turned away, aside
svicolare to elude
svincolarsi to free oneself, to disengage oneself
svogliatezza listlessness

svoltare to turn
svuotarsi to empty, to become
empty

tacchino turkey
tacco heel
taccuino writing pad, tablet
tacere to be silent
tafferuglio brawl, scuffle
tagliacarte *m.* letter opener
tappo cork
tartassare to vex, to disturb
tastare to touch
tastiera keyboard
tasto key (of music)
temporale *m.* storm
tenebre *f.pl.* darkness
tenere to hold
tentare to try, to tempt
tetto roof
tiglioso tough
timidezza timidity, shyness
timpano eardrum
tintinnio tinkle
tintura coloring
tirare to pull
tirare (su) to grow, to bring
(up)
tiro a segno shooting gallery
tizio a fellow
tizzo brand, fire-brand
toletta dressing-table
tonante thundering
tondo round
tonfo splash
tonto stupid, dull, silly
tormenta storm
tossire to cough
tosto immediately, soon

tozzo stocky, thick-set
tracciato section
tradimento treason, betrayal
trafelato breathless, panting
tramonto sunset
transitorio temporary
tranviere *m.* busdriver
trapasso change
trapelare to appear, to leak out
trappoco in a short time
trappola trap
trarre to take something out,
to draw
trascorrere to go, to drift away
trascurare to neglect
trasognato dreamlike
trattenere to hold
tratto: ad un — all of a sudden
trattoria restaurant
travedere to be mistaken
traverso: di— slanted, askance
travolgere to sweep away
trazione *f.* traction
tregua rest, respite
trepidare to be anxious, to
tremble
tripolino from Tripoli
triste sad
tritume *m.* bits
trucco trick, deceit
truffare to cheat, to swindle
tubetto tube
tuffarsi to plunge, to dive
tulipano tulip
tuorlo yolk
turbante *m.* turban
turbamento agitation, excite-
ment
turbato agitated, perturbed
turbinio whirling
turchino blue

ubriacare (ubbriacare) to
  intoxicate
ubriaco drunk
uccidere to kill
uggiolare to whine
ungersi to apply (something
  oily on oneself)
urlo shout
usciere m. clerk
uscio door

vacillare to flicker
valle f. valley
vaneggiamento raving
vanni m.pl. wings
vantaggio advantage
vanteria bragging, boasting
vasca pond
vascello ship
vassoio tray
vedere to see
vela sail
velina tissue paper
velluto velvet
velo veil
ventola fan
ventre m. stomach, belly
vergogna shame
vergognarsi to be ashamed
vergognoso ashamed
vernice f. varnish, paint
versare to pour
vestaglia gown

vetrina shop-window
vezzoso graceful, charming
viaggiatore: commesso —
  traveling salesman
viale m. avenue
viavai m. going and coming
vicendevole mutual, reciprocal
vicolo lane
vigna vineyard
villania rudeness
villeggiatura holiday (in the
  country)
villoso hairy
viltà f. cowardice
vino wine
viscere f.pl. bowels, depth
vispo lively, brisk
vitello veal
vivanda food
vizio vice, bad habit
volante m. steering wheel
volere (bene) to love
volpino fox terrier
voltarsi to turn
volteggiare to turn

zampa paw
zampillo jet (of liquid)
zingara gipsy
zitto silent
zolfanello match
zolla clod, sod
zoppicare to limp

COLLEGE OF MARIN

3 2555 00120594 2